# CHINA IN THE ERA
# OF XI JINPING

# ★ CHINA
# IN THE ERA OF
# XI JINPING

## DOMESTIC AND FOREIGN
## POLICY CHALLENGES

Robert S. Ross

AND

Jo Inge Bekkevold, Editors

Georgetown University Press / Washington, DC

Library of Congress Cataloging-in-Publication Data
China in the era of Xi Jinping : domestic and foreign policy challenges / Robert S. Ross and Jo Inge Bekkevold, editors.
      pages cm
This volume is the result of the conference on China's rise and its fifth generation leaders hosted by the Centre for Asian Security Studies at the Norwegian Institute for Defence Studies in Oslo, May 2013.
   Includes bibliographical references and index.
   ISBN 978-1-62616-297-6 (hardcover : alk. paper) —
ISBN 978-1-62616-298-3 (pbk. : alk. paper) — ISBN 978-1-62616-299-0 (ebook)
   1. China—Politics and government—2002– —Congresses.   2. China—Foreign relations—21st century—Congresses.   3. China—Economic conditions   2000– —Congresses.   4. China—Economic policy—2000– —Congresses.   5. Xi, Jinping.   I. Ross, Robert S., 1954– editor.   II. Bekkevold, Jo Inge, editor.
   DS779.36.C47   2016
   320.60951—dc23            2015022058

17 16      9 8 7 6 5 4 3 2 First printing

Printed in the United States of America

Cover design by Trudi Gershenov, TG Design
Cover image: epa european pressphoto agency b.v. / Alamy

# CONTENTS

# TIME LINE OF THE PEOPLE'S REPUBLIC OF CHINA

| | |
|---|---|
| 1949 | Proclamation of the People's Republic of China. Nationalists retreat to the island of Taiwan and set up a government there. Mao Zedong travels to Moscow to negotiate Sino-Soviet Treaty of Friendship. |
| 1950 | China intervenes in the Korean War. The People's Liberation Army marches into Tibet. |
| 1950s | Soviet-style land reforms, heavy industries, and education system are introduced. |
| 1954 | First meeting of National People's Congress is convened and the first constitution is ratified. China signs an agreement with India regarding Tibet and the Five Principles of Peaceful Coexistence in China's foreign policy. |
| 1956–1957 | Hundred Flowers anti-rightist campaign begins. |
| 1958–1961 | Great Leap Forward and people's communes appear, then result in economic breakdown and famine. |
| 1959 | Chinese military forces suppress large-scale revolt in Tibet. |
| 1961–1965 | Readjustment and recovery period, including Agriculture First policy. Food situation improves. |
| 1960 | Sino-Soviet split. |
| 1962 | Border war with India. |
| 1964 | Test of first nuclear bomb in China. |
| 1966–1976 | The Great Proletarian Cultural Revolution commences. |
| 1970 | First satellite is launched (Long March). |
| 1971 | The People's Republic replaces the Republic of China (Taiwan) in the United Nations Security Council. |
| 1972 | US president Richard Nixon visits Beijing. China and Japan establish diplomatic relations. |

| 1976 | Death of Premier Zhou Enlai. Tangshan earthquake. Chairman Mao dies. Gang of Four are arrested. |
|------|---|
| 1978 | Government imposes one-child policy. Deng Xiaoping introduces economic reforms and The Four Modernizations program. Democracy Wall movement in Beijing calls for a "fifth" modernization. |
| 1979 | Diplomatic relations with the United States are established and Deng Xiaoping visits the United States. China invades Vietnam (for twenty-nine days) following Vietnam's ouster of the pro-Beijing Pol Pot regime in Cambodia. |
| 1980 | Special Economic Zones are created. China joins the International Monetary Fund, the World Bank, and the Conference on Disarmament. |
| 1984 | China joins the International Atomic Energy Agency. Sino-British Joint Declaration is signed, with agreement to return Hong Kong to China in 1997. |
| 1987 | CCP secretary general Hu Yaobang is forced to resign and is replaced by Zhao Ziyang. |
| 1989 | Hu Yaobang dies. Students demonstrate in Tiananmen Square, leading to military crackdown followed by a tightened political atmosphere. International sanctions ensue. Jiang Zemin replaces Zhao Ziyang as CCP secretary general. Mikhail Gorbachev visits China, the first Soviet leader to visit in three decades, which paves the way for normalized Sino-Russian relations. |
| 1990 | Stock markets open in Shanghai and Shenzhen. |
| 1992 | Deng Xiaoping's Southern Tour accelerates further market reforms. |
| | China joins the Nuclear Non-Proliferation Treaty. Diplomatic relations with South Korea are established. |
| 1993–1995 | Finance recentralization and taxation reforms strengthen revenues. |
| 1995–1996 | Taiwan Strait Crisis. |
| 1996 | China, Russia, Kazakhstan, Kyrgyzstan, and Tajikistan (the "Shanghai Five") agree to cooperate to combat ethnic and religious tensions. China signs the Comprehensive Nuclear |

Test-Ban Treaty. China ratifies the United Nations Convention on the Law of the Sea.

1997      Deng Xiaoping dies at age ninety-two. Hong Kong reverts to Chinese rule.

1998      The World Health Organization reports that seven of the ten most polluted cities in the world are located in China. China signs the International Covenant on Civil and Political Rights.

1999      NATO forces bomb the Chinese embassy in Belgrade. The Falun Gong movement is declared a threat to national security. Macau reverts to Chinese rule.

2001      Diplomatic standoff occurs over the detention of an American military plane and crew following a midair collision with a Chinese fighter jet. The Shanghai Cooperation Organization is established. China joins the World Trade Organization. China ratifies the International Covenant on Economic, Social, and Cultural Rights.

2002      Hu Jintao replaces Jiang Zemin as CCP secretary general.

2003      SARS crisis. Five hundred thousand people in Hong Kong march against Article 23 anti-subversion law, leading the Chinese government to shelve the bill. Launch of China's first manned spacecraft.

2003      China hosts the first Six-Party talks (among China, Japan, the two Koreas, Russia, and the United States) to roll back North Korea's nuclear program.

2004      Agreement signed with Russia settling border conflicts. Landmark free trade agreement signed with ASEAN.

2005      Zhao Ziyang dies. First direct airplane flight between China and Taiwan since 1949. New law calls for use of force should Taipei declare independence from mainland China. Taiwan's Nationalist Party (KMT) leader Lien Chan, visits China for the first meeting between Nationalist and Communist Party leaders since 1949. Anti-Japanese protests in China are sparked by a Japanese textbook that China says glosses over Japan's World War II record. China and Russia hold first joint military exercises.

2006      Work on Three Gorges Dam is completed. China surpasses the United States in carbon dioxide emissions. China responds to North Korea's first nuclear test by voting in favor of UN Security Council Resolution 1718 (which imposes sanctions), but only after negotiating away any threat of military action against North Korea. African heads of state gather in Beijing for a first-ever China-Africa summit.

2007    China shoots down an old weather satellite, demonstrating the capability of destroying hostile spy satellites. China launches both its first moon orbiter and its first domestically developed passenger jet, the *Xiang Feng*. Premier Wen Jiabao characterizes China's economic growth model as "unsustainable, uncoordinated, unbalanced, and unstable."

2008    Tibetan uprisings. Sichuan earthquake. Beijing hosts the Summer Olympic Games. Japan and China reach a deal for joint development of a gas field in the East China Sea. Astronaut Zhai Zhigang completes China's first spacewalk. The global financial crisis has a worse-than-expected effect on China; Chinese government announces a $586B stimulus package to avoid economic slowdown.

2009    China and Russia sign $25B oil deal. Hillary Clinton, US secretary of state, calls for deeper US-China partnership during her first overseas tour. The USS *Impeccable* incident in the South China Sea. US president Barack Obama makes his first visit to China. Ethnic violence erupts in Xinjiang province. China becomes the largest automobile market in the world.

2010    China overtakes Japan as the world's second-largest economy, and overtakes Germany as the world's biggest exporter. Diplomatic row occurs over Japan's arrest of a Chinese trawler crew found in disputed waters in the East China Sea. Shanghai hosts World Expo. Jailed Chinese dissident Liu Xiaobo is awarded the Nobel Peace Prize. "Stick to the Path of Peaceful Development" speech is given by State Councilor Dai Bingguo.

2011    China unveils its first J-20 stealth fighter jet. China's urban population is larger than its rural population for the first time. Pivot to Asia by United States is seen by Beijing as encirclement.

2012    Bo Xilai political scandal. Territorial disputes fan tensions in the East China Sea and South China Sea. China launches its first aircraft carrier, the *Liaoning*. China completes its first-ever manual docking of a spacecraft with another space module. Xi Jinping appointed new CCP secretary general.

2013     China Defense Ministry's white paper identifies Japan as a potential adversary. China legally abolishes "reeducation through labor" camps. China successfully lands the *Yutu* (Jade Rabbit) robotic rover on the surface of the moon, the first soft landing by any country in thirty-seven years. Barack Obama and Xi Jinping hold California Summit to help reset bilateral relations. China announces the air defense identification zone in the East China Sea. China's top leadership chairs the Periphery Diplomacy Conference, the largest foreign policy strategy meeting in decades.

2014     China signs a thirty-year $400B gas deal with Russia. The Ukraine Crisis tilts Russia closer to China. China hosts the APEC Summit in Beijing. The United States and China make joint announcement on climate change.

2015     China issues Silk Road Action Plan, implementing the Silk Road Economic Belt and Twenty-First-Century Maritime Silk Road initiatives. The China-led Asian Infrastructure Investment Bank (AIIB) established. China's RMB included in the IMF's basket of Special Drawing Rights (SDR) currencies. Xi Jinping met with KMT leader Ma Ying-jeou in Singapore. China's one-child policy abolished.

# INTRODUCTION

## China's New Leadership in Domestic and International Politics

### Jo Inge Bekkevold and Robert S. Ross

In 2010 China surpassed Japan to become the world's second-largest economy. Based on the purchasing-power-parity valuation (PPP) of a country's Gross Domestic Product (GDP), China's economy even surpassed the US economy in 2014. Based on nominal figures, China's economy is still less than 60 percent of the size of the US economy, but by 2019 it is estimated it will be 70 percent of the size of the US economy.[1] The balance in military expenditures between China and the United States is also changing. Based on figures from the SIPRI military expenditures database, US military expenditures in 2000 were ten times larger than China's military expenditures. In 2011, US military expenditures were five times larger than China's; by 2014 US military expenditures ($580 billion) were three times China's expenditures.[2]

China's rise has been impressive, but it has also created challenges for the Chinese leadership, in both its domestic and foreign policies. China needs wise and mature leadership as never before. November 2012 witnessed China's second orderly power succession, when Xi Jinping replaced Hu Jintao as the general secretary of the Communist Party of China (CPC) and chairman of the Central Military Commission at the Eighteenth Party Congress. Whereas Jiang Zemin and the late Deng Xiaoping retained leadership of the Central Military Commission, Hu Jintao's retirement from all leadership posts enabled a smoother power transition and a stronger mandate for Xi Jinping. In March 2013 Xi formally ascended to the Chinese presidency and Li Keqiang became premier. Xi and Li have been chosen to captain the Chinese ship through 2022.

The Third Plenum of the Central Committee frequently provides the opportunity for China's new leadership to announce its policy priorities in a formal way. This was the case with Xi Jinping. At the Third Plenum of the Eighteenth Central Committee in November 2013, Xi signaled his economic policy preferences regarding the balance of state and market. He also announced the establishment of two new high-level policy coordination institutions, one for overseeing economic reform policies and one for enforcing security policies. Xi Jinping is heading both of these new institutions, which gives him a solid platform for launching his policy agenda. Xi Jinping has emerged as a leader who is stronger than his recent predecessors.

The three most urgent and interrelated domestic challenges faced by China's new leaders are: sustaining economic growth, fighting corruption, and maintaining social stability. Hu Jintao and former premier Wen Jiabao addressed the domestic challenges created by China's successes, but with only mixed results. At the National People's Congress held in March 2007, Wen acknowledged that China's economy was still "unstable, unbalanced, uncoordinated and unsustainable."[3] Over time these challenges have become more acute, and the next ten years will be critical for China. If China's economy continues to expand at 6 to 8 percent annual growth, China will most likely surpass the United States' growth rate within the next ten to twenty years and eventually become the world's largest economy. This scenario, however, will depend on a reform of China's economic model. If Xi Jinping wants to deliver on his "China Dream," he and his lieutenants will have to exercise strong leadership and make bold decisions.

China's new leadership is also responsible for steering the Chinese ship in international waters. As a consequence of China's rise, this has become an increasingly challenging task. China's growth has increased expectations at home for a tougher stance in international affairs. Simultaneously, China's increasing capabilities and its evolving policies have created increasingly larger waves across the international system. Under Hu Jintao's leadership, China's rise and its nationalist diplomacy elicited increased apprehension among its neighboring countries and contributed to greater US efforts to consolidate its presence in Asia. What can we expect from China as a foreign policy actor in the coming decade? Foreign policy is often an extension of domestic policies and domestic structures. Does the Chinese leadership have a clear vision or grand strategy for utilizing China's emerging position as a global powerhouse? What is the Chinese worldview? Does the Chinese leadership view the world through lenses shaded by revisionist ideas or through lenses with a vision of China finding its rightful place as a great power within the current international order? How well will the new leadership handle growing nationalism, as influenced by China's patriotic education campaign and an outspoken and influential debate over China's foreign policy, which is currently taking place within China's Internet society?

Now that Xi has been secretary of the Chinese Communist Party and president of China for well over three years, we can develop an assessment of his policy priorities and his leadership abilities. The contributors to this volume take a close look at China's new generation of leaders and explore the challenges facing the new leadership, as it relates to both reforms at home and China's role in the wider world.

## NEW LEADERS, NEW CHALLENGES

The challenges Xi Jinping and his Politburo colleagues face today are different from the challenges their predecessors faced. A brief look at the changing environment of Chinese politics and foreign policy making since the founding of the People's Republic clearly illustrates this point. When Mao Zedong proclaimed the founding of the People's Republic of China in October 1949, his country had been ravaged by Japanese occupation and a civil war that had lasted more than twenty years. The Nationalists had retreated to Taiwan with the intention of regaining power on the Chinese mainland sometime in the future. Chiang Kai-shek was never able to regain control over China, but his government represented China in the United Nations for another twenty-two years. In December 1949, with the world on the verge of a cold war, Mao traveled to Moscow to negotiate a friendship treaty with Joseph Stalin. A few months after returning from Moscow, Mao ordered his People's Volunteer Army troops across the Yalu River to support North Korea against the United States and to defend China's security. The Korean War brought the Cold War to Asia, and China was "leaning to the one side": the socialist camp. During the next three decades China was able to enforce control of its borders but Chinese politics was marked by ongoing political upheavals and campaigns and the Sino-Soviet split in 1960 added further pressure on an already relatively isolated country.[4]

When Deng Xiaoping emerged as the leading figure of China's post-Mao era in the late 1970s, he took charge of a country with a bureaucracy in tatters and an economy in dire straits. China's GDP in 1980 was one-fifth of Japan's, half of the United Kingdom's, and less than one-tenth of the United States'.[5] Measured according to the United Nations Human Development Index, China ranked alongside Ghana and Cameroon, was well behind Lesotho and Zambia, and was equivalent to the score of today's Rwanda, Malawi,

and Sudan.[6] China had been economically outrun by Japan's rapid modernization in the 1960s and 1970s and also by the four "tiger economies" of
South Korea, Taiwan, Singapore, and Hong Kong. In particular, the growth
in the Chinese communities of Taiwan, Singapore, and Hong Kong stood in
stark contrast to the situation on mainland China.

   While Deng Xiaoping faced an ideological battle at home in trying to
convince his Party colleagues to embrace the market economy and strengthen
the state's capacity to handle his proposed reform programs, his task was
greatly supported by China's much-improved international standing. Even
though the Sino-Soviet rivalry still played a decisive role in Chinese foreign
policy, the People's Republic of China had joined the United Nations in late
1971 and US president Richard Nixon's visit to China in 1972 had paved the
way toward normalization of US-China relations. By the time Deng Xiaoping traveled to the United States in January 1979, full diplomatic relations
between the two countries had been established and China was regarded as
a partner in Cold War politics. The country was able to access credit, advice,
and support from international organizations like the World Bank and the
International Monetary Fund (IMF), and an increasing number of foreign
enterprises were eager to take part in China's anticipated economic growth.
The many Chinese living overseas soon became an important tool in China's
economic turnaround. And in 1985 Deng Xiaoping declared that the Soviet
Union no longer posed a threat to the country.

   When Jiang Zemin came to power in 1989, China's GDP had fallen even
further below Japan's and the United States', equaling only one-eighth of
Japan's and one-fifteenth of the United States'.[7] By 1990 China was still only
the fourth-largest exporter and fifth-largest importer in Asia, and its trade was
only one-fifth the size of Japan's.[8] Furthermore, China was in the middle of a
domestic crisis, and even though the United States sent early signals to Beijing about continued cooperation following the events at Tiananmen Square,
the military crackdown on the June 1989 demonstrations led to international
outrage and sanctions. The breaking up of the Soviet Union caused alarm in
Beijing. China was turning inward, and the economic reform program was
at risk.

   Deng Xiaoping, however, pushed for further reforms, and the economic
liberalization that had taken place earlier in the 1980s proved to be a basis
for an economic miracle. When Deng Xiaoping passed away in 1997, Jiang
Zemin and Zhu Rongji gained a firm grip on Chinese politics and economics. The taxation and fiscal reforms spearheaded by Zhu Rongji in the early
and mid-1990s strengthened the central government's control over the economy. Soon thousands of state-owned enterprises faced massive restructuring

and countless foreign enterprises began moving their production facilities to China in increasing numbers.

The end of the Cold War changed the global balance of power in favor of the United States, but it also enabled China to normalize relations with Russia, establish diplomatic ties with South Korea in 1992, and pursue closer relations with countries in Southeast Asia. The revolution in military affairs showcased by the United States during Operation Desert Storm in the 1991 Gulf War, however, convinced China's leaders that its armed forces needed modernization. Despite construction efforts on Mischief Reef in the South China Sea in 1995 and the crisis in the Taiwan Strait in 1995 to 1996, the People's Liberation Army was still a secondary fighting force with a military expenditure in 1995 only one-fourth that of Japan's.

When Hu Jintao became Party secretary in 2002, Beijing had just been awarded the 2008 Olympic Games, China had entered the World Trade Organization, and the country was well established as the world's factory. An increasingly uneven economic development between China's coastal and inner provinces, between urban and rural areas, and between the rich and the poor led Hu Jintao and Wen Jiabao to launch slogans such as "new socialist countryside" and "harmonious society." Double-digit growth figures and new policy initiatives made China's government seem both able and willing to address these challenges. China had in the late 1990s also signed the International Covenant on Civil and Political Rights, and in 2001 it ratified the International Covenant on Economic, Social, and Cultural Rights.

Despite the efforts of Hu and Wen to change China's growth model, the old model was rolling ahead and the stimulus package launched during the financial crisis contributed to further consolidation of the old investment-driven model. As several of the authors in this volume show, it is now even more difficult for the Xi Jinping leadership group to make the necessary adjustments in China's growth model.

"China's Peaceful Rise"—a modern version of Deng Xiaoping's mantra, *taoguang yanghui* (keep a low profile in international politics)—became a guiding principle in China's foreign policy in the mid-2000s. However, as late as the year 2000 China was still only ranked as the world's seventh-largest exporter, after the United States, Germany, Japan, France, the United Kingdom, and Canada. In 2000 China's trade was still roughly half that of Japan's; its GDP was only one-fourth of Japan's.[9] At the time, both the size of its economy and total military expenditures were only one-tenth the size of the US economy and military expenditures.

Fast forward ten years: China had overtaken Germany as the world's biggest exporter, its economy had overtaken Japan's as the second largest in the world, and its military spending was also the second largest, with a defense budget more than double that of Japan and Russia. China now also ranked as an upper-middle-income economy according to World Bank criteria.[10] In 2008 Beijing hosted a successful Olympic Games, with China winning more gold medals than the United States. In 2010 Shanghai hosted the most expensive World Expo in modern times, and in the meantime China had played a constructive role in contributing to the rescue of the world economy from its worst recession since the 1930s. In this context China developed more proactive defense and foreign policies. The Hu Jintao leadership launched China's first aircraft carrier and unveiled its new J-20 stealth fighter jet. When Xi Jinping took the helm in 2012, China was a quite different place from when Hu Jintao became Party secretary only ten years earlier.

## THE STRUCTURE OF THE VOLUME

The book is divided into two parts. Part 1 addresses the domestic challenges faced by Xi Jinping and his team. In chapter 1 Bo Zhiyue introduces China's new leadership and political elite: their characteristics, their individual pathways to leadership, and the implications for their presumed policy preferences. The early history of the People's Republic of China was largely synonymous with the history of Mao Zedong and Deng Xiaoping. The policy choices of these two leaders shaped the lives of generations of Chinese, for better or for worse. Joseph S. Nye reminds us in his recent book that from the very beginning of the creation of the United States, US presidents have undoubtedly shaped US policy.[11] We should expect China's new leaders to have the same ambition. Their personal qualifications, or their "demography," is thus important. China's "new generation" leaders differ in noteworthy ways from their predecessors, and these differences will influence their political behaviors and policy preferences.

But leadership has its limits, and studies of leadership sometimes fail to acknowledge the structural and cultural frameworks at work. J. G. March and J. P. Olsen have labeled this approach "reductionism," indicating its analytical inadequacy.[12] Structures normally refer to a government's formal organization, including governmental institutions and political hierarchies. Structures typically develop gradually over time as a result of negotiations and compromises and they lead to a strong vested interest in the status quo, which in turn makes it highly problematic for a leader to make substantial changes. Structures and related cultures, norms, and values are often a mix of the traditional and the modern as well as the native and the foreign.[13] In the case of

China, formal and informal "phenomena" encircle the leadership, including legacies from the Imperial Era like Confucianism and Legalism, as well as imported concepts like Soviet-style socialism and Western-style market liberalism. Nothing illustrates this better than the full name of the formal political doctrine in China: Marxism-Leninism, Mao Zedong Thought, Deng Xiaoping Theory, the Three Represents (developed by Jiang Zemin), and Scientific Development (formulated under the guidance of the fourth generation leaders). Similarly, China pursues "socialism with Chinese characteristics." Each new generation of leaders has added a perspective overlaying these traditional Chinese and Marxist-Leninist values.

As a political system takes shape, its structural and cultural features are consolidated. Each generation of leaders confronts greater structural constraints than its predecessors did, and any changes that occur proceed within a given path shaped by those predecessors.[14] While Deng Xiaoping was able to exceed the limits of structure and choose a new path for China in the late 1970s, later leaders have been more pressured to follow paths trodden by their predecessors. Will Xi Jinping be able to overcome structural and cultural obstacles, as Deng did three decades ago, to chart a new course for China that will enable the country to reach its place as a high-income prosperous society? In chapter 2 Zheng Yongnian and Weng Cuifen analyze the development of formal political structures in China and how these may empower or constrain the new leadership's autonomy in decision making.

In chapter 3 Barry Naughton examines the challenges of economic growth in China and the urgent need to change the economic model. China's rapid economic transformation has created enormous stresses and strains, and the low-hanging fruits have been reaped. China's impressive growth has also created complacency, and Naughton questions whether China's new leaders will be able to overcome strong vested interests that are linked to the old growth model. Naughton analyzes the choices these new leaders face in confronting a reform agenda and in finding the right balance between initiating reforms and consolidating reforms.

Joseph Fewsmith, in chapter 4, explores the challenges posed by growing social instability. Fewsmith argues that the economic success that China has enjoyed over the past three decades has not yet generated the "harmonious society" desired by the leadership. Despite efforts by the former administration under Hu Jintao and Wen Jiabao to address China's uneven economic development by shifting to a more service-oriented government, the fear of social instability continues to be a major challenge. Moreover, Fewsmith elaborates on the fact that even though China's century-old dream of "wealth and power" has been achieved, China broods on the injustices of

the past. Fewsmith foresees that growing nationalism will increasingly influence China's foreign policy making.

Part 2 of the volume explores the foreign policy challenges facing China's
new generation of leaders. China's foreign policy-making process has become
increasingly complex. In chapter 5 Chen Gang and Stig Stenslie explore
China's strategic thinking and discuss the obstacles China confronts in developing and carrying out any grand strategy. The combination of China's complex domestic challenges and the fast-changing international environment
requires daily "firefighting" and reactive policy making that makes it difficult
to turn strategy into policy.

The fragmentation of the Chinese policy-making bureaucracy imposes a
second significant challenge to foreign policy. Through the 1970s China's foreign policy was crafted by a small handful of leaders with Mao at the top and
Zhou Enlai acting concurrently as premier and foreign minister. Later Deng
Xiaoping guided Chinese foreign policy. Since the late 1990s, however, a
wider range of institutions, economic enterprises, and leaders have started to
gain influence over China's foreign policy. China's Ministry of Foreign Affairs,
for example, is staffed with highly professional diplomats but it lacks leverage
within the Chinese political system. In the United States the secretary of
state is one of the president's most important advisors; in China the foreign
minister and the state councilor responsible for foreign affairs are not members of the twenty-five-member Politburo. The US National Security Council
has a crucial role in coordinating US foreign policy; in China, despite the
recent creation of a National Security Commission, the leadership still lacks
a government institution that can coordinate foreign policy. In chapter 6
Linda Jakobson analyzes the impact of fragmentation and an increasingly
wide range of foreign policy actors have on China's foreign policy making and
on China's maritime policies in particular.

Chinese leaders must also set foreign policy in response to the institutional
structure of international politics and the foreign policies of other states.
Although China's influence in international politics has grown, the post–
World War II institutional structure remains intact, constraining China's policy-making autonomy. And, as a trading state, Chinese interdependence with
the global economy as well as its bilateral relationships constrain its policy
choices. In chapter 7 Andrew Nathan examines the role of China in international regimes. In chapter 8 Helge Hveem and T. J. Pempel discuss the impact
of international interdependence in trade and finance and bilateral economic
relations between the United States and China, the world's two largest economies, has on Chinese foreign policy choices. They consider possible scenarios
for the future development of China's policy posture.

Chinese security policy also faces pressure from the international system. Although China is considerably more powerful than it was a mere ten years ago, the United States still poses a significant challenge to Chinese security. The US strategic presence on China's maritime perimeter constrains its policy options and Japanese nationalism and Sino-Japanese territorial disputes challenge its ability to manage Chinese nationalism and sustain stable relations with Japan. In Southeast Asia numerous claimants to disputed maritime territories contest Chinese sovereignty claims, exacerbate Chinese domestic demands for a hardline foreign policy, and test the leadership's ability both to defend Chinese interests and maintain regional stability. In chapter 9 Mingjiang Li and Robert S. Ross discuss the challenges to Chinese security policy. They find that before Xi Jinping assumed the Chinese presidency in March 2013, Hu Jintao's heavy-handed approach toward regional security had deepened many regional states' apprehension over Chinese intentions, so much so that China's relations with much of the region were "in a worse state" than they had been anytime during the previous two decades. Li and Ross argue that China's challenge of sustaining improved relations with its neighbors will be especially difficult within the context of China's increasingly complex policy-making environment, the persistence of nationalism, and the politics of foreign policy making.

This volume is the result of the conference China's Rise and Its Fifth-Generation Leaders, hosted by the Centre for Asian Security Studies at the Norwegian Institute for Defence Studies in May 2013. We would like to thank the staff at the institute who organized and participated in the conference and made invaluable contributions, and to William Mayborn of Boston College for his assistance in the preparation of the manuscript. We are also grateful to Donald Jacobs and his staff at Georgetown University Press for their support and patience in the publication process.

## NOTES

1. These figures (GDP, current prices in US dollars) are based on International Monetary Fund estimates derived from official Chinese statistics; downloaded March 16, 2015 from http://www.imf.org/external/pubs/ft/weo/2014/02/weo data/index.aspx.
2. These figures are based on the SIPRI (Stockholm International Peace Research Institute) military expenditure database, downloaded September 12, 2015, from http://milexdata.sipri.org/.
3. "Premier: China Confident in Maintaining Economic Growth," Xinhua News Agency, March 16, 2007, accessed August 12, 2013, at http://news.xinhuanet .com/english/2007-03/16/content_5856569.htm.

4.  The United Kingdom acknowledged the Communist leadership in Beijing by the beginning of 1950, while France waited until 1964 to establish diplomatic relations with China. Japan established diplomatic relations with China in 1972, and the United States did the same in 1979.

5.  International Monetary Fund statistics, downloaded March 15, 2015, from http://www.imf.org/external/pubs/ft/weo/2014/02/weodata.

6.  The Human Development Index (HDI) is a tool for monitoring human development trends and developments in a country's GDP as well as in its health and education sectors. For further information see Human Development Report 2010, Twentieth Anniversary Edition, *The Real Wealth of Nations: Pathways to Human Development*, United Nations Development Programme.

7.  International Monetary Fund statistics, downloaded March 15, 2015, from http://www.imf.org/external/pubs/ft/weo/2014/02/weodata.

8.  WTO international trade statistics of 2001, in World Trade Organization, Geneva (2001), downloaded March 15, 2015, from https://www.wto.org/english/res_e/statis_e/its2001_e/stats2001_e.pdf.

9.  WTO international trade statistics of 2001, World Trade Organization, Geneva (2001), downloaded March 15, 2015, from https://www.wto.org/english/res_e/statis_e/its2001_e/stats2001_e.pdf; and International Monetary Fund statistics, downloaded March 15, 2015, from http://www.imf.org/external/pubs/ft/weo/2014/02/weodata.

10.  See http://data.worldbank.org/about/country-and-lending-groups.

11.  Joseph S. Nye Jr., *Presidential Leadership and the Creation of the American Era* (Princeton, NJ: Princeton University Press, 2013).

12.  J. G. March and J. P. Olsen, "The New Institutionalism: Organizational Factors in Political Life," *American Political Science Review* 78, no. 3 (1984): 734–49.

13.  Kathleen Thelen, "Historical Institutionalism in Comparative Politics," *Annual Review of Political Science* 2 (1999): 369–404.

14.  Philip Selznick, *Leadership in Administration: A Sociological Interpretation* (New York: Harper and Row, 1957).

# PART I

## Domestic Challenges
## for the Chinese Leadership

# 1

# CHINA'S FIFTH-GENERATION LEADERS

## Characteristics of the New Elite and Pathways to Leadership

### Bo Zhiyue

Until 1989, the concept of "generations" within the Chinese Communist Party (CCP) leadership did not exist. The founding fathers of the People's Republic of China had been invariably referred to as "old generation revolutionaries" (*lao yi dai ge ming jia*), but no further delineation was made to differentiate veteran leaders. "First-generation leadership" was posthumously reconstructed by Deng Xiaoping. According to Deng, the CCP's leaders from 1921 to 1935 were not worth consideration because none of them had been mature enough. The first mature CCP leadership started with Mao Zedong, Liu Shaoqi, Zhou Enlai, and Zhu De.[1]

Deng also dismissed Mao's successor, Hua Guofeng, as a transitional figure since he did not have his own ideology. Hua was simply an advocate of Maoism and he adopted a policy of whateverism (seen in his statement "We will resolutely uphold whatever policy decisions Chairman Mao made, and unswervingly follow whatever instructions Chairman Mao gave"). According to Deng, the "second generation" refers to the CCP leadership that initiated reforms and opening policies, that is, Deng's own generation. Though Deng himself belonged to the first-generation leadership, he played an important role in starting new policies of reform and the country's opening to the West.

Deng's point of framing the CCP history in terms of generations was meant to introduce a new leadership, the post-Tiananmen group, who would take over from his generation and move forward. At the Fourteenth National Congress of the CCP in October 1992, Deng wanted to both retain the services of the third-generation leadership with Jiang Zemin at the helm and also select a candidate, Hu Jintao, as the core of the fourth-generation leadership. Ten years later, at the Sixteenth National Congress held in November 2002, the baton was passed from the third to the fourth-generation leadership. In the meantime, China was also grooming the fifth-generation leadership

The first individual to be considered a candidate for the fifth-generation leadership was Li Keqiang (born July 1955). At the age of thirty-seven in 1992, he was poised to succeed Song Defu (born February 1946) as the first secretary of the Central Committee of the Chinese Communist Youth League (CCYL) at the forthcoming Thirteenth National Congress of the CCYL the following year.[2] In 1992 Li was nominated as a candidate for alternate membership in the Fourteenth Central Committee of the CCP while he was still a member of the secretariat of the Central Committee of the CCYL. However, Li failed in the election partly because deputies to the Fourteenth National Congress did not feel the need to elect an alternate member in addition to a full member (Song Defu) from the CCYL.[3]

Two fifth-generation candidates emerged during the Fifteenth Party Congress held in September 1997: Li Keqiang, who was elected to be a full member of the Central Committee of the CCP in his capacity as first secretary of the Central Committee of the CCYL without a glitch; and Xi Jinping (born June 1953), a young candidate who also almost failed to enter the Fifteenth Central Committee of the CCP as an alternate. As deputy secretary of Fujian province beginning in 1995, Xi's image as a "princeling" (as the son of Xi Zhongxun) was probably a liability. Among the candidates for alternate membership, Xi was ranked number 151, one place short of the originally planned number of alternate members. Xi was eventually included as an alternate member of the Fifteenth Central Committee of the CCP through his selection as a candidate for the fifth-generation leadership.[4]

The majority of fifth-generation leaders entered the Sixteenth Central Committee of the CCP in 2002 as full members, many of whom entered the Seventeenth Politburo in 2007 and the Eighteenth Politburo Standing Committee in 2012. It will be instructive to understand these fifth-generation leaders in terms of their demographic characteristics (age, education, home province, ethnicity, and gender). We will then analyze their pathways to leadership in terms of political endowments, political origins, training grounds, and launching pads.

# CHARACTERISTICS OF FIFTH-GENERATION LEADERS

## Age and Generation Cohorts

The CCP has developed two norms for Politburo members: "age sixty-eight" and "age sixty-four." "Age sixty-eight" refers to the norm that those who are sixty-eight or older are not eligible for election to a new Politburo term; "age sixty-four" refers to the norm that those who are sixty-four or older are not eligible for election as new Politburo members.

It is widely believed that the age sixty-eight norm began in 2002 when Li Ruihuan, a then-standing member of the Politburo and chairman of the Chinese People's Political Consultative Conference (CPPCC), was retired at the age of sixty-eight.[5] However, another Politburo member, Li Tieying (son of Li Weihan), was also retired from the Politburo in 2002 even though he was only sixty-six years old (born in September 1936). Li Tieying had been a member of the Politburo for three consecutive terms and was retired probably because he was considered a member of the third-generation leadership. Two people who were one year older than Li Tieying were either promoted to the Politburo Standing Committee or made new members of the Politburo: Luo Gan (born in July 1935), a member of the Fifteenth Politburo, was promoted to the Sixteenth Politburo Standing Committee; and Gen. Cao Gangchuan (born in December 1935), a member of the Central Military Commission, was made a member of the Sixteenth Politburo.

The norm of age sixty-eight was enforced in 2007 when Zeng Qinghong, the vice president of China, was retired, while Jia Qinglin, the chairman of the CPPCC, was retained. Jia is only eight months younger than Zeng: Zeng was born in July 1939 and Jia in March 1940. The same norm was also enforced at the Eighteenth Party Congress in 2012: Wang Lequan (born in December 1944) was retired, while Yu Zhengsheng (born in April 1945) was promoted to the Politburo Standing Committee. Yu is merely four months younger than Wang, and in fact Wang was still only sixty-seven years old at the time of the Eighteenth Party Congress in November 2012.

China's top political leaders can be divided into different generations according to birth year vis-à-vis age sixty-eight. Generations are usually separated by ten-year increments, and two cohorts can be identified within each generation. In this sense the third-generation cohort refers to those who were born between 1930 and 1934; third-and-a-half-generation cohort refers to those who were born between 1935 and 1939; the fourth-generation cohort refers to those who were born between 1940 and 1944; and so on (see table 1.1).[6]

**Table 1.1** Generation Cohorts for Politburo Members in China

| Generation Cohort | Year of Birth | Year of Retirement | Party Congress |
|---|---|---|---|
| 3.0 | 1930–1934 | 2002 | Sixteenth |
| 3.5 | 1935–1939 | 2007 | Seventeenth |
| 4.0 | 1940–1944 | 2012 | Eighteenth |
| 4.5 | 1945–1949 | 2017 | Nineteenth |
| 5.0 | 1950–1954 | 2022 | Twentieth |
| 5.5 | 1955–1959 | 2027 | Twenty-First |
| 6.0 | 1960–1964 | 2032 | Twenty-Second |
| 6.5 | 1965–1969 | 2037 | Twenty-Third |

Apparently the norm of age sixty-four—which was introduced in 2007—was not enforced in 2012, because five new members of the Eighteenth Politburo were age sixty-five or older. These five were Fan Changlong (sixty-five), Guo Jinlong (sixty-five), Meng Jianzhu (sixty-five), Ma Kai (sixty-six), and Li Jianguo (sixty-six). In fact, the last two, who had been skipped five years earlier, were installed as new members of the Politburo at age sixty-six.

As a result, the new leadership that was produced by the Eighteenth National Party Congress is a mix of four cohorts, all of whom were born in the late 1940s through the early 1960s. It seems that the largest cohort of the Eighteenth Politburo is not the 5.0 generation cohort but rather the 4.5 generation cohort. Of the twenty-five members, eleven belong to the 4.5 generation cohort, or 44 percent of the total (see table 1.2). The second largest cohort is the 5.0 generation, equaling 32 percent of the total. Four people belong to the 5.5 generation cohort and two to the 6.0 generation cohort.

**Table 1.2** Generation Cohorts of the Eighteenth Politburo

| Generation Cohort | Freq. | Percent | Cumulative Percent |
|---|---|---|---|
| 4.5 | 11 | 44 | 44 |
| 5.0 | 8 | 32 | 76 |
| 5.5 | 4 | 16 | 92 |
| 6.0 | 2 | 8 | 100 |
| Total | 25 | 100 | |

Source: Author's database.

In fact, of the seven members of the Eighteenth Politburo Standing Committee, only Xi Jinping can be considered a fifth-generation leader. Five other members are 4.5-generation leaders, and one is a 5.5-generation leader.

Interestingly, President Xi Jinping and Premier Li Keqiang belong to different cohorts, although they are only two years apart in age. Xi was born in 1953 (thus belonging to the 5.0-generation cohort) and Li was born in 1955 (belonging to the 5.5-generation cohort). The political implication is that while Xi will have to retire in 2022 when he is sixty-nine years old, Li will not have to because he will be only sixty-seven years old by then. In other words, Li Keqiang, Wang Yang, and Wang Huning could work for another five years beyond 2022, and Hu Chunhua and Sun Zhengcai could work for another ten years after 2022.

Due to the retention and admission of many members of the 4.5-generation cohort, in 2012 the average age of the Eighteenth Politburo membership was a bit older than that of the Sixteenth Politburo in 2002. The former was just over sixty-one years old; the latter was not yet sixty-one years old. Since all five new members of the Eighteenth Politburo Standing Committee are from the 4.5-generation cohort, their average age is sixty-five-and-a-half years old and almost six years older than the average age of the two oldest standing members.

Compared to Politburo members produced by national party congresses since 1982, however, the average age of the Eighteenth Politburo is only marginally different from that of its predecessors (see table 1.3). Because of the structure of generation cohorts in the Politburo, another major turnover will occur during the Nineteenth National Party Congress in 2017, when at least eleven Politburo members (including five standing members and six full members) will have to retire.

**Table 1.3** Average Age of Politburo Members (1982–2012)

| The Politburo | Alternate | Full | Standing | Total |
| --- | --- | --- | --- | --- |
| Twelfth (1982) | 64.7 | 71.2 | 73.8 | 71.0 |
| Thirteenth (1987) | 58.0 | 64.8 | 63.6 | 64.1 |
| Fourteenth (1992) | 58.5 | 61.8 | 63.7 | 62.1 |
| Fifteenth (1997) | 58.5 | 62.5 | 65.4 | 63.0 |
| Sixteenth (2002) | 60.0 | 59.9 | 62.1 | 60.7 |
| Seventeenth (2007) | | 61.4 | 62.3 | 61.8 |
| Eighteenth (2012) | | 60.3 | 63.4 | 61.2 |

## Education

Educational credentials have always been an important symbol for Chinese politicians. A college degree is a must for anyone who wants to make it to the Central Committee of the CCP. But it has become fashionable for ambitious politicians to go further and obtain master's degrees and even doctoral degrees as well.

The Eighteenth Politburo could be classified according to its members' formal college education. One group did not go to college on a full-time basis, one group went to college as "worker-peasant-soldier" students during the Cultural Revolution, and one group went to college either before the Cultural Revolution had begun or after it had concluded.

Surprisingly, even thirty-five years after Deng Xiaoping reopened colleges to qualified students through competitive national college entrance examinations, less than a quarter of Politburo members are products of this system (see table 1.4). Of the twenty-five members, only six received formal academic training through this competitive system. Li Keqiang, Li Yuanchao, Hu Chunhua, and Sun Zhengcai were admitted to universities after 1977; Wang Huning and Ma Kai skipped college and went straight to graduate programs after 1977.

Another 24 percent of that group received their college educations during the Cultural Revolution, and their educational programs were shorter than members who studied either before or after it. These include Zhang Dejiang, Liu Qibao, Wang Qishan, Xi Jinping, Zhang Chunxian, and Zhao Leji. Zhao Leji and Li Keqiang, for instance, went to the same institution of higher learning: Peking University. Zhao was enrolled in the Department of Philosophy from February 1977 to January 1980, or a period of three years. Li was enrolled in the Department of Law from March 1978 to January 1982, or nearly four years. Xi Jinping and Liu Yandong attended the same department at the same university: the Department of Chemical Engineering at Tsinghua

**Table 1.4** College Educational Experience of Eighteenth Politburo Members

| College Education | Freq. | Percent | Cumulative Percent |
|---|---|---|---|
| No formal education | 8 | 32 | 32 |
| Before the Cultural Revolution | 5 | 20 | 52 |
| During the Cultural Revolution | 6 | 24 | 76 |
| After the Cultural Revolution | 6 | 24 | 100 |
| Total | 25 | 100 | |

Source: Author's database.

University. Xi was there from October 1975 to March 1979, or three-and-a-half years. Liu studied in the same department from September 1964 to March 1970 for five-and-a-half years.

In this context, Li Yuanchao's experience is rather unique. He studied mathematics at Shanghai Normal University from 1972 to 1974, during the Cultural Revolution. But he decided to go back to school again through the competitive national college entrance examinations and was admitted to the Department of Mathematics at Fudan University in February 1978.

Twenty percent of the Eighteenth Politburo members entered college before the Cultural Revolution: Yu Zhengsheng, Liu Yandong, Li Jianguo, Guo Jinlong, and Zhang Gaoli. Unfortunately, shortly after their enrollment the Cultural Revolution began, interrupting their academic training. In this group, Yu went to college the earliest. He was admitted to Harbin Institute of Military Engineering in August 1963. Liu, Li, and Guo went to college in 1964, and Zhang enrolled in 1965. The Cultural Revolution broke out in May 1966, at which point education at all universities in China was brought to a halt.

Most surprisingly, almost one-third of the Eighteenth Politburo members did not go to college on a full-time basis at all. Eight members (including one standing member) did not attend college on a full-time basis in their early years. They are Liu Yunshan, Wang Yang, Han Zheng, Li Zhanshu, Sun Chunlan, Meng Jianzhu, Xu Qiliang, and Fan Changlong.

In fact, one standing member of the Eighteenth Politburo never went to college at all: Liu Yunshan. After graduating from middle school Liu was admitted to Jining Normal School in Inner Mongolia in 1964. Jining Normal School is not a college but a teachers training school (*zhongzhuan* in Chinese).[7] Similarly, Sun Chunlan began studies at a technical school in Liaoning at the age of fifteen, then after her graduation went to work in a factory. Gen. Xu Qiliang followed a similar path. He joined the People's Liberation Army (PLA) at the age of sixteen as a cadet of Air Force No. 1 Aeronautic Preparatory School and became a pilot after intensive training at air force aeronautic schools No. 8 and No. 5. Similarly, Li Zhanshu spent a year in a finance and commerce school in Shijiazhuang of Hebei province in the early 1970s before he joined the workforce in December 1972.

Fan Changlong, Han Zheng, Meng Jianzhu, and Wang Yang did not attend either college or any kind of technical school. After two months as an "educated youth" in Liaoning, Fan joined the PLA in January 1969. Han started working in Shanghai at the age of twenty-one. Meng began his work on a farm in Shanghai in August 1968. And after losing his father at a young age, in 1972 Wang inherited his father's job in a food processing factory in Suxian of Anhui province at the age of seventeen.[8]

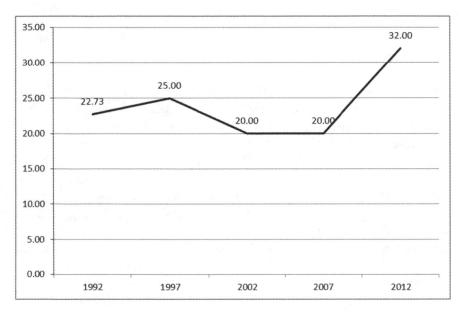

**Figure 1.1** Percentage of Politburo Members with No Full-Time College Education

Historically speaking, the current Politburo is the least educated. The percentage of Politburo members with no full-time college education is the highest since 1992 (see figure 1.1). However, while it is understandable that some political leaders of earlier generations did not get a chance to go to college on a full-time basis because they were professional revolutionaries, in a year when China produced almost seven million college graduates it is almost inconceivable that almost one-third of its top leaders had never attended college on a full-time basis. Clearly, these top elites are not social elites in today's China.

For those who did attend college to obtain an undergraduate or graduate degree, the majority went for humanities and social sciences. Ten of the seventeen members, or 58 percent, studied humanities and social sciences (see table 1.5). Only seven people studied the sciences and engineering. Six people undertook subjects in humanities: Li Jianguo and Hu Chunhua both studied Chinese literature; Wang Qishan and Liu Qibao studied history; Zhao Leji studied philosophy; and Zhang Dejiang first studied the Korean language in China and then took courses on economics at the Kim Il-sung Comprehensive University in North Korea. Four leaders were social sciences majors: Li Keqiang studied law; Zhang Gaoli and Ma Kai, economics; and Wang Huning, international politics. Seven leaders were enrolled in sciences or engineering: Yu Zhengsheng studied ballistic missiles; Liu Yandong and

**Table 1.5** College Majors of Eighteenth Politburo Members

| College Majors | Freq. | Percent | Cumulative Percent |
|---|---|---|---|
| Humanities | 6 | 35.29 | 35.29 |
| Social sciences | 4 | 25.53 | 58.82 |
| Sciences and engineering | 7 | 41.18 | 100.00 |
| Total | 17 | 100.00 | |

Source: Author's database.

Xi Jinping, chemical engineering; Li Yuanchao, mathematics; Sun Zhengcai, agriculture; Zhang Chunxian, machine building; and Guo Jinlong, physics. Again, considering Politburo membership over the past two decades, the Eighteenth Politburo has the lowest percentage of members with engineering backgrounds (see figure 1.2). With relatively more people trained in the social sciences and humanities, the new leadership is better prepared to handle social and economic issues.

Through remedial courses, members who did not have a chance to attend college on a full-time basis were able to obtain college degrees and even graduate degrees later on. According to their official biographies, the present leadership is highly educated (see table 1.6).

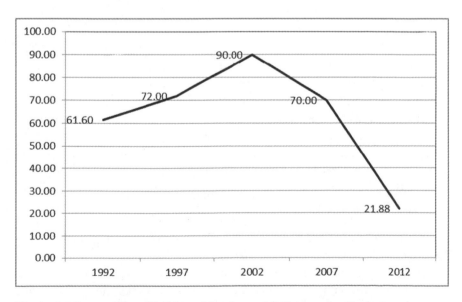

**Figure 1.2** Percentages of Politburo Members with Engineering Backgrounds

**Table 1.6** Educational Achievements of the 18th Politburo Members

| Degree | Freq. | Percent | Cumulative Percent |
|---|---|---|---|
| Three-year college | 1 | 4 | 4 |
| Four-year college | 8 | 32 | 36 |
| Graduate | 2 | 8 | 44 |
| Master's | 9 | 36 | 80 |
| PhD | 5 | 20 | 100 |
| Total | 25 | 100 | |

Source: Author's database.

Almost two-thirds of the current leaders have obtained postgraduate degrees, including nine master's degrees and five PhDs. Two members—Sun Chunlan and Zhao Leji—obtained their graduate diplomas through Party schools.[9] Except for Ma Kai and Wang Huning, seven obtained their master's degrees through part-time studies. And, with the exception of Sun Zhengcai, four others—Li Keqiang, Li Yuanchao, Liu Yandong, and Xi Jinping—received their doctoral degrees through part-time studies. Xi Jinping in particular was directly matriculated into a doctoral program without having to obtain a master's degree first.

## Home Province

"Home province" is a complicated concept.[10] Traditionally the term refers to one's ancestral home. But it can also refer to one's birthplace or a place where one grew up. The problem is that these three often are not the same. Xi Jinping's ancestral home, for instance, is Shaanxi, but he was born and grew up in Beijing. Wang Qishan's ancestral home is Shanxi but he was born in Shandong and grew up in Beijing. Yu Zhengsheng's ancestral home is Zhejiang but he was born either in Shaanxi or Hebei and grew up in Tianjin and Beijing.[11] For the current discussion, "home province" will refer to the locale used in the official biographies of these leaders.

It is clear from the data in table 1.7 that three provinces are prominent as home provinces. Shandong and Jiangsu each have produced four members of the Eighteenth Politburo: Sun Zhengcai, Xu Qiliang, Li Jianguo, and Wang Huning are all from Shandong; Li Yuanchao, Liu Yandong, Guo Jinlong, and Meng Jianzhu are from Jiangsu. Sun Zhengcai, Xu Qiliang, and Li Jianguo were all born and grew up in their home province of Shandong. But Wang Huning was born in Shanghai and grew up there.[12] Li Yuanchao was born in Jiangsu but grew up in Shanghai. Liu Yandong was also born in Jiangsu but grew up in Shanghai and Beijing. Guo Jinlong was born and grew up in Jiangsu. Meng Jianzhu was probably born in Shanghai and grew up there.[13] Anhui is also prominent as a home province and has produced three members of the Eighteenth Politburo: Li Keqiang, Liu Qibang, and Wang Yang. All three were born and grew up in their home province.

Although only one person—Ma Kai—has identified Shanghai as his home province, Shanghai is an important place for four other members: Wang Huning, Li Yuanchao, Meng Jianzhu, and Han Zheng all grew up there. A native of Zhejiang, Han Zheng attended elementary and middle schools in Shanghai.[14] As for Ma Kai, he was actually born in Shanxi and grew up in Shaanxi and Beijing.[15] In 1953 he went to an elementary school in Xi'an and then moved to Beijing in 1955, eventually graduating from No. 4 Middle School in Beijing.

Beijing is a significant place for five members of the Eighteenth Politburo: Yu Zhengsheng, Wang Qishan, Liu Yandong, Ma Kai, and Xi Jinping grew up there. Yu Zhengsheng and Ma Kai went to the same middle school (No. 4 Middle School) and Liu Yandong went to the Middle School of Tsinghua University.[16] Xi Jinping went to Bayi School and No. 25 Middle School.[17] Wang Qishan went to No. 35 Middle School.[18]

**Table 1.7** Home Provinces of the 18th Politburo Members

| Home Province | Freq. | Percent | Cumulative Percent |
|---|---|---|---|
| Anhui | 3 | 12 | 12 |
| Fujian | 1 | 4 | 16 |
| Hebei | 2 | 8 | 24 |
| Henan | 1 | 4 | 28 |
| Hubei | 1 | 4 | 32 |
| Jiangsu | 4 | 16 | 48 |
| Liaoning | 2 | 8 | 56 |
| Shaanxi | 2 | 8 | 64 |
| Shandong | 4 | 16 | 80 |
| Shanghai | 1 | 4 | 84 |
| Shanxi | 2 | 8 | 92 |
| Zhejiang | 2 | 8 | 100 |
| Total | 25 | 100 | |

Source: Author's database.

After recalculation based on the above information, it's clear that Beijing and Shanghai are very important for the Eighteenth Politburo members. They are "home" for nine of them, including three standing members and six full members. In contrast, Shaanxi has disappeared from the list because neither Xi Jinping nor Zhao Leji grew up there.

## Ethnicity and Gender

Eighteenth Politburo members are all from the Han ethnic majority. Not one member is from a minority ethnic group. In the entire history of the CCP since 1945, only four people with ethnic Mongol backgrounds have ever been named to the Politburo.

Ulanhu, a Mongol, was the first minority person to be admitted to the Politburo. He is commonly considered the founding father of Inner Mongolia under the leadership of the CCP, and was made an alternate member of the Eighth Politburo in 1956. Serving concurrently as vice premier of the state council with a military rank of full general, Ulanhu was the most powerful leader having a minority background. After initial sufferings at the beginning of the Cultural Revolution, Ulanhu came back to power in 1973 and was made a full member of the Eleventh Politburo in 1977. He was reelected into the Twelfth Politburo in 1982, was subsequently elected vice president of China in 1983, and retired from the Politburo two years later.

Wei Guoqing, a Zhuang, and Seypidin Ezizi, a Uyghur, were both admitted to the Politburo in 1973. Wei, the first party secretary of Guangxi Zhuang Autonomous Region and the first political commissar of the Guangzhou Military Region, was a full member of the Tenth, Eleventh, and Twelfth Politburos. He also retired from the Politburo in 1985. Seypidin, the first party secretary of Xinjiang Uyghur Autonomous Region, was an alternate member of the Tenth and Eleventh Politburos.

Since 1985 only one person from a minority ethnic group was a member of the Politburo: Hui Liangyu, a native of Jilin, is of Hui ethnicity. In Jilin, chances for being a Hui are very small. Over 90 percent of the population in Jilin is of Han origin, and less than 10 percent are ethnic minorities. Among the minorities, Koreans and Manchus are the largest groups, together accounting for 87 percent of all minorities in the province. These two are followed by Mongols and Hui, 7 percent and 5 percent of the minorities in Jilin, respectively.[19] As an ethnic group, the Hui in Jilin are not significantly different from the Han there. But even with this background, Hui Liangyu was able to enter the Politburo in 2002 and served two consecutive terms. He was also vice premier in charge of agriculture for two terms.

There are two female members in the Eighteenth Politburo: Liu Yandong, currently vice premier of the state council, is serving a second term as a Politburo member; and Sun Chunlan, former party secretary of Tianjin and currently director of the Central United Front Department, is a new member. In the history of the Chinese Communist Party only eight females have served as members of the Politburo. Jiang Qing and Ye Qun were the first. They were installed as members of the Ninth Politburo in 1969 because of their special relationship with other top leaders (Jiang Qing was Mao Zedong's wife and Ye Qun was Lin Biao's wife). The third female member of the Politburo, Wu Guixian, was a textile worker from Shaanxi. She was an alternate member of the Tenth Politburo. Deng Yingchao (Zhou Enlai's wife) and Chen Muhua were members of the Eleventh Politburo. Deng was a full member of the Politburo from October 1978 to September 1985, and Chen was an alternate member of the Politburo from August 1977 to November 1987.

Due to the age sixty-eight rule, Liu Yandong must retire in 2017 but Sun Chunlan is likely to stay. If she is doing well in her current position, in a few years Sun could become the first female standing member of the Politburo.

## PATHWAYS TO LEADERSHIP

### Political Endowments

"Political endowments" refer to the initial political capital one is able to garner as a foundation for a possible political career. This capital includes at least three aspects, beginning with membership in the CCP. The very first step in anyone's political career in China is to become a CCP member. Even though members of the Eighteenth Politburo are all members of the CCP, we should not underestimate their early efforts to join the Party. Xi Jinping, for instance, wrote eight applications before he was admitted to the Chinese Communist Youth League and ten applications before he was admitted to the CCP.[20] It is also erroneous to presume that people like Xi Jinping possess huge political endowments because of their family backgrounds. In fact, Xi had to make extra efforts because his father was more of a political liability than a political asset at the time.

Eighteenth Politburo members joined the CCP in different years. Three people joined the Party before the Cultural Revolution: Liu Yandong, Yu Zhengsheng, and Ma Kai. Liu, daughter of Liu Ruilong, joined the CCP in July 1964 at the age of eighteen while she was still a high school student.[21] Yu Zhengsheng joined the Party in November 1964 at the age of nineteen when he was a sophomore at the Harbin Institute of Military Engineering. Ma Kai also joined the Party as a high school student, in August 1965. He was retained as a schoolteacher one month later.

Fifteen members (60 percent) joined the CCP during the decade of the Cultural Revolution (1966–1976). Xu Qiliang and Fan Changlong both became Party members after joining the People's Liberation Army (PLA). Though not yet eighteen years old, Xu joined the Party one year after he became a cadet in the Air Force No. 1 Aeronautic Preparatory School in July 1967. Fan joined the PLA in January 1969 and joined the Party in September 1969, a short nine months later.

Zhang Dejiang, Liu Yunshan, Meng Jianzhu, Li Jianguo, and Liu Qibao all joined the Party in 1971. Zhang joined when he was a staff member of the Propaganda Group under the Revolutionary Committee of Wangqing County in Jilin. Liu joined in April 1971 when he was a staff member of Tomd Right Banner Party Committee in Inner Mongolia. Meng joined in June of the year while he was working at a state farm in Shanghai. Li joined in June of the year after he was sent to Tianjin for physical labor. And Liu joined in December of the year when he was working as a farmer in his hometown of Anhui.

Zhang Chunxian, Zhang Gaoli, and Sun Chunlan all joined the Party in 1973. Zhang Chunxian joined when he was a PLA soldier; Zhang Gaoli joined when he was working for Maoming Oil Company in Guangdong; and Sun joined while working in a factory in Liaoning. After great efforts, Xi joined the Party in January 1974. Li Zhanshu, Zhao Leji, and Wang Yang all joined the Party in 1975: Li as a staff member of the Commerce Bureau in Shijianzhuang, Hebei; Zhao in July 1975 at the age of eighteen while an "educated youth" in Tsinghua; and Wang Yang in August 1975 while a factory worker in Anhui. Li Keqiang joined the Party in May 1976 at the age of twenty when he was an educated youth in his home province of Anhui.

Seven Politburo members joined the Party after 1978. Li Yuanchao joined in March 1978, right before he was enrolled in the Department of Mathematics at Fudan University. Already twenty-seven years old, he was a teacher at a technical school in Shanghai at the time. Han Zheng and Guo Jinlong both joined the Party in 1979. Guo was already thirty-one years old when he joined the Party in April 1979. He was a coach in the Sports Committee in Zhongxian, Sichuan. Han joined the Party in May 1979 when he was working for Shanghai Xuhui Crane Installation Team. Wang Qishan and Hu Chunhua both joined the Party in 1983, though Wang is fifteen years older than Hu. Hu joined the Party in April 1983, a few months before his graduation from Peking University. He was twenty years old.

Wang Qishan joined the Party in February 1983 at the age of thirty-four. It is not clear how many applications he had submitted but, regardless, his earlier attempts to join the Party had been unsuccessful. Like Xi Jinping, Wang also went to Shaanxi in January 1969 as an educated youth; Xi went to Yanchuan County and Wang to Yan'an County. Xi stayed in Shaanxi for almost seven years while Wang stayed for less than three years. Wang was recruited as an interpreter by the Shaanxi Museum in late 1971 and was enrolled at Northwestern University (Xibei Daxue) in 1973. After graduating he returned to the Shaanxi Museum and in 1979 was transferred to the Modern History Institute of the Chinese Academy of Social Sciences as an intern. In 1982 he was recruited by the Research Office of Agricultural Policies under the secretariat of the CCP Central Committee and within a year he was admitted to the Party.

Wang Huning also joined the Party quite late. He did not join the Party until April 1984, eight years later than Li Keqiang, who was also born in 1955. Wang was admitted to the Party while a teacher at Fudan University. Immediately after his admission to the Party he was promoted to associate professor, the youngest associate professor at the time. Sun Zhengcai joined the Party in July 1988, one year after he began to work in the Beijing Academy of Agriculture and Forestry. He was twenty-four years old.

Since 80 percent of the Eighteenth Politburo members were admitted to the Party at the age of twenty-five or younger, we may be able to calculate their political endowments in terms of Party membership by subtracting from twenty-five the age they joined the Party. It is clear that different people have different political endowments in terms of Party membership. Xu Qiliang, Zhao Leji, Liu Qibao, Liu Yandong, Yu Zhengsheng, Ma Kai, Zhang Chunxian, Wang Yang, and Hu Chunhua have huge advantages because they joined the Party early. Li Zhanshu, Li Jianguo, Zhang Dejiang, Han Zheng, and Sun Zhengcai did not obtain any advantages by becoming CCP members. And Zhao Gaoli, Li Yuanchao, Wang Huning, Guo Jinlong, and especially Wang Qishan suffered some disadvantages because of their late Party membership.

A second aspect to be understood regarding political endowments is professional background. Of the twenty-five Politburo members, only four can be identified as having engineering backgrounds. Yu Zhengsheng, a typical technocrat with an engineering background, spent at least sixteen years as an engineer in two factories and one research institute. After graduation from the Department of Chemical Engineering at Tsinghua University, Liu Yandong worked in two chemical factories for a total of ten years. Zhang Chunxian became a technician in a factory under the No. 3 Machine Building Ministry upon his graduation from college in 1980 and was promoted to assistant engineer a few years later. Zhang soon moved to the political track by becoming a deputy director of the Organization Department of No. 10 Research Institute Party Committee of the Ministry. Guo Jinlong became a technician in the Hydropower Bureau in Zhongxian, Sichuan, but he soon switched to be a coach in the Sports Bureau.

Five Politburo members began as academics. Ma Kai became an assistant researcher in September 1982 after he obtained his master's degree in political economy from Renmin University of China. Wang Huning taught at Fudan University for fourteen years. Sun Zhengcai worked for ten years in the Beijing Academy of Agriculture and Forestry after his graduation with a master's degree from the same institute. Zhang Dejiang worked as an administrator at Yanbian University for a total of six years during two separate periods. Interestingly, Wang Yang could be classified as an academic because he was an instructor in two different schools for four years even though he probably did not even have a high school diploma.[22]

Five leaders served as personal secretaries to other politicians. Xi Jinping was personal secretary to Geng Biao for three years; Liu Qibao worked in the general office of the Anhui Provincial Party Committee for three years; Li Jianguo worked in the general office of the Tianjin Municipal Party Committee for eleven years; Li Zhanshu worked in two general offices for eleven years total; and Wang Qishan worked as a staff member for Du Runsheng in the Research Office of Agricultural Policies.

Four leaders began their careers as youth league cadres.[23] Han Zheng started off as a storekeeper in the Shanghai Xuhui Crane Installation Team in December 1975, but he became a youth league cadre soon after he joined the Party in May 1979. Li Yuanchao became a youth league cadre after he had obtained a degree in mathematics. Li Keqiang became a youth league cadre after he had obtained a degree in law. Hu Chunhua traveled to Tibet after his graduation and he began as a youth league cadre there.

Three leaders began their careers in factories or on state farms. Sun Chunlan began as a factory worker in Anshan, Liaoning, in November 1969 and spent the subsequent nineteen years in two separate factories and at the bureau that supervised light industries. Zhang Gaoli spent fifteen years in the Maoming Oil Company in Guangdong between 1970 and 1985. Meng Jianzhu started off as a sailor at the Qianwei State Farm in Shanghai in August 1968 and worked in the same place for eighteen years.

In addition to two professional soldiers—Xu Qiliang and Fan Changlong—two Politburo members belong to separate categories. Zhao Leji spent almost two decades in one government organization: the Department of Commerce of Qinghai Provincial Government. He started off as a receptionist in the general office of the department in July 1975 and was promoted to be a staff member of the department's political bureau after his graduation from Peking University. After a three-year stint at the Commerce Training School under the department, Zhao was promoted to deputy head of the department's political bureau in November 1983. Eight years later he was made head of the department.

Liu Yunshan's background is also unique among the Eighteenth Politburo members. Although he was initially trained as a schoolteacher, Liu turned out to be a reporter. Upon his graduation from Jining Normal School, Liu taught at a school in Tomd Left Banner (a county) in Inner Mongolia for only one semester and then was sent down to the countryside for physical labor. In 1969 he was recruited by the Tomd Right Banner to be a propaganda staff member responsible for writing articles on local news for newspapers and radio stations of Inner Mongolia. Liu was officially hired by Xinhua News Agency as a reporter in 1975 and worked in that capacity until 1982.[24]

None of the Eighteenth Politburo members can be described as a *haigui*, or someone who studied abroad and then returned to China although three people did have foreign learning experiences. Zhang Dejiang, for instance, studied in North Korea for two years. He was enrolled in the Department of Economics at the Kim Il-sung Comprehensive University from 1978 to 1980. Wang Huning was a visiting scholar at two universities in the United States. He visited the University of Iowa and the University of California at Berkeley from 1988 to 1989. Sun Zhengcai spent six months in the United Kingdom as a visiting scholar, visiting Rothamsted Experimental Station (now Rothamsted Research) from January to July 1991. Though brief, these limited experiences may still offer these three somewhat different perspectives.

A third aspect of political endowments is social network. In every Chinese person's social circle, the father is the most important. Having a father who has enormous political capital and a strong social network is critical for a successful political career. Oftentimes one's mother plays the role of facilitator on behalf of the father. The father-in-law ranks second, and having the right wife is also important. But one's patron could also be someone who is not related. Most important, one needs more than one patron to move ahead.

In this regard princelings enjoy great advantages. In China there are two types of princeling: princeling by birth and princeling by marriage. "Princeling by birth" refers to those whose parents are high-ranking officials. "Princeling by marriage" refers to those whose parents-in-law are high-ranking officials. Of the Eighteenth Politburo members, six are princelings, five by birth and one by marriage: Xi Jinping, Yu Zhengsheng, Liu Yandong, Li Jianguo, and Li Yuanchao belong to the former and Wang Qishan belongs to the latter. Xi Jinping's critical promotion from party secretary of Zhengding County in Hebei to vice mayor of Xiamen in June 1985 is certainly due to his father's connections.[25] Wang Qishan's uplift in April 1982 from being an intern at the Chinese Academy of Social Sciences to being a researcher with the chief county rank at the Research Office of Agricultural Policies without having a CCP membership could be traced to the fact that his father-in-law is Yao Yilin, a member of the secretariat of the CCP Central Committee, a vice premier of the state council, and the director of the general office of the CCP Central Committee. Obviously Wang Qishan's social networks are more than enough to compensate for his late arrival to party membership.

However, it is not always easy to attribute the promotions of these leaders to their fathers or fathers-in-law. Yu Zhengsheng, for instance, could not rely on his father for his political career because his father, Huang Jing, passed away in 1958 when Yu was only thirteen years old. Another example is Li Jianguo: his father, Li Yunchuan, was a former ambassador to a number of countries but he has not been visibly influential in Li's political promotions.

## Political Origin

"Political origin" refers to the locale where a first significant political office is obtained. Political elites do not always have to start from scratch. Their first significant political appointment could be anywhere between deputy county level and deputy provincial level.

Political elites with youth league backgrounds tend to have relatively higher initial positions, and they experience more rapid promotions. Liu Qibao's first significant appointment was as deputy director of the propaganda department of the Anhui Provincial Youth League Committee in June 1980, a position equivalent to the deputy county level. He was promoted to the deputy secretary position in May 1982 and to the secretary position in August 1983. Clearly Anhui was Liu's political origin, and specifically the Youth League Committee of Anhui province.

Following in Liu Qibao's footsteps was Wang Yang, another native of Anhui. Wang's first significant political appointment was in October 1980 to deputy secretary of the Xuxian Prefecture Youth League Committee (the deputy county level). Wang succeeded Liu Qibao as director of the propaganda department of the Youth League Committee of Anhui in October 1982 and then as deputy secretary of the Youth League Committee of Anhui in August 1983.

Li Yuanchao's first significant appointment was as deputy secretary (the deputy department level) of the Shanghai Municipal Youth League Committee in April 1983. He was promoted to its secretary the very next month and was further promoted to be a member of the secretariat of the central committee of the Chinese Communist Youth League (CCYL) in December 1983 (the vice-ministerial level). Li's rapid promotions within a year were probably due to his connection to Chen Pixian, a then-member of the secretariat of the CCP Central Committee and the former first party secretary of Shanghai.[26]

One of Li Yuanchao's successors as secretary of the Shanghai Youth League Committee, Han Zheng, succeeded Huang Yuejin, Li Yuanchao's successor, in May 1991. Since Huang had left in April 1990 for a position in Hongkou District of Shanghai, Han had been in charge of the Shanghai Youth League Committee through his capacity as its deputy secretary since June 1990.[27] Han was appointed acting head of Luwan District in Shanghai in November 1992.

Liu Yandong also experienced rapid promotions in the early 1980s. She was appointed deputy secretary of the Chaoyang District in Beijing in 1981 (the deputy department level), but was promoted to be a member of the secretariat of the Central Committee of the CCYL in December 1982. She skipped the chief department level and went straight to the vice-ministerial level.

Upon graduation from the Department of Law at Peking University, Li Keqiang was appointed secretary of its Youth League Committee (probably the deputy department level) in January 1982. He was soon promoted to alternate membership of the secretariat of the CCYL Central Committee in December 1983 and then to full membership of the secretariat in November 1985.

Hu Chunhua's political origins could be traced to the Youth League Committee of Tibet. Four years after he was sent as a clerk in the organization department of the Youth League Committee of Tibet, he was made its deputy secretary with a rank of chief county level. Three years later he was promoted to the deputy department level in the same position, and two years after that he was promoted to secretary of the chief department level.

Initially a reporter, Liu Yunshan also had experiences as a Youth League cadre. He was appointed deputy secretary of the Inner Mongolia Youth League Committee in July 1982 and subsequently became a member of the Eleventh Central Committee of the CCYL in December of the same year. In less than two years and with the recommendations of his patron, Tian Congming, the then–secretary general of the Inner Mongolia Party Committee, Liu was made deputy director of the propaganda department of the Inner Mongolia Party Committee in February 1984. Due to his age advantage, Liu was installed as an alternate member of the CCP Central Committee at the National Party Conference in September 1985. He was thirty-eight years old at the time and the only candidate from Inner Mongolia under age forty.[28] Liu's seniority in terms of the CCP Central Committee membership is unparalleled among Eighteenth Politburo members. As an alternate member, Liu was twelve years ahead of Xi Jinping, Wang Qishan, and Liu Yandong and seventeen years ahead of Li Yuanchao and Wang Yang.

Several members of the Eighteenth Politburo started at the county level and moved up one step at a time. Xi Jinping started off as a deputy county party secretary in Zhengding, Hebei, in March 1982. He initially intended to become a party secretary of a people's commune (a township), but the first party secretary of Hebei, Jin Ming, decided to appoint him deputy secretary of Zhengding because he was the son of Xi Zhongxun.[29] Xi was promoted to party secretary of Zhengding in November 1983 and in June 1985 was promoted to be a standing member and vice mayor of Xiamen. It took him only thirty-nine months to reach the deputy department level from the deputy county level.

Xi's career trajectory is much faster than normal promotions. According to regulations on the appointment of leaders at the county level and above, candidates must meet some basic requirements. For positions at the county level, candidates must have at least five years of work experience and two years of experience at the grassroots level; for positions above the county level, candidates must have experience holding at least two positions at a lower level. Candidates for chief positions must have at least two years of experience at deputy positions; candidates for deputy positions of a next-higher level must have three years of experience at chief positions of a lower level.[30] In other words, it should have taken Xi at least five years to move from deputy secretary of Zhengding to vice mayor of Xiamen but he completed the process in less than three and a half years.

Li Zhanshu also began as party secretary of a county in Hebei. In 1982 Li wrote a letter to General Secretary Hu Yaobang proposing to promote the song "Socialism Is Good,"[31] and he was subsequently appointed party secretary of Wuji County in Hebei in October 1983.[32] Li was soon promoted to deputy secretary of Shijiazhuang Prefecture in November 1985 and to secretary of the Youth League Committee of Hebei in April 1986. Compared to Xi, Li's promotions happened even quicker: he skipped the deputy county level and rose to chief department level in two and a half years.

Meng Jianzhu also began as party secretary of a county in Shanghai, but because that county enjoys the chief department level, his initial rank was at the chief department level. Meng was appointed party secretary of Chuansha County in Shanghai in 1986 and was transferred to Jiading County as party secretary in 1990.

Similarly, Sun Zhengcai also began as the head of a chief department level county in Beijing. He was appointed acting head of Shunyi County in Beijing in September 1997 and was later promoted to party secretary of Shunyi

District in February 2002. Three months later he was elected as a standing member of the Beijing Municipal Party Committee "by accident."

Zhang Dejiang's first political appointment was also as deputy party secretary of a county-level city, but he soon skipped several levels and became a vice minister. With recommendations from Li Dezhu, the party secretary of Yanbian Prefecture from November 1983 to October 1990, Zhang was appointed deputy secretary of Yanji City in March 1983 and was soon made a standing member of the Yanbian Prefecture Party Committee in 1984. He was promoted to deputy secretary of Yanbian Prefecture in April 1985 and to vice minister of Civil Affairs in August 1986. It took Zhang only three years and five months to rise from the deputy county level to the vice-ministerial level. His last jump to the Ministry of Civil Affairs was probably due to a nomination by Hu Yaobang because Zhang reportedly accompanied Hu during Hu's visits to North Korea in 1984 and 1985.[33]

A number of other Politburo members also experienced rapid promotions in the 1980s. Wang Qishan's first appointment in the Research Office of Agricultural Policies under the secretariat of the CCP Central Committee in April 1982 was at the chief county level. He skipped three levels: deputy township level, chief township level, and deputy county level. In another four years he became a researcher with a chief department rank. Ordinarily it should have taken him at least five years to get to the chief department level from the chief county level. Li Jianguo also skipped levels during his early career. He was appointed deputy head of the General Office (level 2) under the General Office of the Tianjin Municipal Party Committee (level 1) in 1981 but was promoted to the deputy head of the General Office (level 1) in 1982. In the former position Li was at the deputy county level; in the latter position he was at the deputy department level. He was able to skip one level.

In the race to the top, youth league cadres have huge advantages and many of them get to the vice-ministerial level at younger ages than princelings. Li Keqiang was appointed to a vice-ministerial level position in 1991 at the age of thirty-six. He was two years ahead of Xi Jinping but also four years younger than Xi was in getting to this level. Liu Yandong was the first among the group to get to the vice-ministerial level. She got it in 1982 when she was only thirty-seven. Yu Zhengsheng, who was born in the same year as Liu Yandong, didn't reach the same level until a full ten years later. Li Yuanchao and Hu Chunhua attained the vice-ministerial level before their thirty-sixth birthdays.

While not strictly comparable to other party leaders because of different ranking systems, PLA generals nevertheless can be compared with one another. In this regard, Xu Qiliang has been a shining star in the military. He was appointed to a deputy division commander in 1980 at the age of thirty, five years ahead of Fan Changlong. Three years later he was promoted to chief division commander, which was seven years ahead of Fan Changlong. And he was appointed deputy army commander in 1984 at the age of thirty-four, nine years ahead of Fan. Since Xu is three years younger than Fan, Xu was in fact twelve years younger than Fan when they obtained the rank of deputy army commander. Moreover, Xu entered the CCP Central Committee as an alternate member in 1992, ten years earlier than Fan did.

## Training Grounds

Political elites in China are often sent to different places to be tested before receiving further promotions, and China's provinces are usually useful training grounds for them.[34] Of the twenty-five members of the Eighteenth Politburo, a full twenty had leadership experiences in the provinces (see figure 1.3). Since some political leaders are trained and tested in more than one province, there are altogether fifty-three cases.

Clearly, Guangdong stands out as a training ground for future national leaders because one in five of current Politburo members have been trained there. Shanghai is the second most important training ground for the current

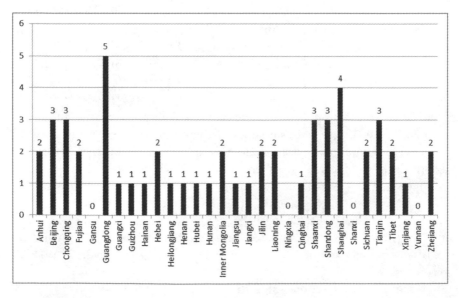

**Figure 1.3** Training Political Leaders in Provinces

leadership; it has provided training opportunities for four national leaders. There are significant differences between Guangdong and Shanghai, however. Shanghai, a stronghold of the Shanghai Gang, has succeeded in promoting its locals to top positions in the municipality. In contrast, Guangdong has been mostly subdued by the central leadership but has been used by outsiders as a major stepping-stone for their further promotions.

Beijing, Tianjin, Chongqing, Shaanxi, and Shandong are also important training ground provinces. Each produced three future national leaders. Beijing has enjoyed a special status in Chinese politics since the founding of the People's Republic of China (PRC). For a long time after the founding of the PRC, Beijing was the only provincial-level unit that was managed by a Politburo member. Since the 1980s, however, Beijing's mayor has always been a grade higher than his provincial counterparts in other provincial units and only Beijing mayors could be directly promoted to state councilors or Politburo members. In the history of the PRC, Tianjin has changed its status several times but has become important in recent years. It has been managed by six Politburo members since 1984. Chongqing has also become important in Chinese politics in recent years; it has produced two Politburo members and has been managed by four others. Shaanxi also has become an important place for grooming national leaders and has produced enough national politicians to form a "clique."[35] One of the largest provinces, Shandong, has produced many national leaders. It is not surprising to find it on the list of top producers. However, Shandong has not been able to maintain its status as a Politburo-level unit.

Among those who were trained in provinces, three members worked in only one provincial unit: Han Zheng never left Shanghai; Li Yuanchao worked in Jiangsu only; and Liu Yunshan hailed from Inner Mongolia. Five members worked in two provinces: Li Keqiang, Liu Qibao, Meng Jianzhu, Zhang Chunxian, and Zhao Leji. Eight members worked in three provinces: Li Jianguo, Sun Chunlan, Sun Zhengcai, Wang Qishan, Wang Yang, Xi Jinping, Yu Zhengsheng, and Zhang Gaoli. And four members worked in four provinces: Guo Jinlong, Hu Chunhua, Li Zhanshu, and Zhang Dejiang.

As for the two PLA generals, they were also trained and tested in different military units and regions. Fan Changlong worked in the Shenyang Military Region and the Jinan Military Region as well as the PLA General Staff Department; Xu Qiliang was trained in the PLA Air Force and the Shenyang Military Region as well as the PLA General Staff Department.

Only three people—Ma Kai, Liu Yandong, and Wang Huning—were not sent to provinces after they obtained the vice-ministerial rank.

## Launching Pads

It is noteworthy to learn where these political elites were "launched" (promoted) to the center. These places are referred to here as launching pads. Clearly, the provinces have served as major launching pads and Shanghai is preeminent in this regard. Three members of the Eighteenth Politburo were launched from Shanghai, including two standing members and one full member. Beijing and Chongqing are also important: each has sent two Politburo members. Of course, these were not sent to the Politburo in the same year. In the case of Beijing, one was sent to the Politburo in 2007 and another in 2012. In the case of Chongqing, one was sent to the Politburo in 2007 and another was sent to the Politburo Standing Committee in 2012. Jilin and Liaoning, the major producers of political elites in the northeast, are visible on the list, as well as the coastal provinces of Fujian and Jiangsu. One may also find the western regions such as Sichuan, Guizhou, and Shaanxi, as well as minority regions such as Inner Mongolia and Xinjiang, as significant. However, Guangdong, the most important economic powerhouse in China, is absent from the list and also missing from the list is Tibet.

The state council also managed to send two new members to the Politburo in 2012. Meng Jianzhu and Ma Kai were both state councilors from 2008 to 2013.

# CONCLUSION

In the past twenty-six years, political generations have become institutionalized in the Chinese leadership system. It is now easy to identify certain individuals as people of a certain "generation" by simply looking at their years of birth. Since age sixty-eight has become a strong norm in Politburo membership turnover, half a generation could be identified in terms of political leadership in China. Interestingly, the current political leadership in China is generally viewed as fifth-generation leaders. Yet the majority of the current leadership group does not necessarily belong to the fifth generation cohort. Of the twenty-five current members of the Eighteenth Politburo, only eight (32 percent) fall in this category. Of the seven members of the current Politburo Standing Committee, only one person is technically a member of the fifth generation. Since the largest cohort belongs to the 4.5 generation, a large turnover can be expected from the next National Party Congress in 2017.

In terms of educational background, one would expect that the majority of the top leaders would be products of the college education system following the Cultural Revolution. However, less than one in four Politburo members belong to this group. Almost one-third did not receive any formal tertiary education and another one-fourth were products of the Cultural Revolution educational system. Those who attended college before the Cultural Revolution were also adversely affected at the outbreak of the Cultural Revolution. Overall, among those who did attend college, humanities and social sciences majors dominate. Their official biographies look impressive, because officially a majority of current leadership have postgraduate degrees, including five PhDs and nine master's degrees.

A major distinction can be seen between one's ancestral home and where one grew up in terms of home province. In terms of ancestral home, Shandong, Jiangsu, and Anhui are prominent; using a home province definition, Beijing and Shanghai are more significant. These metropolitan cities are home to nine members of the Eighteenth Politburo, including three standing members and six full members.

The Eighteenth Politburo is primarily composed of people of the Han majority. Not one member is from a minority ethnic group. Females fare better: there are two female Politburo members but not a female standing member.

China's fifth-generation leaders rose to the top through different pathways. Each leader started off with a different political endowment in terms of three different elements: CCP membership, professional career, and social network. It is clear that those who joined the CCP early had huge advantages. Using age twenty-five as a benchmark, joining the Party at a young age bestows a lot of political capital, and joining the Party late is a political liability. While members of the Eighteenth Politburo followed different professional careers—initially working as engineers, academics, personal secretaries, youth league cadres, factory or state farm workers, professional soldiers, government staff, or reporters—the whole group can hardly be described as "technocratic" because only slightly more than one-third possess either engineering or academic backgrounds and only one person is fully qualified to be considered a technocrat. There are no returnees from western countries nor are there any lawyers. Regarding social networks, the father is the most important, followed by the father-in-law. Princelings enjoy great advantages because they have either a father who is a high-ranking official or a powerful father-in-law. A strong social network is often more than enough to compensate for deficiencies in other aspects of political endowments.

In terms of political origins (i.e., places where one obtained his or her first significant political office), a wide variety in localities and career paths is observable. Many leaders followed a path as youth league cadres, but a number of others moved up from county-level positions. In a race to the top, though, youth league cadres have a huge advantage and can obtain a high rank at relatively young ages. In this regard, youth league cadres have fared better than princelings. Li Keqiang achieved the rank of vice minister eight years earlier than Xi Jinping did; Liu Yandong obtained a vice-ministerial rank ten years earlier than Yu Zhengsheng.

Once political elites have become candidates for future leadership positions, they are usually sent to the provinces to gain credentials. Guangdong and Shanghai are the most important places for training future leaders. Guangdong is typically a training ground for outsiders, while Shanghai appears able to send its own people to the center. Beijing, Chongqing, Shaanxi, and Shandong are also important training grounds. Among those who have worked in provinces, the majority have worked in more than one province.

These political leaders have also been launched to the Politburo from different provinces or central organizations. Again, centrally administered municipalities such as Shanghai, Beijing, Chongqing, and Tianjin have played an important role as launching pads. Shanghai alone has sent three people to the Eighteenth Politburo, including two standing members and one full member. It's noteworthy that Guangdong and Tibet, as well as many other provincial units, are completely absent from the list.

Compared to their predecessors, especially the third-generation leaders, fifth-generation leaders are less internationally focused. In contrast to the Politburo Standing Committee elected in 1992, which had two of seven members who had studied overseas (in the Soviet Union), the Eighteenth Politburo Standing Committee has only one member who studied overseas (in North Korea). Moreover, the formative years of many fifth-generation leaders were spent during the Cultural Revolution so they probably tend to be more sympathetic to Maoism. It is understandable that some of them might want to imitate Mao as both a nationalist and a populist. So, in their foreign policies they likely would become more assertive and in their domestic policies they would adopt more populist measures to improve people's livelihood.

Compared to other members of the Politburo, Xi Jinping is not particularly outstanding in terms of his social network and power bases. He was chosen to be the successor to Hu Jintao not because of his strong ties with other princelings and power bases in the provinces of Hebei, Fujian, or Zhejiang, as well as Shanghai. On the contrary, he was chosen primarily because he had been known to possess weak factional links and shallow power bases.[36]

## NOTES

1. Deng Xiaoping, "We Must Form a Promising Collective Leadership That Will Carry Out Reform," in *Selected Works of Deng Xiaoping*, 3rd ed, 296–301 (Beijing: Renmin Chubanshe, 1993), May 31, 1989.
2. For information on the Thirteenth National Congress of the CCYL, see http://www.gqt.org.cn/695/gqt_tuanshi/gqt_ghlc/lcdbdh/200612/t20061211_5640.htm.
3. For details see Zong Hairen, *Disidai* (The fourth generation) (Carle Place, NY: Mirror Books, 2002), 398.
4. Ibid, 398–99. Xi emerged as the first preference for general secretary of the CCP in 2007 partly due to the power manipulations of Jiang Zemin and Zeng Qinghong and not necessarily because of dramatic changes in public sentiment toward princelings.
5. This norm has nothing to do with Deng Xiaoping. Deng had long passed away by the time the new leadership under Jiang Zemin was trying to figure out an age limit for Politburo membership. The initial age limit for Politburo members was set at seventy in 1997, with Jiang Zemin as an exception. It is widely believed that Jiang introduced the age limit to eliminate his rival, Qian Shi, who was two years older than Jiang.
6. Unfortunately, Bo Xilai belongs to the 4.5th-generation cohort because he was born in 1949. The 18th Party Congress in 2012 was his last chance to get it to the Politburo Standing Committee, yet his overreach backfired and landed him in jail.
7. For details see Xiang Jiangsu, *Li Keqiang Bandi* (Li Keqiang's men) (Carle Place, NY: Mirror Books, 2009), 160–62.
8. Dou Zijia, *Wang Yang Zhuang: Zhongguo Zheng Tan Na Pi Lang* (Biography of Wong Yang: A wolf in Chinese politics) (Carle Place, NY: Mirror Books, 2009), 13–16.
9. It has become a trend among high-ranking officials to obtain a graduate diploma through Party schools. These diplomas are useful for obtaining promotions but their qualities are questioned by the Ministry of Education.
10. "Home province" is a source of political identity among political elites in China. During the Ming and Qing periods, a rule was introduced to prevent government officials from abusing their powers in favor of their relatives and friends in their home provinces. The rule is the rule of avoidance. It is important to know what a "home province" in contemporary context really means politically. It is often misleading to identify Shanghai as the home province of the members of the Shanghai Gang because a majority of them are either from Zhejiang or Jiangsu.

11. For Yu Zhengsheng's information, see Gao Yuan Peng, *Yu Zhengsheng He Tade Jiaozu* (Yu Zhengsheng and his family) (Carle Place, NY: Mirror Books, 2009), 240–79.

12. Qiu Ping, *Zhonggong Di Wudai* (Fifth-generation leadership) (Hong Kong: Xiafeier Chuban Youxian Gongsi, 2005), 182.

13. Meng Jianzhu graduated from Xinzhong Middle School in Shanghai. He is recognized as one of the school's outstanding alumni. See http://www.baike.com /wiki/%E4%B8%8A%E6%B5%B7%E5%B8%82%E6%96%B0%E4%B8% AD%E9%AB%98%E7%BA%A7%E4%B8%AD%E5%AD%A6.

14. Han Zheng went to Wukanglu Elementary School and Liming Middle School in Shanghai. See http://www.boxun.com/news/gb/china/2007/03/200703262325 .shtml.

15. http://book.jd.com/10578075.html; http://zh.wikipedia.org/zh/%E9%A9% AC%E5%87%AF_(%E6%94%BF%E6%B2%BB%E4%BA%BA%E7% 89%A9).

16. Qiu Ping, *Zhonggong Di Wudai*, 296.

17. Wu Ming, *Zhongguo Xinlingxiu: Xi Jinping Zhuan* (China's new leader: Xi Jinping) (Hong Kong: Xianggang Wenhua Yishu Chubanshe, 2010), 41–61.

18. See http://www.21ccom.net/articles/rwcq/article_2012112371601.html.

19. For details see https://zh.wikipedia.org/zh/%E5%90%89%E6%9E%97%E7% 9C%81%E6%B0%91%E6%97%8F%E6%9E%84%E6%88%90%E5%88% 97%E8%A1%A8.

20. Xi Jinping, "Wo Shi Ruhe Kuaru Zhengjie De" (How did I get into a political career) in Wu, *Zhongguo Xinlingxiu*, 576–94.

21. According to Qiu Ping, Liu Yandong joined the Party during her first year at Tsinghua University. This is unlikely. Liu joined the Party in July 1964 and began her studies at Tsinghua in September 1964. For more on the first version see Qiu Ping, *Zhonggong Di Wudai*, 298.

22. Dou Zijia, *Wang Yang Zhuan*, 13–16.

23. It should be noted that in their early years many more people of the Eighteenth Politburo worked as youth league cadres at various levels and in different capacities.

24. For details see Gao Xin, *Lingdao Zhongguo de Xin Renwu* (China's top leaders: Biographies of China's politburo members) 2 (Carle Place, NY: Mirror Books, 2003), 484–86.

25. For details see Wu Ming, *Zhongguo Xinlingxiu*, 158–61.

26. See http://news.creaders.net/china/2013/03/13/1242083.html.

27. For details see http://www.wang-shi.com/html/53/t-1753.html.

28. For details see Gao Xin, *Lingdao Zhongguo de Xin Renwu*, 488–91.

29. For details see Wu Ming, *Zhongguo Xinlingxiu*, 129–30.

30. See Article 7 of "Dang Zheng Lingdao Ganbu Xuanba Renyong Gongzuo Tiaoli" (2002) (Regulations on appointments of leading party and government leaders), at http://www.people.com.cn/GB/shizheng/16/20020723/782504.html.e

31. For a reference see http://news.creaders.net/china/2013/03/17/1243326.html.

32. *Hebei Xianzhen Nianjian* (1990) (Beijing: Zhongguo Tongji Chubanshe, 1990), 305.

33. For details see Gao Xin, *Lingdao Zhongguo de Xin Renwu*, 557–58. For a chronicle of visits to North Korea by Chinese leaders before 2000, see http://www.people.com.cn/GB/shizheng/19/20010903/550493.html.

34. There is no central directive regarding sending officials to lower levels for training but it has been a common practice since the 1960s. In theory these people are sent to different places to have their capacities tested. In reality they are sent to these places to gain credentials. In many cases their future prospects depend less on their performance than on the power of their patrons.

35. The Shaanxi clique might include those who worked as educated youths, such as Xi Jinping and Wang Qishan, and those who worked as top leaders, such as Zhao Leji, Li Jianguo, and Li Zhanshu.

36. This is a separate topic that should be considered for further research.

# 2

# THE DEVELOPMENT OF CHINA'S FORMAL POLITICAL STRUCTURES

## Zheng Yongnian and Weng Cuifen

In this chapter we aim to answer a key question on contemporary China by narrating the evolution of China's formal political structures since the reform and open door policy of the late 1970s: To what extent have China's formal political structures developed to either constrain or empower China's political leadership in policy making and implementation in their response to a changing political environment, in particular the responses by the new leadership under the helm of Xi Jinping? In the pre-reform era, Mao Zedong's personal dictatorship caused political disaster for China, both during the Great Leap Forward (1958–1961) and during the Cultural Revolution (1966–1976). In the post-Mao era the Chinese Communist Party (CCP) leadership has placed much emphasis on formal institution building, and these new institutions have played an important role in policy making for all major issues. Indeed, one of the important legacies of Deng Xiaoping was to strengthen China's political institutions and bureaucracy.

However, formal institutions must be changed to adapt to a changing political environment. China is now facing a totally new environment compared to what existed during the Deng era. The new leadership under Xi is facing enormous problems: deteriorating environmental conditions, imbalances in the economy, a housing bubble, financial instability, political corruption, rising unemployment, social instability, and growing Internet accessibility and resulting social unrest. The list is endless. One thing is clear: none of these problems has an easy solution and all will require a strong leadership to resolve. Against this backdrop, the research question raised above can be divided into several subquestions, including: Does China's current political system work? Does the system empower or weaken leaders in their decision making and policy implementation, at both the central and local levels? How do political leaders overcome the bureaucracy's resistance to getting things done? What institutional barriers constrain leaders in their efforts to introduce reforms to formal institutions?

Central to China's formal institutions is the CCP, which indeed is the pillar of China's political system. However, the Party is not almighty and it relies on other formal institutions to assist in decision making and policy implementation. It will be useful to examine the evolution of the CCP as an organization and also understand its relations with other formal institutions like the government (the state council), the people's congress system, the military, and the judiciary. Additionally, it will be useful to examine the changing relationship between the CCP and society since the CCP's challenges do not only come from within (that is, from other institutions) but also from without (from society itself).

The first part of the discussion focuses on the relationship between the CCP and the state. China has long been regarded as a Party-state. However, the Party and the state are two separate institutional entities and two parallel systems. The relationship between the Party and the state evolved during the reform era and in the following sections key aspects of reforms and changes that have been introduced into the Party and the state will be scrutinized. The Party's relations with other key institutions, including the people's congress system, the military, the judiciary, and civil society, will be examined. Throughout these discussions the main purpose is to look into how the Party has maintained its domination over state institutions and society while adjusting to the continually changing environment. By doing so, we hope to answer the question of whether China's formal institutions are capable of providing effective governance in a new age.

## PARTY-STATE RELATIONS AS THE CORE OF CHINA'S POLITICAL STRUCTURE

Central to China's political system is the CCP, which claims absolute domination over the state and society. There are two parallel systems in China's governance: the Party and the state (or government). Such a dual political structure exists from the center through the province /city to the county and the township. The Party system is called *dangwu xitong* (Party affairs system) and the state system is *zhengwu xitong* (state affairs system). The relationship of these two systems forms the most important institutional infrastructure of China's formal political structure and shapes its characteristics. While a historical review of the evolution of Party-state relations might be of interest, here the focus will be on the development of the Party-state relationship in the contemporary era.

In the scholarly community, efforts have been made to treat the Party and the state as two separate political structures and to explore the relationship between the two.[1] A proper analogy to the relationship between the CCP and the state is one between a property owner and a property manager. Considering itself as the owner of the territory of China, the CCP claims its domination over the state. Generally, the state council system can be seen as comparable to the bureaucratic systems of other political systems. In China, the Party leadership holds key decision-making powers and the state council implements the decisions made by the Party leadership. The key institutions through which the CCP dominates the state in a new socioeconomic environment include the *nomenklatura* system: the central leading small groups (CLSGs), the *dangzu* (Party groups), and the *xitong* (systems).[2] These institutions have remained influential over the past decades in facilitating the CCP's domination over the state, and some of them have been upgraded and strengthened, particularly the CLSGs. In a general sense the government includes the state administrative system, where the locus of power resides in the state council, the national and local people's congresses, the Chinese People's Political Consultative Conference (CPPCC), and the judiciary system.

In addition to its efforts to strengthen these traditional organizational pillars, the CCP has also continuously adjusted its political system according to a changing political environment at the societal level.[3] Many factors—such as globalization, the rise of the Internet, and the development of civil society—have placed the CCP in a totally new political situation. The CCP leadership has thus created many new institutions to cope with this changing environment and to maintain its domination. For instance, new institutions have been set up to regulate the Internet and other forms of new communication and to contain their social consequences.[4] There are also new institutions to control new information technologies and maintain social stability under the powerful Political and Legal Commission.[5]

## EVOLUTION OF PARTY-STATE RELATIONS

The evolution of the Party-state relationship can be examined from two aspects: one is changes in the Party organization itself; the other is the changing relationship between the Party system and the government system. Since establishment of the reform and open-door policy, changes in China's political-institutional system have been limited to reforms of the government organization system rather than reform of the Party system. Consequently, the Party structure remains unchanged while drastic changes have been introduced into the state bureaucratic system.[6] However, to cope with changes in state institutions, the Party has had to create new institutions to regulate its relations with the state.

During the Zhao Ziyang era in the 1980s, there were discussions about reforming the Party organizations and some reform measures were introduced. Nevertheless, since the crackdown on the 1989 pro-democracy movement, the discourse of Party organization reform has completely disappeared. In China's political system, where the boundary between the Party and the state is blurred, the Party organization is essentially part of the whole governance system and constitutes a large part of the state organization system. If the Party organization is unable to be reformed and streamlined, it will be difficult for any meaningful or real political reform to take place.

The second aspect of the relations between the Party and the state is an old and complicated one, namely, vertical fragmentation. From the central level down to the township level, the Party system and the state system are paralleled and often argue against each other, leading to what in China is called "infighting." The head of the state bureaucracy, which itself is a part of the Party leadership at the same level, is often reluctant and may even refuse to take an order from the head of the Party. This is because the head of the state bureaucracy is not appointed by the head of the Party at the same level; instead, heads of the Party and the state bureaucracy are each appointed by the higher-level Party organization. For instance, the governor in a province is not appointed by the Party secretary in the same province; instead, both the governor and the Party secretary are appointed by the Central Organizational Department under the Central Committee of the CCP. Such appointments are often the result of factional politics at the top, meaning that the governor and the Party secretary belong to different political factions within the Party. Therefore, while in theory the governor takes orders from the Party secretary, in reality this is often not the case. The efficiency of public administration has been seriously jeopardized. Two observations can be made from this arrangement. First, it explains why the Party leadership at different levels must continuously strengthen its power over the state bureaucracy. Second, it reaffirms the fact that in order to establish an effective government, any political system reform should include reform of the Party system either to allow greater administrative independence or to mark a clearer boundary between the Party and the state.

In the mid-1980s Deng Xiaoping and Zhao Ziyang set the separation of the Party from the government as the core of the reform discourse. Such discourse was rather conservative because the purpose of the separation was to strengthen the effectiveness of the leadership of the Party rather than change the domination of the Party over the state. This discourse did lead to a short period of so-called political liberalization, since some reform measures were introduced to allow greater local and administrative autonomy. For instance, the two-level-down personnel appointment and management system was changed to a one-level-down system in terms of central-local relations. This change empowered local governments in managing local affairs. Another was that all central ministers were assigned a more important role than Party heads in managing daily affairs of their respective ministries. However, after the 1989 crackdown on the pro-democracy movement, the need to separate the Party from the government disappeared from the discourse of Jiang Zemin (1989–2002), Hu Jintao (2002–2012), and Xi Jinping (2012 to present); instead, at the center of reform discourse is the opposite: how to strengthen the domination of the Party over the government.

While the separation of the Party from the government is no longer on the reform agenda, in the post-Deng era the Party leadership has also attempted to rationalize the relations between the two bodies. In fact, considering China's one-party system, it is unrealistic to expect a clear-cut separation of the Party from the state. The issue of the Party-state relations is not whether, but how the CCP will exercise domination over the state while allowing more space for the latter in managing daily state affairs. The CCP has devoted a great deal of effort to adjusting—through institutionalization and rationalization—its relations with the state. The term "rigid flexibility" describes the overall development of China's formal political system: the overall structure remains intact while its content and function continually undergo change. It is thus important to see China's new Party-state relationship in the light of these functional changes, despite a seemingly unchanged one-party structure.

In retrospect, the goal of separating the Party from the state in the 1980s was too idealistic and not feasible within the Chinese political climate of the time. While a clearer boundary between the two bodies may occur, it is difficult to imagine their total separation. In recent years a new line of thinking has appeared in the reform discourse as well as in practice in some localities: considering China's reality, it is not necessary to implement the same Party-state parallel systems from the center down to the local levels, and Party-state relationship can vary at different administrative levels.

At the central and provincial levels, a "division of functions" could be established between the Party and the state, while at the subprovincial level the Party system and the state system could be gradually integrated into one single system. This is feasible because at the central and provincial levels there are sufficient complicated affairs for the Party and the state to deal with separately due to the size of the country and the provinces. In fact, such "division of functions" has been generally established at these highest two levels of China's political system. The Party system is now mainly in charge of political affairs, while the state system is in charge of administrative affairs on a day-to-day basis. Comparatively speaking, at the highest levels China's political system is similar to the semi-presidential system in France and the presidential system in Russia. In both of these systems the president and the prime minister hail from the same ruling Party but a division of labor exists between them.

Since the passing of Deng Xiaoping, China has entered what can be called a "post-strongman" era. While strongman leaders like Mao and Deng acquired legitimacy from their revolutionary experiences, post-strongman leaders do not have such experiences and must earn their legitimacy by holding political offices and building institutions. The Party Congress (deciding who gets what) now becomes a platform for political bargaining among political leaders and all the decisions are the result of power compromises among the top leaders. Under such a pluralist leadership, institutions become increasingly important for the regulation of their relations. Without the support of a top political strongman, top leaders resort to the institutions to maximize the power of their positions; without formal institutions bitter power struggles take place. For example, under Hu Jintao (2002–2012) there was division of labor among the nine members of the Standing Committee of the Political Bureau and each claimed his own territory of power and tried to institutionalize the claim. Under such a system the state council gained more autonomy in administering economic and social affairs on a day-to-day basis. While the structure allowed for little change, the functional levels became increasingly important. To some extent the division of functions between the Party and the state at the top level makes China's political system similar to the dual leadership of the Party and the state. However, the "division of labor" system at the top has led to another important political problem, namely, internal pluralism. The Party leadership does not have a sound mechanism to coordinate individual leaders' power and responsibilities and the unity of the leadership is often called into question.

## RATIONALIZING PARTY-STATE RELATIONS

Though the Party has maintained its domination over the government, it has also made great efforts to rationalize or better coordinate their relationship. Over the years, neither the Party nor the government has been satisfied with the current structure of their relationship. The parallel system of the Party and the government, from national to local levels, has led to political and administrative inefficiency. The boundary between the Party and the government blurs, and the two remain in constant conflict. What in China is called *wolidou* (literally, infighting) could paralyze the governance system, especially during the time of a crisis such as the pro-democracy movement in 1989, the SARS crisis in 2003, and the Sichuan earthquake in 2008. This paralysis seems inevitable, since the blurring of the boundary between the Party and the government makes responsibilities less clear. Despite the division of labor between political leaders, knowing who should bear what responsibilities continues to be a major problem since dealing with social realities is a multi-faceted task that requires efficient coordination. For example, if each member of the Standing Committee of the Political Bureau (SCPB) looks after his or her own functional area only, then a responsibility to other functional areas will be missing. Without support from other members of the SCPB, each member can hardly fulfill the responsibilities of his or her own territory. For example, following the 2008 Sichuan earthquake, Premier Wen Jiabao, who was responsible for rescuing affected people in the region, was not able to mobilize military support since the state council does not have any legal basis for exercising command over the military force; this power is in the hands of the head of the Party leadership, namely Hu Jintao. To achieve better coordination, many reform measures have been carried out, particularly since Xi came to power in 2012. Needless to say, these reforms also aim to establish the means by which the Party maintains its domination over the government.

### The Three-in-One System

In today's China the general secretary (the head of the ruling party) is concurrently the head of state (state president) and the commander in chief of the military (CMC chairman). This three-in-one system, in which the role of state president and the CMC chairmanship are tied to the position of Party general secretary, somewhat resembles the semi-presidential system is other countries. Prior to Jiang Zemin's accession to the post of state president in 1993, the state president office was insignificant and was usually filled by a revolutionary elder or political noble. Previous officeholders included

Madame Sun Yat-sen (Soong Ch'ing-ling), Li Xiannian, and Yang Shangkun. The current state president is Xi Jinping.

In an attempt to institutionalize Party-state relations, the state presidency and state vice presidency are now the most important positions in the Chinese leadership. Hu Jintao was vice president for several years before he succeeded Jiang. This is also the case for Xi, before he succeeded Hu. Institutionalization has brought about some level of "division of functions" between important public offices and has conferred the benefit of legitimizing the Party's command over the military. While the basic principle that "the party commands the gun" remains largely unchanged, this power is now vested in a formal office that acts on behalf of the Party. This is evident in the institutional arrangement of the CMC: while the CMC is one organization, it has two names in public, namely, the Party's CMC and the state's CMC.

The positions of state president and CMC chairman give the Party general secretary and his office a legitimate institutional base to perform governmental functions. Nevertheless, there is an informal "division of labor" between the state president's office and the premier's office. The state president's office is in charge of foreign affairs, national defense, national security, and public security, while the state council (the official arm of the premier) is in charge of economic and civil affairs. Thus several ministries—the Ministry of National Defense, the Ministry of State Security, the Ministry of Public Security, and the Ministry of Foreign Affairs—are under the jurisdiction of the state president's office even though technically they are located within the state council.[7] This implies that major decisions in these areas are made by the Party (i.e., the general secretary's office) in the name of the state president's office. Of course, the state council must bear the responsibility of policy implementation. In this sense, a clear boundary exists between the Party and the state. For example, as the head of the Small Leading Group over Foreign Affairs, the general Party secretary makes all important decisions but the state council, where the Ministry of Foreign Affairs is located, must implement them.

The three-in-one system was consolidated further after the CCP's Eighteenth National Congress in 2012. When Jiang Zemin finished his second term as general Party secretary at the Sixteenth National Congress in 2002, he retained his position as the chairman of the CMC for another two years, meaning that the power transition from Jiang to Hu Jintao was not complete at the Sixteenth Congress. The fact that Jiang did not give up his military power for two more years greatly constrained Hu Jintao's leadership. Indeed, the fact that Hu Jintao's leadership group did not make substantial reform progress during its ten-year tenure is partly due to the constraints imposed by the previous Jiang leadership. At the CCP's Eighteenth National Congress,

Hu discontinued Jiang's practice and gave up the three positions at the same time, which immediately completed the power transition from the Hu leadership to Xi Jinping's leadership. The one-step power transition has enabled Xi to consolidate his power after the Eighteenth Congress. Few could have guessed that Xi would be as forceful and capable as he has been since the congress convened, and it is widely expected that from now on, the one-step power transition will continue.

## Party Secretary as the Head of the People's Congress

At the provincial level, the secretary of the provincial Party committee simultaneously acts as the head of the people's congress. This institutional arrangement is true for most of China's provinces and cities. While the arrangement is often interpreted as efforts on the part of the CCP to strengthen the control of the Party over the people's congress, the underlying rationale behind it can be explained in terms of the rationalization of the Party-state relationship.

According to China's constitution, the National People's Congress (NPC) is the "highest organ of state power" (article 57) and "the NPC and the local people's congress at various levels are the organs through which the people exercise state power" (article 2). However, in reality the NPC and the local people's congresses often act as rubber stamps of the Party; the Party organizations make major decisions first and later ask the NPC and the local people's congress simply to "approve." This is particularly reflected in the timing of the Party's National Congress and the NPC session: the former takes place in late September or early October of each year while the latter is held the following March.

In both Mao's and Deng's eras, the NPC and the local people's congresses were usually headed by a powerless retired senior Party cadre or government official. The situation changed following the 1989 pro-democracy movement, when many NPC leaders (under the leadership of Wan Li) revealed their sympathy toward the movement. Hu Jiwei, then editor of the *People's Daily* and a member of the NPC standing committee, even attempted to use the NPC to nullify the martial law imposed by the state council (under Li Peng). After the crackdown, the Party leadership began to strengthen the Party's control over the NPC and the local people's congresses. Since the early 1990s the NPC standing committee has been headed by a member of the Standing Committee of the Political Bureau of the CCP Central Committee, such as Qiao Shi, Li Peng, and Wu Bangguo. The current head of the NPC, Zhang Dejiang, is also a member of the SCPB.

The provincial people's congresses are headed by the secretary of the provincial Party committee. Indeed, according to Zhao Ziyang, this arrangement was initiated in the 1980s, when political reform became an important agenda for the Party leadership with the expectation that it would be helpful in reconciling the two contradictory sources of power: the NPC, in theory the highest organ of state power, and the CCP, in reality the owner of the highest power.[8] Zhao's assessment can be interpreted in the following way: the Party secretary, as the head of the people's congress, gives the Party a legitimate means to influence the government. The CCP, as the only ruling party, has thus maintained its domination over the government. Political reforms of the 1980s focused on the separation of the Party from the government. But if the Party and the government were actually two separate bodies, so the thinking went, then how could the Party exercise control over the government? According to China's state constitution, the NPC and the local people's congresses have similar functions because the NPC and the local congresses are required to supervise the government at different levels. By being actively involved in the activities of the NPC, the Party establishes a legitimate means for "supervising" and maintaining its domination over the government. This new tie-in has led the CCP to exercise direct control over provincial people's congresses and there is little doubt that the provincial Party secretaries, as representatives of the central leadership, must deal directly with the local people's representatives. The provincial Party secretaries now must listen to and take into consideration the representatives' opinions before the Party committees can make important decisions.

To a degree this institutional reform has changed the NPC's traditional image as a "rubber stamp" body. The role of the NPC and the structure of the NPC's relationship with local congresses are now more complicated. On the one hand, the CCP continues to dominate the NPC system by controlling personnel appointments and setting NPC agendas, so the NPC system can hardly be considered independent of the CCP. On the other hand, the NPC has been empowered in its relationship with the state council and in local congresses' relationship with local state bureaucracies. NPC representatives can now have their voices heard and can openly question ministers of the state council. But one thing is clear from this development: the CCP is able to exercise more effective control over the state via the NPC system.

## LOCAL EXPERIMENTS

China's recent practices show that although it is difficult to separate the Party from the state or vice versa, it is possible to observe functional division between the two. However, though the division of labor between the Party and the state seems to work well at the central level, this divide has caused increasing conflict at the local level.

In recent years some localities, particularly in the eastern coastal provinces, have begun to better coordinate the functions and responsibilities among the Party and the state. Reforms in Guangdong province are significant, specifically reforms in Shunde. Shunde, a county-level government, has made institutional innovations to gradually form a Party-state integration system. For example, the six agencies of the Party committee are integrated into corresponding government agencies at the same level. Hypothetically the relations between the Party and the state are the same at all administrative levels. However, although there is a trend toward clearer "division of functions" between the Party and the state at the central level, the boundary between the two bodies at the local/county level has been increasingly blurred. At the county level, both the Party and the state are faced with daily issues of people's livelihoods. The infighting of power caused by the parallel Party-and-state system at the local level has severely hindered administrative efficiencies and has served to alienate the Party and state from the people. Shunde's experiment of Party-state integration has aimed at improving governance efficiency while at the same time effectively integrating both administrative (vis-à-vis the state) and political (the Party) responsibilities.

The rationale behind the move in Shunde was that infighting had led to poor administrative efficiencies. Given the fact that at the local level both the Party and the state are always competing for greater administrative power, a major portion of the Party's responsibilities can be integrated into the state bureaucracy. In the past few years this reform in Shunde has greatly reduced the size of both the Party and the state organizations, which has further pushed the Party and the state to decentralize power to local social organizations. In Guangdong the concurrent rise of nongovernmental organizations (NGOs) has been rapid. Social organizations now bear greater responsibilities in organizing themselves and providing public services. The development of civil society has also generated increasingly high pressure on the local Party leadership. To facilitate better and more efficient communication between the Party and society, the Shunde Party leadership has initiated a new program to regulate the local Party cadres. Local People's Congress representatives and local Chinese People's Political Consultative Conference members regularly meet with their constituents. The new program, based on the Singapore experience (where parliament members meet weekly with the people in their respective constituencies), aims to reduce the tension between the state and society. Indeed, under the leadership of Wang Yang (2008–2013), Guangdong initiated a great reform program that integrated administrative reform with social reform.[9] While the former aimed at reducing the size of the government by decentralizing power to society, the latter aimed at the expansion of social forces by allowing the rise of civil society.[10] The Shunde experiment has been regarded as a model for China's next step of administrative reforms, particularly at the local level.[11] In fact, some aspects of the Guangdong reform experience have become national reform agendas. Based on the Guangdong experiments, the state council under Premier Li Keqiang has announced two reform programs to decentralize power to society.[12] In the long run this kind of local political system is favorable for the emergence of a responsible and clear government.

Of course, one must be realistic about local experiments. Some local experiments aimed to empower the Party and weaken society. The Chongqing experiment is one example. During Bo Xilai's tenure from 2008 to 2012, the power of the Party was greatly strengthened. The local Party leadership appealed to the Maoist ideology and sought political means for cracking down on so-called local gangsters. Many private entrepreneurs were deprived of their property and put into jail. Following the removal of Bo Xilai in March 2012, the Chongqing model was disgraced and a modified new development model has emerged.[13]

## THE PARTY SYSTEM: RADICAL ADJUSTMENT UNDER XI

While the structure of the Party system remains intact in most ways, radical adjustments have taken place since Xi Jinping took the reins of power in 2012. The most significant development after the Eighteenth Party Congress was the downsizing of the number of Political Bureau members, from nine to seven. As the core leadership group of the entire country, the Political Bureau is composed of the top leaders of the Party, the state, and the military.[14]

According to the constitution of the CCP, the general secretary of the CCP Central Committee must be elected from the Political Bureau and be first among political bureau members. The constitution does not specify the order of positions of the rest of the Political Bureau's members, but according to the CCP's general practice, these members are ranked by seniority and position in order to reflect each leader's power in the Party and in the state.

The most powerful body is the Standing Committee of the Political Bureau. In the post-Deng era, the SCPB includes the president of the state; the premier of the state council; the chairmen of the NPC, the CMC, and the CPPCC; the first vice premier of the state council; the first secretary of the central secretariat; the secretary of the CDIC; and the general secretary of the Party.

Between the Sixteenth and the Seventeenth Party Congresses, Li Chang-chun, the then-chairman of the CCP Central Ideological Construction Steering Committee (CICSC), served on the Political Bureau for ten years. The positions of vice state president and secretary of the Central Political and Legal Commission were also filled by the members of the SCPB between the Fifteenth and the Seventeenth Party Congresses and the Sixteenth to the Seventeenth Party Congresses, respectively.

There is also no specific regulation on the number of SCPB members nor their responsibilities. For instance, the SCPB had eight members at the Thirteenth Party Congress in 1987, but the Fourteenth and Fifteenth Party Congresses each had seven, and the Sixteenth and Seventeenth had nine. In 2012 the number was again reduced to seven for the Eighteenth Party Congress, and the scope of responsibilities for some members changed. The positions of the premier of the state council (Li Keqiang), the chairman of the CPPCC (Yu Zhengsheng), the secretary of the CDIC (Wang Qishan), and the first vice premier of the state council (Zhang Gaoli) are still filled by the members and their responsibilities and functions remain unchanged.

Xi Jinping concurrently holds the positions of general secretary of the CCP, president of the state, and chairman of the CMC of the CCP, as well as the CMC of the state, just as Jiang Zemin and Hu Jintao did. As mentioned earlier, Hu Jintao gave up all three positions at his retirement during the Eighteenth Party Congress, which made it possible for Xi to take over all powers from Hu. Zhang Dejiang, the chairman of the NPC, was also appointed the head of the Central Coordination Group of Hong Kong and Macau Affairs. In the past decade this position had been held by the vice president of the state, who was also a member of the SCPB. When the number of SCPB members was reduced to seven, for the first time the state vice president, Li Yuanchao, was not a member of the SCPB and he only served as deputy head of the Central Coordination Group. In July 2003, following the July 1st protest against the CCP in Hong Kong, the Party established a coordination group of leaders from eighteen organs to handle the Hong Kong and Macau affairs. Zeng Qinghong, a then-member of the SCPB and vice state president, was named head of the group. In October 2007, after Zeng retired from the SCPB during the Seventeenth Party Congress, Xi Jinping, then a new member of the SCPB, replaced Zeng to lead Hong Kong and Macau affairs. After Xi became the General Party Secretary, he transferred this authority to Zhang Dejiang and Li Yuanchao.

Liu Yunshan, who had been the chief of the propaganda department of the CCP before the Eighteenth Party Congress, took over power from Li

Chuangchun, meaning that Liu continued to be in charge of propaganda. However, Liu's responsibility was expanded when he was also named president of the Central Party School, a position formerly held by the vice state president, Xi Jinping.

At the Eighteenth Party Congress in 2012 the most significant change of the Party system SCPB was the downgrading of the position of the Central Political and Legal Commission (CPLC). In the previous Party Congress the position of the secretary of the CPLC was held by Zhou Yongkang, then a member of the SCPB. However, this position was taken by Meng Jianzhu, a member of the Political Bureau, at the Eighteenth Party Congress. Under Zhou, the CPLC had come to be regarded as an independent "kingdom" and one of the most corrupt Party sectors. After the fall of Zhou, a number of high-ranking government officials in this sector came under investigation, including Deputy Minister of Public Security Li Dongsheng. The power of this body has been greatly reduced and is now under the direct control of Xi Jinping.

The most radical political change Xi has established is the drastic expansion of his institutional base of power. Like his predecessors, Xi now concurrently holds the three most important positions in China's political system: general secretary of the CCP, state president, and chairman of the Central Military Commission. However, past experience has demonstrated that to hold the three positions does not mean that officeholder will be powerful enough to engage meaningful reforms. Hu Jintao's leadership failed to accomplish what it had planned when it originally came to power. Xi did not want the same to continue during his tenure. In the name of deepening reform, during the Third Plenum in 2013 Xi decided to establish two new bodies, both of which resulted in empowering Xi himself.

First, the plenum announced the establishment of the Central Leading Group on Comprehensively Deepening Reforms (*zhongyang quanmian shenhua gaige lingdao xiaozu*), which was responsible for overall reform. This move indicated Xi's determination to push through the marketization process that had been halted since the outbreak of the global financial crisis in 2008. Xi himself is now the head of this body. More important, the Third Plenum also established a new National Security Council or National Security Commission (*guojia anquan weiyuanhui*). Xi also named himself the head of this body, which will serve to strengthen his control over the military, over domestic security forces, over propaganda, and over all foreign policy. In 2014 Xi established another new body, the Small Leading Group on the Internet and Informatization, and again named himself its head.

While the CCP has had many small leading groups before, the creation of these new bodies is politically significant. Three points should be stressed.

First, even though these new bodies empower Xi, they are different from earlier small informal leading groups because these are transparent formal institutions. Previous small leading groups were informal, so they were not transparent and often became the tools for individual leaders to manipulate power relations among top leaders. Second, while Xi is the head of all three bodies, Premier Li Keqiang is the deputy so Xi must bear the overall responsibilities in all three areas. Third, these new bodies have changed the power configuration at the top. As mentioned earlier, before the Eighteenth Party Congress there was a "division of functions" system among the members of the SCPB. Though aiming to realize the so-called collective leadership, such a power structure often led to too many "checks and balances" among the top leaders and inefficiency in decision making. Under the new system, members of the SCPB are allocated into different bodies, which has changed the system of "one man, one territory." It is expected that the new system will be able to improve coordination in decision making and policy implementation.

It is worth elaborating on this point by considering the National Security Commission as an example. This new body is primarily based on the American model: it consists of a highly empowered group of security experts who can work the levers of the country's vast security apparatus. But the Chinese body will differ from the US National Security Council in one crucial aspect: the Chinese version has the dual duties of responsibility over both domestic security and foreign policy.

Before the establishment of the National Security Commission, China's highest-level decision-making apparatus with responsibility over external relations and security issues was scattered among the Central Military Commission, which controlled the armed forces, and two separate but in some ways overlapping leading panels at the top: the Foreign Affairs Leading Small Group (FALSG) and the National Security Leading Small Group (NSLSG). The strength of these two groups has been constantly impaired by horizontal conflicts with formidable institutional players in other systems during a time when Chinese foreign and security policymaking has been undergoing dramatic changes like pluralization, decentralization, and fragmentation.

In Hu Jintao's time much of the job of domestic security and stability maintenance (*weiwen*) was done by the powerful Central Political and Legal Commission (*zhongyang zhengfawei*), which was presided over by Zhou Yongkang, then a SCPB member. Currently the Central Political and Legal Commission is headed by Meng Jianzhu, a lower-ranking Political Bureau member. The CCP is confronting an increasingly demanding domestic security situation, with more violent attacks rooted in civic grievances among the citizenry and heightened ethnic conflicts. To address this worsening domestic security, the country needs a more centralized system.

As China has become further integrated with the globalized world, the number and type of pressure groups involved in security and foreign policy making has expanded substantially. Most ministries at the national level, the military, intelligence, big business, the media, local governments, nongovernment organizations, and even individuals are playing increasingly significant roles in the whole process.

As the final arbiters of foreign policy making, the paramount leaders who served immediately prior to Xi's tenure tended to be more consultative and consensual than their predecessors, due to the decreasing authority within the Political Bureau in the post-Mao era. The core leader today faces a much more complicated external and internal context with many other responsibilities; he depends on others to help plan and implement Chinese foreign and security policy, which further reduces his personal influence but magnifies his institutional and pluralistic effect upon the whole process. Two of Xi's predecessors, Jiang Zemin and Hu Jintao, had contemplated forming a coordinating group, like the US National Security Council, but bureaucratic resistance, particularly from the military, had prevented its creation.

Xi is now strong enough to formally set up this new organization. The new council, which would likely focus on domestic security to a greater extent than its US counterpart, is meant to uplift Xi's position from being first-among-equals in the SCPB to an all-powerful leader with absolute authority in handling domestic and external affairs. The move grants Xi a level of authority that eluded his two predecessors, Jiang and Hu, and reverses the trend toward a collective leadership since Deng Xiaoping.

With the three newly established bodies, Xi now enjoys unparalleled power. This could undermine the CCP's mechanism for collective leadership, in which the power of paramount leader is not absolute and is constrained by other SCPB members, all of whom are vested with almost equal political authority. On the one hand such power concentration may facilitate bold reforms and forestall policy deadlocks, but on the other it may break the existing power sharing and balance among competing political camps and lead to extreme policies. Moreover, without a sound system of intra-party democracy, a high concentration of power could lead to resistance from other powerful leaders and power struggles among them. For Xi, the biggest political challenge is how to solicit cooperation from other leaders while concentrating all powers in his own hands.

# STATE SYSTEM REFORMS

During the reform era the CCP leadership has gradually realized that in strengthening its domination over the state and society, it is equally important to introduce institutional changes to state-society relations. Without institutional reforms the state will not be able to assist the Party to govern society effectively. If the state is weakened in the views of society, the Party will face ever-greater challenges from society. To achieve that goal, the CCP has initiated several rounds of state system reform to improve the governance system. But it has not been a smooth process.

China's administrative reform has gone through two phases. The first phase covered the 1980s to the early twenty-first century, when the theme of reform was economic decentralization through an administrative management system compatible with a market economy. The second phase began with the Sixteenth Party Congress in 2002 and concluded at the Eighteenth Party Congress in 2012; the goal then was to establish a regulatory regime of super-ministries to effectively regulate the economic activities of enterprises. These two phases of administrative reform were aimed at facilitating the policy of market economic reform.

Under the planned economy of the first phase, the administrative system was responsible for managing both society and the economy. In China, having a market economy meant that the government gradually would be released from direct economic activities and the power in the economic arena was to be decentralized and shifted to the economic actors, i.e., the individual economic enterprises. This has been a tough process. Although the administrative reforms of the 1980s abolished many departments that directly participated in and managed economic activity, many local governments were reluctant to decentralize their economic power to the enterprises and as a result the major economic power is still in the hand of the local governments.

The government's decentralization of economic power, especially the power held by the local governments, took place following Deng Xiaoping's southern tour in 1992 and the Fourteenth Party Congress that same year. The concept of a "socialist market economy" was officially established. Economic decentralization reached its peak during Zhu Rongji's tenure as vice premier (1993–1998) and then as premier (1998–2003). In the mid 1990s the state council formed a strategy of "retaining the large, while releasing the small" (*zhuada fangxiao*). Under the guidance of such strategy the government reorganized large SOEs into modern corporations (*zhuada*) and privatized all small- and medium-sized enterprises (*fangxiao*).

"Releasing" the small SOEs decentralized power from the government to the enterprises. After the privatization of the small SOEs, local governments retained only a small number of SOEs. However, the degree of "privatization" varied significantly. In some localities, such as Guangdong and Jiangsu, "privatization" was thorough; in other areas, such as in the northeast, "privatization" made small progress and many local SOEs still exist. The strategy of "retaining the large" reorganized the central SOEs into corporations and began the process of changing traditional SOEs that had not separated political, economic, and social functions into real corporations.

The success of economic decentralization became the main precondition for effective political administrative reforms. Government must retreat from the economic field before enterprises can become the real actors of economic activity and the size of government can be reduced. In 1998 the administrative system reform led by Zhu Rongji reduced the number of central ministries and commissions from forty to twenty-nine. Such reforms laid the institutional foundation for the subsequent reform initiatives that were needed to build a regulatory government.

After the Sixteenth Party Congress in 2002, China began a new wave of large-scale administrative system reforms. These new reforms, led by Premier Wen Jiabao in 2003, had two objectives. The first was to turn the government into a regulatory regime by establishing "super-ministries." The second goal was to transform the government into a service-oriented authority in accordance with the policy concepts of "harmonious society" and "scientific outlook on development."

In developed countries the purpose of such a "super-ministry" reform would typically be with the intention of building a regulatory government that emphasizes the governance structure and regulates economic and social activities and sets the "rule of law." In China, although the super-ministry reform has been officially going on for years, there is still no consensus on the meaning and goal of the reform and administrative efficiency has not improved. Most officials understand that the super-ministry reform aims to legitimize and rationalize the administrative structure. But only by integrating administrative organizations with related functions will the reform be able to reduce duplication and settle disputes between bureaucratic agencies, thereby increasing governance efficiency. Furthermore, decentralization of power from the government to the enterprises and the society is still not complete. In some areas, especially in the official SOEs, the government or the agents of the government are still the main forces behind most economic activities. It is almost impossible to establish a regulatory regime in the context of incomplete economic decentralization. As long as the government is still the lead actor of economic activities, the so-called government regulation is nothing but "the left hand regulating the right hand." This is even more the case in the social arena. Decentralization of power from the government to society has just begun in some localities such as Guangdong, but it has yet to become accepted nationwide. At the same time, the issue of how to administratively establish the government's regulatory capability over society has not yet reached the level of a reform agenda.

The Xi administration has so far followed the same gradual approach of the Hu-Wen leadership of 2003 and 2008: rounds of state administrative system reform to build a regulatory regime by furthering the "super-ministry" reform, particularly at the local levels. The 2013 reform plan emphasized the transformation of government functions and aimed to work out a new division of labor between the state, the market, and society. Although the idea of transforming the government was raised during the 1988 state council reforms under Li Peng, the results have been limited, unstable, and reversible. What is relatively new in Xi's administrative reform is the intention to fortify similar reforms within the pipeline of legislation. Building a law-based public administration is the direction to go and is consistent with the general orientation of Xi's leadership, based on the idea that there must be clear boundaries and responsibilities among different government departments and the Party must enhance its capacity to coordinate functions among them.[15] Under the previous leadership, China had suffered from the weakening rule of law and rampant power abuse by public administrators, which resulted in increasing tensions between the government and society. To contain rising social movements, the Xi leadership must appeal to the rule of law so that citizens can trust decisions will be made according to established law.

A more important point of development during the latest round of reform is the emphasis on social welfare policies. While economic decentralization during the 1980s and 1990s and regulatory reforms during the Hu-Wen administration mainly focused on the relations between the market and the state, social development is now regarded as an important component of administrative reform. This emphasis was first given voice during the Hu-Wen leadership under the policy concept of "harmonious society." The Hu-Wen leadership made some serious attempts to develop a set of social policies regarding social security, healthcare, education, and public housing. The Guangdong model of social reform was an example of this kind of reform. The Xi leadership continues to encourage the development of social organizations. As discussed earlier, several aspects of the Guangdong model have been placed on national reform agendas. The government has enforced a social organizations policy that can be called "selective liberalization." Several types of social organizations, such as those in the areas of trade unions, science and technology, charities, environmental protection, and community service are allowed to enjoy a greater degree of autonomy. But tight control continues in other areas, including those related to political, religious, and ethnic issues that are regarded as politically sensitive.

A trend toward professionalism is another observable state system reform. Rapid economic development and social changes have led Chinese society to become increasingly complicated. To boost effective governance, the CCP gradually has transformed itself from a revolutionary party to a normal ruling party, and ideological reliability is slowly giving way to allow more professionalism in the ranks of government officials. Since the mid-1990s the CCP has begun to loosen its grip on the state to give professionals more autonomy in the day-to-day running of the country. In other words, the state has become more powerful in its own "field." This trend has continued since the Xi leadership came to power.

The most visible signs, however, are those within the state council itself. Over the years the council has become a body of economic and social management by professionals. The posts of premier, vice premier, state councilors, minister, and vice minister are all filled by professionals, especially at the ministerial and vice-ministerial level. The rise of professionalism largely reflects the increasing need for special expertise in dealing with the complexities of new social and economic issues. In 2007 China made its first two noncommunist cabinet appointments, namely Wan Gang, minister of science and technology, and Chen Zhu, minister of health. However, the political implications of these two appointments should not be exaggerated since the Party organization continues to exercise influence in overall decision making. However, it does mean that professionals now play an increasingly important role in handling daily state affairs.

Effective leadership requires effective decision making and policy implementation. Professionals play an important role in both, but they need strong political backing. The new economic and foreign policy teams appointed during the 2013 *lianghui* (NPC and CPPCC 2013 annual sessions) show this trend. While the role of professionals in the state system has been enhanced, political backing has also become stronger and more important compared to the previous leadership. The governor of China's central bank and the heads of China's three economic regulatory commissions are all economic and financial professionals experienced in managing financial and economic systems. The appointments of Wang Yang as vice premier in charge of commerce and regulations and of Ma Kai as vice premier in charge of industry and finance lend strong political support to the economic team. Wang Yang, an experienced political leader, initiated a great reform program during his tenure in Guangdong. Ma Kai is an experienced top bureaucrat. Both have assisted Premier Li Keqiang in making economic decisions.[16]

## NPC AND CPPCC
## AS REPRESENTATIVE INSTITUTIONS

The rapid development of the market economy has led to an increasingly pluralistic Chinese society. How to integrate pluralistic interests into the system has been a major challenge for the CCP leadership. To better these interests, the CCP has introduced institutional reforms into the two key representative bodies: the NPC and the CPPCC. These two bodies have become the institutional links between the CCP and the state and society. The key issue is whether the CCP can represent both the social interests and also organize and supervise the government through the NPC and CPPCC. The NPC and the CPPCC will play an increasingly important role in the political system.

Professionalism has been injected into local people's congresses as well. The NPC is largely an inefficient platform due to its massive size, which hovers around three thousand members. It annually convenes for only a short period, usually somewhere between ten and fourteen days. Moreover, the structure of its meetings, which are made up of full-day plenary sessions, is not suited for lengthy deliberations. To overcome these shortcomings, NPC reforms since the early 1990s have focused on expanding its Standing Committee and establishing special committees.

Over the years the Standing Committee has been expanded to its present strength of 176 members. This expanded group functions as a "miniature NPC" and its small size allows more frequent and efficient consultations than the NPC as a whole. Yet the committee is large enough to accommodate different social and political bases, particularly those of non-CCP members. The expansion of this group of "first among equals" allows follow-up on NPC decisions when the need arises.

Currently the NPC has nine special committees that govern the areas of foreign affairs, finance, education, minorities, and agricultural and rural affairs. The number of committees continues to increase. Special committees usually draw their members from two sources: government officials who have previously served in various state organizations and specialists in particular fields. These special committees provide expertise and public office experience, both in the law-making process and in the supervision of the daily functioning of the government (i.e., the state council and its various ministries).

To a degree, professionalization has altered the role of the NPC from that of a "rubber stamp" to one that is capable of overseeing governmental operations. As mentioned earlier, the CCP has actively employed the NPC as a means of exercising checks on the government. But the NPC itself continues to be dependent on the Party.

The CPPCC is also trying to have more say in policy suggestions. For example, 5,641 proposals were submitted during the first session of the Twelfth CPPCC in March 2013. Since 2008 as many as 6,000 proposals have been submitted by members during each CPPCC session. Compared to the number of proposals submitted at the first session of the Eleventh CPPCC in 2008 (4,772), the per-session number of proposals submitted by just the eight so-called democratic parties and the national trade and commerce union has continually increased, from 223 in 2008 to 352 in 2013. According to Wan Gang, the vice chairman of the CPPCC, CPPCC members submitted a total 25,114 proposals during the Eleventh CPPCC; this is an average of 2.2 proposals per member.[17] Most of these proposals are in the social and economic areas.

A review of the number of proposals submitted in the period of 2008 to 2013 shows that 10 percent of the members did not submit any proposals in every session of the conference. For instance, at the third session of the Eleventh CPPCC in March 2011, 88.82 percent of the members submitted proposals. The number in 2013 was down to 87.9 percent.[18] The reduction may be due to the fact that most members are not professionals or experts on political and social issues. They come from different walks of life and some are not familiar with the procedure and rules.

In the post-strongman era, as the institutions have become more and more important in Chinese politics, the NPC and CPPCC have gradually played an increasingly important role in China's political system. Nevertheless, their functions are to co-op rather than challenge the domination of the CCP. Given the fact that the NPC and CPPCC are both chaired by members of the SCPB, institutional-based factions tend to arise. In this sense, all are now more aware of their own interests and will participate more actively in China's politics.

## THE PARTY AND THE JUDICIARY SYSTEM

Since the onset of economic reforms in 1978-1979, there has been ongoing debate about which is superior, the Party or the law. Although the Chinese constitution stipulates that "no organization or individual may enjoy the privilege of being above the constitution and the law," and notwithstanding statements by the CCP leadership, which has repeatedly emphasized that like all others, the Party must act within the Chinese legal and constitutional framework, the Party in reality has dominated the country's judiciary through various institutional mechanisms.

The most powerful mechanism that enables the CCP to dominate all legal affairs is the Central Political and Legal Commission (CPLC). The CPLC, founded in 1980, is a specialized organ within the Party in charge of political and legal work (*zhengfa gongzuo*). In the 1980s the body was employed by powerful political figures like Peng Zhen and Chen Pixian to build China's legal system, which was completely destroyed under Mao Zedong. The CPLC was headed by a member of the Political Bureau. After the 1989 prodemocracy movement, this arrangement was highly institutionalized. From 1992 to 2012 the body was headed by a number of SCPB members, including Qiao Shi, Luo Gan, and Zhou Yongkang. During Zhou Yongkang's tenure (2007–2012) the role of the CPLC was greatly expanded. A task force in charge of maintaining social stability was set up within the CPLC and its head answers directly to the SCPB. This institutional arrangement guarantees that the Party maintains its leadership over the CPLC's political and legal work—as well as the relationship between and among various political and legal organs—by linking the Party's center to the political and legal front lines. The CPLC performs many governmental functions and is actively involved in judicial work, especially in giving instructions to the relevant court on how to handle cases. It has the power to jointly issue legal documents together with the court and the procurator. On the political side, the CPLC often takes initiatives in launching so-called strike-hard (*yanda*) campaigns.

Moreover, most of the court cadres are CCP members who are inclined to obey Party decisions and policies when deciding cases, particularly those that have political implications. Apart from the Party membership, the Party has its committees and Party groups within courts and procurates.

The increasingly important role of the CPLC has led to serious power abuses as well. Under the "maintaining stability" policy goal, the CPLC relied too heavily on coercive measures against society and thus created enormous tension between the Party and society. This led to the recent change of the CPLC at the Eighteenth Party Congress. The body was downgraded from the SCPB to the political bureau level, meaning that it is no longer headed by a SCPB member. The latest change is thus a positive sign for the future development of the judiciary system. When the CPLC was led by Zhou Yongkang, a member of the seventeenth SCPB, both the judiciary and social management were under the control of the CPLC. After Meng Jianzhu, a Political

Bureau member, replaced Zhou as the new head of the CPLC, he put an emphasis on further rationalizing the relations of the CPLC with other political and legal organizations. Meng believed that the CPLC should support the independence of the judiciary system in its jurisdiction and responsibilities.[19] This is in contrast to Zhou Yongkang, who emphasized that the CPLC should strengthen its supervision and administration over all organizations that conducted political and legal work.

The latest move of reform has also indicated that the CCP leadership wants to reduce arbitrary intervention into legal affairs by Party cadres and government officials and increase the professional integrity of the judiciary. In the Chinese Communist Party's Fourth Plenum of the Eighteenth Congress (October 2014), the CCP leadership passed a reform plan regarding the legal system. Titled "Decision on Several Important Issues Regarding the All-Around Promotion of Ruling the State According to Law," the plan vows to build the "rule of law" in the country.[20] This marks a first for the Central Committee: never before was this topic a focal point of discussions at a plenum. Three major reform initiatives are proposed as part of the decision. First, Beijing is directed to establish circuit courts and cross-region courts. This will serve to sever the connection between judges and local political interests and will weaken the authority of local Party cadres over the legal system. Second, interventions into legal affairs by Party cadres and government officials at different levels will be recorded, and officials will have to bear responsibility for intervention during their lifetimes. Third, Chinese authorities will promote professionalism within the judicial system. Judges must be recruited from among law graduates or law professionals, and they must start their careers working in low-level courts and they must work their way up based on performance and ability.[21]

The Central Discipline Inspection Commission (CDIC) was established in 1978 with the intent of enhancing Party discipline, but it has also frequently intervened in judicial work. With its wide range of duties, the CDIC inevitably has performed tasks that rightfully belong to the government. Anticorruption campaigns are one example. The CDIC usually initiates and leads anticorruption campaigns, but since January 1993 the CDIC and the Ministry of Supervision share joint offices, that is, two different official names but one working team. No real boundary exists between the Party and the government in the judicial system.

A significant change also happened to the CDIC after the Xi leadership took power. At the Eighteenth Congress a powerful figure, Wang Qishan, was promoted to the SCPB and was appointed to be in charge of Party discipline. Since then the CCP has initiated an unprecedented anticorruption campaign. Often when a new leadership group comes to power it initiates a new anticorruption campaign. In the past such campaigns would become a powerful political means to use against one's political competitors and also to solicit support and loyalty from Party cadres and government officials. Consequently, these campaigns have not been effective and corruption continues to be rampant. Corruption undermines the legitimacy of the CCP and weakens the state's capacity to govern society. The new Xi leadership is determined to bring down corrupt Party cadres and government officials.

The tenacity and ferocity of Xi's drive to eliminate graft has surprised many observers at home and abroad. An unprecedented number of officials at the vice-ministerial level or above, the "tigers," in Xi's words, have been investigated or detained under corruption charges since Xi came to power in November 2012 (see table 2.1). For example, thirty-six senior officials, including four state-level leaders—Zhou Yongkang, Xu Caihou, Su Rong, and Ling Jihua—were investigated in 2014 by the CPC's disciplinary inspection departments. Probes on Zhou and Xu have far-reaching political implications, as these investigations totally changed the power-sharing structure at the top level and influenced the transition from collective leadership to Xi's strongman politics. Such a transition could be politically risky because it poses challenges to the interests and safety of other strong leaders, particularly those in the SCPB who previously enjoyed immunity from the threat of corruption charges during their incumbencies or retirement. The six leaders investigated during Hu Jintao's second term (2008–2012) paled by comparison.[22]

This anticorruption campaign is indicative of Xi's more assertive and authoritarian governing style as compared to the styles of his predecessors. It may help to overcome resistance from long-entrenched interest groups and bring further market reforms. Xi's battle against corruption is still raging unremittingly. But it is unclear whether the probes on Zhou and Xu will involve other retired or incumbent Party oligarchies or their family members and close political allies. Nevertheless, there is no sign that Xi's campaign against mid-level bureaucrats or SOE leaders will subside anytime in the near future.

If the CDIC anticorruption campaign can be integrated into Xi Jinping's "rule of law" campaign, it is expected that China's governance will be greatly improved during Xi's tenure as the head of the CCP. However, more often than not, expectations are not the reality because anticorruption campaigns still remain political. Such campaigns frequently undermine the independence of the judiciary. And while the involvement of the CDIC may help such a campaign to effectively probe into high-ranking Party cadres such as Zhou Yongkang, it can also help some Party members escape criminal justice. The anticorruption practice is therefore quite arbitrary and as long as

**Table 2.1** Vice Ministerial-Level-or-Above Officials Under Investigation in 2014

| Name | Position | Time of Dismissal or Investigation |
|---|---|---|
| Ji Wenlin (冀文林) | Vice governor of Hainan province | February 2014 |
| Jin Daoming(金道铭) | Vice chairman of Shanxi Provincial People's Congress | February 2014 |
| Zhu Zuoli (祝作利) | Vice chairman of People's Political Consultative Conference of Shaanxi province | February 2014 |
| Shen Peiping (沈培平) | Vice governor of Yunnan province | March 2014 |
| Yao Mugen (姚木根) | Vice governor of Jiangxi province | March 2014 |
| Shen Weichen(申维辰) | Vice chairman of Chinese Association for Science and Technology | April 2014 |
| Song Lin (宋林) | Chairman of China Resources Holdings | April 2014 |
| Mao Xiaobing (毛小兵) | Party secretary of Xining city, Qinghai province | April 2014 |
| Tan Xiwei (谭栖伟) | Vice chairman of Chongqing People's Congress | May 2014 |
| Yang Baohua (阳宝华) | Vice chairman of People's Political Consultative Conference of Hunan province | May 2014 |
| Zhao Zhiyong (赵智勇) | Secretary general of Jiangxi Provincial Party Committee | June 2014 |
| Su Rong (苏荣) | Vice chairman of Chinese People's Political Consultative Conference | June 2014 |
| Du Shanxue (杜善学) | Vice governor of Shanxi province | June 2014 |
| *Ling Zhengce (令政策) | Vice chairman of Shanxi CPPCC | June 2014* |
| Ling Jihua (令计划) | Member of the Political Bureau of CCP, Head of the CCP's United Front Work Department | December 2014 |

*Ling Zhengce is the brother of Ling Jihua, a key aide to former president Hu Jintao and now vice chairman of the CPPCC. Ling Jihua's son was killed in a scandalous Ferrari crash in March 2012. Ling Jihua then failed to join the Politburo at the Eighteenth Party Congress. It is still not clear whether the probe on Ling Zhengce will incriminate Ling Jihua, who is also heading the Party's United Front Work Department.

Source: Compiled by the authors.

the Party treats its own members without reference to any legal process, it is unlikely that China will move toward a depoliticized legal system.

## LEGALIZING THE COMMAND OVER THE MILITARY

With the passing of the old guard it has become increasingly important for the younger generation of Party leaders to institutionalize an effective civil-military relationship. At a certain point personal control was no longer a viable method of maintaining control, so institutions had to be established to do so. However, establishing effective mechanisms for exercising Party control over the military has not been an easy task for the post-Deng leadership. Before Jiang Zemin firmly established himself as CMC chairman in the mid-1990s, he had experienced great difficulties in coping with military intervention in civilian affairs. Jiang replaced Zhao Ziyang as general secretary of the CCP in the aftermath of the pro-democracy movement in 1989, at which point he turned to being conservative and initiated no reforms. However, Deng's southern tour in 1992 targeted Jiang's conservative political line, which had placed social stability above further reforms. In initiating a new wave of reform Deng relied on local governments and the military, particularly Yang Shangkun, the president of the state, and his brother general, Yang Baibing. Unfortunately, this also created a political condition for the military to intervene in civilian affairs. Prior to the Fourteenth Party Congress, the Yang brothers argued that the military had to play the role of *baojia huhang* (escort to the reform process) but it was regarded as a serious attempt by the military to intervene in civilian affairs. Following his southern tour Deng attempted to address this problem. He believed that the Yang brothers could form a second power center to challenge Jiang's authority and threaten the CCP as a unified organization. Deng removed the Yangs from their military posts at the Fourteenth Party Congress in 1994, despite the fact that for years they had been his most loyal followers. It is worth noting that Deng successfully forced Jiang to alter his policy preferences. Deng also decided at the Fourteenth Party Congress that the three top posts in the Party, the state and the military should be concentrated in the hands of the Party leader, namely Jiang, with the sole aim of strengthening Deng's authority. This had not happened since Mao's state presidency in 1962. As noted earlier, this three-in-one system has been highly institutionalized since 1992 simply to assist the civilian leader to consolidate his power over the military.

As the personal authority of civilian leaders has decreased, they have had to rely more heavily on institutions to control the military. In 1997 China passed the National Defense Law, the first of its kind in the country. The major objective of the new law was to legalize the command of the Party over the military. Legalizing the relationship between the Party and the military is in fact the rational method to institutionalizing control of the Party over the gun, which in the past depended largely on an individual strongman's personal power rather than on the institutional power that defined civil-military relations.

The passage of the National Defense Law undoubtedly indicated progress toward civilian control over the military. However, it does not mean that the civilian leadership is actually able to control the gun. The Party leadership since Jiang has also appealed to many other mechanisms to accomplish this, such as reshuffling military personnel (i.e., the appointment or removal of generals); using ideological tools (i.e., the military must demonstrate its loyalty to the Party); controlling budgetary allocation; and even enhancing personal ties. For instance, at the Fourteenth Party Congress, Gen. Liu Huaqing exited peacefully from the SCPB and no military general has since been promoted to this most important decision-making body. After becoming CMC chairman, Jiang restored the growth of the military budget, which eased accumulated anger among senior military officers toward Deng Xiaoping and Zhao Ziyang, the latter of whom heavy-handedly decreased defense spending during the 1980s. During Jiang's thirteen-year reign the military instituted a large number of reforms, such as the separation of the military from business and greater professionalization among its officers.

In 2008 another important law, the National Defense Mobilization Law, was promulgated by the NPC. This law endorsed giving more power to the state council in order to be able to mobilize the military in emergencies or times of disaster. Before the publication of this law, the general secretary of the CCP was the only person in the SCPB who had the power to command the military and there was no legal basis for the other members to do so. In 2008, when the first Sichuan earthquake hit, Premier Wen Jiabao failed to mobilize the military to implement immediate rescue and help was delayed. This incident undoubtedly provided the impetus for the passage of the mobilization law.

The National Defense Mobilization Law has also given the government (i.e., the state council) a larger legal basis and platform upon which it can coordinate with the military in dealing with nonmilitary affairs, such as coping with disasters. By the time of the Sichuan Ya'an earthquake in 2013, the state council and the military were better coordinated and able to implement timely rescue help at the scene. The new law also gives the state council greater power in managing other military-related tasks, including peace-keeping missions under the auspices of the United Nations. However, it does not give the state council the power to mobilize the military for waging war or warlike activities.

The professionalization of the military has made the PLA similar to other military forces in the West. In many democracies the military exercises powerful influence over the policy-making process, especially concerning matters of national security and defense. The issue in China, however, is whether this will ultimately produce a nationalized military and soldiers of political neutrality. While this is a legitimate question, it is too early to search for an answer. The task of the Party leadership for the foreseeable future is still to build institutions that enable the Party to exercise effective control over the military while also institutionalizing an efficient Party-military relationship. Without strong support from the Party, the civilian government will face great uncertainties in exercising control over the military. In the minds of the CCP, the prevalence of military rule in many developing countries, whether democratic or authoritarian, justifies the Party's control over the military. As long as the CCP remains an "organizational emperor," the military will continue to be a "royal" army. In this sense the nationalization of the military depends on changing relations between the Party and the government. Also, in a scenario similar to what happened in the former Soviet Union and its Eastern European confederates, there is no substantial evidence to indicate that the Party's control over the military will be a major barrier for political reform, or even democratization.

Indeed, the CCP's main challenge remains the same: it must figure out how to continue to exercise effective control. It is not an easy task for the CCP to control the military since institutional links between the CCP and the military have remained weak. At the institutional level, the Political Bureau is charged with responsibility for political affairs, while the CMC is in full command of military affairs. However, the general Party secretary is the only SCPB member who sits on the CMC (as the commander in chief surrounded by top generals) so it will always be a big question as to whether the general Party secretary can exercise effective control. For example, during Hu Jintao's tenure, weak civilian oversight was greatly compromised by the reign-without-rule practice of Hu in managing the PLA. Hu basically adopted a hands-off approach due to the lingering influence of Jiang, who kept the top military post for two years after retiring from the paramount Party post. Hu's complete exit from both the Party and the military in 2012 became a turning point for reshaping Party-military relations and granted Xi formidable power in handling PLA affairs.

Just as in the Party and government apparatus, Xi had to consolidate his power in the military through daunting anticorruption investigations. The downfall of Xu Caihou caught many observers by surprise, as he was the first CMC vice chairman purged for corruption charges during the reform era. Xu had placed a large number of his favored senior officers in strategic positions inside the PLA, many of whom are now being implicated in the unprecedented anti-graft campaign in the military.[23]

Guo Boxiong, the other former CMC vice chairman during Hu's time, has also been placed under investigation for allegedly taking bribes.[24] The military was running on a "dual leadership" system, where a general's promotion had to be approved by both Xu and Guo when they were CMC vice chairmen. So far more than a dozen PLA generals, including Gu Junshan, the former deputy commander of the PLA's General Logistics Department, and Yang Jinshan, the former deputy commander of the PLA's Chengdu Military Area Command, have been put into custody (see table 2.2). Several suicides by PLA generals have also been reported since Xu's case was exposed to the public in June 2014.

Throughout the year Xi has repeatedly emphasized the importance of the PLA's absolute loyalty and firm faith in the Party leadership, even when large-scale anti-graft purges were being carried out within the PLA. He reiterated the Party's supremacy over the PLA during a military political work conference held on October 30 at Gutian township in Shanghang County, Fujian. The meeting was held in the same place as the famous Gutian Conference of 1929, which was considered a milestone for both the Party and the PLA because it established the fundamental principle of the "Party leading the army."[25]

Compared with Hu's weak style of leadership over the PLA, Xi has been able to sway the pendulum toward the other end of excessive personal control. Xi's authoritarian approach may have addressed some of the accumulated negative effects of weak civilian oversight, but the structural difficulties in achieving an appropriate degree of civilian control still remain.

## CONCLUSION

China's formal institutions, particularly the Communist Party's relations with the state, the judiciary, and the military, have developed and changed over time. While China continues to be an authoritarian system, its political system has nevertheless been flexible. Rapid economic developments since the reform and open-door policies arose has created a new socioeconomic environment for the CCP. The CCP has thus had to consistently adjust its relations with the government and other state institutions in order to survive.

**Table 2.2** PLA Generals (Admirals) Under Investigation in 2014

| | |
|---|---|
| Gu Junshan (谷俊山) | Deputy commander of PLA's General Logistics Department |
| Xu Caihou (徐才厚) | Retired CMC vice chairman |
| Guo Boxiong (郭伯雄) (not confirmed) | Retired CMC vice chairman |
| Yang Jinshan (杨金山) | Deputy commander of People's Liberation Army's Chengdu Military Area Command |
| Ye Wanyong (叶万勇) | Sichuan military commissar |
| *Jiang Zhonghua (姜中华) | Chief of PLA Navy's South Sea Fleet Armaments Department |
| *Ma Faxiang (马发祥) | Deputy commissar of PLA Navy |
| *Song Yuwen (宋玉文) | Deputy commissar of Jilin Military Area Command |
| Zhang Shutian (张树田) | Retired secretary of CMC Discipline and Inspection Committee |
| Zhang Gongxian (张贡献) | Chief of political department of Jinan Military Area Command |
| Li Bin (李斌) | Deputy chief of PLA Navy's Political Department |
| Kang Xiaohui (康晓辉) | Commissar of Shenyang Military Area Command Communications and Logistics Department |
| Qi Changming (齐长明) | Deputy chief of staff of Beijing Military Area Command |
| Gao Xiaoyan (高小燕) | Deputy commissar of PLA Information Engineering University |

*PLA officers who reportedly committed suicide.

Source: compiled by the authors.

A close examination reveals that the Party's domination over the state has not always been absolute. While the whole political-institutional structure remains intact, the functions of the entities within the structure have gradually evolved over time. The increasing functionary differentiation between the Party and the state, as well as the trend of increasing professionalism within state ranks, indicate that the state enjoys certain degree of autonomy outside the Party. The power of the state is not simply delegated by the Party; instead, the state has its own field of power. This is also true in terms of the CCP's relations with the judiciary and the military. Even while institutionalization between the CCP and other institutions has taken place, this level of institutionalization remains low.

Furthermore, China's successful transition to modern, effective governance is dependent both on changing the Party's relationship with the state and on changing the state's relationship with civil society. China's market economy and modernization attempts have served to empower the citizenry. At the local levels, different experiments have been implemented to give citizens more space and a greater degree of autonomy. Conversely, at the national level the empowerment of civil society has been either too reluctant or too slow. So far the CCP has placed its reform emphasis on formal institutions and it has largely ignored how civil society can become a part of new or reformed formal state institutions. Today all state institutions are facing different challenges from society. China's effective governance depends on whether and how civil society is given the institutional channels needed to allow participation in governance. Facing a rising civil society: this is the major political challenge for the Xi Jinping leadership.

## NOTES

1. Shiping Zheng, *Party vs. State in Post-1949 China: The Institutional Dilemma* (Cambridge, UK: Cambridge University Press, 1997); and Andre Laliberte and Marc Lanteigne, eds., *The Chinese Party-State in the Twenty-First Century* (London: Routledge, 2007).

2. For a detailed examination of how the CCP utilizes these institutions to control the state see Zheng Yongnian, *The Chinese Communist Party as Organizational Emperor: Culture, Reproduction, and Transformation* (London: Routledge 2010).

3. For example, David Shambaugh, *China's Communist Party: Atrophy and Adaptation* (Washington, DC: Woodrow Wilson Center Press and University of California Press, 2008).

4. Yongnian Zheng, *Technological Empowerment: The Internet, State, and Society in China* (Stanford, CA: Stanford University Press, 2008); Guobin Yang, *The Power of the Internet in China: Citizen Activism Online* (New York: Columbia University Press, 2009); Zhang Xiaoling and Zheng Yongnian, eds., *China's Information and Communication Technology Revolution* (London: Routledge, 2009); and Wong Tong, *The Power of Social Media in China: The Government, Websites, and Netizens on Weibo* (Singapore: National University of Singapore Department of Political Science, 2012).

5. Xie Yue and Shan Wei, *China Struggles to Maintain Stability: Strengthening Its Public Security Apparatus*, EAI Background Brief no. 615 (Singapore: National

University of Singapore East Asian Institute, April 8, 2011); and Shan Wei, *Social Management: China Goes Beyond Maintaining Social Stability*, EAI Background Brief no. 763 (Singapore: National University of Singapore East Asian Institute, October 22, 2012).

6. For a detailed discussion of bureaucratic reforms see, Yongnian Zheng, *Globalization and State Transformation in China* (New York: Cambridge University Press, 2004); and for an update see Yongnian Zheng, *Contemporary China: A History since 1978* (Oxford: Wiley-Blackwell, 2014), chap. 10.

7. See Linda Jakobson's chapter in this volume.

8. Zheng, *Chinese Communist Party as Organizational Emperor*, 119.

9. Wang Yang was appointed vice premier in 2013.

10. For a discussion on the Guangdong model see Zheng Yongnian, "Shichang jingji yu Guangdong de gaige kaifang" (The market economy, the reform, and open-door policy in Guangdong) in *Kaifang hidai* (Open times) 238 (April 2012): 5–22. See also Lance L. P. Gore, *Wang Yang's Reform Program in Guangdong*, EAI Background Brief no. 727 (Singapore: National University of Singapore East Asian Institute, June 2012).

11. This is based on our fieldwork in Shunde in 2012.

12. Xinhua News Agency, April 24 and July 31, 2013.

13. Bo Zhiyue, "Chongqing after Bo Xilai," EAI Background Brief no. 742 (Singapore: National University of Singapore East Asian Institute, August 2012); and Lance L. P. Gore, *China in Search of a New Development Model: Guangdong or Chongqing*, EAI Background Brief no. 701 (Singapore: National University of Singapore East Asian Institute, February 2012). For more on the modified model see Zhao Litao and Qian Jiwei, *Chongqing under Sun Zhengcai*, EAI Background Brief no. 972 (Singapore: National University of Singapore East Asian Institute, November 2014).

14. See Bo Zhiyue's chapter in this volume.

15. Lance L. P. Gore, "China's New State Council and the 'Super-Ministry' Reform," EAI Background Brief no. 801 (Singapore: National University of Singapore East Asian Institute, March 2013).

16. For a detailed report of the profiles of the new economic team see Yang Mu and Yao Jielu, *China's New Economic Leadership Team: Implications for Reforms*, EAI Background Brief no. 807 (Singapore: National University of Singapore East Asian Institute, April 2013).

17. Tian Xianghua, "The CPPCC Proposals Are About to Be Processed," *The First Financial and Economic Daily*, March 13, 2013, http://news.ifeng.com/main land/special/2013lianghui/content-3/detail_2013_03/13/23047770_0.shtml, accessed April 6, 2013.

18. Ibid.

19. Shen Xinwang, "Analyzing the Direction of the CPLC Reform," *China News Weekly*, April 28, 2013.

20. https://chinacopyrightandmedia.wordpress.com/2014/10/28/ccp-central-committee-decision-concerning-some-major-questions-in-comprehensively-moving-governing-the-country-according-to-the-law forward/.

21. See Zheng Yongnian and Shan Wei, "Understanding Xi Jiping's 'Rule of Law' Campaign," EAI Background Brief no. 1,000 (Singapore: National University of Singapore East Asian Institute, February 2015).

22. "Working Report of Supreme People's Procuratorate of China in 2013," *People's Daily*, March 22, 2013, 2.

23. You Ji, "The Lessons of Xu Caihou," *EAI Bulletin* 16, no. 2 (2014): 3.

24. "Chinese Ex-Military Leader Guo Boxiong Under Graft Investigation: Report," *AFP News*, August 12, 2014.

25. Xinhua News Agency, "Quanjun zhengzhi gongzuo huiyi zai Gutian zhaokai, Xi Jinping Chuxi huiyi bing fabiao zhongyao jianghua" (The PLA conference of political work was held in Gutian, and Xi Jinping attended the conference and made an important speech), December 1, 2014.

# 3

# THE CHALLENGES OF ECONOMIC GROWTH AND REFORM

## Barry Naughton

China's new leaders inherit an economy that has experienced unprecedented economic success over the last thirty years, but they also face profound economic and political challenges. The first part of this chapter sketches China's current economic landscape, noting a few political landmarks as well. It describes the achievements and the rapidly changing economic conditions and emphasizes that both the achievements and the changes have contributed to a crisis of confidence in the ability of China's new leaders to get out in front of change and implement reforms. The second part analyzes the choices the new leaders face in confronting a reform agenda, based on a distinction between initiating reform and consolidating reform. Xi Jinping and Li Keqiang have generally made a strong start in initiating reform, and many of their early moves can be understood in terms of the need to overcome the pervasive crisis of credibility. However, it is uncertain whether this will translate into success in consolidating reform since reform consolidation requires a different set of leadership characteristics than does initiating reform.

## SUCCESS AND COMPLACENCY

At first look, it seems that China's new leadership assumed power in 2012 at the pinnacle of economic success. As soon as Xi Jinping and Li Keqiang put in place their new administration, they made clear their belief that China's economic clout entitles it to a position of respect and global influence greater than ever before. In fact, China's economy had already been a certifiable "growth miracle" when the previous Hu Jintao–Wen Jiabao administration had taken over in 2003. At that time, China's economy had already sustained a torrid annual growth rate of 9.6 percent for twenty-four years, since the beginning of economic reform. But in the subsequent 2003–2012 decade—which included the global financial crisis— China's growth actually accelerated, reaching a 10.4 percent annual growth rate.[1] China overcame the global crisis by pouring resources into investment and accelerating the already eye-watering speed of its infrastructure build-out. Per capita GDP pushed over the upper-middle-income threshold in 2010, when it surpassed US $4,000.[2] Not surprisingly, then, an air of triumphalism began to creep into Chinese attitudes and government proclamations, and a particular point of pride came when the aggregate size of the Chinese economy surpassed that of Japan, making China's the second largest in the world.

Transformation at this pace inevitably created enormous stresses and strains. Besides the inequities, dislocation, and environmental costs, headlong growth also led to another problem: as incomes grew, the impetus for market-oriented economic reforms diminished. As Wu Jinglian, the dean of China's reform-oriented economists, put it, "As life got comfortable, reforms stopped."[3] During the 1990s, driven by profound economic and political crises, the Chinese government pushed through a procession of fundamental economic reforms. Under Premier Zhu Rongji, between 1993 and 1999 China enacted a series of deep and difficult reforms of the fiscal, financial, and market systems. These reforms culminated in the massive downsizing of the Chinese state enterprises sector (1996–2001) and were sealed by China's entry into the World Trade Organization in 2001, which locked in many of the most important reforms. As a result of these reforms, the Hu-Wen administration inherited a highly favorable economic position: the previous administration had paid a substantial price to break down the old system and lay the foundation for a new, better-functioning economic system but had only just begun to enjoy the benefits. Hu and Wen were poised to, as the Chinese saying puts it, "enjoy the shade of the trees planted by the ancestors."

At first, the Hu-Wen administration seemed ready to follow and continue the reform trajectory of the previous Jiang-Zhu administration. Many of the economic technocrats of the Zhu administration had stayed on and the administration's initial economic proposals were full of good ideas. Despite this robust program for a continuation of reform, nothing much happened and there was no follow-through.[4] Today, in Beijing, the perception is widespread that the past ten years have been a "lost decade" insofar as market-oriented economic reform is concerned. This doesn't mean that Premier Wen

Jiabao presided over a do-nothing administration. On the contrary, Wen accomplished much on the social front: he cut taxes on the rural economy and boosted spending on education and medical care; he also created the foundation for rudimentary national systems of health insurance and pensions. Wen also increased defense outlays, which contributed to a stronger military and is certainly seen as a positive by most Chinese. This administration was energetic in spending money, which was acceptable because, as discussed below, they had the money to spend. However, in terms of creating the institutional framework on which future prosperity would depend, the outgoing administration achieved almost nothing.

## FROM COMPLACENCY TO VESTED INTERESTS

It is common in China to find individuals who explain reform stagnation, or the defeat of individual reform initiatives, by referring to the increased strength of "vested interests." Even the current premier, Li Keqiang, refers regularly to the need to manage and minimize interest group opposition if his current reform proposals are to advance successfully.[5] But who, exactly, are these vested interests? The idea of "vested interests" covers a broad spectrum. At one extreme, the opposition of interest groups to reforms shades into and becomes identical with the problem of corruption. Some vested interests are well-connected families; corrupt officials; or even criminal gangs. At the other end of the spectrum, though, the problem of vested interests is a problem created by the stabilization of the entire Communist Party–dominated economic and governmental system. The easiest way to see this is through the prism of China's budgetary situation (see fig. 3.1). From the beginning of reform in 1978 until 1995—well into the Zhu Rongji reform era—budgetary revenues as a share of GDP declined nearly every year. Indeed, the productive era of 1990s reforms described earlier was driven by an acute budgetary crisis. Zhu's reforms included a new tax system and a new level of financial discipline that staunched losses in the state enterprise sector. As state firms were chopped back and restructured, the few that survived made a sustained return to profitability, which increased resources available to national leaders both directly and indirectly. Figure 3.1 also shows that the trend turned dramatically after 1995, and budgetary revenues as a share of GDP *increased* every year between 1995 and 2013. The result was an enormous increase in the volume of resources available to the system.

A few numbers can give a sense of the magnitude of this transformation. As Figure 3.1 also shows, Chinese budget revenues increased from 10.8 percent

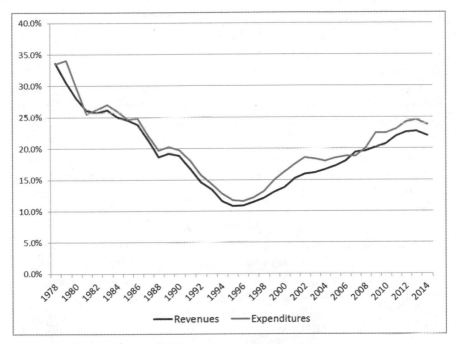

**Figure 3.1** Budget Share in GDP

Source: National Bureau of Statistics, *Zhongguo Tongji Nianjian* (China Statistical Yearbook) 2014 (Beijing: Zhongguo Tongji. 50, 190); and Ministry of Finance, "Report on Implementation of the 2014 Budget and Preparation for 2015 Budget," March 17, 2015, accessed at http://www.mof.gov.cn/zhengwuxinxi/caizhengxinwen/201503/t20150317_1203481.html.

of GDP in 1995 to 22.7 percent of GDP in 2013.[6] Doubling the budget's take of GDP is a substantial achievement in itself, and one that becomes even more impressive when the rapid growth of GDP and the increasing value of the Chinese currency are taken into consideration. In 2012 constant US dollars, the value of China's budgetary revenues increased from $113 billion in 1995 to $2,045 billion in 2013 (that is, $2 trillion). These numbers look like some kind of spreadsheet error, but they are not.[7] Chinese government revenues (central and local consolidated) are roughly equal to the US federal government on-budget revenues: excluding Social Security, the CBO estimates these to be $1.97 trillion for 2012.

Less than two decades since the country faced a potential crisis of state capacity, the Chinese system is now awash in cash. Money is available not just for the critical necessities but for elective projects as well: technology megaprojects; culture vanity projects; global propaganda initiatives; and what have you. If a top leader wants it badly enough, the money can be found. Even the universities have plenty of money. Virtually everyone in a position of authority has a bigger budget, is better off, and has plenty to do. Bitter disputes over resource allocation are less salient, and side payments can be made to buy off dissenters. As the flow of resources through the Party and state-dominated sectors of the economy has increased and stabilized, the system naturally has become organized more stably around that flow. State-owned enterprises, now returned to financial health, are benefiting from the radical downsizing and restructuring that Zhu Rongji had pushed through at such cost in the late 1990s. With a little manipulation, a few strategic entry barriers, and genuine bottom-up economic growth, the state-owned enterprises have been transformed from a burden to an asset. The most extreme example is China Mobile, the state-run company that not only is by far the largest telecom operator in the world, with eight hundred million subscribers, but also sits on the biggest cash pile in Asia, with $64 billion in the bank.[8]

At the same time, the reconstruction of the Party apparatus and the rationalization of Party-state career paths have given the system a new stability and predictability. Career trajectories are knowable; opportunities are significant and increase predictably with promotion. Students in elite universities have increasingly come to see a government career as the most attractive option. In other words, reform stagnation has not been simply a matter of short-term complacency, consisting of deferring urgently needed reforms. Instead, it reflects the long-term stabilization of the system. This system, which in the 1980s and 1990s had been constantly remaking itself in order to adapt to new challenges, has developed into a system that (like most systems in the world) is engaged primarily in reproducing itself more or less as it is. The biggest vested interest, then, is the interest represented by the Communist Party itself. The system is no longer driven by an *internal, immediate* sense of crisis, as it was repeatedly in the 1970s, 1980s, and even 1990s.

## The Crisis of Confidence

The new stability of the system is viewed warily by those outside its embrace. In the first place, there is a widespread perception—both inside and outside China—that it is increasingly difficult to do business in China without political connections. Of course, at the same time, the private sector has grown tremendously along with the overall economy; and, while the state sector has stopped shrinking in absolute terms, its share of the growing economy has continued to erode. However, private business owners now sense increased competition with state firms and an increased need for accommodation with power holders—with "vested interests"—who are increasingly savvy about ways to extract benefits from the booming economy and from private firms.

Even more important, from the outside the Chinese system looks increasingly impervious to change. This has led to an interesting disconnect. Over the past ten years, the government's propaganda organs have continued to trumpet the indispensability of economic reform. Every few years, major new reforms are discussed and policies are implemented, but they have little impact. The result has been a loss in the credibility of official pronouncements. This loss of credibility, combined with the increasing stabilization of China's system and the greater influence of interest groups, has led to a crisis of confidence in China's ability to change. This credibility crisis is something quite new in China, although it has infected for a long time the United States and other developed economy societies, where the idea has spread that problems are peculiarly entrenched and intractable, that there's really nothing that can be done about them, and that only the extremely naïve believe that things can be changed. Until recently this type of cynicism was almost completely absent in China. Because China has been changing so rapidly, everyone believed that its future was full of different possibilities even though the present was difficult and impoverished. That sense of confidence about the future seems to have vanished.

## THE REFORMERS' ARGUMENT

Despite this waning of confidence, economic reform in China is not dead. Reformers hold important positions in the new government and in the country's most influential business media. At the core, these reformers have only one argument to make, but that argument is a powerful one: the current economic situation and policy trajectory are not sustainable. The current way of doing things simply will not work. Economic conditions are changing rapidly, and carrying on with business as usual risks serious crisis. Although it may seem that there is no impetus to change, the reality is that change will come whether policy makers want it or not. If they do not preempt the changes that are coming, then change will be disruptive and potentially devastating. But there is still time to act. The argument about unsustainability has four key components, and these lead into a broader discussion about the nature of Chinese society and the economy.

First, the failure to substantially improve the quality of China's economic institutions will begin to gradually erode the pace of productivity improvement. China's total factor productivity has increased dramatically during the reform era, including over the past decade. This productivity improvement has been diffuse and attributable to multiple causes, to learning and adoption of new technologies, but also to improved institutions. A key link has been the willingness to let underperforming entities fail, concentrating production in the most competitive, highest-productivity firms. The strength of this competitive mechanism seems to have waned in recent years; a new wave of reform is needed to expand the best while shutting down the rest. Productivity is not simple to measure; there are time lags both in the appearance of the productivity effects and in the measuring of them. So by the time the economists have an academically rigorous judgment it is usually too late to do anything about it. But in the interim, policy makers will look at growth rates compared to investment rates. There are many reasons why growth should slow (as I discuss later). But as long as investment rates stay high policy makers will take declining growth rates as evidence that something is wrong with their system's productivity and will be motivated to push harder for reforms.

Second, the limits to investment-driven growth are beginning to appear. China was able to sidestep the worst of the 2008 global financial crisis by increasing domestic investment. GDP growth scarcely dropped because the increase in domestic investment almost completely offset the drop in net exports. But this success was achieved at substantial cost: because the stimulus program was rushed, an unknown proportion of new investment was doubtless wasted on useless projects, although there is no way of knowing how large that proportion is. More fundamentally, as figure 3.2 shows, the investment surge of 2009 was not a "one-off" stimulus. Instead, China's investment rate moved more or less permanently to a higher level. Since 2009, China has been investing a remarkable 48 percent of GDP. An investment effort of this magnitude is completely unprecedented for a large economy. Japan and Korea drove growth with investment, but even so, their investment rates rarely exceeded 40 percent for more than a year or two. Back in 2007, Premier Wen Jiabao described China's economy as "unstable, unbalanced, uncoordinated and unsustainable," but since that time it has become more unbalanced, in the sense that the economy is even more dependent on investment than it ever has been.

What is wrong with this investment-driven, unbalanced growth? After all, investment-led growth has served the Chinese economy well over the past two decades. One of the great paradoxes of the Chinese economy is that although household consumption is an unusually low share of total GDP (35 percent), household consumption has also grown extremely rapidly over the past decade (just not as fast as overall GDP). If you can have *both* more

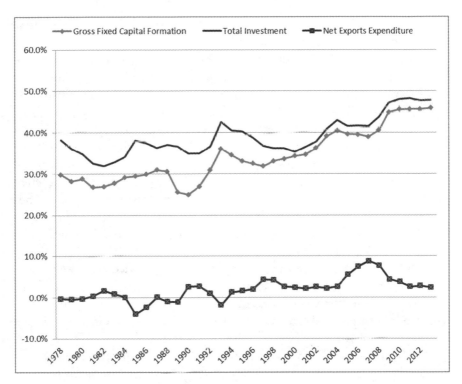

**Figure 3.2** Investment and Net Exports (Share of GDP)

Source: National Bureau of Statistics, Zhongguo Tongji Nianjian (China Statistical Yearbook) 2014. Beijing: Zhongguo Tongji, 68.

consumption and more investment, why not have it all? Because it is probably just not possible. Economists can't provide any logical limit to how high a country's investment rate can be, nor how long it can be sustained. All previous high-growth economies have eventually come to a point where investment rates subside, and it is usually at levels well below the current Chinese level. Investment has an inherent tendency toward instability since it is driven by investors' expectations of the future. While consumption is relatively stable, investment is subject to the "animal spirits" of those making decisions. In China, the government's willingness to act as the reliable investor of last resort has kept the investment propensity of private businesses high as well. The two have been in a productive symbiosis that thus far has served the economy well. But as the fundamental copy-cat infrastructure gets built out, and excess capacity emerges in many industrial sectors, there is almost certainly a limit to this growth strategy. Once the momentum of the economy slows down, there is a danger that investment coming from the private sector will drop faster than the government can pick up the slack.

Third, past investment excesses have already created financial fragility. The huge quantity of new fixed assets the Chinese economy has created over the past five years are just now coming onstream. Many of these assets are housed in corporate structures that have no good business model. The extreme example is China's gleaming high-speed rail system. The railroad system currently has a debt that's the equivalent of US $429 billion. Whether or not the high-speed rail is worth building on this scale is one question (about which opinions differ). An altogether different question is whether there is a revenue model to service this enormous debt. Other than a few high-capacity lines like Beijing-Shanghai, most observers doubt it. This situation is replicated by literally thousands of smaller local government projects and "funding platforms" around the country. Encouraged to invest following the global financial crisis, these vehicles now face debts they cannot service with the income streams they can plausibly generate through user fees and sales revenues. Chinese regulators and financial sector officials are well aware of these problems. They have been pushing China's state banks to increase bad loan provisions and raise capital. They will not be caught by surprise.

Nonetheless, the hard work of actually restructuring these corporations has barely begun. Indeed, it can hardly proceed in an environment in which credit is still flowing freely and in which shambolic state-backed corporations have easy access not just to bank loans but also to nascent bond markets, which have been growing quickly. It is difficult to see how a financial restructuring can be driven forward without a corresponding credit squeeze. But without some kind of financial restructuring, the danger is that resources continue to flow into low-productivity or no-productivity projects and corporations. The creation of a vast sector of "zombie firms" that are neither dead nor alive will ultimately create a far larger and more dangerous risk of financial panic and collapse. In this respect, the relevant experience is that of Japan in the 1990s, when the delay of financial restructuring kept numerous zombie firms alive and prevented the economy from recovering for an entire "lost decade."

Fourth, China is going through profound changes in its labor markets that point to substantially slower growth. For decades, employers had been able to hire new workers at will, at an offered wage that changed little through the 1990s and early 2000s. But some time after the mid-2000s, competition for workers began to drive up unskilled wages. By 2012, real wages for migrant workers were two and a half times what they had been in 2003, increasing by 10.8 percent annually. This dramatic change in labor market conditions led many observers to proclaim "the end of cheap China." The sudden change also revived interest in a so-called Lewis turning point, which is a structural shift that occurs when the reservoir of surplus labor in the countryside is finally drawn down and employers are forced to pay higher wages to draw people out of agricultural work.[9] In past Asian growth "miracles," the arrival of the Lewis turning point often presaged the end of the very high growth period. At a minimum, rapid growth of unskilled wages tends to force economies off the path of labor-intensive export orientation. Economies start to lose comparative advantage in light manufactures—in clothing, shoes, and toys—and the rapid expansion of exports that has driven rapid growth becomes less important. It is clear that these forces are now becoming important for China. Moreover, since export demand from the European Union, Japan, and the United States is likely to be weak for the immediate future, exports will probably make a much smaller contribution to China's growth in the future than they have over the past decade.

Changes occurring in the Chinese labor force are not due solely to the mopping up of surplus rural labor. The year 2012 saw another crucial turning point, as the Chinese population of working age began to decline. This is an entirely different type of demographic transition, driven in this case by China's draconian birth control policies. Typically, developing economies experience a "demographic dividend" when the population at working age is growing more rapidly than the overall population: dependency ratios decrease and the work force becomes younger and (it is hoped) better educated. But the demographic dividend is inevitably exhausted eventually, and economies begin to age and experience a higher (-aged) dependency ratio. China today has an unusually low dependency ratio (since the populations of both children and the elderly are small), and it has been enjoying this demographic dividend for the past twenty-five years. Today, however, it is over, and dependency rates are beginning to grow. Moreover, the absolute size of the labor force is now decreasing. The fact that these two completely different types of transition are occurring simultaneously means that the shift in labor force conditions will be unusually abrupt. For comparison, Japan's labor force began to shrink about twenty-five years after the end of its high-growth era—when the country was already quite rich—and Korea's labor force began to shrink about fifteen years after the end of its high-growth era. But in China, the Lewis turning point and the overall shrinkage of the labor force are occurring simultaneously.

The structural changes in China's labor force mean growth is bound to slow down. This does not have to be a bad thing. After all, higher wages mean that incomes are growing, that people are better off, and that there is an opportunity to shift the pattern of economic development so that it provides a greater share of output for household consumption. Moreover, China is a huge continental economy and does not have to tie its economic growth only to its export strategy. Chinese incomes overall are still relatively low and there is still plenty of room for catch-up. While this structural population change is a huge challenge, it is not necessarily a looming disaster. If it is managed carefully, it could lead to a much more productive and capable society overall. Here, though, the record of Asia's earlier "miracle economies" should provide a cautionary example. When economies such as Japan, Korea, and Taiwan moved out of their very-high-growth phases, they each faced major challenges to their growth models. Japan's growth rate dropped sharply in 1973 and then again in the 1990s. Never again did Japan come anywhere close to replicating the high growth rates of the 1950s and 1960s. Similarly, the end of Korea's high-growth phase (in 1997) came along with the Asian financial crisis, massive financial distress and restructuring, and a permanently lower growth rate. The evidence is clear that if China does *not* handle this transition well there could be a substantial economic price to pay.

Here is where the broader argument about the nature of China's economy and society comes into play. Typically, as forerunner economies have reached the end of their high-growth phases, they have upgraded into high technology and more sophisticated sectors. China clearly hopes to follow this lead. To prepare, China has invested massively in university education (since 2001) and also begun to pour government money into research and development in promising "emerging" industrial sectors. Investment in research and development has now sustained rapid growth for over a decade and surpassed 2 percent of GDP in 2013, a much higher level than that of other economies at comparable levels of GDP per capita. But, typically, forerunner economies aid this upgrading process by transitioning into a much more "light touch" role for government and a broader liberalization of economic and social conditions. Thus, the government typically hands off more of the responsibility for development to the private sector and relies on dispersed entrepreneurship to identify and exploit promising new sectors. In China, the movement in recent years has *not* been in this direction. Government, flush with money, has stepped up its own direct role in technology research and innovation. Entry barriers that have long since fallen away for ordinary manufacturing sectors are still in place for high-value services such as finance and information (including Internet businesses). Will the emphasis on a top-down, state-directed program of innovation, combined with state control of large swathes of the economy, actually end up retarding China's essential move toward an innovative, diverse, and resilient economy?

Today's China faces a set of challenges that are clearly different from those of the past. The current changes in the external economic environment are obvious for all to see. Slowing labor force growth, soaring wages, and rapidly changing cost structures and competitiveness are part of daily life for all Chinese. These changes directly imply that the existing economic strategy has reached its limits. In the past, with unlimited supplies of labor, investment was the key growth driver. All that was needed to bring that labor out of the countryside was new industrial plants and infrastructure. Moreover, as a follower economy, planners and businesses could focus on transplanting business models, technologies, and infrastructure patterns from developed countries. The institutional setup was adapted, in myriad ways, to support the high-investment imperative. The system delivered investment and investment delivered growth. That equation is no longer so simple. Matching the right investment to the evolving needs of the economy has become much more difficult. Now China needs to upgrade the quality of its human resources; identify the sectors, products, and services where opportunities lie; move to the global frontier in numerous sectors where it has long been a follower; and promote innovation across the board. Can it do those things without also further scaling back the power of the state, eliminating visible and invisible barriers to the growth of innovative businesses, and empowering households to make more of the fundamental economic decisions? That seems extremely unlikely. To achieve their long-term goals, China's leaders will need to reinvigorate their program of economic reforms.

In the broadest sense, economic reforms are those changes that increase the scope of the market and reduce the scope of bureaucratic and political control. Policies that permit improved entry and that increase fair competition—or that create institutions that will subsequently support fair competition—are the essence of economic reform. Positive reforms can be "destructive" (tearing down barriers) or "constructive" (creating lasting institutions).[10] Reforms are necessary not only to achieve long-term goals but also to reduce the immediate risks to the economic system that are high due to the financial fragility (referred to earlier). Massive investment increases were used to defer the inevitable slowdown of the economy due to long-term structural changes. The post-2009 investment surge created problems—underperforming investment and fragile financial structures—that had been deferred for too long already. The financial system desperately needs restructuring in which some debts are written off, some companies are declared bankrupt, and some (many?) financial institutions are recapitalized with government money. However, without substantial reforms of the financial system, such restructuring would just amount to government bailouts with no end in sight. New debts would continue to accumulate and eventually unpredictable and uncontrolled defaults would lead to a broader loss of confidence. In that sense, a credible commitment to reform is also necessary just to preserve the system's ability to stably reproduce itself.

In a sense, Xi Jinping and Li Keqiang inherited an economic situation that was exactly the opposite of what Hu Jintao and Wen Jiabao faced when they took the reins ten years ago. The Xi-Li economy looks good on the surface, but it comes with a legacy of deferred problems and unresolved issues. It is still entirely within their power to address these problems and move China toward a path of sustained (but slower) growth, but they must do so promptly and before a host of bills come due. In the end the argument of the reformers is compelling: without further market-oriented reform it will be impossible to resolve these challenges and propel China toward its long-term goals.

## NEW LEADERS FACE THE ECONOMIC CHALLENGES

China's new leadership faced these economic challenges when they took power in November 2012. The top leader, Xi Jinping, the general secretary of the Communist Party, and Li Keqiang, the premier and head of the government, had both signaled their support for economic reforms repeatedly in the months before the formal transfer of power. As they stepped into the top jobs, Xi and Li made key personnel choices that strongly indicated their commitment to reforms. Xi elevated the economist Liu He to be in charge of the office of the Finance and Economics Leadership Small Group, which was in charge of drafting the key programmatic document on economic reform for the Communist Party Third Plenum in November 2013. Liu He's economic views are well known, and he has called for a "top-level design" of economic reform in order to restart a serious market-reform process.[11] On the government side, Zhou Xiaochuan was asked to stay on as head of the central bank, even though he had already reached retirement age (a workaround was found), and Lou Jiwei was promoted to minister of finance. These two experienced technocrats have long histories as proponents of reform and as designers of specific reform measures and initiatives going back to the 1980s. The two most important economic management systems, the financial and the fiscal, are thus headed by highly capable and committed reformers. The personnel choices of both Xi and Li were a good start in resuming progress in economic reform.

Despite these promising indications, though, Xi Jinping and Li Keqiang seem to be rather unlikely candidates to push through radical changes. Xi shows undeniable personal charm. He is attentive to political allies and elders and willing to invest time and emotional energy to defuse rivalries and manage opponents. Xi is the opposite of "prickly": he appears comfortable accepting things that he can't control and doesn't let little things escalate. He seems to like the good life and is married to an attractive and glamorous woman. Li Keqiang has a much different personality. Li is widely regarded as a prodigy and most everybody agrees that he is very smart. However, he is also regarded as glib and has been known to mouth platitudes even when he is actually saying something of interest. His record in the provinces was competent but undistinguished. In short, there is little evidence that these are the type of men who, as leaders, are willing to rock the boat.

However, in the short time since he came to power, Xi has accumulated power more rapidly and he has followed a much more ambitious and proactive policy agenda than anyone anticipated. Economic reform has in fact been an important part of this agenda, but it has not dominated it. Instead, during his first years in office, Xi pushed forward multiple policy initiatives. First, and most prominently, he launched an attack on corruption that has included both the arrest of individuals implicated in blatant corruption cases and a sustained campaign against conspicuous consumption, luxury gift-giving, and wasteful entertainment by ordinary officials. Second, he launched a program of ideological tightening and nationalist propaganda. The ideological centerpiece of the program is Central Document No. 9, which lays out several new ideological taboos as well as stricter preferred locutions.[12] The most controversial actions were the arrests of a number of prominent civil society activists and *weibo* (Chinese Twitter) celebrities. These first two items are linked through a kind of Maoist-influenced revivalism, by which the intensified supervision of the masses is invoked to restrain the special privileges of an elite group of Party and government functionaries. Xi has unmistakably moved to the left in these areas, which makes for an especially jarring juxtaposition with the third initiative, that is, commitment to serious economic reform. In July 2013, prefiguring the important Third Plenum of that year, Xi declared "the main direction for deepening reform [should be to] bring into play the fundamental role of the market in resource allocation; [to] speed up the creation of a market system that is unified and open, with competitive procedures; and [to] exert efforts to get rid of market barriers and raise the efficiency of resource allocation."[13] This definitely does not sound like Mao.

Xi's different policy initiatives may well contradict each other, and we should expect the tensions among different strands of the policy agenda to play out over time. For now, it is enough to note that Xi's policy agenda can be understood as a response to the popular mood described earlier, that is, the widespread sense that China's dynamic processes of economic and social change are slowing down and that change is becoming increasingly difficult. Clearly, the new leaders are aware of the public mood of skepticism. They feel the need to roll out dramatic programs to signal that the game is different now; the anticorruption campaign dramatically signals such a change. Xi wants to revive belief in the regime and rekindle a sense of purpose and dynamism. At the same time, though, the new leaders have been careful not to over-promise. Both Xi Jinping and Li Keqiang have made statements that are implicit criticisms of the gap between rhetoric and action in the reform policy of their predecessors. For example, Xi repeatedly denounces "empty talk." But isn't it clear that those engaging in empty talk are in fact Xi's predecessors? These general pressures are fully in play in the area of economic reform: How can Xi and Li rekindle a sense that economic reforms are achievable and, in fact, moving forward?

## THE THIRD PLENUM

The first crucial test of the new leadership's economic program came at the Third Plenum of the Eighteenth Party Congress, which took place November 9–12, 2013.[14] By conventional arrangement, the third plenary session of any party congress takes place a year after that congress convenes to allow time for the new administration to draw up a full economic program. Important programs of economic reform were presented at past Third Plenums, particularly those held in 1978, 1984, and 1992. The pressure was thus on the new Xi-Li leadership to deliver at the Third Plenum in 2013. In fact, the Xi-Li "resolution" from the plenum was a sprawling, impressive document that altered the political environment and directly confronted the reform credibility problem by drawing a clear line between the old Hu-Wen administration and the new Xi Jinping administration. The "resolution" was designed to demonstrate a credible leadership commitment to a renewed reform process.

First, the resolution was unprecedented in scope and contained a kind of "shock and awe" element that was designed to impress through the sheer breadth of the undertaking. The measure was organized around sixty articles, but each article in fact contained several specific policy initiatives, leading to what ultimately was determined to be 336 separate policy initiatives.[15] Moreover, the resolution, though not very specific, has none of the airiness and vagueness of many Party documents. In fact, many of the initiatives are quite concrete and are therefore observable and verifiable from outside. For example, by the year 2020, state-owned enterprises must turn over 30 percent of their profits to the government, which will use an increased portion of the remitted profits for social services. Such a precise statement sits rather oddly within the context and tone of the rest of the document, but it makes sense because it expresses concrete deliverables that can be easily monitored from the outside and lends credibility by providing specific observable benchmarks.

Xi personally claimed the Third Plenum output as an expression of his leadership, thereby tying his own personal prestige to the development of economic reforms. Xi also established an authoritative new Communist Party body, the Central Leadership Small Group for the Comprehensive Deepening of Reform, to oversee the reforms. This powerful group, ranking above government ministries and chaired by Xi himself, has responsibility for the "comprehensive design, all-inclusive coordination, overall progress, and supervision of implementation." This furthers the personal linkage between Xi and the reform process and provides a powerful instrument to ensure that reforms actually get implemented.

This approach started the reform process off with a bang. However, it also involved the creation of a rather unwieldy structure that may have initially slowed down the implementation process. The leadership small group itself, consisting of most top leaders and all key technocrats, meets once every couple of months. Most of the concrete work is farmed out to six specialized groups, the most important of which has the ungainly name of Economic System and Ecological Civilization System Reform Specialized Group, which is headed by the redoubtable Liu He. Indeed, of the 336 initiatives laid out by the Third Plenum resolution, 181 have been delegated to one of these six specialized groups and 118 have been assigned to Liu He's group. The specialized groups have a tough job: they must "design" a practical program to carry out their assigned initiative, but they must also get a degree of buy-in from their most important constituents. Then, "as reform initiatives mature," they are passed up to the full central leadership small group for discussion and ratification. Clearly, juggling more than a hundred of such initiatives is a daunting task.

As this complicated structure was being put in place, during the year following the Third Plenum, not many really dramatic reforms were announced. Those that were—such as a program to relax household registration rules— were easily traced to decisions that had been in the pipeline for a while. Not until the fall of 2014 did significant initiatives really begin to emerge from the leadership small group. The first indication that implementation was seriously under way came as important fiscal reforms were approved and then as a host of international economic agreements were initialed at the November

2014 meetings of the Asia-Pacific Economic Cooperation (APEC), held in Beijing. It is easy to see why these specific reforms are early into the implementation phase: fiscal provisions are under the control of Finance Minister Lou Jiwei, who has long experience and clear ideas about what he wants to do. International economic agreements are emerging as a key plank of Xi Jinping's agenda for a strong and influential China. Neither set of reforms emerged because of their logical priority within a reform program; there is no "top-level design." Instead, reforms in 2014 began rolling out of a centralized process designed to move reforms through the pipeline, maintaining pressure and momentum. How is this process likely to develop?

## THE CHOICES FOR ECONOMIC REFORM

What are the choices open to a leadership group committed to economic reform? Because the economic challenges facing China are unusually complex, the scope for reform is unusually broad. But policy makers cannot do everything at once, so they will be forced to pick and choose, trying to identify a few crucial objectives for priority implementation. Indeed, the problems are so complex, and involve so many interconnected issues, that initial reforms will inevitably be selective and incremental. The objective will be to build a credible list of measures from a menu of options designed to reduce distortions and create a better-functioning market environment. There are as many options as there as distortions in the economy, and the specific configuration is impossible to predict. Financial reforms will indeed make up an important component. The fiscal and financial regulatory bureaucracies are headed by capable, committed reformers. More fundamentally, financial reforms are necessary in order to clear away distortions and allow for healthier market development. What will they attempt to do?

Financial and fiscal reforms are essential to creating a more fair and competitive overall environment; they have many strands and they help drive concrete reforms in specific sectors. Restructuring of debt is an essential prerequisite to a successful overall reform program. Indeed, as part of the initial "shock and awe" approach to reform, policy makers chose to attack the most central and difficult financial problem: the indebtedness of "local government funding vehicles" (LGFV). LGFVs are corporations set up by local governments to borrow money and carry out investments, which were especially popular during the global financial crisis of 2008–2010. Finance Minister Lou Jiwei laid out an ambitious—but only vaguely specific—three-stage program of fiscal reforms in mid-2014. The most important initial step was an assault on the local government debt problem. Lou initiated a process at the end of 2014 through which the bank debt of LGFVs would be capped (during 2015 and 2016) and much of their debt gradually transferred into local government bonds. (Local governments did not previously have the right to borrow money of their own accord.) The objective was not only to resolve the thorny local government debt problem but also to create a huge 10 trillion RMB pool of local government bonds to serve as the basis for future capital market development.

Financial reforms are the next piece of the reform puzzle. Policymakers expect to have interest rate liberalization completed within the 2015–2016 time frame. This will likely occur through a gradual decontrol of bank lending and deposit rates and an expansion of the scope of market-price capital markets. Financial sector technocrats—first and foremost Zhou Xiaochuan, the central bank head— have long had such an objective in mind, only to have this objective pushed continuously back into the future due to weak support from top policy makers and fears about financial risks. Now the objective is once again within sight. Gradual international liberalization has emerged as an important part in China's domestic financial liberalization. Since mid-2014, China has opened up channels linking the Hong Kong and Shanghai stock markets, thus allowing stock purchasers on either side of the border access to the market on the other side. The Shanghai free trade zone has been experimenting with off-shore financial services with unregulated interest rates, and these provisions are being expanded to three other free trade zones in 2015. Moreover, the proliferation of new non-bank entities—including Internet-based finance—is creating new forms of competition for traditional bank practices.

However, a financial system is not something that can be transformed simply by tearing down barriers and allowing credit to suddenly flow freely to all qualified borrowers. The risks of financial fragility are already significant, and any program of financial liberalization inevitably creates additional risks, at least initially. As money is allowed to escape the banking system and flow into "capital market" assets like bonds, stocks, and commercial paper, it creates a whole new set of regulatory challenges (e.g., what to do when bond issuers can't or won't pay on time). The banks could suffer big declines in profitability as their monopoly status erodes, just at a time when they need capital reinforcement to deal with potentially large nonperforming loans. The very act of opening capital markets creates moral hazard because banks, which have implicit guarantees from the government, are often early movers into this environment and they may be willing to take on excessive risk.

Financial market reforms are technically difficult and fraught with potential problems, but they are going forward. Fiscal and financial reforms will, in an incremental manner, make the overall market environment in which all firms operate more fair and competitive. They are important parts of the process of removing distortions, lowering entry barriers, and making China a more competitive market. Moreover, fiscal and financial reforms are likely to act as a substitute for a frontal assault on the problem of state-owned enterprises (SOEs). SOEs are substantially less efficient than private firms, and they drain resources from the system through their privileged access to finance and government officials' attention. The Third Plenum resolution clearly expressed the need to reform SOEs, proposing that they be converted to "mixed-ownership" firms with more transparency and valuations determined by the stock market. Despite this bold declaration, SOE reform is lagging.

Part of the problem is that there is simply no obvious pressing financial need for state enterprise reform. Unlike the case in the 1990s, when the state enterprise sector was in financial crisis, today's firms are comfortably profitable. In 2012, the firms subordinate to the central government SASAC (State Asset Supervision and Administration Commission) recorded a total of 1.3 trillion RMB in profit, equal to 2.5 percent of GDP. Moreover, policy makers are happy to use state enterprises for diverse public and private purposes. The high technology agenda that many in China support relies on significant SOE investments. For example, China Mobile invests heavily in China's domestic 3G and now 4G telecommunications standards, a centerpiece of the "indigenous innovation" policies. With bureaucrats' careers increasingly governed by term limits, age limits, and regular promotion, SOEs have become one of the important pathways of upward mobility for ambitious bureaucrats. Beginning in the mid-2000s, official documents began to refer to SOEs as "an important foundation of the Communist Party's ability to govern," and Xi Jinping himself used this terminology in a 2009 speech.[16] Powerful families have been able to enrich themselves through their connections to these SOEs. There has long been evidence of close ties between Li Peng's family and the electric power industry, and between Jiang Zemin's son and the telecom industry.

To a certain extent, the anticorruption campaign is clearly upsetting the entrenched position of SOEs with lucrative monopolies and is thus doing some of the work of an SOE reform program. Chief corruption target Zhou Yongkang, a retired standing committee member, built his alleged web of corruption around the single most profitable SOE, the China National Petroleum Corporation (CNPC). Zhou spent thirty-two years in the petroleum industry before moving on to other top posts. Li Peng's daughter, Li Xiaolin, lost her position as board chairman of an important company in the electricity sector during 2015. SASAC, the government organization that nominally "owns" big central firms, has seen its most recent leader arrested, and a new leader, who has come in from the disciplinary inspection network, spent days in continuous meetings "rectifying" operations within the organization.[17]

A reform initiative closely associated with Premier Li Keqiang is the push to ease the government approval process. Designed both to complement the anticorruption campaign (by reducing rent-seeking opportunities) and to redefine the relationship between the government and private business, Li's campaign is primarily responsible for a huge increase in the number of private businesses registered in 2014 (because the registration process is now so much less onerous). These measures together create an emerging view of the economic reform process under Xi and Li: a series of measures will be implemented to create a better-functioning and more fair market. They will also intensify the competitive pressures that come initially from a slowing economy. At the same time, local officials and other interest groups are being kept passive by an intense anticorruption campaign. These top-down pressures are driving an economic reform process forward.

## WILL XI JINPING CARRY THROUGH A PROGRAM OF ECONOMIC REFORM?

Xi Jinping has clearly committed to a program of economic reform and has assembled an effective team and a credible implementation body to push reforms forward. Still, there are doubts about the process because of the multiple competing policy objectives that Xi has laid out. In particular, Xi's commitment to a kind of political revivalism, to increased ideological controls and nationalism, and above all to his emphasis on the role of leadership and the Communist Party, all sit uneasily with the commitment to thorough economic reforms. Moreover, serious lapses in reform implementation during 2015 raised questions about whether Xi Jinping would carry through on economic reform.

The question of Xi's ability to carry reforms through is best addressed by referring to an important distinction made by Stephan Haggard and Robert Kaufman, between *initiating* reform and *consolidating* reform. The initiation of reform, Haggard and Kaufman tell us, "depends on rulers who have personal control over economic decision-making; the security to recruit and back a cohesive 'reform team,' and the political authority to override bureaucratic and political opposition to policy change." By contrast, reform consolidation "rests on conditions that are different from, and in certain respects antithetical to, those associated with the initiation phase. . . . First . . . potential for predatory or arbitrary behavior on the part of the executive is reduced through the evolution of checks on executive discretion and the delegation of authority to policy-making agencies. . . . [and] Second . . . reforms must eventually appeal to a new coalition of beneficiaries."[18] With this distinction in mind, we can return to the challenges laid out in the first part of this chapter. Overcoming the complacency, vested interests, and crisis of confidence described above is identical to the challenge of initiating reform. Well aware of the obstacles they need to overcome, Xi and Li have indeed asserted personal control over economic decision making and assembled a coherent team of technocrats. Tearing down barriers to financial markets and eliminating government approvals clearly qualify as effective reform initiation devises. Moreover, the anticorruption campaign makes measures to override bureaucratic and interest group opposition much more effective. For this reason, some argue that Xi's policy choices are those of a leader who needs to overcome opposition to economic reform and who is concentrating power in his own hands in order to launch far-reaching market reforms.[19]

However, the reality is more complex. Xi's multiple policy objectives, and particularly his stress on leadership, on the Communist Party, and on the revival of ideological mobilization and control clearly conflict with the needs of reform consolidation. Reform consolidation requires the creation of new, independent power centers. It requires institutionalization and restraints on the power of officials. Thus far, measures that fit into this category have been extremely scarce. As of mid-2015, there have been virtually no reforms that strengthen regulatory agencies or create independent credentialing or supervisory authorities. Nor has Xi provided support for the private sector in a way that would mobilize their political support. Indeed, virtually all of Xi's policy choices are consistent with those of an autocrat seeking to maximize his own personal power, or for that matter, even of a sentimental Maoist who believes that there is a version of Maoism that can be consistent with China's contemporary market economy and middle-income society. We simply cannot tell what Xi Jinping's ultimate objectives are from his actions thus far.

However, two things seem clear. First, Xi's actions grow naturally out of the conditions and dilemmas outlined in the first half of this chapter. The sense of complacency and self-satisfaction, the corruption, the entrenched interests, and the crisis of belief that many see engulfing China would challenge any leader, no matter what his ultimate objectives. Xi has sought to overcome those obstacles through whatever measures he has at hand. He is unlikely to be overly troubled by any ultimate inconsistency in his methods if he feels that they can deliver the revival of belief he desires and the concentration of power that he demands. Second, while Xi Jinping accepts the necessity of economic reforms, he is much more personally engaged with the project of making China a great power and himself a great leader. Therefore, to the extent that ultimate decision-making power is concentrated in Xi's hands, economic reforms are likely to be sporadic and uneven because the claim they have on Xi's attention and his use of political resources will generally be secondary to his more immediate strategic and political goals. Exceptions will come in response to pressing economic problems that can only be solved by a deepening of the reform process.

China's growth slowdown is ongoing, and as of 2015, GDP growth had dropped to 7 percent, and was threatening to go lower. This slowdown places pressure on economic decision making: budgetary revenues as a share of GDP declined in 2014 after increasing for eighteen straight years (again, see figure 3.1). Massive investment programs in "strategic emerging industries" have produced meager returns so far, while serious excess capacity is evident in many traditional industries. Financial restructuring has barely begun. If the experience of other East Asian miracle economies is a guide, the end of the miracle growth period is likely to be accompanied by financial crises and a sharp (but potentially short) recession. There is substantial chance that China will also experience such turbulence, particularly as the financial system is opened up and cleaned up. When that happens, China's leaders will have to decide whether to forge ahead with even more thorough reforms or retreat and try to control the situation through government fiat. Only then are we likely to see the ultimate form of Xi Jinping's economic reforms emerge.

The experience of economic reform in 2015 was disheartening for proponents of reform. Finance Minister Lou Jiwei's program of local debt restructuring was made substantially less ambitious after bond markets balked at accepting local government debt without substantially higher interest rates. The state enterprise reform document, when it finally emerged in September 2015 after more than a year delay, was disappointing. Most important, the fiasco of the government intervening in the stock market seriously set back progress in that area. Not only did the government pump money into the market, effectively bailing out speculative investors, it also froze many accounts and prevented normal market operations, greatly undermining the tentative progress that had been made. In two of these cases (local government debt and stock market intervention), top-down decision making created a pattern of inconsistent policy and abrupt changes in direction. In the third (state enterprise reform), lack of a clear signal from top policy makers led to a drawn-out and inconclusive process of consensus building. The obstacles to reform and the limitations on the Xi Jinping decision-making model were very much in evidence.

# CONCLUSION

China's new leaders moved quickly to put into place the tools they needed to qualify as effective reform "initiators" (using Haggard and Kaufman's definition). In the process, they created uncertainty, and sometimes confusion, but certainly changed the game and opened up new possibilities. Their actions seem most easily understandable in light of the complacency, vested interests, and emerging challenges to the Chinese economy. What is less clear is whether these leaders will be willing and able to take the next steps and promote the consolidation of economic reforms as well. The two top leaders must continue to work together if reform consolidation is to occur. Xi seems far more committed and engaged on the political side than on the economic; he listens to good economic advisers, but, after all, advisers can always be changed. Li is personally engaged in the details of economic policy making and is intellectually committed to the idea of broad-based market-oriented reforms, but his political skills seem less well developed than Xi's. In terms of leadership politics, there are many ways in which things could start to unravel.

On the economic side, though, the pressures pushing toward more profound economic reform are very strong. For, at the end of the day, the reformers are right: only major institutional changes that make the economy more open, competitive, and rules-bound can avoid the serious problems that otherwise loom. Even these will require adept policy maneuvering to avoid submerged obstacles. China must continue economic reforms in order to become a technologically creative and institutionally flexible economy with a high standard of living for a majority of its citizens. China can make a transition to a lower growth rate in the context of a wealthier, better-off society. It will depend on this group of leaders, though, to muster the will and determination to initiate reform, and, even after that is achieved, to open themselves to new political alliances and limitations on executive authority. Only then do they have a chance to be regarded as significant "consolidators" of genuine reform.

## NOTES

Portions of this chapter were previously published in Barry Naughton, "China's Economy: Complacency, Crisis, and the Challenge of Reform," *Daedalus* 143, no. 2 (Spring 2014).

1. Official Chinese data, as reported in China Statistical Abstract, *Zhongguo Tongji Zhaiyao* (Beijing: Zhongguo Tongji, Annual).
2. According to World Bank benchmarks, which are calculated using the "Atlas method" (which smooths over exchange rate fluctuations but does not adjust

for purchasing power parity), the dividing line between lower and upper middle income in 2010 was $3,976, which China clearly surpassed.

3. Wu Jinglian, "Toward a Renewal of Reform," January 5, 2012, in Barry Naughton, ed., *Wu Jinglian: Voice of Reform in China* (Cambridge, MA: MIT Press, 2013), 12. Wu is quoting his close friend Zhang Zhuoyuan.

4. For example, the state council published an ambitious "Nine Articles" on capital market reform and development in January 2004, which called for rapid, market-driven expansion in the quantity and variety of debt and equity instruments. The expansion didn't happen. In fact, in May 2014, the (new) state council issued "New Nine Articles" on capital market reform that called for many of the same innovations. The documents can be compared at http://www.people.com.cn/GB/jingji/1037/2314920.html and http://www.gov.cn/zhengce/content/2014-05/09/content_8798.htm. In 2005, Wen Jiabao promoted the Tianjin Binhai district as a comprehensive reform area that would include financial liberalization, but this experiment went nowhere. Transformation of the state enterprise corporate governance system got off to a good start in 2004 with the creation of the State Asset Supervision and Administration Commission (SASAC), but SASAC's corporate governance agenda had clearly run out of steam by 2006–7. In some regions, such as the oil fields in northern Shaanxi and the coal mines in Shanxi, some enterprises that previously had been privatized were "renationalized."

5. Li Keqiang's remarks were reported in Du Yongtao, Fu Yingnan, Wei Xi, and Liu Yang, in "Li Keqiang Qiangdiao: Gaige shi Zhonguo Cuida de Hongli" (Li Keqiang emphasizes that the biggest dividend that China enjoys is the reform dividend), *Renmin Wang* (People's daily online), November 22, 2012, at http://finance.people.com.cn/n/2012/1122/c1004-19667962.html.

6. This does not include certain types of social security funds, adding of which would make the contrast even bigger. This is a consolidated budget that includes local governments.

7. Chinese currency values have been converted to US dollars at prevailing exchange rates, and deflated by the US Consumer Price Index.

8. According to SP Capital it excludes natural resource and financial firms. Cited in Daisuke Wakabayashi and Min-jeong Lee, "Samsung's 'Good' Problem: A Growing Cash Pile," *Wall Street Journal*, May 8, 2013, at http://www.wsj.com/articles/SB10001424127887323798104578454440307100754.

9. Migrant wages are from Feng Lu, "Consolidation or Stimulation? Remarks on China's Macro-Economic Situation and Policy," US-China Economics Dialogue, Beijing, June 19, 2013. For methodology and earlier data see Feng Lu, "Wage Trends for Chinese Migrant Workers: 1979–2010" [in Chinese], *Zhongguo Shehui Kexue* (China Social Sciences) 7 (2012): 47–67. For a good collection

of academic articles on the Lewis turning point see the 2011 special issue of *China Economic Review,* especially the article by the leading proponents of this view, Cai Fang and Du Yang, in "Wage Increases, Wage Convergence, and the Lewis Turning Point in China," *China Economic Review* 21 (2011): 601–10. The empirical evidence in favor of the Lewis theory in other developing economies is mixed, but China fits many of the Lewis model's predictions. Moreover, China has unique institutions that make the basic Lewis assumption of surplus rural labor more plausible, including collective land ownership and institutional barriers that retard rural-to-urban migration.

10. Economic reforms are quite different from political reforms (and the relationship between them is highly contested and beyond the scope of this short chapter), and they are also quite different from generally good economic policy.

11. Liu He's evolving role as an advisor to Xi Jinping is described in my "Leadership Transition and the 'Top-Level Design' of Economic Reform," *China Leadership Monitor* 37; and "Signaling Change: New Leaders Begin the Search for Economic Reform," *China Leadership Monitor* 40, both accessible at http://www .hoover.org/publications/china-leadership-monitor.

12. Chen Xi, "The Full Content of Document Number 9," *Mingjing Yuekan* (Mirror Monthly), August 2013, at http://www.mingjingnews.com/news /?action-viewnews-itemid-96736-page-3=.

13. Xinhua News Agency, "Xi's Speech Underlines Commitment to Reform," July 29, 2013, at http://english.cpc.people.com.cn/206972/206976/8344326.html; "Xi Jinping zai Wuhan Zhaokai Bufen Sheng Shi Fuze Ren Zuotan Hui" (Xi Jinping convenes a meeting in Wuhan with some of the leaders of provinces and cities), *Renmin Ribao* (People's Daily), July 25, 2013, at http://cpc.people.com .cn/n/2013/0725/c64094-22317375.html.

14. See, in particular, Barry Naughton, "Signaling Change: New Leaders Begin the Search for Economic Reform," *China Leadership Monitor* 40 (Winter 2013), at http://www.hoover.org/sites/default/files/uploads/documents/CLM40BN.pdf.

15. Note that even the choice of sixty articles can be taken as a statement that the resolution will be even more important than the "fifty articles" of the breakthrough 1993 resolution of the Third Plenum of the Fourteenth Party Congress.

16. Xi Jinping, "Speech at the Fiftieth Anniversary of the Discovery of Daqing Oilfield," September 22, 2009, accessed at http://news.cnpc.com.cn/system /2009/09/23/001259157.shtml.

17. This new leader is Zhang Yi, who arrived at SASAC in March 2013 after spending nearly all his career in the discipline inspection system. See Office of the SASAC Party Committee Organ on Practical Education, "The SASAC Party Committee Will Strictly Rectify Problems That Have Arisen with Respect to the

'Four Workstyles,'" posted September 17, 2013 on the SASAC website, http://www.sasac.gov.cn/n1180/n15066072/n15390580/n15390689/15522145.html.

18. Stephan Haggard and Robert Kaufman. *The Political Economy of Democratic Transitions* (Princeton, NJ: Princeton University Press, 1995), 9–10.

19. The argument is made in, among others, Lim, Benjamin Kang, and Adam Rose, "China's Xi Stamps Authority on Party with Bo Verdict," Reuters News Service, September 23, 2013, at http://www.reuters.com/article/2013/09/23/china-politics-bo-idUSL4N0HJ02C20130923.

# 4

# THE CHALLENGES OF STABILITY AND LEGITIMACY

## Joseph Fewsmith

China's domestic situation presents what seem like glaring contradictions. On the one hand Chinese citizens express considerable optimism about their own lives. For instance, some 70 percent of Chinese say that they and their families are better off now than they were five years ago, and nearly as many believe they will be better off five years from now.[1] Although a growing number of Chinese (50 percent, compared to 39 percent of four years prior) see corruption as a major problem, 45 percent agree that most will succeed if they work hard (though 33 percent believe hard work is no guarantee of success).[2] A 2009 survey found that over 85 percent of Chinese were "relatively" or "extremely" satisfied with the central government, a result consistent with other surveys.[3]

On the other hand, other survey data suggest important areas of concern. For instance, the Pew center found that the percentage of Chinese citizens who identified corruption as a major problem had increased from 39 percent in 2008 to 50 percent in 2012. Similarly, those who thought the income gap between the wealthy and poor was a major problem increased from 41 percent to 48 percent during the same time period. And those who identified food safety as a major issue increased from only 5 percent in 2003 to 41 percent in 2012. Moreover, the number of protests in China has grown: in 1993 there were some 8,700 "mass incidents"—protests involving move than five people—but by 2005—when the Public Security Bureau stopped publishing figures—there were 87,000 of them. In 2010, according to one widely cited figure, there were some 180,000 mass incidents.[4]

Moreover, the economic success that China has enjoyed over the past three decades combined with its growing military strength has caused nationalistic sentiment in China to grow, as manifested in the anti-Japanese demonstrations of 2012 and the apparent popularity of "leftist" thinking. Whereas one might guess that as China grew into the world's second-largest economy and found itself with secure borders, there might be a sense of accomplishment and satisfaction. The century-old dream of "wealth and power" has been achieved, but rather than celebrate this genuine success, China continues to brood on the injustices of the past. The new exhibit at the National History Museum on Tiananmen Square, the first stop by Xi Jinping after being named general secretary of the Chinese Communist Party (CCP) at the Eighteenth Party Congress, is called "The Road to Renaissance" (*Fuxing zhi lu*) but the main message is one of victimization and the idea that "those who fall behind are trampled under" (*louhou jiuyao aida*). China has territorial disputes with several countries, including Japan, but these conflicts cannot explain the harsh Chinese rhetoric of recent years. Although many factors seem to account for this nationalistic attitude, domestic concerns seem to figure prominently.

It is apparent that China's growing economy has not, or at least has not yet, generated the "harmonious society" desired by the leadership; despite individual optimism about personal prospects, there is much dissatisfaction. Much of this instability is rooted in systemic factors and is thus not likely to diminish even if China's economy continues to grow steadily, and a slowdown or other disruption in the economy could well exacerbate these social tensions.

Four basic sources of discontent and instability can be identified in contemporary China. First, the broad changes in state-society relations have loosened the omnipresent restrictions on life that began during the Maoist period and created space for criminal activity that did not previously exist. Second, the continuation of the old political system, including its politicization and the cadre management system, stand in tension with a changing society and this tension has led to petitions, collective petitions, and mass incidents. Third, fading ideological beliefs have created a new category of political dissidence: not just the few who explicitly call for the ouster of the CCP but, and more important, those who shape the public discourse on both the "left" and the "right." Finally, there seems to be a degree of regime insecurity and political uncertainty—both of which are admittedly difficult to define and measure—within the Party.

# THE CHANGING STATE-SOCIETY RELATIONSHIP

When Mao Zedong finally died and a more pragmatic leadership group was installed (and led by Deng Xiaoping), China began a period in which the state simply had to pull back from society. At the height of the Cultural Revolution, one could say (with only a bit of exaggeration) that society had disappeared, subsumed as it was by a highly politicized state, albeit one that was itself decentralized and disaggregated. Society needed to catch its breath and the Party-state needed to reconstitute itself. The Gang of Four and many acolytes were arrested or sidelined, and society began to emerge from under the shadow of the state. Part of this process was political. Deng Xiaoping, in thinking of China's need to turn its attention to economic development as well as of his own legitimacy (he had been purged twice by Mao), argued that Mao's ideas needed to be understood "comprehensively" and that the key to doing so was to understand the principle of "practice." Thus, the Third Plenum of the Eleventh Central Committee Meeting in December 1978, which turned the Party's attention from class struggle to economic construction, was preceded by a wide-ranging debate on the concept that "practice is the sole criterion of truth."

Another part of the resuscitation of society was sociological. Many youth who had been sent down to the countryside to "learn from the peasants" began to return to the cities of their childhoods but there were no jobs for them to return to. The state-owned economy was facing many problems and it was often said at the time that the economy was on the "brink of collapse." Unemployed youth were permitted to find their own way in the world—and thus began the entrepreneurial economy in which individuals were permitted to open their own, often primitive, businesses. City streets were lined with people repairing bicycle tires, cutting hair, or simply waiting to be hired for the day. Part of this gradual emergence of the private economy was regional and local. Some areas simply did not have the land resources needed to feed the people. Wenzhou, with its long tradition of entrepreneurial success, is the most famous case. As the Cultural Revolution faded, entrepreneurs began to emerge and lead a revolution in ownership.

This growing entrepreneurial activity generated serious debates within the Party, and different leaders in different places reacted differently. In the case of Wenzhou, the private economy was set back when eight major private enterprise leaders were jailed in 1980. But, given the pressures to expand the economy, the non-state sector expanded rapidly. Wenzhou freed the entrepreneurs and embarked on a rapid expansion of the private economy. In the countryside, the Household Responsibility System freed labor to go into township and village enterprises. By the end of the 1980s, some 130 million people were working in such factories and many millions more had migrated to the cities, either to take jobs or to open new enterprises. By the first decade of the new century there were some 250 million economic migrants throughout the country. The work unit (*danwei*) system, with its invasive social controls, was losing strength.

## Crime

While many controls remained—people still had *hukou* and personnel files, and many continued to work in *danwei*—the controls were not as tight as they had been during the Maoist era. When the controls loosened the population's mobility increased, so it was inevitable that there would be an increase in crime. Some of this rising crime was a legacy of the Cultural Revolution. One should not exaggerate this increase in antisocial behavior; China's crime rate then and now is modest by international standards. But the growth in crime was unsettling for a system obsessed with stability.[5] In the 1950s there were only 20 criminal acts per 100,000 people, but in 1981 that number suddenly jumped to 80 acts per 100,000. Some of the cases that appeared during this period were particularly shocking. For instance, in 1981 three female students were raped in Beihai Park, which is located just north of the leadership compound of the Chinese Communist Party (CCP). In 1983 a plane taking off from Shenyang was hijacked and eventually forced to land in South Korea, which refused to extradite the hijackers and instead sentenced them in accordance with Korean law. Also in 1983 two people in Shenyang killed four people and then fled southward, killing ten others along their route, including police officers and PLA soldiers.[6]

Such incidents led to the first and most severe "strike hard" (*yanda*) campaign against crime, which lasted from August 1983 to January 1987. Altogether more than 1.7 million people were arrested, including 876,000 people involved in some 197,000 criminal gangs.[7] This first campaign was followed by three others: April 1996 to February 1997; April 2001 to April 2003; and June to December 2010. The importance of these campaigns is not that they reflect a deteriorating social order but rather that they reflect a particular approach to law and order that views crime through a political lens (i.e., that if left unchecked, crime has the potential to create political opposition that ultimately leads to the CCP's loss of power). Hence the use of political campaign–style tactics to control crime. This is an approach to public order that can be seen in the current efforts to "maintain stability" (*weiwen*), whether or not such movements are officially called "strike hard" campaigns. The hallmark of such campaigns is to mobilize all the powers of China's domestic security apparatus—the Public Security Bureau, the Procuratoriate, the courts, the judiciary, and the State Security Bureau—under the control of the political-legal committees at various levels.

## The Cadre Management System

The Chinese constitution specifies four levels of government in China (central, provincial, county, and township), though there have generally been five levels since the 1980s, when China placed the counties under the supervision of the municipalities.[8] Villages could be considered a sixth level of government, but the constitution calls the villages "autonomous" because their cadres are not funded by the state. Nevertheless, they are still managed by the CCP through local branches. Holding these different levels of government together is the cadre management system by which one level appoints the officials below it and then proceeds to evaluate those cadres. Given the centralization of power upon which the Chinese system is based, in practice the cadre management system gives the Party secretary at one level the ultimate authority to decide on cadres at the next-lower level. The Party secretary may consult others, but traditionally such consultations do not cast a wide net and would be sought within the Party secretary's own network.

The cadre management system developed over the course of China's revolution. Highly centralized management was simply not possible to achieve during the course of a contest between guerilla bases that were spread over a wide geographical area and had little communication with Party headquarters. Moreover, Party headquarters could never be sure of conditions in faraway locales. The cadre management system evolved out of the need for task assignments and mobilization. Local populations were mobilized to recruit soldiers, to pursue "class enemies," to carry out land reforms, and so forth. The system placed a great deal of authority in the hands of local cadres and it was up to those cadres' superiors to decide whether or not tasks had been adequately performed. This high-pressure system combined centralization of policy making with considerable decentralization and flexibility in the execution of those policies. Although the Party system is a vast bureaucracy, power can still be exercised through a surprisingly personal hierarchy of ties and connections. The personal nature of those ties breeds networks through which power is exercised and in which favoritism and corruption grow.[9]

Certainly, the personnel who staff China's cadres system have changed dramatically over the past three decades. Today they are younger, better educated, often quite professional, and not ideologically inclined. They go to

Party schools for training in management rather than ideology (though they are updated on Party policy and ideological interpretations).[10] The goals on which cadres are judged have changed too, from class struggle to economic development (though other tasks such as family planning and social stability play an important role as well). Nevertheless, the cadre system itself has changed remarkably little. It continues to be a hierarchical, task-oriented system that puts pressure on lower-level cadres to perform the tasks demanded by their superiors, primarily economic development. Because of the fading of ideology and the absence of political campaigns, cronyism is more prevalent than ever. And the temptation to use power over the personnel system to solicit favors and bribes is perhaps greater than before as well. Indeed, the buying or selling of office is not a rare occurrence.

The clash between this hierarchical cadre system and a changing society has become the basis for much of today's social instability. Because cadres are under pressure to develop the economy, they must raise funds for paving roads, building factories, and other development projects. In areas with little industry, this means collecting taxes, indeed often forcefully. Prior to the elimination of the agricultural and miscellaneous taxes in 2006, Party policy limited such taxes to 5 percent of income. Such a light tax burden, however, was not sufficient to cover cadre salaries at the village level (which are paid out of village, not state, funds) much less carry out economic development projects. So local cadres collected more, often 30 or 40 percent, of peasants' incomes. Particularly after the 1994 tax reform, which directed more funds to the central government, counties and townships were desperate for funds. It is not surprising that local cadres put pressures on peasants—or that peasants fought back.[11]

This period brought the rapid growth of mass incidents. Mass incidents, though technically defined as having more than five people, can of course be much larger; protests involving thousands of people are not rare. In any event, the number of mass incidents grew from 8,700 in 1992 to 87,000 in 2005, to perhaps some 180,000 mass incidents in 2010.[12] This is an average of nearly 500 incidents every day. The number of mass incidents can be debated, but there is widespread agreement that the numbers have continued to increase, that the average number of participants is larger, and that more violence is involved.[13]

There is little likelihood that mass incidents will pose a real threat to the regime. The specific tensions that set off an incident in one place rarely exist in another, at least at the same time, so incidents do not spread from place to place. Incidents tend to be very cause-specific—for example, when a local government seizes a piece of land, or a local official absconds with funds, or an accidental clash sets tempers aflame—and protest is a high-risk activity. Protest leaders are frequently jailed, so peasants are reluctant to join in the action. The result is that a lot of protests occur and some are successful. But most are contained and protests rarely, if ever, spread beyond the places where they start. The state is particularly vigilant to ensure that the sort of horizontal organization that could link local protests does not develop.

Nevertheless, protests take their toll on the system. The fact that public opinion polls consistently rate corruption as a leading concern reflects the belief that citizens have little regard for their local leaders and suggests that political legitimacy is eroding over time. The central government is clearly aware of such opinion trends and makes considerable effort to encourage citizens to focus their ire on the local governments rather than on the central government. For instance, the central government frequently publicizes the policy that limits tax collections to 5 percent of income, even though it is understood that local governments need to collect more than that in order to develop the economy. Frequently this results in a coalition of sorts between citizens and the central government against local government, but even under such circumstances the citizenry rarely wins these conflicts—the cost to local government is just too high. In the rare instances where a conflict receives wide publicity (such as in Dingzhou, Hebei province, when a peasant recorded on video the violence unleashed by thugs hired by the government), the government can step in and remove the offending officials (as it did in Dingzhou), thus appearing heroic in the eyes of local residents.[14] So, even though it is clear that the actions of local officials result from the pressures of the cadre management system, public opinion seems to absolve the central government from responsibility—which in turn explains the high level of trust revealed in public opinion surveys.

## Political Dissidents

China has few openly political dissidents calling for the organization of an opposition party or the overthrow of the CCP. Indeed, China does not even have people willing to take the label "outside the Party" (*dangwai*) like the opposition to the Kuomintang did in Taiwan in the 1970s and 1980s. When that has happened on the mainland, those who do take a stance critical of the Party have been jailed, such as Liu Xiaobo, the drafter of "Charter 08" (which, among other things, called for amending the constitution to guarantee human rights, separation of powers, and freedom of assembly). The CCP is obviously vigilant against dissidents and willing to take harsh measures to prevent the emergence of any organized opposition.

However, if the understanding of "dissident" is recast to mean people who believe that the CCP is failing in one way or another and therefore should move in a direction to recapture legitimacy—whether democratic, socialist, or nationalist—then the number expands and includes those who appear most influential in setting the parameters of public debate. This suggests the Party has a substantial problem of legitimacy. The CCP sees such people as a threat and has responded in kind.

Over the past decade or so, nonofficial political discourse has been dominated by liberals, by the "New Left," and by neo-Maoists. Chinese liberals have long advocated the rule of law and, by implication, opposed the CCP's ability to exist outside and above the law. Liberals have argued, in theory and in practice, that the CCP should live up to its own laws. The 1982 constitution declared that the Party should act within the bounds of the law, and Jiang Zemin's report to the Fifteenth Party Congress in 1997 declared "rule by law" a major theme of the congress.

Since the early part of this century, some of China's lawyers have tried to push the government to live up to its promises. In 2003 an unemployed college graduate by the name of Sun Zhigang went to Guangzhou in an effort to find employment. Police, thinking he was a migrant worker, demanded to see his identification card (the prejudice against workers from the countryside being real and deep). Unfortunately the young Sun had forgotten to bring it with him and he was detained under the rules of the country's custody and repatriation system. While in detention he was beaten and died of his injuries.

In response, three young PhDs in law—Yu Jiang, Teng Biao, and Xu Zhiyong—wrote an open letter to the National People's Congress (NPC) that argued that the custody and repatriation system violated China's constitution. The system had come under debate within China's security system, so some sympathy already existed for the views expressed by the young legal experts. Regardless, in a surprising move the government agreed with the petition and abolished the custody and repatriation system.

The Sun Zhigang case marked the beginning of the rights protection movement (*weiquan yundong*), which has tried to limit the arbitrary use of power by the state by intervening on behalf of aggrieved citizens. This is a legal strategy to make the Party and state live up to its laws. Needless to say, despite the victory in the Sun Zhigang case, the Rights Protection Movement soon clashed with party-state authority, which, despite repeated promises to uphold the law, regarded itself as beyond legal reproach.

The point is that the Party-state has correctly perceived the rights protection movement as a movement against its interests; if "rule of law" would truly be implemented, the role of the CCP would fundamentally change and

it would perhaps be driven from power. The gap between the state's protes-
tations that it was in fact upholding the law in the Sun case, and the lawyers'
demand that the state must change and uphold the law, not only increased
but also soon attracted the attention of journalists and others who would like
to see significant political reform.

If liberals who have supported the rule of law are considered dissidents—
not in the sense of organizing protests or calling for the ouster of the CCP
but only in the way they push against the Party's prevailing ideology and
pressure it to undertake significant reform—then their ideological opponents, the so-called New Left, should also be considered dissidents. The New
Left is not a homogenous group: some are populist nationalists, others more
statist, and still others advocate for implementing various sorts of "socialist"
policies. But all reject mainstream reform and argue that it is too collusive
with global capital. They see China's entry into the World Trade Organization (WTO) as a way of supporting China's moneyed elite against the
Chinese people. In contrast with China's "conventional" liberals, the New
Left are more concerned with social policy than law. Neo-Maoists might be
considered yet another group, and one that is even farther left than the New
Left. Neo-Maoists hope for a repeat of the Cultural Revolution and exhibit
violent proclivities.

Debates between liberals and the New Left heated up China's Internet in
the mid-1990s before being exhausted by the end of the decade. Then Bo
Xilai's populist policies in Chongqing reenergized the New Left; those policies combined with the global financial crisis to generate discussions of the
so-called China model.

Three points need to be made with regard to these debates. First, there is
no middle ground between the New Left (not to mention the neo-Maoists)
and liberal intellectuals. There really is no true "debate" between the two
sides, merely assertions of one's point of view and complete dismissal of the
other's. Although the New Left and liberals have never agreed, the polariza-
tion between them has become even more apparent. Second, neither side
accepts mainstream reform and both are sharply critical of China's political
system, believing that it needs to embrace socialist policies (the New Left)
or liberal policies (the liberals). In this sense they all dissent from official
ideology and from the regime's point of view. The existence of intellectual
discourse driven by such groups that reject mainstream ideology and policy is
corrosive of legitimacy. Finally, both groups seem to have their supporters in
policy circles that, to one extent or another, agree with either the New Left or
the liberals. In other words, this is not just an intellectual discussion but also
a political tug-of-war over policy direction.[15] This politicization of intellectual

debates again suggests the erosion of official ideology. It also suggests the possibility of deeper political struggles in the future.

# THE STATE FIGHTS BACK

Understanding the domestic landscape—the way society has changed, the pressures local cadres face, rising nationalism, and the evolving debates among China's intellectuals—makes the state's response more comprehensible. The state's response has revolved around three poles: patriotic education, preservation of "stability," and formation of a "service-oriented government." This is to say that the state has so far accomplished three things: use propaganda to frame issues and persuade people that the state represents their interests; use the police and other security forces to slow collective petitions, particularly petitions trying to reach Beijing, and respond to mass incidents; and, perhaps surprisingly, address tensions in state-society relations by adopting policies that respond to grievances (such as building the health care system, creating a pension system, adopting a basic income program, and so forth). What the state has not done is adopt the sort of political programs that might allow for more horizontal or bottom-up accountability and change the basic pattern of the cadre management system—like greater press freedom, a larger role for civil society and greater participation for the public, much less expanded voting rights.

## Patriotic Education

In the wake of the 1989 Tiananmen demonstrations and subsequent government crackdown, the Chinese Party-state concluded that the younger generation needed a strong dose of history education. In 1991 it launched the Patriotic Education Campaign. The campaign got off the ground slowly, but by 1994, when the "Outline on Implementing Patriotic Education" was released, the campaign was in high gear. Perhaps the remarkable thing about this education campaign was that it changed the narrative of China's history, from one of victory in a hundred-year domestic class struggle to one of victimization of foreign aggression.[16]

US foreign policy, however unintentionally, has worked to support China's new narrative. A turning point of sorts came in 1993, when China made a bid to host the Olympic Games in 2000. The often-inept Propaganda Department played its hand beautifully. It built up popular expectations by emphasizing how China deserved the games—expectations that were disappointed when the international community, led by the United States, awarded the games to Australia. Suddenly a new meme was launched: the United States was not opposed to China because of human rights violations (the Tiananmen crackdown), it was simply against China. Soon popular books like *China Can Say No* appeared and a new strain of popular nationalism was launched. Popular nationalism was, of course, a two-edged sword: it bolstered the legitimacy of the government as the defender of the national interest on the one hand but presented a critique of the government if it did not adequately defend China's interests on the other. No doubt the Chinese government welcomed the popular support, but it had to walk a thin line in the coming years.

The US bombing of the Chinese embassy in Belgrade in 1998 occasioned another understandable outburst of popular nationalism, as did the collision between a Chinese military aircraft and a US EP-3 intelligence plane over the South China Sea in 2001. These incidents gave rise to a new narrative: the United States was trying to "contain" China. This new narrative soon overtook the theme that had dominated during China's bid to join the WTO, namely that China was trying to "join tracks" (*jiegui*) with the international community. The collapse of Lehman Brothers in 2008 triggered a financial crisis in the United States, which quickly spread to become a global crisis. But through a massive stimulus package China was able to resume strong growth remarkably quickly, and it became widely believed in China that the United States was losing its dominance and China was rising faster than anyone had anticipated. Indeed, mockery of US ineptitude soon followed, and by 2010 there was an assertion of the superiority of the "China model."[17]

Together these international events have bolstered China's nationalistic narrative. There were—and still are—many weaknesses in China, but nationalism has clearly emerged as a force in both popular and official circles. Indeed, in some circles the populist economic policies are seen as a solution to those weaknesses.

## Preserving Stability

The notion of "preserving stability" (*weiwen*) is based on a political calculus that sees challenges to the social order, whether criminal, social, economic, or political, as harmful to the image of the Party-state and ultimately threatening of the position of the CCP. Although the notion of "core interests" applies primarily to foreign policy, authoritative Chinese statements have made clear that the most important of China's core interests is preserving China's form of government and political system, meaning "the CCP leadership, the socialist system and socialism with Chinese characteristics."[18] *Weiwen* is not just police work; however professionalized it might become, it remains a highly politicized task, and this political feature links what might be considered ordinary police work to the *yanda* campaigns mentioned earlier.

The term *weiwen* emerged in public discourse at the Twentieth National Public Security Work Conference in 2003 and reflected a shift from a focus on serious crime to a broader concern about social instability and citizen protest. This shift in focus reflected research that showed that social conflict revolved around "contradictions" between officials and the "masses" in which corruption played a central role. According to one research report, corruption in the years 1995–2000 amounted to 13 to 16.8 percent of GDP.[19] In other words, the emergence of *weiwen* marked a routinization of police work in the service of a much broader agenda than simply fighting crime; social stability was seen as facing serious problems, and the Ministry of Public Security had to respond accordingly.

In 1991, believing that maintaining social order required broader coordination among departments of the state council, the CCP established the Central Commission on Comprehensive Social Order (*Zhongyang shehui zhi'an zonghe zhili weiyuanhui*). This commission was headed concurrently by the heads of both the political commission and the legal commission; the responsibilities of the two organs largely overlapped but the legal commission had a broader mandate. In 1993 nine new ministries were added as members of the Commission on Comprehensive Social Order, including: Post and Telecommunications, Communications, People's Bank of China, and Ministry of Personnel. In 1995 the scope of the commission was expanded again to include the Central Discipline Inspection Commission, the Ministry of Supervision, the Family Planning Commission, and others.[20] In 2003 the 610 Office was added; its duties are the handling of "heterodox religions" (*xie jiao*). In 2011 the commission was expanded yet again, adding eleven new departments and changing its name to the Central Commission on Comprehensive Social Management (*Zhongyang shehui guanli zonghe zhili weiyuanhui*). This new and broader concept of "social management" reflects increasing concern over social-order issues, including fear that the Arab Spring might spread to China.[21]

This continual expansion of the *weiwen* apparatus surely reflects the state's increasing concerns with domestic security in all its dimensions, ranging from the influence of "color evolutions" and the Arab Spring to the development of NGOs, to the rise of the Internet (including blogs and then *weibo*) and the increasing number of petitions and mass incidents. From the state's point of view, society looks more difficult—though by no means impossible—to control.

As the commission responded, its budget rose accordingly. For instance, in 1996 the budget expenditures for public security in Guangdong province were only 30 percent of the province's total spending. In Qinghai and Gansu, 40 percent of county-level expenditures were financed through fines and penalties.[22] Overall, according to official figures, from 1995 to 2009 spending on public security increased more than tenfold, from $28 billion yuan to $390 billion yuan.[23] (It should be noted that accurate figures are difficult to obtain in part because so many security expenditures are off-budget and come from funds obtained through fines and penalties.) By 2013 the public security budget had risen to $769 billion yuan ($123 billion), exceeding China's announced defense budget of $720 billion yuan.[24] It is difficult to make international comparisons, but the rapidity of the increase in spending in China suggests the seriousness with which authorities view the potential for protest and perhaps violence.

Nevertheless, despite the increase in the amount of money and personnel devoted to maintaining social stability, there was no evidence that the number of mass incidents decreased until, perhaps, the Xi Jinping administration began. There have been no publicly available figures, but some argue that the number of incidents have decreased. But the reason for this decrease, if it does in fact exist, is that the campaign against corruption has slowed local investment—and, with it, the requisitioning of land that was the source of so much protest.

## Service-Oriented Government

A very different way of addressing societal issues has been the effort to build a "service-oriented government." The 2003 epidemic of SARS (Severe Acute Respiratory Syndrome) was a turning point in making officials realize that growth alone could not solve problems—the government had to address societal issues better. The change in leadership was also a factor, as a new leadership team brought in new concerns. Hu Jintao and Wen Jiabao took over Party and state leadership positions in the fall and spring of 2002 and 2003, respectively, and began shifting policy priorities. Whereas Jiang Zemin and Zhu Rongji had focused on the economy and bringing China into the world both economically and diplomatically (after acquiring near-pariah status following the Tiananmen crackdown), Hu and Wen began focusing on what might be called "fairness" issues. During this period the "three rural" (*san nong*) issues (agriculture, countryside, and peasants) moved into prominence in public discussions. Similarly, the issues of education, social security, and health care began to receive belated attention as well.

In 2006 the Chinese government abolished agricultural taxes and unveiled plans to build a "new socialist countryside"; the plans focused on infrastructure construction and on improving the income of rural residents. By 2011 the government's expenditures on rural and agricultural issues reached $2,974 billion yuan, which was ten times more than was spent in 2004. In less than ten years the Chinese government had successfully built a basic social safety net for the rural area. The New Rural Cooperative Medical System, initiated in 2003, had more than 830 million rural participants in 2010. The New Rural Social Pension system, another key policy of the Hu-Wen administration, was implemented nationwide in 2012, shortly after its first experimentation in 2009. In addition to such new policies, the central government also increased the standard of public services. For instance, in 2011 it increased the poverty line of the Minimum Living Security System in Rural Areas to $2,300 yuan per household per year, which is a full 92 percent higher than it was only two years earlier.[25]

The implementation of such policies has often been less than ideal. Local governments sometimes remain focused on economic development rather than on providing services. Even when the central government earmarks funds for special projects that would benefit the people, local officials often find ways to divert those funds to construction projects from which they (local officials) could benefit.

However one evaluates the accomplishments of these service-oriented measures, they reflect a government concerned with social discontent. Social policies can be viewed as the mirror image of the *weiwen* efforts, that is, trying to secure popular support by providing services versus building a network of security measures to suppress protest. The rapidity with which the central government provided funds for creating a service-oriented government on the one hand—removing burdens like the agricultural tax on peasants, providing a minimum income for both rural and urban residents, building at least a skeletal rural health-care system, and putting a basic social security system in place—versus building a *weiwen* apparatus on the other suggests a very high degree of concern with social stability. Perhaps even more remarkable is the fact that the scale and scope of protest, both petitions and mass incidents, continued to climb during this period despite the risk protesters took in registering their complaints.

## Nationalism and Protest

The program of patriotic education put in place in the 1990s has perhaps worked beyond the expectations of the government—there is no denying the widespread patriotic feelings of the Chinese people. Undoubtedly there are reasons for this trend that go beyond teaching patriotic values: the economy has grown quickly, which has imparted a sense of optimism in the people about their futures and helped build a reservoir of trust in the central government; global successes such as hosting the Olympics in 2008 have made people proud; the United States and other economies stumbled badly in 2008, which lent credence to claims for the superiority (or at least viability) of the "China model"; and, most important, the case for liberal political reform cannot be discussed publicly, which truncates the consideration of alternative paths. This distortion of the public discourse is perhaps the most negative and long-lasting outcome of the Tiananmen crackdown.

However, it is not only patriotic education that has fed into a new nationalism. Ironically, discontent with the current political situation has contributed as well. Patriotism in China (and perhaps elsewhere) is a two-edged sword, providing support for the government but also holding up a standard that is perhaps impossible for the government to attain. The New Left (and other leftists as well) believe that mainstream reform has abandoned socialist values in favor of pursuing capitalism and entanglement in the international financial system. But these beliefs are bound up with highly nationalist viewpoints as well. Since socialism and nationalism are privileged within contemporary China, they have gotten a great deal of public attention in recent years. It seems apparent that leftist views have become more mainstream in the past decade or so.[26]

Given the deep reservoirs of resentment against Japan—both for its aggression during World War II (and before) and for its economic success afterward—protests against Japan have become a fairly legitimate outlet for nationalist passions. Many Chinese activists protested the "occupation" of the Diaoyu/Senkaku Islands by Japanese activists in 2004, and widespread anti-Japanese demonstrations were held in 2005 to protest the revision of textbooks and Japan's bid to join the United Nations Security Council. More demonstrations followed a clash between a Chinese fishing boat and a Japanese coast guard ship in 2010, and in 2012 there were protests against the Japanese government's purchase of three of the Diaoyu Islands.[27] More recently, the government organized a major military parade in Beijing in September 2015 to mark the seventieth anniversary of the end of the War of Resistance against Japan.

The issue of nationalism, especially when combined with public protest, raises three questions: (1) Will popular nationalism push the Chinese government to take more nationalistic foreign policy positions? (2) Will popular nationalism prevent the Chinese government from adopting more conciliatory positions once an issue has appeared? and (3) Is nationalism a legitimating or a de-legitimating force for the Chinese government?

As the patriotic education campaign suggests, the Chinese government has fed the Chinese populace a steady diet of nationalism, and raises the possibility that it has created an "echo chamber" in which the voices the government hears are simply amplified versions of the messages that the government sent.[28] There is no evidence that popular opinion has pushed, much less forced, the government to take positions that the government does not want to take, but the growth of nationalistic attitudes, especially combined with the growth of social media, will make it more difficult to retreat from positions it has staked out. In the past China has allowed demonstrations against Japan and the United States to go forward (after the Belgrade bombing and the EP-3 incident), but then relations were fairly quickly normalized. But it is not clear that this pattern can be repeated indefinitely in the future.

The Chinese government seems to have turned more "assertive" since 2010, particularly after 2012 when it declared it would create a "new status quo" in the Diaoyu/Senkaku Islands dispute and in fact continued to send ships into waters surrounding the islands. If this marks a changed approach to Sino-Japanese relations, and to foreign policy in general, then one reason may indeed be that the "echo chamber" has finally taken effect. Another reason not incompatible with the former is that the Chinese leadership has itself become more nationalistic as new leaders like Xi Jinping have come to the fore. Xi's rhetoric about the China dream and his endorsement of the Road to Renaissance exhibit does suggest so.

## The Fight for Legitimacy

The three years following Xi Jinping's rise to power have revealed that the problems felt by the regime are serious and the issues of legitimacy and power are at the core. This has been expressed directly by Xi Jinping, who once asked rhetorically, "Why did the Soviet Union disintegrate? Why did the Soviet Communist Party collapse? An important reason was that their ideals and convictions wavered. . . . Finally, all it took was one quiet word from Gorbachev to declare the dissolution of the Soviet Communist Party, and a great party was gone. . . . In the end nobody was a real man, nobody came out to resist."[29]

Xi's expression of concern was followed by an October 2013 article by "Ren Zhongping" in *People's Daily* titled "Important Commentary from People's Daily" (Renmin ribao zhongyao pinglun). The commentary said, in an unusually blunt way, "Today, the Soviet Union, with its history of seventy-four years, has been gone for twenty-two years. For more than two decades, China has never stopped reflecting on how the Communist Party and nation were lost by the Soviet Communists."[30]

One month later Li Zhanshu, the head of the general office and reportedly a close friend of Xi Jinping, wrote an article in *People's Daily* in which he said that the Soviet Union and the countries of Eastern Europe had undertaken "reform" (the ironic quotation marks appeared in the original) but that the reform had gone astray and led to the "burying of the socialist enterprise." "The lesson is extremely deep," Li declared.[31]

If the fate of the former Soviet Union is on the minds of China's leaders, it is in part because internal disagreements—factionalism—are increasingly a part of the fabric of the CCP. Party divisions are seen most clearly in Bo Xilai's apparent effort to gain a seat on the Politburo Standing Committee and his subsequent prosecution. In carrying out the prosecution the government carefully avoided mentioning ideological issues, and instead charged him with corruption (and a relatively modest amount of corruption at that). But it was Bo's challenge to the decisions that the Party had already made that lay at the core of the case.

Since the prosecution of Bo in September 2012, other prosecutions have occurred: first was the prosecution of Zhou Yongkang, the former PBSC member in charge of security, and more recently the detention and the prosecution of Ling Jihua, the former head of the Party's general office and a close aide to former general secretary Hu Jintao. During the prosecution of both of these people, the central authorities detained many of their close followers, exposing the factionalism within the CCP.[32] A December 2014 Politburo meeting underscored the problem by emphasizing that "forming groups, working together for private interests, and creating factions will not be tolerated in the party."[33]

The broader campaign against corruption that has been carried out since the Eighteenth Party Congress was convened in November 2012 has netted, by spring 2015, some sixty-one officials at the ministerial level and above, several hundred at the department level, and many thousands of lower-level cadres. This campaign, like the formation of groups around Zhou Yongkang and Ling Jihua, strongly suggests that over time the Party organizations are becoming more personal and less impervious to higher-level demands. There has always been a tension between hierarchical discipline and the authority of individual leaders at lower levels, but the campaign against corruption suggests that the balance has shifted away from the organizational needs of the Party. Xi's efforts to deal with corruption seek to redress this balance and restore Party legitimacy.

The effort to strengthen Party discipline in the face of centrifugal tendencies has meant that Xi has adopted some "leftist" vocabulary even while his prosecution of the left seemed to silence, at least for a while, the populist supporters of Bo Xilai. Indeed, to a certain extent Xi has adopted many of the approaches favored by Bo. He ate dumplings at a popular restaurant, which gave him a common touch, and his air of self-confidence has created some thing of a personality cult (though nothing like that associated with Mao). Even his use of Maoist vocabulary evokes a past that somehow seems simpler and more pure than the current era rife with corruption and inequality.

All these tendencies were reinforced by ideological strikes against the "right." "Document No. 9" (entitled "Notice on the Situation in the Ideological Field at Present"), issued in April 2013, suggested the government was deeply concerned with the spread of liberal ideas. The document laid out seven ideological trends that must be resisted, including promoting "constitutional government," "universal values," "civil society," "media freedom," and "judicial independence." Fighting against "rightist" ideological trends is not new to reform in China, as the campaigns against "spiritual pollution" (in 1983) and "bourgeois liberalization" (in 1987) suggest. But the current campaign highlights some differences. Contemporary "rightists" are not really the successors to the "establishment intellectuals" that were targeted in the campaigns in the 1980s. They are much farther from the political center and often not Party members—and they are far more numerous. They reflect the very real and profound changes that have taken place in Chinese society. They have grown up to be lawyers, professors, journalists, and so forth, and they tend to be more loyal to their professions and their understanding of "the people" than to the political system. They see the political system as creating a world of privilege and corruption that exploits the common people (*laobaixing*). They believe that only substantial political change can move Chinese society forward, beliefs that are threatening to the CCP.

The Party recently issued "Document No. 30," which is a sequel to Document No. 9. Like its predecessor, Document No. 30 is critical of liberal ideas, this time demanding that they be eliminated from universities and other cultural institutions.[34]

## CONCLUSION

China is some three years into Xi Jinping's administration and it is clear that the country faces enormous challenges in the domestic realm. This can be seen not only in the rising number of mass incidents but also in the evident disregard for mainstream reform that has been manifested on both the left and the right. Whatever else the Bo Xilai case illustrates, it suggests that a high-ranking member of the political elite—a Politburo member—was willing to champion an ideological program that challenged mainstream thinking. While the Chinese people have directed their discontent primarily toward local government and seem to retain a reservoir of goodwill for the central leadership, the Chinese government has demonstrated clearly through its spending of resources that it perceives a significant political challenge in maintaining social stability and suppressing challenges from both the left and right.

The creation of a rudimentary welfare state was also clear evidence that the government perceived that the unfairness built into the system—the urban bias, the neglected health-care system, the lack of a pension system—fed into societal discontent. The government responded to this discontent by starting to build a "service-oriented" government in 2003 and by abolishing agricultural and miscellaneous taxes in 2006. Still it is striking that, despite efforts to address societal concerns and to build a security network that can maintain social stability, the number of mass incidents, particularly large mass incidents, continued to rise. No figures are publicly available, but private comments suggest that the number of mass incidents may have begun to subside in the last couple years. If so, this trend appears to be a by-product of the campaign against corruption: local officials are reluctant to undertake projects that might lead to a charge of misconduct and therefore they have not requisitioned as much land—a major cause of mass incidents. If so, there may well be a backlog of investment projects that might get under way if and when the campaign against corruption slows. If so, the cycle of pressuring local cadres to carry out economic development that leads to mass incidents may then be repeated.

Both the government's efforts to build support through patriotic education and the nationalistic discontent of many unsatisfied with either government domestic policy or its defense of China's global interests have led to support for more assertive international policies. The attitude of China's leaders seems to be changing; Xi Jinping's remarks since taking over as Party head in November 2012 have betrayed a new level of nationalist sentiment that seems quite related to his palpable concern over domestic issues, including and especially the legitimacy of the CCP.

Whereas in the past domestic passions were allowed to cool as international incidents passed—allowing the government greater flexibility in managing its foreign policy—the growth of social media, the desire to bolster domestic legitimacy, and the increasing nationalism of the governing elite may constrict the space China has available for adjusting its foreign policy, which in the end will make international tensions of one sort or another a common feature of the landscape. And things will not get any easier as the economy slows and domestic unhappiness grows.

Perhaps what is most eye-catching is the government's insistence that China must follow its "own path." This may not seem a particularly nationalistic or antagonistic posture; indeed, it may sound like something that every country does. But when one looks at the evolution of Chinese rhetoric, from the relative cosmopolitanism of the 1980s, to the desire to "join tracks" (*jiegui*) with the outside world by joining the WTO, to the juxtaposition of the so-called Beijing consensus against the Washington consensus, to the espousal of the "China model," it is quite apparent that the government has been trying to move away from the outside world, at least ideationally. The rejection of "universal values" (*pushi jiazhi*) in favor of a Chinese path sees the outside world as threatening in various ways, even if its economy is increasingly intertwined with the global economy. The apparent tension between globalization and domestic challenges suggests that the Chinese government will face enormous difficulties in the years ahead.

## NOTES

1. "Growing Concerns in China about Inequality, Corruption," Pew Research Center Global Attitudes Project, October 16, 2012; Martin King Whyte, *Myth of the Social Volcano: Perceptions of Inequality and Distributive Justice in Contemporary China* (Stanford, CA: Stanford University Press, 2010).

2. "Growing Concerns in China about Inequality, Corruption."

3. Tony Saich, "Chinese Governance Seen through the People's Eyes," *East Asia Forum*, July 24, 2011, available at http://www.eastasiaforum.org/2011/07/24 /chinese-governance-seen-through-the-people-s-eyes/); and Wenfang Tang, Michael S. Lewis-Beck, and Nicholas Martini, "A Chinese Popularity Function: Sources of Government Support," *Political Research Quarterly* 66, no. 4 (December 2013).

4. Sun Liping, "Shehui zhixu shi dangxia de yanjun tiaozhan" (Social order is a critical challenge at present), *Jingji Guanchabao*, February 25, 2011, available at http://opinion.hexun.com/2011-02-25/127571301.html.

5. For comparative statistics see "Crime and Criminal Justice Statistics," United Nations Office on Drugs and Crime, at http://www.unodc.org/unodc/en /data-and-analysis/statistics/crime.html.

6. Xie Yue, *Weiwen de Zhengzhi Luoji* (The political logic of stability preservation) (Hong Kong: Tsinghua shuju, 2013), 49.

7. Ibid., 51.

8. In the 1980s China began to implement the "cities control the counties" system (*shi guan xian*), which inserted the municipality (sometimes the prefecture) between the province and the county. This policy, in force for three decades, was never incorporated into the constitution. Zhejiang province implemented it only briefly before returning to the system in which the province took direct control over the counties.

9. On the cadre management system see Zhuang Guobo, *Lingdao Ganbu Zhengji Pingjia de Lilun yu Shijian* (The theory and practice of evaluating the political achievements of leading cadres) (Beijing: Zhongguo jingji chubanshe, 2007); Maria Edin, "State Capacity and Local Agent Control in China," *The China Quarterly* 173 (March 2003): 35–52; and Susan H. Whiting, "The Cadre Evaluation System at the Grass Roots," in Barry Naughton and Dali Yang, *Holding China Together: Diversity and National Integration in the Post-Deng Era* (New York: Cambridge University Press, 2004).

10. Charlotte P. Lee, *Training the Party: Party Adaptation in Reform-Era China* (Cambridge: Cambridge University Press, 2015).

11. Kevin O'Brien and Lianjiang Li, *Rightful Resistance in Rural China* (New York: Cambridge University Press, 2006).

12. Sun Liping, "Shehui Zhixu Shi Dangxia de Yankun Tiaozhan" (Social order is a critical challenge at present), *Jingji Kaochabao*, February 25, 2011, available at http://opinion.hexun.com/2011-02-25/127571301.html, last accessed November 24, 2011.

13. Joseph Fewsmith, *The Logic and Limits of Political Reform in China* (New York: Cambridge University Press, 2013).

14. Minnie Chan, "Recent Land Disputes That Have Resulted in Violence," *South China Morning Post*, March 24, 2007.

15. Joseph Fewsmith, "Debating Constitutional Government," *China Leadership Monitor* 42 (Fall 2013), Available at http://www.hoover.org/research/debating-constitutional-government

16. Suisheng Zhao, "State-Led Nationalism: The Patriotic Education Campaign in Post-Tiananmen China," *Communist and Post-Communist Studies* 31, no. 3 (September 1998): 287–302; Wang Zheng, "National Humiliation, History Education, and the Politics of Historical Memory: Patriotic Education Campaign in China," *International Studies Quarterly* 52, no. 4 (December 2008): 783–806.

17. Joseph Fewsmith, "Debating the China Model," *China Leadership Monitor*, 35 (Summer 2011).

18. Dai Bingguo, "We Must Stick to the Path of Peaceful Development," December 6, 2010.

19. Tian Quanhu and Ren Hongjie, "Xin xingshixia Woguo Shehui Maodunde Yanbian dui Shehui Wending de Yingxiang (The evolution of social contradictions under the new conditions and their impact on China's social stability), cited in Susan Trevaskes, "Rationalizing Stability Preservation through Mao's Not So Invisible Hand," *Journal of Current Chinese* Affairs 2 (2013): 67.

20. Xie Yue, Weiwen de zhengzhi luoji, 141–42.

21. "Cong zhi'an dao guanli: Zhongyang Zongzhi'an Gcngming tixian Zhongyang dui Shehui Guanli Zhongshi" (From security to management: The Central Commission on Comprehensive Security changes its name to reflect the center's concern with social management), *Jiancha ribao*, September 8, 2013, available at http://politics .people.com.cn/GB/1026/15760578.html#; "Zhongyang zongzhiwei gengming bing zengjia 11 ge chengyuan danwei" (The Central Commission on Comprehensive Security changes its name and adds 11 member units), *Xinjingbao*, September 8, 2013, available at http://news.163.com/11/1009/03/7FT64GVS00014AED .html; and Joseph Fewsmith, "'Social Management' as a Way of Coping with Heightened Social Tensions," *China Leadership Monitor* 36 (Winter 2012).

22. Xie Yue, "Rising Central Spending on Public Security and the Dilemmas Facing Grassroots Officials in China," *Journal of Current Chinese* Affairs 2 (2013): 83.

23. Ibid., 88.

24. Andrew Jacobs and Chris Buckley, "China's Wen Warns of Inequality and Vows to Continue Military Buildup," *New York Times*, March 5, 2013.

25. Joseph Fewsmith and Gao Xiang, "Local Government in China: Incentives and Tensions," *Daedalus* (forthcoming).

26. Peter Hayes Gries, *China's New Nationalism: Pride, Politics, and Diplomacy* (Berkeley: University of California Press, 2004).

27. James Reilly, *Strong Society, Smart State: The Rise of Public Opinion in China's Japan Policy* (New York: Columbia University Press, 2012).

28. The term "echo chamber" comes from Susan L. Shirk, *Fragile Superpower* (Oxford: Oxford University Press, 2007). See also Susan L. Shirk, ed., *Changing Media, Changing China* (Oxford: Oxford University Press, 2011).

29. Christopher Buckley, "Vows of Change Belie Private Warning," *New York Times*, February 15, 2013.

30. Ren Zhongping, "Shouhu Renmin Zhengdang de Shengmingxian" (Protect the lifeline of the people's party), *People's Daily*, October 14, 2013, retrieved from http://opinion.people.com.cn/n/2013/1014/c1003-23187114.html.

31. Li Zhanshu, "Zunxun Sige Jianchi de Gaige Jingyan" (Follow the reform experience of the "four persistents"), *People's Daily*, November 26, 2013.

32. Joseph Fewsmith, "China's Political Ecology and the Fight against Corruption," *China Leadership Monitor* 46 (Winter 2015), available at: http://www.hoover .org/research/debating-constitutional-government.

33. "Zhonggong Zhongyang Zhengzhiju Zhaokai Huiyi" (The Politburo convenes meeting), Xinhua Wang (Xinhua News Agency website), December 29, 2014, retrieved from http://3g.news.cn/html/731/80603.html.

34. Chris Buckley and Andrew Jacobs, "Maoists in China, Given New Life, Attack Dissent," *New York Times*, January 4, 2015.

# PART II

# International Challenges to Rising China

# 5

# XI JINPING'S GRAND STRATEGY

## From Vision to Implementation

Stig Stenslie and Chen Gang

In the wake of the Eighteenth Party Congress, a growing call rose within Chinese policy-making circles for the adoption of a "grand strategy" by the incoming leadership of Xi Jinping. China already has five- and ten-year plans, but many believed the country lacked an overall plan for its rising international standing and expanding global interests. The demand was voiced from both within and outside the Communist Party. Outspoken international affairs scholars debated this issue in public and proposed various grand strategies for the new leadership.[1] It is broadly believed that the adoption of a grand strategy by the Chinese leadership would be highly beneficial: on the domestic level, such a strategy will have a unifying effect, which is needed at a time when rapid growth is creating considerable national stress on the international level, a grand strategy could make China more appealing and undermine increasingly widespread notions of the "China threat." While the advantages of a grand strategy for a rising power like China would seem obvious, neither its formulation nor its implementation will be easy.

In this chapter we argue that Xi Jinping has taken small but important steps in the direction of formulating a grand strategy for China. Unlike his two predecessors, Jiang Zemin and Hu Jintao—both of whom were lackluster in theorizing a national strategy—Xi has formulated his own vision under different slogans such as "China Dream," "Asia-Pacific Dream," and "One Belt, One Road" (Silk Road Economic Belt and Maritime Silk Road). The essence of Xi Jinping's emerging grand strategy is state prosperity, collective pride and collective happiness, and national rejuvenation.

Yet Xi is likely to face significant structural obstacles when it comes to the implementation of his vision for rising China. Xi is already being referred to as China's most powerful leader since Deng Xiaoping. The *Economist* has argued that Xi is even the most powerful since Mao Zedong.[2] Elisabeth Economy referred to Xi as "China's imperial president" in an article in *Foreign Affairs* magazine.[3] By immediately taking over all the three key leadership positions in China—head of the Communist Party, president and head of state, and head of the Central Military Commission—Xi has from the outset been awarded with a much stronger mandate than either of his predecessors enjoyed. Although Xi has arguable established himself as the paramount leader within a tightly centralized political system, he is far from almighty.[4] Neither the internal nor the external environments are favorable for a smooth implementation of Xi's grand strategy.

## DEBATING CHINA'S GRAND STRATEGY

An agreed-on definition of "grand strategy" does not exist. Sir Basil Henry Liddell Hart is an important reference. According to Liddell Hart, "the role of grand strategy is to coordinate and direct all the resources of a nation, or band of nations, towards the attainment of the political object of war."[5] Liddell Hart looked at grand strategy as the war's political goal rather than war being part of a larger national strategy. In times of peace, in other words, states have no grand strategy. Paul Kennedy of Yale University expanded the concept of grand strategy to also apply in peacetime. He stated:

> The crux of grand strategy lies . . . in *policy*, that is, in the capacity of the nation's leaders to bring together all of the elements [of national power], both military and non-military, for the preservation and enhancement of the nation's long-term (i.e., in wartime and peacetime) best interests.[6]

Kennedy's "long-term" reference is important. Unlike a particularly military or economic strategy, grand strategy is both comprehensive and long term. Such a strategy is intended to channel all the elements of national power in order to maximize the nation's future security and welfare. This requires a policy that has a horizon of decades rather than years.

Historically, many grand strategies have not been written or have existed as fragmented manifestos, such as the grand strategy of Louis XIV.[7] Some grand strategies were written but kept secret, as was the case with "The National Security Council Report 68" (NSC-68), signed by US president Harry S. Truman in 1950. This top-secret policy paper (declassified in 1975) was one of the most significant statements of US policy during the Cold War, and it largely shaped American foreign policy for twenty years.[8] Other grand strategies have been made known to the public in the form of official written documents that detail end-state conditions and outline the path to get there. As an example, the main elements of President George W. Bush's grand strategy, also known as the "Bush Doctrine," was delineated in "The National Security Strategy of the United States of America" and published on September 17, 2002.[9]

Some scholars allow for the usefulness of having an implicit or de facto grand strategy that is actualized in political practices. Such a strategy is implanted in the "official mind," a concept introduced by Ronald E. Robinson and John Gallagher in their study of British imperialism.[10] Likewise, George Friedman argues that "[a] country's grand strategy is so deeply embedded in the nation's DNA, and appears so natural and obvious, that politicians and generals are not always aware of it."[11] According to Edward Luttwak,

> All states have a grand strategy, whether they know it or not. That is inevitable because grand strategy is simply the level at which knowledge and persuasion, or in modern terms intelligence and diplomacy, interact with military strength to determine outcomes in a world of other states with their own "grand strategies."[12]

While many Chinese are calling for their government to adopt a grand strategy, many Western observers believe that China already does have such a strategy. (Likewise, Chinese pundits tend to suspect that the United States also has a grand strategy, although American critics of the Obama Administration question this[13]).

China watchers tend to emphasize distinct cultural and institutional norms that support the idea of a Chinese grand strategy. It is often said that "long-term thinking" and "strategic patience" are deeply rooted in Chinese culture.[14] As Zbigniew Brzezinski writes, "Prudence and patience are part of China's imperial DNA."[15] Moreover, China's one-party system is considered a favorable condition for the formulation and implementation of a grand strategy. Some refer to the benefits of the one-party system—with a certain degree of admiration—in their criticism of Western democratic systems, which are often accused of fostering short-term policy only.[16]

China has had a written grand strategy in the past. This was Mao Zedong's strategy of "leaning to one side."[17] In 1948 Mao proclaimed that China would

lean to the socialist camp headed by the Soviet Union, and oppose the impe-
rialist camp headed by the United States. This strategy was stipulated in the
"Common Program," which served as China's provisional constitution after
it was adopted in 1949:

> The People's Republic of China shall unite with all peace-loving and free-
> dom-loving countries and peoples throughout the world, first of all with the
> USSR, all People's Democracies[,] and all oppressed nations. It shall take its
> stand in the camp of international peace and democracy, to oppose imperialist
> aggression and to defend lasting world peace.[18]

Mao abandoned his grand strategy as a result of the Sino-Soviet split in
1960, and China has not had an officially known written grand strategy since.
Still, it is claimed that China's remarkably consistent foreign policy indicates
that its leadership does have a long-term plan. As an example, Aaron L. Friedberg argues that the leadership in Beijing has "stayed on the path he [Deng
Xiaoping] set for them thirty years ago," as summarized by the catchphrase
"keep a low profile" (*taoguang yanghui*).[19] In the absence of a written "formal
and detailed plan contained in a 'smoking gun document' issued by the Chinese Communist Party's Central Committee," observers have resorted to various methods to unveil China's secret—or de facto—grand strategy.[20] Some
scholars have tried to deduce the strategy through a systematic study of Chinese history, of the behavior of earlier rising powers, and of the basic structure
and logic of international power relations. Michael Swaine and Ashley Tellis,
as an example, have described China's strategy on the basis of "its historical
experiences, its political interests, and its geostrategic environment."[21] Other
pundits like Friedberg and Avery Goldstein have tried to postulate a "broad
underlying consensus" that top-leaders of the Communist Party are being
socialized into through an interpretation of public statements and documents
combined with a substantial number of interviews with civil servants, military officers, and analysts at Chinese think tanks.[22]

These studies suggest that as China grows stronger, it likely will become
more assertive globally. In other words, China is likely to move away from
Deng's "keep a low profile" strategy (to the extent that it makes sense to refer
to this as "strategy" rather than as pure "tactics") and will adopt a grand strategy with more revisionist aims. According to Goldstein, China's overall goal
is to replace the current unipolar world order dominated by the United States
with a new multi-polar order; Friedberg argues that Beijing's ultimate goal
is to push the United States out of East Asia and eventually reestablish the
Sino-centric order that prevailed during the great Chinese empires.

These studies are all well researched and make important contributions to an understanding of strategic thinking in China, and their conclusions might be right. China's rise is a fact—and most Chinese would certainly like to see their country restored as a great power. Yet whether Beijing has had a grand strategy, in the sense of a detailed plan to become great, is questionable. The notion that China has a de facto grand strategy—although this term is so elastic that it is hard to argue against it—is also debatable. One problem, as Feng Zhang has pointed out, is that studies based on the premise that China does have a grand strategy "have a strong feel of *post hoc* scholarly rationalization." A study of Chinese foreign policy over the past decades can hardly be said to reveal a consistent strategy, as is often claimed, and suggests that there does not exist an overall plan.[23] Another problem is that the cited studies do not take into account the limits on the Chinese leadership's freedom when it comes to formulating and implementing grand strategy.

# FORMULATION OF GRAND STRATEGY

Xi Jinping has so far proved to be more of a political visionary and strategic thinker than many China observers had expected him to be as the heir to the Dragon Throne.[24] As the world's largest economy in purchasing-power-parity terms, under the leadership of Xi China has shown far more confidence in its political and economic model;[25] it does not hesitate to display its ambition to project its influence on other parts of the world. In this respect Xi appears as a much more visionary leader than his two predecessors, both of whom were lackluster in theorizing a national strategy.

## Xi's Vision for China

Xi has established his own doctrines, including "China Dream," "Asia-Pacific Dream," and "One Belt, One Road" (a combination of "Silk Road Economic Belt" and "Twenty-First Century Maritime Silk Road"). Xi's emphasis on national rejuvenation and international aid suggests a link between his China Dream doctrine and a grand strategy of becoming the world's dominant superpower with a super-strong economy and military.[26] The expansive schemes of Silk Road Economic Belt and Twenty-First Century Maritime Silk Road, which were first proposed by Xi in September and October 2013, are crucial pillars of the emerging grand strategy that Xi has crystallized in the first three years of his tenure.[27]

A few days after he became the Party's general secretary at the Eighteenth Party Congress in 2012, Xi visited the exhibition "The Road to Rejuvenation" in Beijing and defined for the first time the "Chinese Dream" of "achieving national rejuvenation."[28] He told the National People's Congress that "the Chinese dream of the rejuvenation of the Chinese nation means that we will make China prosperous and strong" and that "we should be guided by the strategic thinking that only development will make a difference."[29] Xi offered an expansion of his own catchphrase "China Dream" (*zhongguo meng*) and underlined his country's growing global clout when he introduced a Chinese-driven "Asia-Pacific Dream" (*yatai meng*) at the Beijing-hosted annual Asia-Pacific Economic Cooperation (APEC) leaders' gathering in November of that year.[30] "We have the responsibility to create and realize an Asia-Pacific dream for the people of the region," Xi told the APEC leaders. The rise of China thus represents both opportunity and anxiety to neighboring countries that are eager to benefit from China's economic expansion but are wary of its hegemonic political intentions.

The essence of Xi's China Dream is state prosperity, collective pride and happiness, and national rejuvenation.[31] Since slogans matter in the arcane world of Chinese politics, the China Dream may reveal clues to the understanding of the new leadership's long-term strategic goals. In essence, the populist and accessible nature of China Dream differs significantly from Xi's predecessors' stodgy ideologies, like Jiang Zemin's "Three Represents" and Hu Jintao's "Scientific Development."

The China Dream seems to be a promise of national restoration that gives the people a more important role in the rise of China. Xi's China Dream, in contrast to its American namesake, is about something more than middle-class material comfort.[32] By extending "the dream" from China to the Asia-Pacific, Xi is leveraging the decades-long economic boom and aiming to increase China's regional and global heft. A string of ambitious outward initiatives included the formation of the Asian Infrastructure Investment Bank (AIIB) proposal and the Free Trade Area of the Asia-Pacific (FTAAP); both of these were labeled by many analysts as a Chinese version of the Marshall Plan, an American initiative to help rebuild European economies after the end of World War II.[33]

On November 29, 2014, Xi Jinping gave an important speech to the Communist Party's work conference on foreign policy. Present were all members of the Politburo's standing committee and the PLA's senior leadership. Xi revealed his foreign policy guidelines and priorities and was remarkably specific in his articulation and elaboration of China's foreign policy objectives and strategic goals. With confidence Xi stressed that China's relationship with the rest of the world is changing and that China must develop an international presence that better reflects its role as a superpower. This implies a more active diplomacy and pressure for reform of international organizations to ensure Chinese representation so that China's interests are safeguarded. Xi also said that it is necessary to build up China's "soft power" in order to make China better able to communicate its message to the rest of the world. It is worth noting that formulations concerning the establishment of "a global network of partners" and "a new kind of superpower relations" is based on "win-win cooperation."[34]

Xi has departed from Deng Xiaoping's low-profile diplomacy methods (*taoguang yanghui*), which warned China against becoming a world leader (*juebu dangtou*), and Xi's new vision relies on increasing China's engagement with other regions. Xi's overtures have greatly reduced the lingering political influence on crucial policy and personnel decisions by retired Party elders like Jiang Zemin, Hu Jintao, and Li Peng. He attempts to link domestic economic activities with an emerging global strategy to export the country's excessive capital, technology, and industrial capacity to others who need them. Xi has fundamentally shifted China's strategic gravity from a three-decades-long focus on domestic economic development to an outward expansion of its influence.

## The Key Strategic Decision Maker

By taking the role as "China's imperial president," Xi Jinping has made China more "normal" in terms of foreign policy making. Strategy formulation is normally a top-down process with a leader (or equivalent) identifying the vision for the future that is then developed by senior advisors, who eventually create the draft strategy. As an example, over the course of US history the president has repeatedly been "the *key* figure in strategic decision making."[35] While the US Constitution places extensive limitations on presidential influence over domestic affairs, the president's role as commander in chief has allowed presidents to minimize the role of Congress in foreign affairs and security making, while the Supreme Court has experienced a tendency to practice self-marginalization when it comes to this sphere.[36] Not all presidents have written themselves into the history books as great strategists, nor have the American people always chosen their presidential candidates based on their foreign policy visions. In many elections—especially those in the immediate wake of the Cold War (1992, 1996, and 2000)—foreign and defense policy have played a minor role and the candidates' perceived ability to master such questions was therefore not decisive for the outcome.[37]

President George H. W. Bush, who had developed significant implementation capacity and experience in foreign affairs, still had no clear grand strategy to position the United States in a post–Cold War world.[38] Nevertheless, the US president has a powerful position that can be used when it comes to formulating and implementing grand strategy.

Arguably, the US president carries more weight when it comes to taking strategic action than is the case for leaders in most other countries, including, somewhat ironically, the leaders of totalitarian or authoritarian states such as China. In the latter it is common that many players have a voice in strategic decision making, so that coalition-building is an essential part of the process.[39] Some earlier studies based on the state-centric assumption of having a traditional realist approach to the study of international politics have revealed that China's foreign policy was often treated as the product of a rational unitary state pursuing and maximizing its national interests under the constraints imposed by the external environment.[40] But whereas past Chinese debates were principally internal deliberations among a narrow Party elite, current research increasingly highlights a more public dimension, with multiple inputs from actors not commonly involved in these traditionally insular processes.[41]

It is true that China's foreign policy-making processes are, to a large extent, still vertically organized, with the core figure of the Communist Party leadership having the last word on all vital issues. However, as the final arbiters of foreign policy making, the paramount leaders are tending to become more consultative and consensual than their predecessors due to their diminished authority within the Politburo in the post-Mao era. As the undisputed leader of the Communist Party and founder of the People's Republic of China, Mao decided China's foreign strategies according to his own understanding of world politics. Although Deng, as the general architect of China's reform and opening policy, still had the final say on foreign policy making, he became more consultative with his Politburo colleagues, mostly because he wielded less political authority than Mao. Jiang Zemin was more consensus oriented than Deng, and Hu Jintao was the most consensual and consultative among all paramount Party leaders.[42] Xi, it is generally agreed among China observers, has reversed this process toward consensus.

## Integrating Interests, Values, and Beliefs

Xi Jinping has formulated a vision for rising China that partly integrates national interests with Chinese values and beliefs, something that is crucial when it comes to grand strategy making. Leaders do not design policies in a moral vacuum. In order to gain the support of its citizens, a grand strategy must reflect nonrational dimensions such as feelings and ideas about right and wrong. Likewise, a strategy must include such noninstrumental elements to make sense to other countries.

History shows that the basis of grand strategies often has been a mix of interests, values, and beliefs. In the case of the United States, ideology is a strong driving force in foreign policy. The US "containment strategy" during the Cold War was focused on stalling and pushing back the spread of communism while at the same time enhancing America's security and influence abroad. Even after the demise of the Soviet Union, ideology and faith has continued to be an important driver in US foreign and security policy, which in particular was expressed during presidency of George W. Bush. A group of so-called neoconservative thinkers used the events of 9/11 to advocate the idea that the United States was locked in a global war—a war of ideology—in which its enemies are bound together in their hatred of democracy. Several notable neocon thinkers obtained powerful positions in the Bush administration, including Paul D. Wolfowitz, Richard Perle, Elliott Abrams, Michael Ledeen, Lewis Libby, and John Bolton. They succeeded in influencing the president with their grand strategic thinking, which came to be known as the Bush Doctrine.[43] Four main points are underlined as the core of this doctrine: preemption, military primacy, new multilateralism, and the spread of democracy.[44]

By contrast, ever since Mao abandoned the "leaning to one side" strategy, ideology has hardly been baked into Chinese foreign policy.[45] Some have referred to the politics of Deng—Mao's successor—as "radical pragmatism," which involved reforming China's moribund economic system and opening up the country to the outside world. "Crossing the river by feeling the stones" (*mozhe shitou guo he*) was Deng's recipe for how China would open up and reform. The ideological dogmas of Marxist Leninism were soon outmaneuvered by the leadership's pragmatic calculations regarding the national interest.[46] The removal of ideology from Chinese politics and the seeming lack of clearly articulated values and beliefs arguably made it more difficult for later leaders to formulate a grand strategy for China.

The essence of Xi Jinping's China Dream is state prosperity, collective pride and happiness, and national rejuvenation. By emphasizing national rejuvenation, Xi differs markedly from his predecessors—Jiang Zemin and Hu Jintao—who carefully avoided appealing to the national feelings of the Chinese people. Nationalism is arguably the strongest ideological currency among contemporary Chinese, but appealing to this tendency is a double-edged sword for Beijing: nationalism can easily turn the people against the leaders if the nationalists begin to feel that the government is not safeguarding national interests. Looking at China's recent history it is easy to understand such fears. The Boxer Rebellion (1898–1901) started out as a protest against foreigners in China. But discontent was soon redirected at the imperial administration and led to the fall of the Qing Empire in 1911. Eight years later, the May Fourth Movement protested what it believed was an unpatriotic government. The movement, a precursor to the Communist Party, contributed to the fall of the nationalist government. Xi, in contrast to his predecessors, seems to be willing to take this risk and is grooming popular support by formulating a grand strategy that incorporates nationalist values and beliefs.

## IMPLEMENTATION OF GRAND STRATEGY

Although Xi seems able to articulate a clear vision for China, he is likely to face a number of major obstacles related to the implementation of his grand strategy. He might find the available institutional tools insufficient, crisis management at home is likely to steal the leader's attention, and neighboring countries in the Asia-Pacific are increasingly wary of China's strategic intentions.

### External Resistance

First, and most important, China's external environment complicates implementation of a grand strategy. The Middle Kingdom's fourteen neighbors constrain Beijing from looking beyond its own region, in contrast to other important powers such as the United Kingdom, the United States, and Japan. Many people in East Asia are alarmed by China's military armament and increasingly assertive attitude on the international stage and they question Beijing's long-term intensions. They fear China is becoming a revisionist power aimed at reorganizing the world exactly as it has done for two thousand years. This view has China as the center: the "Middle Kingdom" (*Zhongguo*), surrounded by kowtowing tributary states. Some alarmists even believe that Beijing's goal is nothing less than to "replace the current *Pax Americana* with a *Pax Sinica*."[47]

By emphasizing national rejuvenation, some alarmed China observers have suggested that there is a link between Xi's China Dream and the hawkish attitude of Liu Mingfu, who in 2010 published *The China Dream: Great Power Thinking and Strategic Posture in the Post-America Era*. Liu, a retired military colonel, stated that the "China Dream" aims to replace the United States as the world's dominant superpower, possessing a super-strong military.[48] Liu discusses the special role played in world history by the most powerful and "champion country" (*guanjun guojia*) during the past five hundred years —including Portugal in the sixteenth century, the Netherlands in the seventeenth century, Great Britain in the eighteenth and nineteenth centuries, and the United States in the twentieth century. He proposes that China should pursue the strategic goal of being the new champion country in the twenty first century through a four-tier nation-building process of establishing security, increasing development, rising ascendance, and, ultimately, achievement of the status of "champion country."[49]

Since the early 2000s Chinese political leaders, scholars, journalists, and pundits have openly discussed the concept of "soft power" and the need to strengthen the country's international reputation.[50] In line with this, Beijing has invested significant resources in charm offensives toward the outside world. Through diplomacy, favorable trade terms, the use of international media, and the promotion of cultural and student exchanges, Chinese authorities have sought to promote good "Chinese values" such as collectivism, self-control, hard work, altruism, and morality.[51] The campaigns, however, have had limited impact if we are to believe recent global opinion polls: in 2013 the Pew Research Center published survey findings that revealed a far higher number hold a positive view of the United States than of China. The Japanese expressed by far the worst view of China: only five percent of Japanese held a favorable view of the historical archrival.[52] According to Professor Yan Xuetong at Tsinghua University in Beijing, a gap exists between the outward humanistic legacy that the authorities seek to show and the authoritarian tendencies, corruption, and near-obsession with money within the Chinese community itself. This leaves the Chinese with a fundamental image problem. Yan advises that only when government is able to demonstrate an ability to govern in accordance with good values at home can it hope to inspire people in other countries. As he states, money makes it easy for the Chinese to buy friends in all corners of the world, but such "friendship" does not stand the test of difficult times."[53]

American strategists are responding to a rising China by advocating containment, while China's highly suspicious neighboring countries are gearing up their military modernization programs and have explicitly asked Washington to reengage in Asia as a counterweight to China. The United States has made it clear that it has both the will and capacity to contain China in Asia. As Hillary R. Clinton declared in *Foreign Policy* in the autumn of 2011, "The future of politics will be decided in Asia, not Afghanistan or Iraq, and the United States will be right at the center of the action."[54] She stressed that over the next decade the United States will bring together in Asia its political, military, and economic power: "The region is eager for our leadership and our business," the secretary of state confidently claimed.[55] Washington has strengthened its relations with India, Indonesia, Singapore, New Zealand, Malaysia, Mongolia, Vietnam, Brunei, and the small states of the Pacific. Joint military exercises have been conducted, which Beijing interprets as an American effort to build an anti-China alliance. The United States has long had formal alliances with Japan, South Korea, Australia, Philippines, and Thailand and is Taiwan's most important backer. In January 2012 President Barack Obama announced a new American military strategy that shifts the focus from Afghanistan and Iraq to Asia and the Pacific.[56] Defense Secretary Leon Panetta followed up in June of that year when he announced that 60 percent of the US Navy will operate in the Pacific by 2020.[57]

At the same time, China's influence is constrained by its neighboring states, including strong military powers such as India, Japan, and Russia. A number of factors lead them to harbor strong skepticism toward China, including historical experience, China's military rearmament and its assertive foreign policy behavior, its general feeling of relative weakness toward the country, and simple prejudices. The Indians fear growing Chinese presence in their Mare Nostrum (the Indian Ocean region); Japan feels vulnerable after being overtaken by China as the world's second largest economy; and the Russians are afraid that the eastern hordes once again will roll westward. Strong forces are in play that will prevent China from achieving a new era of hegemony in East Asia and beyond and will make it difficult for Xi to strengthen regional cooperation and garner support for his vision to implement a grand strategy in China.

## Insufficient Institutions

Successful implementation of grand strategy depends on Xi Jinping's ability to coordinate and direct all resources of the nation toward the objects of his desire. China's size obviously endows it with strength and resources, but it also creates a disadvantage for the leadership when it comes to extracting resources from society, exerting control, or implementing policies. Institutional fragmentation complicates such coordination.

In this fast-changing and increasingly complex world Xi has many responsibilities; he depends on others to help plan and implement foreign policy, which ultimately reduces his personal influence while magnifying institutional and pluralistic impacts upon the whole process. Although issues in Chinese politics are usually organized vertically in what are called *xitong* (systems) as Linda Jakobson discusses in her chapter, the strength of the *waijiao xitong* (diplomatic system) has been constantly impaired by horizontal conflicts with formidable institutional players in other systems.[58] The hierarchical components of the *waijiao xitong* includes the Foreign Affairs Leading Small Group at the top, which formulates foreign strategies and coordinates major diplomatically oriented departments and other relevant entities. The middle includes the Ministry of Foreign Affairs, which is charged with managing official relations with other countries, and the International Department of the Central Committee of the Communist Party of China (*Zhonglianbu*), charged with Party-to-Party diplomacy. Besides the traditional players—like the Ministry of Foreign Affairs, the Ministry of Commerce, and the People's Liberation Army (PLA)—another four institutional actors now expect to have their voices heard in today's Chinese foreign policy making : large SOEs, such as the oil giants and major weapons companies; the media (especially Internet media); other previously marginalized cabinet ministries; and ambitious and internationally oriented local governments. The Communist Party cannot afford to neglect their demands.

In the late 1990s under Jiang Zemin, a debate arose on the establishment of a council similar to the National Security Council of the United States. This council is the principal forum used by the president to formulate long-term foreign policy and serves as the president's principal tool for coordinating policies among different government institutions. Supporters of a Chinese National Security Commission argued that such a body could help the leadership adopt a more coordinated foreign policy, especially in times of crisis. At the time it was decided that such a council should not be created, and the debate was eventually laid dead.[59] However, at the Third Plenum of the Eighteenth Party Congress in November 2013, Xi Jinping managed to establish the National Security Commission (*Guojia anquan weiyuanhui*) based on the American model; it includes a highly empowered group of security experts who can work the levers of the country's vast security apparatus. With increased control over the military forces, the domestic security apparatus, propaganda programs, and intelligence and foreign policy, Xi is expected to be in a better position than his predecessors to implement strategic thinking.

## Domestic Firefighting

Finally, the Chinese leadership is increasingly consumed by shortsighted "firefighting" at home, which is a major obstacle to the success of any long-term policy. The previous leadership literally went from crisis to crisis: On

November 15, 2002, Hu Jintao succeeded Jiang Zemin as general secretary of the Communist Party. The following day an outbreak of what is believed to be severe acute respiratory syndrome (SARS) began in Guangdong province. The SARS epidemic was not simply a public health problem. Indeed, the inept handling of the epidemic triggered the most serious sociopolitical crisis for the Chinese leadership since the days of the 1989 Tiananmen crackdown. A decade later, on November 15, 2012, Hu passed the general secretary post to his successor, Xi Jinping. Only ten days before, on November 4, Chongqing's powerful governor, Bo Xilai, was formally expelled from the Chinese Communist Party; the public revelations in relation to Bo's fall from power set off a political crisis far larger than the SARS epidemic had caused. The crisis revealed a world of power abuse, corruption, and intrigue at the very top of the Communist Party. Several other crises had occurred in the decade between the reigns of Hu and Xi: In 2008, anti-China protests escalated into the worst violence Tibet had seen in two decades, just five months before Beijing was set to host the Olympic Games. Later the same year nearly fifty-three thousand Chinese children fell ill after drinking tainted milk, which forced the former premier, Wen Jiabao, to issue a public apology. And in 2009 the Xinjiang region in the north witnessed its worst ethnic violence in decades.

As Edward Luttwak notes, Chinese leaders are more introverted than most other leaders, whether those from other major countries like the United States or from small countries like Norway and Qatar, simply because they are confronted by domestic realities that are both much larger and potentially more volatile.[60] The striking absence of foreign affairs specialists in the Politburo is symptomatic of the inward-looking nature of China's current leadership. China's minister for foreign affairs holds a relatively low rank in the Party, despite his seat near the top of the state hierarchy. By contrast, the US secretary of state (the US government's equivalent of a minister for foreign affairs) is the highest-ranking member of the cabinet and the third-highest official of the executive branch of the federal government, after the president and vice president.

Challenges at home have grown in line with China's rapid socioeconomic growth. The Ministry of Public Security annually announced the number of "mass incidents"—protests, riots, and other forms of social unrest—until 2005, when the figure had reached 87.000.[61] As the number increased, government reporting stalled. The Chinese Academy of Social Sciences (CASS) think tank estimated that the number had passed 90,000 by the following year, while Professor Sun Liping of Tsinghua University claimed that 180,000 such incidents occurred in 2010.[62] If these figures are reliable, it means that each day there are around 500 protests, demonstrations, or riots across the country. Disgruntled social groups are mushrooming and the intelligentsia has become both politically more conscious and increasingly vocal. The Internet age has globalized protests, from the Arab Spring to Occupy Wall Street. Chinese citizens today are no longer apolitical or passive, their deft usage of social networking sites like Weibo (Twitter-like mini-blogs) to challenge China's political establishment testifies to the fact that China has entered a new age.

Xi Jinping and his leadership team must face these realities. They came to power in the middle of a storm (the Bo Xilai crisis and political scandal), which went hand in hand with other domestic crises. Two reports, one from *Bloomberg* and the other from the *New York Times,* tarnished the incorruptible image of Xi and former premier Wen Jiabao with reports on how members of their extended families have amassed wealth in the range of hundreds of millions of dollars. Undoubtedly there will be more crises. In order to survive the leaders in Beijing will be forced to devote their time to dealing with short-term domestic firefighting rather than on the implementation of a long-term grand strategy.

## CONCLUSION

Xi has taken important steps in the direction of formulating a grand strategy for China, but it is still in the making. In this manner Xi appears as a more visionary and strategic thinker than his predecessors Hu Jintao and Jiang Zemin, neither of whom articulated any grand vision guiding a rising China. In theory Xi's new grand strategy could have a unifying effect domestically, something that is highly needed in an era where rapid growth is creating considerable national stress. In addition, the grand strategy could make China more appealing to the outside world and undermine increasingly widespread notions of the "China threat." Although China's leader has a much stronger position than the one enjoyed by his predecessors, he is doomed to face significant structural obstacles when it comes to the implementation of a grand vision for a rising China. Neither the internal nor the external environments seem to be favorable for a smooth implementation of such a grand strategy. In particular, neighboring states are suspicious of China's strategic intentions, especially in light of the country's military rearmament and recent foreign policy behavior. No doubt this will be a considerable barrier to Xi's grand strategy development and implementation. Moreover, Xi faces formidable challenges related to a massive and partly fragmented state apparatus and rising domestic tensions. This does not mean that China's leader will never see his dream come true for the Middle Kingdom, but the odds are low.

## NOTES

This chapter was adapted from Stig Stenslie, "Questioning the Reality of China's Grand Strategy," *China: An International Journal* 12, no. 2 (August 2014), a publication of the East Asian Institute of the National University of Singapore. Used by permission.

 1. For some important contributions to this debate see: Ye Zicheng, *Inside China's Grand Strategy: The Perspective from the Peoples Republic,* ed. and trans. Steven I. Levine and Guoli Liu (Lexington: University Press of Kentucky, 2011); Wang Jisi, "China's Search for a Grand Strategy: A Rising Great Power Finds Its Way," *Foreign Affairs*, 90, no. 2 (2011): 68–79; and Yan Xuetong, *Ancient Chinese Thought, Modern Chinese Power*, ed. Daniel A. Bell and Sun Zhe, trans. Edmund Ryden (Princeton, NJ: Princeton University Press, 2011).

 2. "The Rise and Rise of Xi Jinping," *Economist*, September 20, 2014, at http://www.economist.com/news/leaders/21618780-most-powerful-and-popular-leader-china-has-had-decades-must-use-these-assets-wisely-xi#, accessed March 23, 2015.

 3. Elizabeth C. Economy, "China's Imperial President: Xi Tightens His Grip," *Foreign Policy*, November-December 2014, at https://www.foreignaffairs.com/articles/142201/elizabeth-c-economy/chinas-imperial-president, accessed March 23, 2015.

 4. Economy, "China's Imperial President"; "The Rise and Rise of Xi Jinping."

 5. Basil Henry Liddell Hart, *Strategy*, 2nd ed. (New York: Meridian,1991), 332.

 6. Paul Kennedy, *Grand Strategies in War and Peace* (New Haven, CT: Yale University Press, 1991), 5.

 7. John A. Lynn II, "The Grand Strategy of the *Grand Siècle*: Learning from the Wars of Louis XIV," in Williamson Murray, Richard Hart Sinnreich, and James Lacey, eds., *The Shaping of Grand Strategy: Policy, Diplomacy, and War* (New York: Cambridge University Press, 2011), 44.

 8. US Department of State, "National Intelligence Council Report 68" (NSC-68), April 1950, http://www.trumanlibrary.org/whistlestop/study_collections/cold war/documents/pdf/10-1.pdf.

 9. US Department of State, "The National Security Strategy of the United States of America," September 2002, http://www.state.gov/documents/organization/63562.pdf.

10. Ronald Ewald Robinson and John Gallagher, *Africa and the Victorians: The Official Mind of Imperialism* (London: Macmillan, 1963), 21–22.

11. George Friedman, *The Next One Hundred Years: A Forecast for the Twenty-First Century* (New York: Doubleday, 2009), 39.

12. Edward Luttwak, *The Grand Strategy of the Byzantine Empire* (Cambridge, MA: Belknap, 2009), 409.

13. See, for example, Jackson Diehl, "Obama's Foreign Policy Needs an Update," *The Washington Post*, November 21, 2010, at http://www.washingtonpost.com /wp-dyn/content/article/2010/11/21/AR2010112102263.html; John Mearsheimer, "Imperial by Design," *National Interest*, January-February 2011, http:// mearsheimer.uchicago.edu/pdfs/A0059.pdf, 16–34; Niall Ferguson, "Wanted: A Grand Strategy for America" *Newsweek*, February 2011, http://www.newsweek .com/2011/02/13/wanted-a-grand-strategy-for-america.html; and Michael Hirsh, "Obama: The No-Doctrine President," *National Journal*, March 29. 2011, http:// news.yahoo.com/blogs/exclusive/obama-no-doctrine-president-004835238.html.

14. See, among others, Kishore Mahbubani, "Smart Power, Chinese-Style," *American Interest*, March-April 2008, 68–77; Martin Jacques, *When China Rules the World: The End of the Western World and the Birth of a New Global Order* (New York: Penguin, 2009); Henry M. Kissinger, *On China* (New York: Penguin, 2011); and Zbigniew Brzezinski, *Strategic Vision: America and the Crisis of Global Power* (New York: Basic, 2012).

15. Brzezinski, *Strategic Vision*, 80–81.

16. See, among others, Mahbubani, "Smart Power, Chinese-Style"; Kissinger, *On China*.

17. Rebecca E. Karl, *Mao Zedong and China in the Twentieth-Century World: A Concise History* (Durham, NC: Duke University Press, 2010), 77.

18. The Ministry of Foreign Affairs, the People's Republic of China, http://www .fmprc.gov.cn/mfa_eng/.

19. Aaron L. Friedberg, *A Contest for Supremacy: China, America, and the Struggle for Mastery in Asia* (New York: W. W. Norton, 2011), 144.

20. Avery Goldstein, *Rising to the Challenge: China's Grand Strategy and International Security* (Stanford, CA: Stanford University Press, 2001).

21. Michael Swaine and Ashley Tellis, *Interpreting China's Grand Strategy: Past, Present, and the Future* (Santa Monica, CA: RAND, 2000), ix–x.

22. Goldstein, *Rising to the Challenge*, 17; and Friedberg, *Contest for Supremacy*.

23. Feng Zhang, "Rethinking China's Grand Strategy: Beijing's Evolving National Interests and Strategic Ideas in the Reform Era," *International Politics* 49 (2012): 319.

24. Stig Stenslie, "Questioning the Reality of China's Grand Strategy," *China—An International Journal* 12, no. 2 (August 2014): 161–78.

25. "The World's Biggest Economies: China's Back," *Economist*, October 11, 2014.

26. Liu Mingfu, *Zhongguomeng: Houmeiguoshidai De Daguosiwei Yu Zhanlued-ingwei* (The China dream: Great power thinking and strategic posture in the post-America era) (Beijing: Zhongguo Youyi Chuban Gongsi, 2010), at http://v.book.ifeng.com/commons/exception/0.htm, accessed December 2, 2013.

27. Xi Jinping, *The Governance of China* (Beijing: Foreign Languages Press, 2014), 315–20.

28. Xi, *Governance of China*, 37–38.

29. Xi, *Governance of China*, 41–43.

30. "Xi Offers Vision of China-Driven 'Asia-Pacific Dream,'" AFP News, November 9, 2014.

31. "Zhongguomeng Qubieyu Meiguomeng de Qida Tezheng" (Seven differences between China dream and American Dream), *Qiushi* (Seek truth), May 20, 2013, at http://theory.people.com.cn/n/2013/0523/c49150-21583458.html, accessed December 1, 2013).

32. "Chasing the Chinese Dream," *Economist*, May 4, 2013, 20.

33. "China's "Marshall Plan" Is Much More," *The Diplomat*, November 10, 2014.

34. Ministry of Foreign Affairs of the People's Republic of China, "The Central Conference on Work Relating to Foreign Affairs Was Held in Beijing," November 29, 2014, at http://www.fmprc.gov.cn/mfa_eng/zxxx_662805/t1215680.shtml, accessed March 26, 2015.

35. C. Dale Walton, *Grand Strategy and the Presidency: Foreign Policy, War, and the American Role in the World* (New York: Routledge, 2012) 8.

36. Walton, *Grand Strategy and the Presidency*, 1.

37. Walton, *Grand Strategy and the Presidency*.

38. Walton, *Grand Strategy and the Presidency*, 64.

39. Walton, *Grand Strategy and the Presidency*, 8.

40. Hao Yufan, "Influence of Societal Factors: A Case of China's American Policy Making," in Yufan Hao and Lin Su, eds., *China's Foreign Policy Making: Societal Force and Chinese American Policy* (Aldershot, UK: Ashgate, 2005), 1–18.

41. Bonnie Glaser and Evan Medeiros, "The Changing Ecology of Foreign Policy-Making in China: The Ascension and Demise of the Theory of 'Peace Rise,'" *China Quarterly* 190 (June 2007): 291.

42. Zheng Yongnian and Chen Gang, "Xi Jinping's Rise and Political Implications," *China: An International Journal*, 7, no. 1 (2009): 8–9.

43. For the development of the "Bush Doctrine" see Lawrence Kaplan and William Kristol, *The War over Iraq: Saddam's Tyranny and America's Mission* (San Francisco: Encounter, 2003); Chris J. Dolan and Betty Glad, eds., *Striking First: The Preventive War Doctrine and the Reshaping of U.S. Foreign Policy* (Basingstoke, UK: Palgrave, 2004); Jim Mann, *Rise of the Vulcans: The History of Bush's War*

*Cabinet* (New York: Penguin, 2004); Chris J. Dolan, *In War We Trust: The Bush Doctrine and the Pursuit of Just War* (Aldershot, UK: Ashgate, 2005); Timothy Shanahan, ed., *Philosophy 9/11: Thinking about the War on Terrorism* (Chicago: Open Court, 2005); Stephen F. Hayes, *The Brain: Paul Wolfowitz and the Making of the Bush Doctrine* (New York: HarperCollins, 2005); and Stephen M. Walt, *Taming American Power: The Global Response to U.S. Primacy* (New York: W. W. Norton, 2006).

44. "National Security Strategy of the United States of America."

45. Suisheng Zhao, "Chinese Foreign Policy: Pragmatism and Strategic Behaviour," in Suisheng Zhao, ed., *Chinese Foreign Policy: Pragmatism and Strategic Behaviour* (Armonk, NY: M. E. Sharpe, 2004), 8.

46. Zhao, "Chinese Foreign Policy."

47. Steven W. Mosher, *Hegemon: China's Plan to Dominate Asia and the World* (San Francisco: Encounter, 2000), 99.

48. Liu, *Zhongguomeng.*

49. Liu, *Zhongguomeng,* chap. 2.

50. Li Mingjiang, ed., *Soft Power: China's Emerging Strategy in International Politics* (Lanham, MD: Lexington, 2009), 22.

51. For an example see Joshua Kurlantzick, *Charm Offensive: How China's Soft Power Is Transforming the World* (New Haven, CT: Yale University Press, 2007).

52. For a recent poll see Pew Research Council, July 18, 2013, http://www.pewglobal.org/2013/07/18/americas-global-image-remains-more-positive-than-chinas/.

53. Yan Xuetong: "How China Can Defeat America," *New York Times,* November 20, 2011, http://www.nytimes.com/glogin?URI=http%3A%2F%2Fwww.nytimes.com%2F2011%2F11%2F21%2Fopinion%2Fhow-china-can-defeat-america.html%3Fpagewanted%3Dall%26_r%3D0.

54. Hillary R. Clinton, "America's Pacific Century," *Foreign Policy,* October 11, 2011, http://foreignpolicy.com/articles/2011/10/11/americas_pacific_century.

55. Clinton, "America's Pacific Century."

56. For the strategy see the *New York Times* at http://graphics8.nytimes.com/packages/pdf/us/20120106-PENTAGON.PDF.

57. See, as an example, BBC News, June 2, 2012, http://www.bbc.co.uk/news/world-us-canada-18305750.

58. David Bachman, "Structure and Process in the Making of Chinese Foreign Policy," in Samuel Kim, ed,. *China and the World: Chinese Foreign Policy Faces the New Millennium* (Boulder, CO: Westview, 1998), 34–54.

59. See, among others, Michael D. Swaine, *The Role of the Chinese Military in National Security Policymaking* (Santa Monica, CA: RAND, 1998), 27; and Richard C. Bush, *The Perils of Proximity: China-Japan Security Relations* (Washington, DC: Brookings Institution, 2010), 308.

60. Edward N. Luttwak, *The Rise of China vs. the Logic of Strategy* (Cambridge, MA: Belknap, 2012), 9–10.

61. Irene Wang: "Incidents of Social Unrest Hit 87,000 in 2005," *South China Morning Post*, January 20, 2006.

62. Will Freeman: "The Accuracy of China's 'Mass Incidents,'" *Financial Times*, March 2, 2010, https://subscribe.ft.com/barrier/logic?location=http%3A%2F%2Fwww.ft.com%2Fcms%2Fs%2F0%2F9ee6fa64-25b5-11df-9bd3-00144feab49a.html%3Fsiteedition%3Duk&referer=&classification=conditional_standard.

# 6

# DOMESTIC ACTORS AND THE FRAGMENTATION OF CHINA'S FOREIGN POLICY

Linda Jakobson

## INTRODUCTION

The emergence of new foreign policy actors in China is transforming the country's decision-making environment.[1] As China has become more powerful—economically, politically, and militarily—its global outreach has expanded. Simultaneously, the number of groups and institutions seeking to influence China's foreign policy has multiplied. Decisions made about China's policies in the international arena, on issues ranging from commerce and investment to anti-piracy and climate change, affect broad sectors of Chinese society and are scrutinized by the numerous actors who wish to advance their own agendas. These actors are both influential organizations or institutions within the official decision-making apparatus of China—the Communist Party of China (CPC), the Chinese government, and the People's Liberation Army (PLA)—and various groups on the margins of the traditional power structure.

The Communist Party of China and the government of the People's Republic of China (PRC) have separate decision-making structures, although some offices overlap in function, authority, and even personnel. The CPC's authority is supreme, hence the CPC's highest body—the Politburo Standing Committee (PSC)—retains the ultimate decision-making power. It exercises this power on key foreign and security policy decisions and seeks to "set the tone for and outline the broad contours of China's foreign policy," but it leaves lower levels to work out implementation details.[2] This structure allows a variety of actors—whether official or on the margins—to exert or attempt to exert influence over foreign policy. Subordinates at various levels interpret instructions from the top in ways that suit their own institutional interests.

Within the Chinese government, the Ministry of Foreign Affairs (MFA) used to be regarded as the leading entity on foreign policy. Today the MFA faces competition for influence from among other bodies: the Ministry of Commerce (MOFCOM), the National Development and Reform Commission (NDRC), the Ministry of Finance, the Ministry of State Security, the Ministry of Public Security, People's Bank of China, and China's Development Bank. Each of these government bodies has expanded its international outreach in its respective field, which has resulted in intense rivalry both with the MFA and with other official foreign policy actors.

The number of official actors in competition for control ranges widely from issue to issue. Official actors can include institutions as varied as the CPC Policy Research Office, the NDRC, or the PLA's Second Artillery Corps.

As for the actors on the margins, in other words outside the traditional confines of the CPC and the government, the most important ones are business executives, especially directors of state-owned enterprises in the resource sector; local governments, especially local leaders in the border and coastal regions; prominent researchers and leading intellectuals who for one reason or another have close ties to individual Politburo members; and prominent media representatives and the online community, the so-called netizens.

Among the new foreign policy actors, netizens are looked upon as the most dynamic.[3] The expansion of the Internet and the commercialization of the media have dramatically transformed interactions between officials and citizens. People in China are permitted to express their views, both on opinion pages in commercial newspapers and on the Internet, more freely than would have been imaginable a decade ago. The perspectives and sources of information available to the ordinary citizen have multiplied greatly, but it does not mean that citizens have genuine freedom of expression. Authorities try to steer public opinion, sometimes by encouraging a certain stance on a given issue and at other times by suppressing public opinion when it is deemed to be detrimental to the government's objectives.

Blog writers on popular foreign affairs websites often criticize Chinese leaders for being weak and bowing to international pressure. Officials are acutely aware of how rapidly a dissatisfaction with foreign policy can give rise to questioning the leadership's ability to govern. Hence, China's leaders at times appear to feel constrained by public opinion and especially by the views of the online community during international crises involving China.

This is especially relevant when Japan or the United States is involved or when international attention focuses on issues related to Taiwan or Tibet.

The pluralization of Chinese society coupled with China's growing interdependence with the international order has put enormous pressure on CPC leaders. They rely on a host of interest groups to maintain social order and economic growth—prerequisites for the CPC's ability to stay in power. As a result, the leadership must accommodate numerous and sometimes competing agendas. This challenge is further complicated by the decentralization of power that has taken place in China over the past three decades and which has been essential to the country's growing economic success. Consensus building (or at least the perception of consensus building) within the Politburo Standing Committee is important to ensure CPC unity and political stability.

At play are *omnidirectional influences* among CPC officials, government bureaucrats, PLA officers, intellectuals, researchers, media representatives, and business executives.[4] Everyone seeks to influence everyone else and public opinion too: they lobby, they write blogs, they take part in televised debates, and they engage in roundtable discussions about the direction of Chinese foreign policy. Developing an awareness of such omnidirectional channels of influence is critical to understanding the complex nature of foreign policy formation in China. It is no longer possible to think of China's decision makers as the one unitary force of days past. On any given foreign policy issue, those seeking China's cooperation must evaluate and engage the potential interests of several groups.

Three broad trends are evident when examining the role of new foreign policy actors in China. First, authority has become fractured. Second, while in general everyone regards China's continued internationalization as inevitable, a variety of views exist among officials and other actors regarding the degree to which China should prioritize this internationalization. Third, the view that China should more actively defend and pursue its international interests is becoming prevalent, especially since Xi Jinping took over as head of the CPC in November 2012. Each of these trends has implications for policy makers outside China.

This chapter strives to shed light on the development of these trends in recent years, in particular on the implications of fractured authority and the manner in which fragmentation is used by actors who advocate China's pursuit of a more robust foreign policy. These actors include both groups within the official foreign policy establishment and actors on the margins. Leadership matters. Regarding the crucial maritime security sphere, there are signs that China's new leaders have acknowledged the problem of fragmentation and are attempting to centralize control over decision making.

# FRACTURED AUTHORITY

Over the past few years Chinese scholars have begun to pay more attention to the phenomenon of fragmentation in foreign policy formulation.[5] They do not explicitly use the term "fractured authority"; rather, they describe a process of fragmentation in foreign policy decision making that has accelerated over the past decade. In open-source literature they refer to the need for weighing the interests of nonstate actors (*fei guojia xingwei ti*) when considering the multifaceted challenges that policy makers face, and they note that "conflicting interests are a common occurrence."[6] In a 2015 opinion piece, Zhao Kejin of Tsinghua University encourages the delegates of the Chinese People's Political Consultative Conference to dare to speak out on diplomatic affairs, noting that the more globalized a country is, the more fragmented the voices are regarding foreign affairs and the more likely it is to hear differing voices.[7]

Wang Yizhou of Peking University writes about an "ever-increasing level of autonomy and overseas contact for all levels of local government." He differentiates between "core diplomacy" and all other kinds of diplomacy, such as "energy diplomacy," "cross-border diplomacy," "party diplomacy," "military diplomacy," "sports diplomacy," "economic diplomacy," "people to people diplomacy," "public diplomacy," "community diplomacy," "union diplomacy," and "women's federation diplomacy." In principle, Wang writes, all organizations conducting diplomacy are meant to report to the Ministry of Foreign Affairs to receive "recognition and guidance." In actual practice, however, there is little oversight of these organizations' actions. They fill the space left open by the often too-busy Ministry of Foreign Affairs and use it to achieve their own interests. It is only natural that contradictions and conflicts arise due to differing interests and perspectives.[8]

The vague policy guidelines emanating from the CPC central agencies and the central government versus the imperative for individual government agencies to make routine policy decisions create a diverse range of policies that are at times contradictory. As Wang Jisi of Peking University notes, "Defining China's core interests according to the three prongs of sovereignty, security, and development, which sometimes are in tension, means that it is almost impossible to devise a straightforward organizing principle [to guide foreign policy]. And the variety of views among Chinese political elites complicates efforts to devise any such grand strategy based on political consensus."[9]

In an article written in 2011, Cui Liru of the China Institutes of Contemporary International Relations refers to this dilemma and laments a lack of strategic coordination in China's diplomacy and foreign policy. He stresses that "China's strategic thinking should move from fuzziness to clarity." Cui writes that "clearly articulated plans, ideas, theories, doctrines, goals and means are needed to link philosophical ideals with concrete actions. Both external and internal coordination are necessary for an extensive diplomatic strategy."[10]

In private conversations Chinese policy makers today, more so than a decade ago, refer to fragmentation to explain turf battles between ministries and the push-pull dynamic between the central government and the provinces and municipalities. Anecdotes about the weakened power of the Ministry of Foreign Affairs abound.[11] The MFA lacks the power to effectively enforce its mandate to coordinate among the various foreign policy actors.

One concrete example of the dysfunctionality of decision making in China is the 2012 decision by the Ministry of Public Security (MPS) to issue new passports with maps that show disputed islands as Chinese territory. Predictably, this caused an outcry by neighboring countries. The foreign ministry had not been consulted on the decision ahead of time, and then–foreign minister Yang Jiechi was described as being "furious" upon hearing the news.[12] Zhu Feng of Peking University said he thought the MPS saw the need "to do something to show their support for China's sovereign claim."[13] The MPS issues passports for ordinary citizens. The MFA issues passports for government officials and these official passports remain unchanged and carry no map.

An examination of the events leading up to the controversial passports being issued by the MPS appear not only to reflect a total lack of communication between the MFA and the MPS but also a signal of the desire by the MPS to repudiate a MFA stance. Speaking at the MFA press conference on February 29, 2012, spokesperson Hong Lei said: "At the core of the South China Sea dispute are the territorial sovereignty dispute over some of the Nansha Islands and the demarcation dispute over part of the waters of the South China Sea. What should be pointed out is that neither China nor any other country lays claim to the entire South China Sea." Many foreign observers interpreted this as a sign that China was slightly softening its stance and acknowledging the damage it was doing to itself by speaking in public about the nine-dash line as though it laid claim to all the territory within it. Three months later the MPS started to produce the passports with maps containing the nine-dash line.[14]

Due to the MFA's weak standing within the Chinese foreign policy decision-making apparatus, the MFA is often not informed by other agencies about incidents or decisions pertaining to China's international relations despite the fact that the MFA is the agency tasked with responding to queries by foreign diplomats and the international media. For example, the MFA was reportedly not informed in November 2012 about Hainan province's new maritime security regulations that authorized the border public security organs to board and search foreign vessels. Exactly what authority the maritime law enforcement organ possesses remains open to interpretation. The frequently used terms "territorial waters" (*linghai*) and "littoral waters" (*yanhai*) appear to refer to Hainan-administered waters, but no clear distinction has ever been made between the customary twelve nautical miles (where domestic law applies) versus the two hundred nautical miles covered by the exclusive economic zone (where China already has a history of boarding and inspecting foreign vessels). Hainan's new regulations entered into effect some months before the realignment of China's various maritime law enforcement agencies. Hence, areas of authority were further blurred when no reference was made to a specific agency and only to "public security frontier defence organs" (*gong'an bianfang jiguan*).[15] When diplomats from other countries sought clarification about the Hainan provincial government's new regulations, the ministry was unaware and unprepared.[16] More important, from the viewpoint of assessing fragmentation in foreign policy decision making, the Hainan government reportedly did not even seek approval from the central government before issuing the regulations.[17]

The Ministry of Public Security's decision to issue the controversial map and the Hainan government's new regulations underline the damage a single government entity can cause for China's international relations. In the case of the passports, the top leadership was presumably caught unaware by a decision taken at some lower level. But even if a senior leader had not approved of the new passports and map it would have been extremely difficult for that leader to publicly retract the decision after the fact. China does, after all, officially claim maritime rights in the waters within the so-called nine-dash line, so issuing a directive that would nullify a decision to promote the nine-dash line would be interpreted as China bowing to outside pressure.[18]

## LACK OF POWERFUL FOREIGN POLICY LEADERSHIP

Appointments at the Eighteenth Party Congress and Twelfth National People's Congress confirmed the weak standing of the MFA and suggested that foreign policy is not the highest priority of the CPC leadership. Those hoping to see a Politburo member placed in charge of foreign policy were disappointed. Instead and yet again, a "mere" central committee (CC) member (Yang Jiechi) was appointed to the post of state councilor in charge of foreign affairs. (The new foreign minister, Wang Yi, is also a member of the CC.) In this regard the Xi Jinping era represents a continuation of the Hu Jintao era; not since Qian Qichen, who was a Politburo member from 1992 to 2002, has China's top diplomat wielded considerable political power within the Party.[19] Yang Jiechi is only one among 205 CC members. In the Party hierarchy, each of the 25 Politburo members outranks Yang, which means that they can overrule any of Yang's decisions. For example, Yang must heed the views of at least five provincial leaders who are significant foreign policy actors "on the margins."[20] The Party secretaries of Beijing, Chongqing, Guangdong, Shanghai, and Xinjiang were all appointed to the Politburo at the Eighteenth National Congress and they all outrank Yang as well. This structure represents a continuation from the Hu era. The Politburo appointed by the Seventeenth CPC Party Congress had six Party secretaries of major provinces or municipalities.

Because the CPC's authority is supreme over the government, some important official decision makers do not necessarily even have a government post. For example, Wang Jiarui, the head of the CPC Central Committee's Organizational Department since 2003 and a consequential decision maker on China's North Korea policy, has not held a government post since 2000.[21] Politburo member Wang Huning has no government title either, but he is regarded as a key foreign policy advisor to Xi Jinping. Ever since 1995, when he was moved by Jiang Zemin to Beijing from Fudan University, he has been considered the intellectual driver of the CC policy research office. As a Politburo member, Wang is certainly Yang Jiechi's superior. Wang was prominently seated beside Xi Jinping at the June 2013 Sunnylands Summit with Barack Obama.

Another Politburo member, Li Zhanshu, heads the CPC Central Committee General Office, which is significant because it controls the flow of information to senior leaders and manages their schedules. Li is believed to be a personal friend of Xi.[22] A third Politburo member without a government position, Liu Qibao, is head of the Central Committee Propaganda Department and responsible for shaping China's public rhetoric on foreign policy, its actions around the globe, and its international image. What Chinese citizens and the rest of the world read in the *People's Daily* or from Xinhua News Agency are what Liu and the leadership want anyone to know and how they desire us to understand events and the Chinese government's intentions.

In the same vein, few leaders who are not also Central Committee members hold influential government posts. All but three (twenty-two of twenty-five) ministerial level posts under the State Council are held by CC members.

The PLA's foreign affairs system further contributes to the problem of fractured authority in foreign policy formulation. As Michael Swaine of the Carnegie Endowment notes:

> Many of the activities undertaken by the military that pose potential problems for the United States—including both the testing of major weapons and deployments of PLA assets beyond China's borders—come under either the Operations Department or the Military Training and Service Arms Department of the PLA General Staff Department (GSD). According to one very knowledgeable Chinese officer, these departments are senior in the PLA hierarchy to those GSD units in charge of foreign affairs and intelligence. As a result, they routinely do not consult with such units when deploying assets or conducting military tests or exercises. In addition, the GSD's foreign affairs office is primarily responsible for military exchanges with foreign countries, not assessments of the diplomatic impact of military actions. In other words, no organization within the PLA has the authority and responsibility to routinely demand and receive notice of PLA activities that might impact China's foreign policy.[23]

Coordination between the PLA and the government generally is even weaker than the coordination among government entities or within the PLA. Public speeches by senior officials and PLA officers as well as articles in open-source literature continuously emphasize the need to improve military-civilian cooperation. One glaring example of the lack of communication between the PLA and the MFA dates back to 2007, when the MFA was caught unaware of the PLA's shooting down of a Chinese weather satellite.[24] In recent years other signs show that in at least some security-related areas the cooperation between civilian and military units is improving. For example, as of 2014 the PLA navy and the new China coast guard have begun to visibly collaborate in China's near seas in the realm of maritime law enforcement and "rights defense."[25] According to some Chinese sources, PLA navy officers participated in the coordination of the escort and defense operations involving numerous Chinese law enforcement vessels when the HYSY 981 oil rig was towed to disputed waters off the Paracel Islands in May 2014.[26] But, based on research interviews in late 2014, communication between the PLA and the Ministry of Foreign Affairs remains poor.

Leaders specifically in charge of foreign policy in China are managers, not crafters of foreign policy. Major decisions on foreign policy during the Hu Jintao era were made by the Politburo Standing Committee, with Hu himself as the head, and this trend has continued under Xi Jinping. While several PSC members have distinct portfolios, not one member has an exclusive foreign policy portfolio. Since taking the helm Xi has apparently not only been the ultimate decision maker on major foreign policy issues but he has been proactive in promoting new foreign policy initiatives. Xi appears to want to be the "prime mover" of Chinese foreign and security policy.[27] However, the less important and so-called second- and third-tier foreign policy issues remain in the hands of government officials in charge of foreign affairs, which leaves ample room for a diverse set of foreign policy actors vying to get their voices heard. Because of the conflicting interests of numerous interest groups and the weak standing of China's top foreign policy officials within the CPC, fractured authority in foreign policy formulation can be expected to continue.

## SUPPORT FOR A TOUGHER FOREIGN POLICY

In the last few years there appears to be growing agreement among various Chinese elites and netizens at large that China should be "less submissive" toward the demands of industrialized countries and more active in its pursuit of its interests internationally.[28] After thirty years of rapid economic growth, many Chinese feel that the country should abandon Deng Xiaoping's dictum of avoiding a leadership role in the international arena. The global financial crisis in particular strengthened this perception among foreign policy actors on the margins (e.g., resource company executives, local officials, influential media commentators, and netizens) as well as official foreign policy decision makers (central CPC and government officials and senior PLA officers). These groups—though in no way organized—seem to share the view that China no longer should acquiesce to outsiders' demands, as China was compelled to do for the sake of the country's modernization during the decades of reform and opening.

An assessment of whether the fragmentation in foreign policy decision making is being used by those advocating a more forceful foreign policy must consider several driving forces. Nationalism is one. Xi Jinping's latest political slogan, "China Dream," alludes not only to the goal of making China strong and prosperous but also to the humiliation that China suffered at the hands of Japan and the West during the "century of shame" from the mid-nineteenth to the mid-twentieth century. This cultural frame of national humiliation is continuously emphasized by the CPC and is a "very deliberate celebration of national insecurity," as William Callahan has so vividly phrased it.[29] According to another scholar, Jing Men, China has a dual identity: a strange combination of self-superiority and self-inferiority.[30] As early as 1969 John K. Fairbank warned, "The tradition of Chinese superiority has now been hyper-activated. . . . It will confront us for a long time to come."[31]

Protecting China's sovereign rights—"rights defense" (*wei quan*)—has become the mantra of today's China.[32] Upholding sovereignty is used as justification for assertive behavior. It is easy to stir up nationalist support among netizens and media commentators for protecting China's territorial integrity, especially regarding disputed waters and maritime rights.

It is noteworthy that while China has not changed its sovereignty claims in its near waters, it has changed its ability and willingness to assert claims to maritime rights in both the South China and East China Seas.[33] According to Chinese analysts, China's moderate policies toward the disputed islands and waters in the first three decades of reform and opening failed to protect China's (perceived) sovereignty and maritime interests against the intensified encroachments by other claimant states. Jian Zhang of the Australian Defense Force Academy argues that recent Chinese actions represent a "major and arguably long-term strategic shift in China's policy regarding the South China Sea, featured by the emergence of an increasingly proactive and purposeful approach to solidify Chinese claims."[34]

A second driving force is commercial interests. It is impossible to determine whether the chief executive officers (CEOs) of resource companies are true nationalists and if they genuinely believe that China should adopt a tougher approach to foreign policy. But it is certainly in the commercial interests of China's large state-owned enterprises (especially those seeking to extract minerals in the East and South China Seas) for Beijing to maintain a rigid stance on its territorial claims. Hence, it is in the interests of CEOs of resource companies to encourage "rights defense."

The South China Sea, in particular, has been the focus of heated competition between Chinese state-owned energy and resource companies and such companies based in other countries. Over the past few years there has been noticeable activity by China National Offshore Oil Corporation (CNOOC) in the region. Since 2009 the CNOOC has called for tenders by foreign companies on at least five batches of oil-exploration blocks in the South China Sea. The June 2012 release on the furthest-out blocks from China's mainland was by far the most controversial. The blocks were located inside the 200-nautical-mile exclusive economic zone (EEZ) of Vietnam, and some of the sites overlapped with areas that Hanoi had awarded to other companies such as Exxon Mobil and Russia's OAO Gazprom.[35] In addition, the claim to at least one individual exploration block—number 65/24, which sits 1 nautical mile from the Paracel Islands (the Xisha Islands in Chinese)—specifically raised the ire of Vietnam. In a March 2012 statement, Vietnam singled out the offer as violating its sovereignty. China and Vietnam fought over this island group in 1974.[36]

If the CNOOC is able to develop these sites there will be the tangible benefit of production growth but also the possibility that it will be able to attract more support from central government actors. Mingjiang Li of Singapore's Nanyang Technological University states: "By playing up nationalism, it could help CNOOC gain more state policy support, more investment."[37] According to a Phoenix News article, a person "close to CNOOC's Zhanjiang Base" said that the June 2012 tenders indicate that China "has officially entered the interior of the South China Sea to exploit oil."[38] The article added that compared to the CNOOC's first failed attempt to move into the area in 1992, this is on a much bigger scale.

Chinese national energy companies currently lack the technical know-how to extract deep-sea oil. One CNOOC senior engineer stated in 2012 that the company's ability to exploit oil at 300 meters down is advanced, but from 300 to 3,000 meters CNOOC is a newcomer.[39] This means that at present, Chinese companies have no choice but to try to partner with foreign firms. As the technical expertise of Chinese companies increases, this impediment to further exploration will be reduced.

There are already signs that the CNOOC is improving its deep-water capabilities. In May 2012 the new CNOOC drilling rig HYSY 981 began drilling in a sea area 320 km southeast of Hong Kong at a water depth of 1,500 meters.[40] "With Chinese offshore drilling technology improving, it is just a matter of time for them to enter the central and southern part of the South China Sea," said Liu Feng of the National Institute for South China Sea Studies.[41] Asked whether the CNOOC would move the rig to disputed waters, Lin Boqiang of Xiamen University said: "I feel they will. . . . If CNOOC does not do it, other countries will do it. So why [should] CNOOC not do it?"[42] Two years later this prediction became reality when the HYSY 981 rig was towed out to the Paracels. The move evoked fury in Vietnam and led to widespread domestic protests, which in some localities turned violent and led to loss of life. According to a well-placed CPC official, the councilor in charge of foreign affairs for years had been under pressure by various actors to sign off on this plan and pass the final decision to the senior leadership.

It is evident that the CNOOC is linking protection of the country's sovereignty rights to its own economic objectives. In the words of CNOOC chairman Wang Yilin in 2012, "Large deep-water drilling rigs are our mobile national territory and strategic weapon for promoting the development of the country's offshore oil industry."[43] The question of what energy and mineral resources lie within disputed waters is also manipulated by those who want to push China's leaders to adopt a tougher foreign policy when it comes to territorial issues. According to a knowledgeable senior Chinese foreign policy official, it is commonplace for senior officials to be given exaggerated figures about the amount of oil and gas China is "forfeiting" in disputed waters.[44]

Official media sources also make the claim that China will lose natural resources if it doesn't assert itself in the South China Sea. One article in the *China Economic Weekly*, which is managed and sponsored by the *People's Daily*, states: "Some insiders believe that geological resources in the central and southern part of the SCS and its extractable resources account for 53 per cent and 66 per cent of China's total maritime oil and gas resources respectively. If [the resources in the SCS] were plundered by other countries, China's maritime area would lose roughly two thirds of its extractable oil and gas resources [there]." The article continues: "Neighboring countries around the SCS have developed 1380 oil wells. The world's major oil companies have shared a slice [of the profits]."[45]

Opening up the Paracel Islands to tourism is another development in which commercial interests are being promoted by officials outside the central government, in this case in Hainan province. This in turn causes tensions with neighboring countries and negatively weighs on China's international image. Tourist excursions to the Paracels were made possible after China's elevation of Sansha City on Woody Island to a prefectural-level city in July 2012. Because it is charged with administering all of China's claims over the South China Sea's hundreds of islets, sandbanks, and reefs, Sansha's new status affords it the "organizational infrastructure for a variety of civilian activities to demonstrate China's sovereignty," including fishing, tourism, and the administration of a small military garrison.[46] At the 2013 Bo'ao Forum, Tan Li, the deputy governor of Hainan province, stated that after the establishment of Sansha City, "China's maritime rights in the South China Sea have been strengthened."[47]

Woody Island's small size, limited access, and minimal infrastructure (such as transportation and sewage treatment) currently restrain the Hainan tourism industry's bold ambitions to unlock "China's Maldives." Nevertheless, the arrival of the eight-hundred-passenger ship *Coconut Princess* (*Yexiang Gongzhu Hao*) at Woody Island is indicative of the market's potential and the strong reactions that the move evokes in neighboring countries. The first group of two hundred Chinese officials and tourists set sail for the Paracels from Haikou in April 2013 on a four-day tour. The launch drew protests from Hanoi, with one Vietnamese media outlet labeling the action Chinese "imperialism." A Chinese foreign ministry spokesperson replied by emphasizing China's undisputed sovereignty over all islands in the South China Sea.[48]

Some estimates claim that opening up the Paracels for Chinese tourism could lead to as much as a 50 percent increase in Hainan's overall tourist income.[49] Furthermore, local authorities have pledged "to create the best conditions possible for travel agencies and investors to begin services in the area, turning Xisha Islands [the Paracels] into a tourism island in the near future."[50] Some Chinese analysts, such as retired rear admiral Yin Zhuo (who is known for his nationalist views on China's maritime claims), see Sansha's uniquely endowed potential as a "special mission" to bring economic development and improvement to the lives of the people while simultaneously serving the "national interest" by "demonstrating sovereignty."[51]

A third driving force is the desire by government agencies to gain prestige and power within the system. It is natural for a government agency to desire greater allocations for equipment acquisition. This context will be discussed in greater detail in the next section.

There is ample evidence—such as media and Internet commentary as well as public remarks by resource company executives and local government officials—that actors on the margins are demanding a tougher foreign policy that staunchly defends China's national interests. Anecdotal evidence based on research interviews also supports the growing tendency by many official actors to emphasize the necessity to be more determined in defending sovereignty when they are charged with articulating policy recommendations or justifying policy decisions.

## RECENTRALIZING A FOREIGN POLICY ISSUE

China's behavior in the maritime sphere since 2009 has complicated China's external relations and in many cases has led to heightened tensions with its neighbors and with the United States. Chinese fishing boats and patrol vessels under the administration of various maritime law enforcement agencies have been embroiled in numerous incidents in the East China and the South China Seas, especially since the September 2010 arrest of a Chinese fishing boat captain by Japanese authorities after he rammed his boat into a Japanese coast guard vessel near the disputed Senkaku/Diaoyu Islands. Following the incident, nationalism surged in both China and Japan, further narrowing the maneuvering room of leaders on both sides. Other 2010 incidents in the South China Sea involving Chinese vessels led to rabid commentary by Chinese netizens, who demanded that China use force to teach Vietnam and the Philippines "a lesson." Chinese leaders were criticized as being too soft.

A lack of attention by China's senior leadership in late 2010 and throughout 2011 could have constituted a plausible explanation for both the increased number of patrols by Chinese law enforcement agency vessels and the country's increasingly assertive actions in pursuit of the mandate to defend its sovereignty in disputed waters. In particular, the harassment of other countries' seismic survey vessels and the detention of fishermen were—and continue to be—a source of contention. One can argue that it is in the agencies' interests to be at center stage in protecting national interests because the uproar has led to increased central government funding to agency budgets, which in turn has led to vastly enlarged maritime law enforcement agency fleets.

However, since 2012, when Xi Jinping was put in charge of a new senior officials group focusing on maritime security, inattention could no longer be the sole explanation for actions by Chinese law enforcement agency vessels in the "near seas." In September 2012, soon after the Japanese government's purchase of the disputed islands, Xi was reportedly made head of the new Office to Respond to the Diaoyu Crisis.[52] It can be assumed that Xi is consulted about the increase in patrols and that he approves of the more robust stance of China toward its neighbors when it comes to defending maritime rights.

Nevertheless, despite Xi's role in important maritime-related bodies, to further understand the fragmentation in Chinese foreign policy decision making two considerations are noteworthy. First, Xi cannot possibly be consulted on every action taken in China's name. This is an important point in light of any assessment of Xi's accumulation of power. Second, it is evident that before Xi came to power someone in the top leadership made the decision that the maritime law-enforcement landscape was too fragmented and not in China's best interests. In other words, the actions of poorly coordinated maritime law enforcement agencies both aggravated relations with its neighbors and the United States and served as an impetus for the central government to take measures to improve coordination and reinstate its power over maritime law enforcement.

## Xi Cannot Control Every Decision

Descriptions of Xi as a strongman who has consolidated more power than any leader since Deng Xiaoping or even Mao Zedong run the risk of conveying a false impression. Just because Xi has amassed power does not mean he has a say in every policy that is crafted or dictates every action that China takes. He does not. Despite Xi's image as a determined leader, systemic problems that have accumulated since the founding of the PRC, as well as the increase of fractured authority, leave substantial room for various actors to push their own agendas, especially in relation to the South China Sea. Although Xi might have provided guidance about the general direction to take in defending what China perceives as its rights, local government officials, large resource company CEOs, coast guard officials, and PLA officers are very much a part of the decision-making processes and formulation of concrete policies, not to mention the implementation of those policies.

China is a one-party authoritarian state, but many types and many layers of official and even unofficial stakeholders influence both policies and actions. An increasingly complex governance structure must continuously adapt to both a more global nation and a more splintered international environment. The central government's loss of power to local governments, due to the decentralization that was imperative for the first phases of economic growth, has been further compounded by the loss of power to many additional stakeholders as a result of the country's increasing dependence on international markets and global forces, especially since the turn of the century.

For example, despite Xi's concentration of power, various actors continue to use for their own personal economic or political advantage his ambiguously two-pronged statement about the necessity to remain steadfast in protecting maritime rights while at the same time maintaining stability. Xi has not stated which is more important. His guidance is classic CPC rhetoric: "Plan as a whole the two overall situations of maintaining stability and safeguarding rights."[53]

Actors who would benefit most from an assertive stance by China in the "near seas" highlight Xi's emphasis on "rights protection." These include the PLA, maritime law enforcement units, local governments, resource companies, and the tourism and fishing industries. A senior CPC official based in Hainan explained in 2014 that "no one can punish us for defending China's maritime rights in a determined manner—our national chairman has said that we should." But actors who see even-keeled relations with the neighbors as better serving their interests—such as companies that trade and invest abroad or those who might lose reduced tourist inflows from Vietnam and the Philippines—repeat Xi's emphasis on "stability maintenance."

## Restructuring Maritime Law Enforcement Agencies

Increasing friction with neighbors was one driver of the central government's 2013 announcement that China's maritime law enforcement agencies were to be restructured. In part the decision reflected the Chinese leadership's desire to consolidate central control over numerous unwieldy local actors that were cooperating poorly and ran the risk of destabilizing the region. Xi wants to stand up for China's (perceived) sovereignty but he does not want chaos. He does not want to be placed in a situation that requires decisions of war and peace. Moreover, any restructuring must be viewed as the result of demands made by several actors on the margins—including maritime scholars associated with maritime law enforcement—that China strengthen its capacity to defend its rights in disputed waters. The consolidation of China's maritime law enforcement agencies had been a long time in the making and was the result of both top-down and bottom-up pressures.

In 2013 the State Oceanic Administration (SOA) under the Ministry of Land and Resources, which previously managed the fleet of the China Marine Surveillance, officially took overall control of four organizations: the maritime police (Gong'an Bianfang Haijing); the Border Control Department (BCD) (Gong'an Bianfang Guanliju), which was previously under the Ministry of Public Security; the Fisheries Law Enforcement Command (Zhongguo Yuzheng), previously administered by the Ministry of Agriculture; and the Maritime Anti-Smuggling Authorities (Haishang Jisi Jingcha Bumen), which was previously administered by the General Administration of Customs.[54]

The SOA remains to a great extent under the administration of the Ministry of Land and Resources, though after 2013 it was decided that China's maritime law enforcement will be performed in the name of the Maritime Police Bureau (Haijing Ju), which is administered by the SOA but operationally guided by the Ministry of Public Security. All of the fleets except that of the Maritime Safety Administration are now incorporated into one fleet called (in English) the China Coast Guard. (It is unclear why one of the previous five law enforcement agencies, the Maritime Safety Administration under the Ministry of Transport, was not included in the consolidation plan.) How this dual leadership structure will work in practice is still unclear. The reorganization that was intended to improve cooperation and communication may have actually created a new set of problems.

## Unhappy Law Enforcement Agencies

Since the mid-2000s, maritime specialists in China have publicly complained about inadequate funding for the five maritime law enforcement agencies, considering the enormous challenges they face in managing a rapidly evolving maritime security environment. Effective maritime law enforcement is repeatedly described by Chinese observers as essential in order to "protect our national maritime security and effectively enforce China's ocean rights."[55]

Moreover, maritime specialists like Zhang Haiwen of the SOA's China Institute for Maritime Affairs have for years stated that the capacity of the agencies does not reflect China's status as a great power.[56] Though the central government has increased its funding and significant improvements have been made by increasing the size of fleets and personnel, the agencies have perceived their own capacity as weak in comparison with other countries in the region. In nearly all research interviews conducted by the author with Chinese maritime analysts and officials prior to 2013, the Japanese Coast Guard was mentioned as an overwhelmingly more powerful actor in the maritime domain.

Complaints have also arisen about inadequate legislation. Li Guoqiang, a researcher within the Chinese Academy of Social Sciences (CASS), writes that "some departments snatch other countries' seized fishing boats and fishermen, but do not know how to manage this. They still need to give them food and water and provide medical treatment if they are sick, lest something bad should happen and cause an even bigger international dispute. . . . But in marine law enforcement we have not specifically established a special decree [on this issue]."[57] This lack of legislation has left China's maritime personnel in envy of the staff in other countries who are able to legally process Chinese fishing crews immediately after apprehending them or who have "established measures and specific provisions to deal with the intrusive claims of the sea areas under jurisdiction."[58]

In addition to a lack of resources and legislation, Chinese maritime specialists have repeatedly criticized the poor coordination that exists among the five maritime enforcement agencies. According to another CASS researcher, Chinese maritime agencies need to "overcome the outdated mindset of selfish departmentalism."[59] Wang Yang, an active-duty PLA officer, alluded to this mentality when noting that cooperation requires "breaking down the barriers, pooling resources and sharing information. But information is precious and resources are exclusive, so this requires cooperating units to have an open mind and generous spirit."[60]

Until March 2013 the urgent need to merge law enforcement agencies into one body to improve coordination was a common theme in Chinese analysts' publications.[61] Wang Hanling, the director of the Centre for Ocean Affairs and the Law of the Sea at CASS, is one of numerous Chinese researchers who cite the US Coast Guard as an "all-in-one force" model that they believe China should adopt to provide military, multi-mission, and maritime services to protect broad national security interests and also to patrol international waters.[62]

In sum, the central government's decision to restructure the maritime law enforcement agencies should be viewed as both an attempt to reassert its control by improving command and control processes within the maritime domain as well as a response to the complaints from within the maritime security specialist community of inadequate capacity and overall weakness of the agencies. The reorganization is still a work in progress and many questions remain unanswered about its implications. These include: How will the restructuring affect China's behavior in its near seas? What kind of a relationship will the strengthened "coast guard" have with the PLA? And what implications will there be for the PLA navy's operational doctrines?

## THE NATIONAL SECURITY COMMISSION

For years the need for China to establish a national security commission (NSC) was debated among Chinese foreign policy scholars. Overlapping lines of authority and weak coordination were often cited as reasons for establishing such a body. For example, Jin Canrong said in a 2011 interview that "China's system has always been stronger at control than coordination. It was difficult enough to coordinate in Mao Zedong's time. Now, because the current leaders' authority is not as strong as before, China's ability to coordinate is even weaker."[63] Another reason, though one mentioned by Chinese scholars in private conversation only, is the limited (if any) regular contact between parts of the Chinese military and the Chinese government's foreign affairs system regarding military activities of relevance to foreign policy. Hao Yufan of Macau University noted in 2012 that an NSC would bring together into one overarching and unified strategic framework the views of the PLA with the views of the numerous government agencies involved in foreign affairs: the Ministry of Foreign Affairs, the Ministry of State Security, the International Department of the CPC Central Committee, the Ministry of Commerce, the Ministry of Education, the Ministry of Science and Technology, the National Energy Administration, the State Oceanic Administration, the State Council Information Office, the Ministry of Environmental Protection, and the People's Bank of China.[64]

In November 2013 the new CPC National Security Commission (NSC) was announced during the Central Committee's Third Plenum. The first NSC meeting, held in April 2014, was prominently reported by official media. Unsurprisingly, Xi is the chair of the commission and Li Keqiang and Zhang Dejun have important roles. The commission is presumed to include leaders from the Central Military Commission (CMC) and its four headquarters (general staff, political work, logistics, and armaments); the Central Discipline and Inspection Commission (Wang Qishan); the ministries of national defense, public security, and state security; and the National Development and Reform Commission.

As with the consolidation of maritime law enforcement agencies, poor coordination was one motive for establishing the NSC. Michael Lampton of Johns Hopkins University presumes that another motive was Xi's critical view of—and possibly his frustration with—the foreign and security policy decision-making system he inherited. Xi's speeches certainly stress the need to improve institutions and mechanisms that deal with foreign affairs and to enhance coordination among different sectors and actors. In a March 2015 article, Lampton writes: "Xi Jinping . . . is trying to construct new institutional pathways to shape policy and bring in new people not so beholden to the previous constellation of interests. He also is using the creation of the NSC to seek to consolidate his personal sway in the domestic security, foreign policy and military realms. In short, Xi is both driving to achieve better policy coordination and greater personal control in the system." [65]

In the past, critical foreign policy decisions were presumed to be deliberated and in some cases made by either the CPC's Foreign Affairs Leading Small Group (FALSG) or National Security Leading Small Group (NSLSG). [66] The membership of the FALSG / NSLSG are not known but are presumed to be identical and include leading officials from the CPC, the government, and the PLA.

According to research interviews by the author in November 2014, the FALSG/NSLSG has almost never been convened under Xi—another indication that the NSC and other new leading groups established by Xi are his attempt to remold the governance system at the top and do away with old practices. It remains to be seen whether it is humanly possible for Xi to stay on top of as much as he has taken on as chair of numerous leading small groups and the NSC. It is possible that by consolidating too much power in his own hands Xi will exacerbate the problems of coordination, which in turn will lead to further fragmentation of authority.

## CONCLUDING THOUGHTS

Xi Jinping is intent on strengthening the CPC and wants Party organs to be at the fore on all major initiatives. Xi is unquestionably the lead person deciding the direction of foreign and security policy. He heads all major foreign policy–related small groups and the NSC. Nevertheless, fractured decision making continues to characterize foreign policy formulation in China. Though Xi Jinping will weigh in on all major foreign policy issues as the head of the CPC, PSC, CMC, and all noteworthy foreign policy–related small groups, collective leadership—or the perception of it—remains important for CPC unity. Xi must build consensus among the PSC members for major policy decisions to ensure political stability. Furthermore, most policy decisions affecting China's international behavior will be taken by a host of actors who do not necessarily share a vision of how to implement policy and who do not communicate efficiently with each other. Actors on the margins—provincial leaders, CEOs of large resource companies, netizens, prominent intellectuals—are either becoming more active in their efforts to influence foreign policy decisions or, as a result of their actions in pursuit of commercial profit or more prestige, are increasingly having an effect on China's foreign policy.

In light of events since September 2010, maritime law enforcement agencies should also be considered foreign policy actors. In addition, the recent focus by China's senior leaders on China's maritime environment has made local governments in maritime provinces more prominent foreign policy actors.

The number of actors who pursue their own agendas in the international sphere, all in the name of China's national interests, is growing. On any given issue several CPC units, government ministries, and PLA units weigh in on the decision-making processes. The picture that emerges of these actors resembles a complex montage.

The implications of fractured foreign policy decision making are manifold. In all political systems there is competition for funding, information, talented people, and, ultimately, power within the system. Sharing power is challenging enough in a political system in which transparency and accountability are guiding principles. In China, decision-making processes are not transparent and the decision makers are not accountable on the basis of publicized rules that can be challenged. The so-called stovepipe syndrome that has its roots in China's centrally planned economy prevails. Collaboration and communication among CPC entities, government ministries, other government units, PLA units, and state-owned enterprises is weak. Lack of communication is often accompanied by mistrust. So, while the government officially encourages cooperation, in reality the weak linkages are a major structural challenge.

One obvious consequence of fragmentation and fractured authority is that resources are scattered, repetitive, and not used efficiently. There is tremendous waste within the system. Another is the impulse among officials to use incoherent or vaguely worded policies to their own advantage. Chinese government directives are usually worded in a manner that can justify a broad range of activities.[67] A third consequence is the risk of miscalculation by a "rogue" foreign policy actor that leads to a serious incident and possibly the loss of life at sea or in the air. There are indications that at times China struggles to control daredevil pilots. The top US Air Force commander in the Pacific, Gen. Herbert Carlisle, said in October 2014 that while inter-actions between Chinese, Japanese, and US aircraft in the area had been to a large extent safe, some unsafe encounters have occurred and these unsafe encounters have generally been isolated to one place and limited to one Chinese unit.[68]

Once a crisis has erupted, the emotionally charged nationalist sentiment that exists among citizens across East Asia, including China, Japan, Viet-nam, and the Philippines, makes it extremely difficult for senior leaders of any country to put forward a proposal that can stabilize a fraught situa-tion. In January 2013 a Chinese official involved in the standoff with Japan said in private conversation that at times Xi Jinping "is intentionally given exaggerated assessments by those who want him to take a tough stance."[69] The official added that the maritime enforcement agencies "independently enforce senior-level directives. And once these agencies have acted it is very difficult for a senior leader to criticize actions which were taken in the spirit of defending China's national interests." The view that China should more actively defend and pursue its interests internationally has become even more prevalent in the past few years. "Rights defense" (*weiquan*) and the need to protect China's sovereign rights are used by numerous actors to jus-tify assertive behavior.

This aspiration—to adopt a more forceful foreign policy—intertwined with the strong nationalist undercurrent running through Chinese society is used by several foreign policy actors to pursue their own interests. In some cases, advocating that China should more forcefully defend what it perceives as its sovereign territory (waters) is useful to substantiate an agency's desire for equipment acquisitions, as in the cases of the China Maritime Surveillance agency and the Fishing Administration. Large resource companies can only benefit from China taking a firm stance on its territorial claims, especially in the South China Sea. For example, CNOOC has spent nearly $1 billion on its ultra-deep water rig to explore disputed areas of the South China Sea. It is highly likely that the rig will continue to explore in disputed waters and there will be renewed standoffs between Vietnamese and Chinese law enforcement agency vessels similar to the standoff in May 2014. One can surmise that CNOOC senior executives are among those lobbying most vig-orously for central government decision makers not to back down on China's territorial claims.

As Wang Jisi points out, "almost all institutions in the central leadership and local governments are involved in foreign relations to varying degrees, and it is virtually impossible for them to see China's national interest the same way or to speak with one voice."[70] The government restructuring measures adopted at the National People's Congress in March 2013, especially the decision to consolidate maritime law enforcement agencies, reflect in part an acknowledgment of the need to improve policy coordination among Chinese government agencies. In practice, however, domestic actors can be expected to continue to push their own agendas, further contributing to fragmentation of China's foreign policy. Considering the fact that CPC legitimacy relies on the ongoing support of several powerful domestic actors, it remains to be seen whether foreign policy leadership under Xi Jinping will be able to balance between being tough and keeping the peace with its neighbors.

## NOTES

This chapter has as its starting point a SIPRI Policy Paper by the author and Dean Knox, *New Foreign Policy Actors in China* (Stockholm International Peace Research Institute, SIPRI Policy Paper 26/2010). It also develops further some of the arguments made in a short draft paper, entitled "Foreign Policy Decision-Making Processes in China, between Fragmentation and Centralisation," which the author presented at a conference (The Hu Jintao Decade in China's Foreign and Security Policy [2002–2012]: Assessments and Implications) organized by the Stockholm International Peace Research Institute (SIPRI) in Stockholm April 18–19, 2013. The author is grateful for research assistance provided by Dirk van der Kley, Jiao Li, Liu Yun, Eva O'Dea, and Harrison Palmer.

1. Linda Jakobson and Dean Knox, *New Foreign Policy Actors in China*, Stockholm International Peace Research Institute, SIPRI Policy Paper 26 (2010), 1–3.
2. Susan Lawrence, "Perspectives on Chinese Foreign Policy," Testimony before the US China Economic and Security Review Commission Hearing on China's Foreign Policy: Challenges and Players, April 13, 2011, at http://www.uscc.gov/sites/default/files/4.13.11Lawrence.pdf.
3. This and the following paragraphs draw from Jakobson and Knox, *New Foreign Policy Actors*, 47–51.
4. Jakobson and Knox, *New Foreign Policy Actors*, 43, 48.
5. See, e.g., Wang Yizhou, "Ruhe Lijie Zhongguo Waijiao (Xia)" (Wang Yizhou: How to understand Chinese diplomacy), part 2, *Fenghuang Wang* (Phoenix news online), March 22, 2013, at http://news.ifeng.com/opinion/politics/detail_2013_03/22/23397854_0.shtml.
6. Hao Yufan, "Yong Da Zhanlue Sikao Zhong Mei Guanxi," (All-encompassing conceptual strategies for considering Sino-US relations), *Meiguo Wenti Yanjiu* (Fudan American Review) 1 (2012): 1–15.

7. Zhao Kejin, "Renmin Waijiao Ying Chengwei Zhengxie De Di Si Zhineng" (People-to-people diplomacy should become fourth function of CPPCC), *Zhongguo Wang* (China.com.cn), March 5, 2015, at http://opinion.china.com .cn/opinion_90_123590.html.

8. Wang, "Ruhe Lijie Zhongguo Waijiao."

9. Wang Jisi, "China's Search for a Grand Strategy?," *Foreign Affairs*, March-April 2011.

10. Cui Liru, "Some Thoughts on China's International Strategy," *Contemporary International Relations* 21, no. 6 (November-December 2011), at http:// www.cicir.ac.cn/english/ArticleView.aspx?nid=4042 (official translation by Ma Zongshi).

11. Author's discussions with Chinese government officials and researchers during six visits to Beijing in 2011, five visits in 2012 and 2013, and three visits in 2014.

12. Author's separate conversations with three officials of China's Ministry of Foreign Affairs in December 2012 and January 2013. See also John Ruwitch, "As China's Clout Grows, Sea Policy Proves Unfathomable," Reuters, December 9, 2012, at http://uk.reuters.com/article/2012/12/09/china-sea-policy-idUKL4N 09H0OZ20121209. The author is aware of conflicting accounts of whether the MFA and MPS communicated about the new passports decision. According to "Dangerous Waters: China-Japan Relations on the Rocks," *Crisis Group Asia Report* 245 (April 8, 2013), 34, "the decision had been made by the Public Security Bureau and the passports went to print over the objection of the foreign ministry, which was told, 'passports are an issue of immigration and not foreign policy.'"

13. Ruwitch, "As China's Clout Grows."

14. "Duoming Gongmin Chi Xinban Huzhao Rujing Yuenan Yu Zu" (A number of Chinese citizens traveling on new passports have difficulty entering Vietnam), *Xingdao Ribao* (Singtao Daily), November 23, 2012, at http://news.singtao .ca/toronto/2012-11-23/china1353663094d4212412.html; Andrew Chubb, "'You Cannot Not Support This': The Passport Saga Impresses China's Online Nationalists," "South Sea Conversations," November 27, 2012, at https:// southseaconversations.wordpress.com/2012/11/27/you-cannot-not-support -this-the-passport-saga-foreign-policy-incoherence-and-impressing-chinas -online-nationalists. The map produced by the MPS is available at http://www .thejakartapost.com/files/images2/p02-b_10.img_assist_custom-560x381.jpg.

15. For the new regulations in full, see Standing Committee of Hainan Provincial People's Congress, "Hainan Sheng Yanhai Bianfang Zhi'an Guanli Tiaoli" (Hainan coastal border security management regulations), December 31, 2012, at http://www.hainanpc.net/hainanrenda/29/43783.html. M. Taylor Fravel is of

the opinion that the law applies to the 12 nautical miles of Hainan's territorial waters being the responsibility of the "province public security border defense organs" (*sheng gong'an bianfang jiguan*). However, this view is open to interpretation. Furthermore, this responsibility, along with those of other maritime law enforcement agencies, appears to have been absorbed by the newly unified Maritime Police Bureau (Hai Jing Ju) under the State Oceanic Administration (SOA). See M. Taylor Fravel, "Hainan's Maritime Regulations: An Update," at M. Taylor Fravel's blog, January 4, 2013, at http://taylorfravel.com/2013/01/hainans-new-maritime-regulations-an-update/. Boarding, inspecting, and expelling ships from Chinese-claimed waters is one of the objectives of the South Sea Fisheries Administration Bureau (also recently incorporated into the police bureau), which escorts Chinese fishing boats into Chinese-claimed exclusive economic zones. See Michael A. McDevitt, M. Taylor Fravel, and Lewis M. Stern, *The Long Littoral Project: South China Sea*, CNA Strategic Studies, March 2013, at https://www.cna.org/CNA_files/PDF/IRP-2012-U-2321-Final.pdf, 46

16. "Dangerous Waters," 36.

17. Author's conversation with a Ministry of Foreign Affairs official in Beijing, January 2013.

18. Linda Jakobson, "China's Foreign Policy Dilemma," Lowy Institute for International Policy, February 2013, at http://www.lowyinstitute.org/files/jakobson_chinas_foreign_policy_dilemma_web3_use_this.pdf.

19. Qian Qichen was foreign minister from 1988 to 1998 and vice premier in charge of foreign affairs from 1993 until he retired in 2003. He was a politburo member from 1992 to 2002.

20. Jakobson and Knox, *New Foreign Policy Actors,* 31–33.

21. Wang Jiarui, *China Vitae*, at www.chinavitae.com/biography/2140.

22. Cheng Li, "Xi Jinping's Inner Circle," part 1: "The Shaanxi Gang," *China Leadership Monitor* 43, Hoover Institution, Spring 2014, at http://www.brookings.edu/~/media/research/files/papers/2014/01/30-xi-jinping-inner-circle-li/xi-jinping-inner-circle.pdf.

23. Michael D. Swaine, "China's Assertive Behavior," part 3: "The Role of the Military in Foreign Policy," *China Leadership Monitor*, November 28, 2011, at http://carnegieendowment.org/files/CLM36MS.pdf.

24. B. Gill and M. Kleiber, "China's Space Odyssey: What the Antisatellite Test Reveals about Decision-Making in Beijing," *Foreign Affairs* 86, no. 3 (May–June 2007).

25. Linda Jakobson, "China's Unpredictable Maritime Security Actors," Lowy Institute for International Policy, December 2014, at http://www.lowyinstitute.org/publications/chinas-unpredictable-maritime-security-actors, 21.

26. Ibid.

27. David M. Lampton, "Xi Jinping and the National Security Commission," *Journal of Contemporary China* 24, no. 95 (2015): 760.

28. Jakobson and Knox, *New Foreign Policy Actors*, 51.

29. William A. Callahan, "National Insecurities: Humiliation, Salvation, and Chinese Nationalism," *Alternatives* 29 (2004): 199.

30. Jing Men, "China's Peaceful Rise?," *Studia Diplomatica* 56, no. 6 (2003): 17.

31. John K. Fairbank, "China's Foreign Policy in Historical Perspective," *Foreign Affairs*, April 1969, 9.

32. "NIDS China Security Report 2011," National Institute for Defense Studies, Tokyo, 2012, at http://www.nids.go.jp/publication/chinareport/pdf/china_report_EN_web_2011_A01.pdf.

33. Taylor Fravel, "Maritime Security in the South China Sea and the Competition over Maritime Rights," "Cooperation from Strength: The United States, China, and the South China Sea," Center for New American Security, January 2012, 41–42.

34. Jian Zhang, "China's Growing Assertiveness in the South China Sea: A Strategic Shift?," in "The South China Sea and Australia's Regional Security Environment," Australian National University National Security College report, no. 5, 2013.

35. "China Offers Oil-Exploration Blocks near Disputed Waters," Bloomberg, August 28, 2012, at http://www.bloomberg.com/news/articles/2012-08-28/china-offers-oil-exploration-blocks-near-disputed-waters-1-.

36. Ibid.

37. Xu Tianran, "Deep-Water Drilling Starts," *Global Times*, May 9, 2012, at http://www.globaltimes.cn/NEWS/tabid/99/ID/708511/Deep-water-drilling-starts.aspx.

38. "Zhonghaiyou Nanhai Qu Kuai Quanqiu Zhaobiao Hazuo Bu Hui Yinwei Jubu Moco Zhongduan" (CNOOC's global tender for partners in the South China Sea will not be interrupted by local frictions), *Fenghuang Wang*, July 3, 2012, at http://finance.ifeng.com/hk/gs/20120703/6696456.shtml.

39. Ibid.

40. "Deep-Water Drilling Begins in South China Sea," China.org.cn, May 9, 2012, at http://www.china.org.cn/business/2012-05/09/content_25339532.htm.

41. "China Tests Troubled Waters with $1 Billion Rig for South China Sea," Reuters, June 21, 2012, at http://www.reuters.com/article/2012/06/21/us-china-southchinasea-idUSBRE85K03Y20120621.

42. "Analysis: China Unveils Oil Offensive in South China Sea Squabble," Reuters, August 1, 2012, at http://www.reuters.com/article/2012/08/01/us-southchinasea-china-idUSBRE8701LM20120801.

43. "Deep-Water Drilling Begins in S. China Sea."
44. Author's discussion with senior foreign policy official in Beijing, January 10, 2013.
45. Yao Dongqin, "Nanhai Baozang: Shiqu Nanhai Jiu Xiangdang Ya Shiqu Zhong-guo Youqi Zong Ziyuan San Fen Zhi Yi" (Treasures in the South China Sea: Losing the South China Sea means losing one-third of China's total oil and gas resources), *Zhongguo Jingji Zhoukan* (China economic weekly), no. 21 (2012), at http://www.ceweekly.cn/html/Article/2012052856700324485.html.
46. McDevitt, Fravel, and Stern, *Long Littoral Project*, 45.
47. Wang Yue, "Hainan Fushengzhang Biaoshi Sansha Jianshihou Nanhai Wei-quan Dedao Jiaqiang" (Vice governor of Hainan province says South China Sea rights defense was strengthened after Sansha City was developed), Guoji Zaixian (China radio international online), April 6, 2013, at http://politics.people.com .cn/n/2013/0406/c14562-21035142.html.
48. Huang Minxue and Zhang Jianfeng, "Zhongguo Tuijin Sansha Luyou Yin Yuenan Buman, Yue Waijiaobu Kangyi" (China efforts of promoting tourism to Sansha has caused dissatisfaction of Vietnam, Vietnamese foreign ministry protest), *Renmin Wang* (People's daily online), May 3, 2013, at http://travel .people.com.cn/n/2013/0503/c41570-21350670.html.
49. "'Zhongguo Ma'erdaifu' Sansha You You Wang 10 Yue Kaifang" (China's Mal-dives—Sansha tourism hopes to bloom by October), "What's on Sanya," Septem-ber 1, 2012, at http://www.whatsonsanya.com/news_msg_cn.php?titleid=23300
50. "Cruise Tours to Sansha Expected to be Launched in October," "What's on Sanya," September 1, 2012, at http://www.whatsonsanya.com/news-23300 -cruise-tours-to-sansha-expected-to-be-launched-in-oct.html.
51. "Sansha Luyou You Wang 'Wu Yi' Chengxing Ke Shang Xisha Qundao Guan-guang" (Sansha tourism hopes to embark by May 1, Opening the Paracels to Sightseeing), *Renmin Wang* (People's daily online), April 4, 2013, at http:// xz.people.com.cn/n/2013/0414/c138901-18460255.html.
52. Author's conversations with two Chinese officials in Beijing, January 2013. The "group" referred to is the CPC Maritime Security Leading Small Group. Jakob-son, "China's Foreign Policy Dilemma."
53. Jakobson, "China's Unpredictable Maritime Security Actors," 34.
54. "Fangwu Duanping: Wu Long Nao Hai Jieshu Zhongguo Ban Hai'an Jingwei Dui Wenshi" (Short defense analysis: The end five dragons disturbing the sea China's coast guard to be formed), *Fenghuang Wang*, May 10, 2013, at http:// news.ifeng.com/mil/forum/detail_2013_03/10/22936298_0.shtml; "China to Restructure Oceanic Administration, Enhance Maritime Law Enforcement," Xinhua News Agency, March 10, 2013, at http://news.xinhuanet.com/english /china/2013-03/10/c_132221768.htm.

55. Li Jie, "Haishang Zhifa Liliang Huhuan Gaoxiao Heyi" (Maritime law enforcement power calling out for efficient unification), *PLA Daily (Expert Report)*, July 3, 2010, at http://www.81.cn/jfjbmap/content/2010-07/03/node_8.htm.
56. Xu Yang, Xu Xiaoqing, and Ma Yang, "Zhuanjia Cheng Zhongguo Chongzu Haiyangju Bingfei Zhuiqiu Haiyang Baquan Weixie Lin Guo" (Experts state that China's reorganized SOA is for harassing neighboring countries as a maritime hegemony), *Zhongguo Xinwen Wang* (China news online), May 10, 2013, at http://www.chinanews.com/gn/2013/03-10/4629982.shtml.
57. Li Guoqiang works at the Chinese Borderland History and Geography Research Centre under CASS. Guo Yina, "Zhongguo Haiyang Weiquan Xingshi Jiang Geng Yanjun" (China's maritime rights situation will become more severe), *Guoji Xianqu Daobao* (International herald leader), May 6, 2011, at http://www.21ccom.net/articles/qqsw/zlwj/article_2011051135233.html.
58. Guo, "Zhongguo Haiyang Weiquan Xingshi Jiang Geng Yanjun."
59. "Changing Tack with Sea Strategy," *People's Daily Online*, May 13, 2011, at http://en.people.cn/90001/90776/90786/6656502.html.
60. Zhang Bolin and Shi Binxin, "Huang Bo Shoujia Haifang Xiezuo Qu Dansheng" (The Yellow–bohai coastal defense cooperation zone is born), *Zhongguo Jun Wang* (China military online), July 28, 2009, at http://www.81.cn/jfjbmap /content/2010-07/03/content_32315.htm.
61. See, e.g., Li, "Haishang Zhifa Liliang; Wang Lirong, "Guanyu Zhongguo Haiyang Zhanlue Wenti de Ruogan Sikao" (Some considerations about China's maritime security problem), *Haiyang Fazhan Yu Guanli* (Maritime development and administration), report no. 4 (June 2011): 19–23.
62. Jiang Huai, Ma Xiaojun, Li Jie, Wang Hanling and Fan Xiaoju, "Zhongguo de Haiyang Quanyi he Haijun" (China's maritime rights and interests and the PLAN), *Shijie Zhishi* (Global knowledge), 1 (2009).
63. Interview transcript of interview with Jin Canrong by *Nanfang Dushi Bao* (Southern Metropolis Daily), reproduced electronically in "Zhong Mei Guanxi Zouxiang Xin Gongshi" (Moving toward a new consensus on China-US relations), *Guanchazhe* (Observer), January 30, 2011, at http://www.guancha.cn /america/2011_01_30_53692.shtml.
64. Hao Yufan, "Yong Da Zhanlue Sikao Zhong Mei Guanxi" (All-encompassing conceptual strategies for consider Sino-US relations), *Meiguo Wenti Yanjiu* 1 (2012): 1–15.
65. Lampton, "Xi Jinping and the National Security Commission," 760.
66. The general understanding of the difference between FALSG and the National Security Leading Small Group (NSLSG) is that it is nonexistent. FALSG/ NSLSG is literally the same organization with two different titles (Yige Jigou Liang Kuai Paizi). See Yun Sun, "Chinese National Security Decision-Making:

Processes and Challenges," Brookings Institution, May 2013, at http://www .brookings.edu/~/media/research/files/papers/2013/05/chinese-national -security-decisionmaking-sun/chinese-national-security-decisionmaking -sun-paper.pdf.

67. For more on this point see Jakobson, "China's Unpredictable Maritime Security Actors," 47.

68. "U.S. General: Most East China Sea Interactions Safe," *Navy Times*, October 10, 2014, at http://www.navytimes.com/article/20141010/NEWS/310100041 /U-S-general-Most-East-China-Sea-interactions-safe.

69. Author's conversation with Chinese official in Beijing, January 2013. The conversation took place under the condition that the official be identified as a "Chinese official involved in the standoff with Japan."

70. Wang, "China's Search for a Grand Strategy?."

# 7

# CHINA'S RISE AND INTERNATIONAL REGIMES

## Does China Seek to Overthrow Global Norms?

Andrew J. Nathan

We live in an age of increasing international normativity. To a degree unprecedented in history, the world is governed by international "regimes," which can be defined as the formal and informal norms and institutions that regulate interactions at the supranational level—that is, on global, regional, multilateral, and bilateral bases, and usually, but not exclusively, among nation-states.[1] After World War II, and then with renewed vigor since the mid-1970s, these international regimes have increased in number, complexity, and scope, and—more controversially, but supported by most scholarship—in actual influence over the behavior of states and other international actors.[2]

The rise of China has coincided with the period during which the international regime system has expanded most dramatically. As China has risen it has also joined and for the most part complied with most international regimes. But it has also, like other major states, worked to influence the way in which regimes have continued to evolve. This chapter asks in what direction China is pushing the international regime system. Is there an ideological, interest-based, or other logic to China's preferences? Does China aim to overthrow existing norms or merely to influence how they evolve in a way that is consistent with China's basic character? With respect to the international regime system, is China behaving as a status quo power or as a revisionist power?

To be sure, there is a sense in which the rise of China, by definition, constitutes a change in the global order—that is, if the global order is defined as
the structural distribution of power among states in the manner described
by Kenneth Waltz.[3] The global order so defined has shifted from a unipolar
structure in the 1990s to what most scholars today would call a multipolar
structure, with China positioned as a powerful pole. This order will be altered
further if China's power continues to increase relative to the power of other
states. But a shift in the structural distribution of power among participating
states is not the same as a shift in the norms that make up global regimes.

International regimes are not static. They have changed throughout history, and have done so especially rapidly in recent decades. If regimes have
any influence at all on the behavior of states, then we can expect that these
states will work to shape and reshape them to better serve their own interests. This will be equally true of incumbent powers as of rising powers, of
the United States as of China. So the question is not whether China tries to
influence the evolution of global regimes; it is whether the changes China
seeks can be characterized as fundamental.

How, then, can the boundary between within-system change and fundamental change be identified? There is no simple benchmark. It requires an
assessment, regime by regime, of whether China's negotiating positions seek
to adapt each regime in ways that benefit China without changing the regime
fundamentally versus instead trying to alter the regime's essential character.
As a rough guideline, we might accept G. John Ikenberry's characterization
of the existing system as a "liberal international order." In this order, states—
using the right (called sovereignty) that they possess to establish by mutual
agreement rules that bind each other's behavior—have created a set of institutions that are open to all states, that promote free trade and other "open"
economic interactions, and that establish rule-bound procedures for settling
disputes peacefully.[4] We can only characterize China's (or any other state's)
position in this liberal order as a snapshot of a moving target, but such a snapshot can tell us whether the posture China has taken so far is one that accepts
or undermines the basic principles of this existing regime system.

## PREVIOUS RESEARCH

Some excellent research has been done on China and international regimes,
but most of it proceeds from a problematic premise that differs in three ways
from the one proposed here.[5] First, instead of viewing international regimes
as essentially contested and evolving, most of the literature views the regimes

as having some stable meaning that is consistent with the American or general Western interpretation of their content. Second, and accordingly, instead of comparing China's negotiating position in each regime to those of other actors, the literature asks how much and why China's position has or has not moved closer to the position of the West. Third, in answering this question, the literature tends to argue that Chinese policies have shifted in response to Western persuasion and socialization rather than exploring the extent to which China's policies might be motivated by the pursuit of its own interests.[6] The approach taken here, by contrast, is to see regimes as continually evolving, to see all actors (including Western actors) as engaged in a contest to shape such norms and institutions, and to pose the same question about China that can in principle be posed about each state actor: What drives its policy toward each regime?[7]

A variety of theories have been proposed for what drives China's foreign policy, including its policy toward international regimes. One sees China promoting a particular ideology or vision of the international system and its role within it, based on such principles as sovereignty, a multi-polar world, Asian values, or Chinese domination.[8] Another suggests that China's policies can be seen as pragmatic responses to specific material interests.[9] An investigation of China's behavior in international regimes can help to clarify what type of goals it is seeking.

An investigation of China's positions within various international regimes can also throw light on the larger question of whether China's rise supports or threatens the liberal international order. Some authors argue that China wants to change that order in fundamental ways. Amitav Acharya, for example, writes, "It is a fallacy to assume that just because China, India, and other rising powers have benefitted from the liberal hegemonic order, they will abide by its norms and institutions. They may not seek to overthrow it but push for changes that might significantly alter the rules and institutions of that order."[10]

Similarly, Mark Leonard writes, "The Chinese . . . do not feel inclined to uphold a Western-led international order that they had no role in shaping. . . . [R]ather than being transformed by global institutions, China has taken part in sophisticated multilateral diplomacy that has changed the global order." Leonard gives the examples of China siding with debtor nations in the G20, helping to doom the Doha Round negotiations of the World Trade Organization by sitting on its hands, pushing against liberal norms at the United Nations (UN), setting up the Shanghai Cooperation Organization, creating bilateral and multilateral trading arrangements with countries around the world, holding summits with the BRICS nations (Brazil, Russia, India,

China, and South Africa), and setting up a BRICS bank. He argues that the weakness of Western-dominated institutions like the UN, the International Monetary Fund, and the World Bank, and their "irrelevance," could "grow worse over time, as rather than working together to reform existing common forums, Western powers try to build 'a world without China' and China and its partners try to create what some analysts call 'a world without the West.'"[11]

The analysis here, however, supports an alternative argument: that the liberal international order is resilient and that China prefers to join it rather than to overturn it. As Ikenberry writes, "[A]lthough the United States' position in the global system is changing, the liberal international order is alive and well. The struggle over international order today is not about fundamental principles. China and other emerging great powers do not want to contest the basic rules and principles of the liberal international order; they wish to gain more authority and leadership within it."[12]

## THE RISE OF REGIMES

International regimes have a long history, dating to the sixteenth century or before, with a period of marked expansion during the nineteenth century. The end of World War II saw a wave of regime creation with the establishment of the United Nations, the Bretton Woods system, and the General Agreement on Tariffs and Trade (GATT); with the expansion of international humanitarian law in the form of the Geneva Conventions; and with the launch of modern international human rights law via the adoption of the Universal Declaration of Human Rights (UDHR). But the bulk of the international normative system that we live under today is less than forty years old. This constitutes a remarkable, and perhaps too little noted, change in the international system. For example, in the international trade regime, the GATT was reformed into the World Trade Organization (WTO) in 1995, a process during and after which the regime added many more rules and more members and took on a more powerful role in resolving international trade disputes through its dispute settlement procedures. Starting in the 1990s and accelerating in the 2000s, the United States and the European Union (EU), plus other states in other regions, concluded a growing series of bilateral and multilateral free trade agreements (FTAs) which grew increasingly complex with the inclusion of human rights and environmental provisions in some of them.[13]

In the arms control and disarmament (ACD) regime, the Nuclear Nonproliferation Treaty entered into force in 1970; the Biological Weapons

Convention in 1975; the UN Conference on Disarmament was established in 1979; the Missile Technology Control Regime in 1987; and the Chemical Weapons Convention entered into force in 1997. The Comprehensive Test Ban Treaty was approved by the UN General Assembly (UNGA) in 1996 but has not yet entered into force. Along with these major enactments came a large number of more technical norms and the establishment of various committees and organizations.

In the field of international humanitarian law (IHL), rules adopted since 1980 include the 1980 United Nations Convention on Prohibitions or Restrictions on the Use of Certain Conventional Weapons Which May Be Deemed to Be Excessively Injurious or to Have Indiscriminate Effects; the 1997 Ottawa Treaty banning the use of landmines; the 1994 San Remo Manual on International Law Applicable to Armed Conflicts at Sea; the 1994 International Committee of the Red Cross/United Nations General Assembly (UNGA) Guidelines for Military Manuals and Instructions on the Protection of the Environment in Time of Armed Conflict; the 1994 UN Convention on the Safety of United Nations and Associated Personnel; the 1996 International Court of Justice advisory opinion on the Legality of the Threat or Use of Nuclear Weapons; the 1997 Convention on the Prohibition of the Use, Stockpiling, Production, and Transfer of Anti-Personnel Mines and on Their Destruction (Ottawa Treaty); the 1998 Rome Statute of the International Criminal Court; the 2000 Optional Protocol on the Involvement of Children in Armed Conflict; and the 2008 Convention on Cluster Munitions.[14]

Regarding international human rights, the UNGA adopted the International Covenant on Civil and Political Rights and the International Covenant on Economic, Social, and Cultural Rights in 1966; the Convention on the Elimination of All Forms of Discrimination Against Women in 1981; the Convention Against Torture in 1987; and the Convention on the Rights of the Child in 1990. The Annan Doctrine (regarding the international community's responsibility to prevent crimes against humanity) was promulgated in 1999; the Global Compact (on business and human rights) was adopted in 2000; the Millennium Development Goals were adopted in 2000; and the Declaration on the Rights of Indigenous Peoples was adopted in 2007. Alongside these norm-establishing enactments came a growth in related institutions: the UN Department of Peace-keeping Operations was established in 1992; the Office of the High Commissioner for Human Rights was established in 1993; and the International Criminal Court was established in 2002. Of the thirty-five thematic mandates created by the United Nations Human Rights Council (formerly Commission), ten were established in the 1990s and twenty-one during the 2000s.

These norms and institutions are only examples of the many that could be mentioned that were newly created during the late– and post–Cold War regime expansion process. Also of note—although there will be no space to discuss them further in this essay—has been the rise of many regional and international forums and associations, such as the G7 (later expanded into the G20), the BRICS grouping, ASEAN (the Association of Southeast Asian Nations), APEC (Asia Pacific Economic Cooperation), the East Asia Summit, and so on.

Why has the international regime system expanded so much in this period? International relations theorists have given a variety of reasons, some of which work better for explaining some regimes than for others. The growth of the international trade regime yields easily to an institutionalist explanation: in an age of globalization, the economic benefits to member states of expanding the trade regime are greater than the costs. The growth in human rights norms and institutions is more often analyzed from a constructivist point of view: governments are pushed by transnational activist networks to accept the legitimacy of new norms.[15] The growth in rules governing arms control and disarmament can be explained by either a constructivist approach—which argues that governing elites learn to regard certain kinds of weapons as abhorrent—or by a realist approach—which says that states can consolidate their strategic advantages by using treaty norms to prevent other states from developing or using weapons that would allow those other states to gain a potential battlefield advantage.[16] For the broad phenomenon of increasing international norm making as a whole, the most powerful explanation is probably that globalization—which has accelerated due to technological change—makes states more interdependent and forces them to regulate their interactions more intensively. In addition, as a contingent factor, the end of the Cold War created the opportunity for the United States and countries in Europe to consolidate their strategic advantages and advance their overlapping visions of world order by codifying in new rules and institutions many of their preferences for the management of international affairs. As a third factor, the end of the Cold War freed the UN bureaucracy, especially under Kofi Annan (secretary-general from 1997 to 2006), to expand its powers by pushing to increase its global role.

International regimes are technical and remote, so we are seldom aware of their impact on our lives or of the struggles that take place within them. But they are important nevertheless. The states that have entered into them use them to manage many consequential affairs. Once the rules are laid down, they tend to persist and to constrain states, because even when a state loses a dispute in a particular regime, the potential gain from abandoning the regime or of trying to redesign it is not worth the loss of the benefits that the regime provides to that state by coordinating its relations with other states. However, the rules are not static. Precisely because they matter, states have an incentive to try to shape the rules in their favor.

## CHINA JOINS

A striking feature of China's rise is that it has moved from a position of almost no participation in international regimes to the current position in which it participates in almost all of the major international regimes in which it is eligible to participate. (This sentence requires some unpacking. The use of "major" regimes acknowledges that at any given time in the international system a number of treaties and other international agreements have attracted participation from a minority of states, including, for example, the Convention on Cybercrime, the Anti-Counterfeiting Trade Agreement, and many conventions of the International Labor Organization. China is often among the majority that have not acceded to such instruments. The use of "almost all" indicates that there is a small number of widely acceded-to treaties that China has not joined—and often these are the same ones that the United States has rejected as well. These include the Rome Statute [the treaty that establishes the International Criminal Court] and the Land Mines Convention; likewise, China and the United States are among the small number of countries that reject the informal international norm that regards the death penalty as a violation of human rights law. The qualifier "in which it is eligible to participate" is meant to exclude such institutions as the Community of Democracies, which bars China on political grounds, the Missile Technology Control Regime, which for security reasons has not invited China to join, and, of course, regional organizations that China is not geographically eligible to join.)

During most of the period of Mao Zedong's rule (1949–1976), China rejected in principle ideas like arms control, international human rights, intellectual property rights protection, the exchange of public health information, and so on. It accepted no foreign direct investment and conducted little foreign trade. The PRC was a member of no international organization except, in the 1950s, those that formed parts of the socialist camp. After the PRC regained the China seat in the UN in 1971, the country began to join international organizations connected to the UN, such as the World Health Organization (WHO) and the Food and Agriculture Organization. It started to take an active role in UN bodies related to human rights. It regained the China seat in bodies such as the World Bank, the International Monetary Fund, the WTO, the Asian Development Bank, the International Olympic Committee, and so on.

As China intensified its embrace of globalization under Deng Xiaoping and his successors, it engaged more and more thoroughly with the international system, which, as noted earlier, was itself expanding at the same time. China applied in 1986 to join the GATT and in 2001 it was accepted into what had by then become the WTO. In the financial field it joined the major global standard–setting organizations, such as the Basel Committee on Banking Supervision, the Committee on Payment and Settlement Systems, and the Financial Stability Board.[17] China acceded to the main international conventions governing intellectual property rights, such as the Berne Convention.[18]

One of the most dramatic shifts came with China's participation in the global arms control and disarmament (ACD) regime. Under Mao, China rejected all international limits on the proliferation of missiles, nuclear weapons, and other weapons of mass destruction, arguing that such restrictions served only to consolidate what China called the "hegemony" of the two superpowers, the United States and the Soviet Union. Starting in the mid-1980s and accelerating during the 1990s, China acceded to a host of ACD treaties—including the Biological Weapons Convention (1984), the Nuclear Nonproliferation Treaty (1992), the Chemical Weapons Convention (1993), and the Comprehensive Test Ban Treaty (1996)—and it joined a long list of additional agreements, institutions, and committees.[19] Through its diplomatic activity, China cooperated with international efforts to prevent or roll back the nuclear weapons programs of North Korea and Iran.

Also noteworthy was China's embrace of the international human rights regime. Besides acknowledging the validity of the UDHR (which is not a treaty and hence cannot be signed by states), China ratified or acceded to the International Covenant on Economic, Social, and Cultural Rights, and the conventions on slavery, genocide, children's rights, women's rights, racial discrimination, torture, and the rights of persons with disabilities, among others. It signed the International Covenant on Civil and Political Rights in 1998, although it has not yet ratified it. In the 1984 Sino-British Joint Declaration on Hong Kong, China agreed to allow the two international covenants on civil and political rights and economic, social, and cultural rights to continue in force in Hong Kong for fifty years after its 1997 retrocession to Chinese sovereignty. China has been an active participant in the UN Human Rights Commission (later Council) and has promoted the codification of the right to development, the rights of indigenous peoples, and the rights of migrant workers, among others. In 1998 China entered into a dialogue with the newly established Office of the United Nations High Commissioner for Human Rights (OHCHR) and in 2000 it signed a memorandum of understanding for a program of technical cooperation on issues like human rights and education.

China's joining behavior is remarkable in a comparative perspective. India, for example, has been far less forthcoming in signing treaties and participating in international institutions. Its engagement has been hampered by its focus on immediate regional security problems, a continuing commitment to "strategic autonomy," a complex and inward-looking domestic political environment, and even a shortage of diplomatic staff. Although India has lobbied for permanent membership on the UN Security Council, it has kept an arms-length relationship with the World Bank and the International Monetary Fund, placed obstacles in the way of agreements in trade and climate negotiations, and avoided international arms control commitments.[20]

Why has China been such a strong joiner? Just as with the puzzle of regimes in general, different theories yield different answers to different parts of the puzzle. China presumably joined the international trade, intellectual property rights, finance, and other economics-related regimes in order to enjoy material benefits, a calculation that seems to have paid off. Although the motives for joining different parts of the arms control and disarmament regime are varied, in general the shift likely reflects Beijing's judgment that the agreements it has joined are beneficial for China's security.[21] In joining the human rights regime, Chinese policy makers probably have calculated that to gain most from its position as a UN Security Council "Permanent Five" state, China needs to position itself as an active participant in all the regimes closely associated with the UN, of which human rights is one. The diplomatic inconvenience of refusing to join one major regime while joining others is greater than the problem of managing participation within that particular regime, a challenge successfully addressed by many other states with human rights problems and with less impressively staffed foreign ministries. China could better manage attacks on its reputation by being within the regime than outside of it.[22]

In joining each regime China has not only achieved specific benefits, whether economic, military, or diplomatic, but has also gained the opportunity to try to shape the future evolution of that regime to its preferences. In joining the system as a whole, China has both gained access to and influence over the system as a whole and made itself a more consequential diplomatic actor with an enhanced ability to trade support and opposition with other states across normative platforms.

# CHINA COMPLIES

A second striking feature of China's rise is that it has complied with the regimes it has joined to approximately the same extent as any other state. This claim requires definition and substantiation. What is compliance? While there is no hard-and-fast answer to this question in the international relations or international law literatures, it will be sufficient for our purposes here to adopt a common-sense way of thinking about the issue.[23]

To begin with, compliance must be assessed differently with respect to hard vs. soft norms. We can conceive of a continuum that stretches from detailed, formal norms (e.g., WTO accession agreements, which are hundreds of pages long) through vague formal norms (human rights treaties, which are usually only a few pages long, or the IMF prohibition of currency manipulation, which consists of no more than a sentence in the organizaton's articles of agreement) to informal norms (e.g., the "level playing field" in international trade or the prohibition of the death penalty), to disputed norms (e.g., the meaning of the right of "innocent passage" in the UN Convention on the Law of the Sea [UNCLOS]), all the way to emerging norms that are not yet widely recognized as binding (e.g., the norm of the Responsibility to Protect [R2P]). Only with the most detailed and strictly defined norms, or those that can be applied to specific issues by an authoritative institution like the WTO or the European Court of Human Rights, can one say that compliance must take the form of implementing the letter of the law as interpreted by an independent authority. These are the "hard" norms. Soft norms are those that are vague enough so that it is hard to know where to draw the boundary between "interpreting" the norm and "violating" it. Even in the context of the WTO, in order to test the validity of an action one must first do something that another WTO member may regard as a violation, and then go through a process of negotiation or adjudication to find out how the WTO dispute settlement system will ultimately apply the norm to the action taken. To take another example of the difficulty of knowing who is complying with a norm and who is violating it, in order to qualify to enter into a negotiation over sovereignty over a land form at sea, one must first establish a claim to that land form under the customary international law principles of (among others) occupation and display of sovereignty—as indeed China and other claimants have done in the South and East China Seas—and vindicate this claim by taking actions that other claimants are likely to call illegal. Who was right and who was wrong will be determined only when the competing claims are resolved, whether through armed conflict, negotiation, or a ruling by an international court. Where norms are informal or vague and an adjudication mechanism is lacking—for example, with the IMF norm against the manipulation of currency exchange rates—the only way to establish what a norm means is to violate another member's claim about it and see whether the other party can force compliance that conforms to its interpretation.

It may seem paradoxical to say that a country or state confirms its membership in a regime by violating one of its norms. But the appearance of paradox is created by fallaciously viewing the norm as more fixed than it is, or as meaning only what one actor says it means, or by imagining the international system as functioning like a domestic legal system to a greater extent than it actually does. Even within a domestic legal system the actors (for example, corporations) test and push forward even very specific rules (such as the tax code) by looking for loopholes and seeing whether their interpretations of those loopholes stand up under administrative review or in court. If we see the essence of norms as contested, interactional, and evolving, then China is "in" by contesting the norm and would only be "out" if it rejected the norm. This is admittedly a difficult distinction, but one that must be made in order to understand how any country relates to the international normative system.

To add to the complexity, for China as for other states, complying with a regime often requires a phase-in period, either as a matter of law (as in the case of China's WTO accession agreement) or as a practical matter (as in the case of bringing diverse domestic actors into line with national commitments on arms control, intellectual property rights, or environmental protections). Compliance may remain a work in progress, if the central government finds it difficult to enforce its international commitments via bureaucratic agencies, local governments, and corporations and other private actors that have an interest in avoiding compliance.[24]

Finally, there are some norms that are so contested that it is difficult to say whether the actors promoting the norm or those resisting them should be considered more compliant. For example, there has been an ongoing struggle over the extent to which the UN Security Council has the power to authorize interventions in the internal affairs of states in pursuit of "international peace and security" (known as Chapter VII powers) or to protect the human rights and humanitarian needs of the domestic populations of states (known as Chapter VI powers, or the so-called R2P norm). China, joined by other actors, including Russia, has often watered down, blocked, and occasionally vetoed Chapter VI and Chapter VII interventions desired by the United

States and some European governments, often citing the norm of state sovereignty as a reason for opposing an intervention. One cannot at this point say which side of this debate is more intensively complying with or violating international norms because the normative balance between sovereignty and intervention remains intensely contested.

With respect to any given norm within any given regime, it is possible to conceptualize a continuum of degrees of compliance that range from explicit refusal (*rejection*), to an obvious or acknowledged breach (*violation*), to acknowledgment of a norm as binding but with significant and substantive noncompliance (*hypocritical compliance*), to an in-between state of significant and substantive compliance paired with significant noncompliance (*partial compliance*), to a state of working to come into compliance (*emerging compliance*), to a state of full formal and substantive compliance (*full compliance*). A residual category must be left for norms like the R2P that are not yet clear enough to enable one to say who is complying and who is not. Using this rough continuum, China's regime-compliance behavior at the present time can be described in the following way.

## Rejection

Although in the Mao period China rejected in principle the legitimacy of all the then-prevailing international regimes, today it does not reject any of them in principle.

## Violation

There are no known regimes that China has joined and has then violated across the board.

## Hypocritical Compliance

China has joined the international human rights regime and complies with it in all formal respects. It attends all necessary meetings and files on time all necessary reports with the relevant treaty bodies. It has undergone the Human Rights Council's process of universal periodic review. It participates in some programs with the Office of the High Commissioner for Human Rights and participates in bilateral human rights dialogues with several Western states. In 2004 the National People's Congress amended the Chinese constitution to say, "The State respects and preserves human rights." Substantively, China has made progress in achieving many economic, social, and cultural rights. But a wide range of its actions at home systematically violate widely recognized civil and political rights.[25] The Chinese government does not acknowledge these acts as violations. It variously says that the acts are in conformity with Chinese law or that it complies with international norms by engaging in a process to eliminate violations that still occur.

A more controversial example is China's alleged noncompliance with the International Monetary Fund's norm against currency manipulation. The IMF's articles of agreement commit members "to assure orderly exchange arrangements and to promote a stable system of exchange rates." Some Western analysts and politicians have accused China of violating its IMF obligation to allow the market to set currency exchange rates. IMF standards are vague, though, and China claims that it does not violate them.[26] China undergoes the required IMF review process and has gradually allowed the exchange value of its currency to appreciate until it reached what the IMF in 2015 deemed a fair-market value; that year it modestly expanded the trading range within which it allowed its currency to trade. Whether these actions bring China into full compliance with IMF rules remains controversial. But, as one commentator has put it, "the accusation that China is today violating the rules [of the international monetary regime] is far-fetched; the rules do not exist."[27]

## Partial Compliance

Because of the secrecy that attends arms transfers, it is hard to be sure how strictly China has complied with its ACD obligations. On the one hand, it is not clear from the public record that China has ever violated an explicit arms control treaty commitment after signing that treaty. Even if China's arms sales were legal under its international law commitments, the United States has often accused China of violating other nontreaty nonproliferation norms or commitments. For example, on the basis that China's arms sales were generally destabilizing, the United States accused China of proliferation when it supplied a nuclear power plant to Algeria, missiles to Syria, Silkworm missiles to Iran, and so on. The fact that until 2007 the United States was still announcing sanctions on specific Chinese companies for prohibited transfers to Iran suggests that there may have been some continuing transfers of chemical weapons precursors and missile-related technologies after China agreed not to make them. So far as we know, however, China eventually complied with US demands in all of those cases.[28]

## Emerging Compliance

This category might apply to China's position with respect to its WTO obligations. China's WTO accession agreement required the country to phase in various changes over the course of five, ten, and fifteen years after 2001, and we know that the central government has in many respects worked to do so. Indeed, even before acceding to the WTO, China had reformed many of its domestic laws and institutions to "join tracks" (*jiegui*) with global trade norms. But the central government has faced resistance from large state enterprises, related ministries, and local governments. A major study of China's record during its first ten years of membership in the WTO concludes, "Beijing is generally engaging in an 'acceptable level of compliance' with its WTO commitments and has demonstrated a willingness to abide by WTO rules and operate within the WTO system."[29] Another study found that, as of April 2013, regarding WTO disputes against China that had reached the panel or appellate body stage and in which China had been found in violation of at least one term of its WTO obligations, China had fully complied with the panel or appellate body recommendations in a timely manner in all but one case compared to twenty-five of fifty-six cases for the United States.[30]

It is characteristic of the WTO regime that every country interprets, stretches, and tests the rules. China and its trading partners, especially the United States and the European Union, have charged each other with numerous violations. It should be considered a sign of compliance rather than noncompliance that China has taken its disputes to the WTO and has complied with most decisions handed down against it by the organization's dispute settlement procedures.[31]

Other regimes in which China seems to be in the midst of the process of coming into compliance are the international public health regime (cooperating more closely to provide timely and accurate information to the WHO on public health events and to share information and samples with foreign partners like the US Centers for Disease Control and Prevention);[32] military transparency (an informal norm with which China increasingly complies by issuing national defense white papers, although these are far from giving as much information as foreign partners desire); environmental protection (China cooperates more than in the past with international agencies and NGOs promoting various elements of environmental protection);[33] and management of financial institutions (as Chinese stock markets, banks, and other financial institutions move closer to international standards).[34]

## Full Compliance

China complies fully and noncontroversially with a large number of regimes. Many are purely functional regimes that involve mutual benefit and have no obvious political component. These include the international postal regime, the air travel regime, the international police regime (e.g., Interpol), the international arbitration regime, international sports law, and the international tourism regime.

If one asks why China complies with some regimes more than with others, the answer seems obvious—it does so when the demonstrable benefits outweigh the economic and political costs. This finding tends to support the realist and institutionalist explanations of compliance and requires little help from constructivist theory to make sense of the pattern of behavior.

Human rights may seem to be the exception to this pattern, since the Chinese government does not believe it can use international civil and political rights standards as a tool to enhance domestic stability nor has it enjoyed much success in its attempts to use international human rights standards to counterattack Western critics. China has had to play the human rights game defensively but it has done so not by opting out but by engaging.[35] However, it has not carried its compliance so far as to grant political rights and freedoms that the leadership believes would endanger its hold on power.

The classifications and examples offered in this section are open to challenges and corrections but the larger point survives: China is broadly similar to every other major state in its pattern of compliance with international regimes, in that it is more compliant than not.

## CHINA'S ROLE IN THE EVOLUTION OF INTERNATIONAL REGIMES

One of the reasons why the question of compliance is hard to evaluate is that, as already noted, no international regime is static. All are in a state of constant change, some of course more dramatically than others. The typology of levels of compliance depends on measuring a state's behavior against a given interpretation of a given set of regime norms at a given point in time. But states are also constantly proposing new interpretations of existing norms as well as new norms to be added to (or occasionally subtracted from) existing regimes, and sometimes seek to establish completely new regimes.

Regimes evolve through processes that could be labeled interpretation, negotiation, contestation, and innovation. Interpretation takes place as the members, involved bureaucracies, and interested civil society actors debate over how to interpret the rules and institutions that exist and seek rulings from international courts, "soft law" authorities like law professors, or via an emerging consensus. Negotiation takes place as actors try to create new rules and institutions; it can take the form of diplomatic discourse or can occur through lobbying, posturing, mobilizing the public, or actions aimed at enforcing norms. Contestation takes place when states undertake tests of strength over the interpretation of regimes, such as threatening trade or financial sanctions over economic disputes or confronting one another militarily over varying interpretations of territorial or security interests.[36] Innovation is the creation of new sets of rules. Although most international regimes are ultimately created by states, other actors—transnational action networks (TANs), NGOs, corporations, aggrieved communities or peoples, UN staff members, UN treaty bodies, academic experts, individual plaintiffs before international human rights courts, and others—may engage in or seek to influence these processes.[37]

Every state with a degree of expertise and staffing related to a particular regime participates in this process of regime evolution, and China is no exception. The overall pattern of Chinese compliance with regimes includes efforts to shape these regimes. As China's power has increased—and its diplomats' sophistication about each regime's rules has grown—it has increasingly become not only a rule follower, but a rule shaper.[38]

This leads to the question: What is China's negotiating position in each regime? (The term "negotiating position" must include not only a country's proposals and its positions for and against other states' proposals, but also the rhetoric and behavior that it uses to interpret the regime.) This topic is hard to study because each regime has unique technical aspects. However, negotiating positions are in another way more easily understood than some other topics: a negotiating position taken within an international regime has to be made known to the international community in order to be effectively pursued (although it may be revealed in stages and is bound to be clothed in the most attractive possible rationale). The study of the Chinese government's negotiating positions should therefore give us a more transparent view of its foreign policy goals than the study of, for example, its military goals, which remain partially secret. We can compare China's known positions to those of other actors, especially those of "the West"—usually understood to be the United States and the EU, although they are sometimes not the same.

Because there are so many international regimes in operation today, only a sample can be addressed here. Given the complexity of each regime it is possible to characterize China's negotiating position only in broad terms. The discussion is roughly organized in categories, starting with economic, security, and human rights, and then touching on a miscellany of regimes in other functional areas.

## International Trade

The Doha Round of negotiations by the WTO was launched in 2001, the same year that China joined the WTO. This round has not reached an agreed-on resolution at the time of writing but is regarded by many commentators as essentially dormant. Although some analysts have blamed China for the lack of progress in the Doha Round, most agree that China has adopted a relatively passive position in these negotiations; some even characterize the Chinese role as moderately helpful.[39] Given that the issues on the table are of peripheral relevance to Chinese trade interests—which generally center on the export of manufactured goods—China has tended to side with other developing countries that have more at stake, thereby fostering diplomatic goodwill. It has backed positions that call for the elimination of agricultural subsidies by developed countries, to allow developing countries' agricultural products to be more competitive on world markets.

In regional trade negotiations, China's position favors further opening world markets to manufactured exports, which would obviously benefit China as a manufacturing powerhouse.[40] China has so far not shown a clear desire to join the Trans Pacific Partnership, a framework that the United States is negotiating with various regional partners, presumably because the TPP would impose environmental and labor rights conditions that Chinese policy makers view as unfavorable to China's interests. China has worked to join or create bilateral and regional FTAs, such as the China-ASEAN Free Trade Area, the Regional Comprehensive Economic Partnership, and the Free Trade Area of the Asia-Pacific, all of which set lower standards for environmental and social protections than the TPP.

In the WTO, China has used its positions as a complainant, a defendant, and an interested party to try to clarify issue areas in its own interest. For example, it has argued that its pricing system does not constitute "dumping" and it has begun to use its domestic laws to exert an influence on the international trading system: with the implementation of its 2008 antimonopoly law China became one of only three markets (along with the United States and the European Union) with the power to regulate mergers of transnational corporations. A wave of investigations of foreign firms operating in China on allegations of monopolistic behavior, fraud, and corruption have been interpreted either as an effort to clean up the Chinese marketplace or as an attempt to use Chinese laws to create advantages for homegrown competitors.

In all, China's negotiating positions in the international trade regime are obviously interest-driven. The interests being protected, and the corresponding negotiating positions, are in some respects compatible with those of other major trading nations—namely, to expand international trade—and in other respects are adverse—namely, to enjoy competitive advantages in its own and in others' markets. The pursuit of these interests by way of trade agreements and institutionalized dispute resolution conforms to the open but rule-bound character of the contemporary international trade regime.

## International Finance

China's positions vis-à-vis the international finance regime likewise appear to be pragmatic and interest-driven, and the changes China seeks appear to be adaptive rather than revolutionary. Within the IMF, China has lobbied for an increase in the quota shares and voting rights of its own and other emerging countries to reflect their growing shares of world GDP. It has sought changes in the IMF's annual review of every country's currency practices as well as changes to the governance and transparency requirements for IMF loan recipients. At the same time it has cooperated with other countries in creating some regional financial institutions that operate independently of the IMF and thereby give China and other cooperating countries the power to act without the approval of the United States and other old-line financial powers. These regional mechanisms include the Chiang Mai Initiative Multilateralization Agreement and the Asian Bond Fund. Such efforts seek to increase China's clout on the international financial stage; they are consistent with its growing economic power but also show that China intends to use this clout to help maintain the global financial stability that is necessary for its foreign trade to prosper.

The United States and other trading partners have lobbied to get China to increase the exchange value of the *yuan* and move toward free convertibility, and Chinese policy makers have done both of these things, although more slowly than the country's trading partners wanted. (China, meanwhile, showed strong concern for the stability of the US dollar during and after the 2008 financial crisis.) By gradually strengthening its currency, creating currency swap arrangements with some trading partners, selling bonds denominated in the Chinese currency (called the *renminbi*), and authorizing *renminbi* clearing and trading operations ("hubs") in several foreign countries, China has begun to challenge the hegemony of the dollar and the euro as international reserve currencies.

China has not pushed any of these initiatives to the point of hampering the functioning of the existing financial system, however. On the contrary, measures taken by China have served to facilitate the international flow of currencies: it continues to use the dollar, the euro, and other international currencies in its trade—as indeed it must if it wishes to conduct a high volume of foreign trade—and continues to hold its foreign exchange reserves in assets chiefly denominated in these currencies. Although some analysts perceive a Chinese intention to replace the dollar with the yuan as the main international reserve currency, most think that China has no such ambition for the foreseeable future.[41] In short, according to one analyst, "[W]hile continuing to call for more substantial reforms on the existing global financial architecture, Beijing has been neither a key policy innovator nor a principal objectionist vetoing major policy initiatives. China has played a constructive role in the institutionalization of the G-20 summit and the reform of the FSF/FSB [Financial Stability Forum/Financial Stability Board] even though it did not take the lead in those global initiatives."[42]

China has recently played a key role in the creation of two development banks outside the previous Bretton Woods framework of the IMF, the World Bank, and the Asian Development Bank. They are the BRICS New Bank, announced in 2012, and the Asian Infrastructure Investment Bank, established in 2014. The mere fact of channeling more money into development loans presents no challenge to the existing international system. It remains to be seen to what extent the operations of these banks will challenge the lending standards of the older institutions.

## Arms Control and Disarmament

China's participation in the existing ACD regime supports the strategic status quo. It has backed opposition to North Korean and Iranian nuclear weapons development and proliferation and supported the further development of the ACD regime in certain respects. In these ways, China's positions support the idea of limiting arms development, proliferation, and utilization by international agreement.

On the other hand, many of its specific negotiating positions related to the development of the regime have served its own strategic interests by weakening or constraining areas of American superiority. For example, China supports the declaration of nuclear-free zones, which the United States—the dominant nuclear power—does not support. China backs treaties that would ban the first use of nuclear weapons, ban the development of antiballistic missiles, and ban an arms race in outer space—all areas in which the United States enjoys advantages. China advocates the "norm of nondiscrimination" by which nonproliferation does not only target certain regimes like Iran and North Korea but is universalistic. Also, China favors persuasive measures instead of coercive ones (e.g., military strikes or sanctions) to enforce nonproliferation commitments, a stance that comports with its maintenance of good relations with Iran and North Korea. As a smaller nuclear power China is less concerned than the United States or Russia with limiting the growth of nuclear arsenals; it is more concerned with agreements on nuclear operations and the ways in which nuclear forces are targeted, alerted, and otherwise prepared for potential use. As a major user of nuclear energy and uranium importer, China is in favor of the establishment of a global nuclear fuel supply mechanism, in which China would probably emerge as a major supplier.[43] In short, China is a supporter of the ACD regime as such, but, like other countries, it pursues its own interests with respect to how that regime is developed and how its rules are applied.

## Human Rights

Over the past quarter-century China has exerted considerable influence over the way the international human rights regime works. As a member of the Human Rights Council, China and cooperating states pushed a principle of universality that reduces the degree to which individual countries are singled out for targeted attention. The current process of universal periodic review, which China helped promote, subjects all states—the United States as much as China—to review by the council, and it does so in a way that allows the state under review and its sympathizers to shape the agenda of the review. Similarly, China was one of the promoters of a council initiative to require each state to submit a human rights action plan—something China has done—to put forward its own interpretation of how international human rights norms should be interpreted for application in that country. China had already been doing this by issuing a series of white papers on the subject in previous years. China has worked to restrict the role of NGOs in the operation of the council and in the treaty bodies and to restrict the length and content of mandates given by the council to the so-called special procedures. The net effect of these efforts has been to position China in compliance with self-set priorities and to insulate it from serious pressure from the Human Rights Council, a posture which it undoubtedly views as an improvement over the pressures it felt from the council's predecessor, the Human Rights Commission, in the early 1990s.[44]

China has found widespread support among other states for the position that it is up to each state to interpret how its international human rights obligations are interpreted and implemented within its domestic political system. China (along with Russia and others) has pioneered regulations and administrative measures that make it difficult for foreign NGOs to carry out their activities inside the country and for domestic NGOs to receive foreign funding without prior government approval. China and like-minded countries have tried to delegitimize international democracy promotion as a form of subversion.[45]

China has sought to establish a norm that government-to-government complaints about human rights issues should be conducted in private and that public airing of such interventions is disruptive of diplomatic courtesy. In the area of state-to-state human rights dialogues, China has promoted the norm that such dialogues should be done in secret, that they should be bilateral rather than multilateral, that foreign dialogue partners should not coordinate with one another, and that nongovernmental specialist components of these dialogues need to be vetted and approved by both sides (i.e., each state can veto participants proposed by the other side). These restrictions have sapped the value of human rights dialogues by frequently postponing them and, when they are held, by reducing them to pro forma exchanges.[46]

China and its partners in the Shanghai Cooperation Organization (SCO) challenged a well-established human rights norm when they concluded secret treaties that allowed for the *refoulement* (defined in international law as the coerced return of a refugee despite a well-founded fear of political persecution) from one SCO member state to another of any of its own citizens that the receiving state has designated as a terrorist.[47] China has also insisted on the *refoulement* of its citizens from other states, including Pakistan, Cambodia, and Thailand, on the grounds that it has designated them as terrorists. However, these actions occurred against a background in which the United States was also challenging the existing norms on torture and "extraordinary rendition" by sending suspected terrorists to countries where they could be expected to be tortured. China was therefore not alone in trying to alter the way in which prevailing due process norms would apply in the new situation of an international "war on terror."

Given its diplomatic achievements in shaping the human rights regime in ways that blunt that regime's ability to embarrass or influence the Chinese government, China does not appear to be aiming either for major changes in the regime or for its abandonment. It appears to be content to work within the existing human rights institutions to shape them to its own interests.

## Humanitarian intervention, R2P, and UN Peacekeeping

As liberal democracies have promoted the expanded use of humanitarian intervention, China is one of many states that have gone along only partially with this normative shift while emphasizing the need to continue to respect the previously (and arguably still) dominant norm of nonintervention in the internal affairs of states. As a permanent, veto-bearing member of the UN Security Council, China has sometimes allowed interventionist resolutions to be adopted (either by abstaining or by voting in favor of them) but it has also often delayed, modified, or blocked such resolutions on the ground that states should settle their internal problems by themselves. When China has allowed such resolutions to go forward, it has usually done so to maintain solidarity with Russia, to align itself with states in an affected region (e.g., it voted with the African Union on the Sudan and with the Arab League on Libya), or to protect its economic interests (e.g., again in the Sudan and Libya), and has insisted on the proviso that the intervention should not be used to overthrow the regime in the targeted country.[48]

With respect to the emergent R2P norm promoted by some UN officials and Western statesmen, Rosemary Foot writes, "Beijing was a full participant in the debate that generated the World Summit Outcome document of September 2005. . . . [Beijing] placed its main efforts behind the state capacity-building functions of the R2P mandate—what is referred to as Pillar I. . . . It has also worked to ensure R2P's focused application and a definition that constrains the operational methods associated with humanitarian intervention. . . . Beijing has aimed to develop the norm in a direction that gives primacy to the preventative aspects . . . in the hope of diminishing the instances where the norm of non-interference . . . is breached. . . . Its interpretation . . . lies at the conservative end of the spectrum when compared with the positions of several of its Asian neighbours."[49]

On UN peacekeeping, China moved from opposing such operations to actively supporting and participating in them, but it emphasizes the principles of host state consent and the use of development projects as part of the peacekeeping process.[50] China seems content to continue to implement its nuanced position regarding this set of norms, accepting the right of the international community acting through the UN to intervene in the domestic affairs of states but under conditions more restrictive than those favored by some other governments. Such a position allows China to position itself as a peacefully rising developing country rather than as an assertive great power and to support or oppose interventions based on its specific interests in each case, including the need to maintain solidarity with regional organizations and the desire to limit as far as possible the United States' use of humanitarian intervention as a pretext for increasing its own influence.

## Other Regimes

Under Hillary Clinton, the US Department of State pursued an initiative to codify a broad concept of information freedom in several international venues. China (and like-minded states) pushed back. In 2011, "delegates from China, Russia, Tajikistan, and Uzbekistan submitted a joint proposal for a 'Code of Conduct for Information Security' at the 66th session of the UN General Assembly. The proposal calls for greater state-based regulation of the Internet rather than the current multistakeholder arrangement."[51] Within the Shanghai Cooperation Organization (SCO), China supported a Russian push to define the concept of "information warfare" and called for a norm of cyber disarmament. At the December 2012 meeting of the International Telecommunications Union, China, Russia, and other states submitted a proposal that would, according to one source, "redefine the Internet as a system of government-controlled, state-supervised networks."[52] It is clear that the Chinese would prefer to define international norms on the Internet in ways that are very different from American ideas of free speech, but given the facts that free speech boundaries vary widely even among Western countries, and that the Internet is relatively new, it is hard to say at this point whether the American position or the position of China and its allies represents a more radical challenge to existing global norms.

The law of the sea is inherently complicated, and China, like all other states, has interpreted the law in its own favor. Having acceded to the UNCLOS in 1996, China has interpreted its provisions on the continental shelf and exclusive economic zones (EEZs) to claim control over large maritime areas. It has based its claims to land forms at sea on customary international law provisions such as first discovery, continued occupation, effective administration, and unchallenged claims. China interprets the UNCLOS provision on "freedom of navigation" differently from the US, seeking to deny US navy ships and air force planes the right to conduct intelligence operations in Chinese EEZs without Chinese permission.[53] (The United States has not acceded to the UNCLOS but says that it respects its provisions, and interprets the innocent passage rule as allowing military noncombat operations within other countries' EEZs.)

China, India, and other developing countries support the Kyoto Protocol principle that says that developed countries should reduce emissions sooner and faster than developing countries and should also provide financial support for developing countries to change their energy economies. Meanwhile, China is actually moving faster on renewables than the United States—not necessarily in response to international requirements, but as part of its own energy security policy.[54]

China resists stricter rules in the World Intellectual Property Organization (WIPO), the institution through which intellectual property rights norms are negotiated. China has less intellectual property to protect and needs to acquire more. The United States has pushed for stricter rules.

China is an "upriver" state, with eleven of its major rivers flowing into neighboring states. However, the underdeveloped international water regime imposes no specific obligation on China to respect the water rights of downriver states. "So far China has been largely unresponsive to the concerns of its [downriver] neighbors, among them India, Kazakhstan, Myanmar, Russia, and Vietnam. Since 1997, China has declined to sign a United Nations water-sharing treaty that would govern the thirteen major transnational rivers on its territory. 'To fight for every drop of water or die' is how China's former water resources minister, Wang Shucheng, once described the nation's water policy."[55]

This quick review supports the view that China's negotiating positions are generally interest-based, and those interests lie in protecting its material well-being, enhancing its influence, and diminishing the influence of rival powers like the United States. China has participated in—and sometimes led—the creation of new agreements and organizations that conduct work similar to the work of existing international organizations but which often do not include the United States and other Western powers. These include the Shanghai Cooperation Organization, the Chiang Mai Initiative Multilateralization, the BRICS New Bank, the Asian Infrastructure Investment Bank, and the Regional Comprehensive Economic Partnership. These institutions may enhance Chinese influence and autonomy but so far they have introduced few operating norms that are different from those of incumbent regimes. For example, the Chiang Mai Initiative attempts to protect exchange rate stability; the RCEP aims to promote free trade. One study of these initiatives concludes, "Chinese foreign policy is not seeking to demolish or exit from current international organizations and multilateral regimes. Instead, it is constructing supplementary—in part complementary, in part competitive—channels for shaping the international order beyond Western claims to leadership."[56] No evidence has been found to support the belief that China seeks to abandon, overthrow, or fundamentally revolutionize any of these regimes.

## CONCLUSION

Chinese behavior does not show a pattern of promoting a distinctive "Chinese model" in the international normative system or an alternative vision of world order. If there is a larger pattern, it is that China tends to be a conservative power that resists efforts by the United States and its partners to shape regimes in ways that are unfavorable to China and its partners. This happens fairly often, because the United States continues to actively try to shape the future evolution of regimes. In its competition with the United States and its allies, China often defends the more old-fashioned interpretation of sovereignty against efforts to reinterpret sovereignty in a more limited way. In this sense China is more of a status quo power than the United States. Given that China usually argues the more traditional position, in these debates over sovereignty existing law is often on its side. In this sense, China's positions on human rights and humanitarian intervention can be seen as nonideological, while those of the United States and its allies are ideological in the sense that they seek to promote certain values that are relatively new to the international system. On the other hand, when China has an interest in challenging the traditional interpretation of a norm or creating a new norm, it does so (e.g., in promoting its interpretation of restrictions on foreign military operations in EEZs under the UNCLOS or promoting the norm of nonweaponization of space). Thus China is not wedded to traditional positions when its interests dictate a change in international norms.

As long as China roughly continues on its current trajectory—that is, politically stable with a growing economy—its stake in various international regimes is unlikely to change dramatically. It likely will continue to gain more than it loses from the trade, finance, and arms control regimes and will resist Western efforts to strengthen the human rights, humanitarian intervention, and information freedom regimes. If China becomes an even stronger power relative to its rivals it is likely to bid for more influence in existing regimes rather than try to overthrow them. If it suffers economic or political setbacks it will have less influence on the evolution of the regimes but it will hardly be able to afford to abandon them. While China will continue to influence the evolution of global norms, it is difficult to imagine a realistic scenario in which it will try to revolutionize or overthrow the liberal international order.

## NOTES

1. "Not exclusively" because, for example, the international Olympic movement is managed by nonstate actors, i.e., the national Olympic committees. This broad definition of regimes serves the purposes of the present inquiry better than a narrow definition, so I include informal as well as formal rules and institutions and both state and nonstate actors.

2. Among others, Jan-Erik Lane, "On the Growth in Normativity in International Relations," *Journal of Politics and Law* 6, no. 1 (2013): 15–23.

3. Kenneth Waltz, *Theory of International Politics* (New York: Random House, 1979).

4. G. John Ikenberry, *Liberal Leviathan: The Origins, Crisis, and Transformation of the American World Order* (Princeton, NJ: Princeton University Press, 2011). In Ikenberry's conception the liberal international order was created under American dominance but can persist even if American hegemony wanes.

5. Examples include Alastair Iain Johnston, *Social States: China in International Relations, 1980–2000* (Princeton, NJ: Princeton University Press, 2008); Rosemary Foot and Andrew Walter, *China, the United States, and Global Order* (New York: Cambridge University Press, 2011); Ann Kent, *Beyond Compliance: China, International Organizations, and Global Security* (Stanford, CA: Stanford University Press, 2007); Joel Wuthnow, *Chinese Diplomacy and the UN Security Council: Beyond the Veto* (New York: Routledge, 2013).

6. An interest-based explanation does not entirely rule out the effects of learning, especially prudential or instrumental learning about the way a given regime works and the opportunities it offers to pursue interests and about security dangers that were not previously salient or appreciated. But an interest-based explanation does not include changes in ultimate goals or values.

7. A similar approach—leading to similar conclusions—is taken by Scott Kennedy and Shuaihua Cheng, *From Rule Takers to Rule Makers: The Growing Role of Chinese in Global Governance* (Bloomington, IN: Indiana University Research Center for Chinese Politics and Business and the International Centre for Trade and Sustainable Development, September 2012), at https://rccpb.indiana.edu /pdf/Chinese%20Rule%20Makers%20RED%20Sept%202012.pdf, accessed February 27, 2015.

8. For example, John J. Mearsheimer, *The Tragedy of Great Power Politics* (New York: W. W. Norton, 2014); Martin Jacques, *When China Rules the World: The End of the Western World and the Birth of a New Global Order* (New York: Penguin, 2009); Henry Kissinger, *On China* (New York: Penguin, 2011); Aaron L. Friedberg, *A Contest for Supremacy: China, America, and the Struggle for Mastery in Asia* (New York: W. W. Norton, 2011); Rex Li, *A Rising China and Security*

*in East Asia: Identity Construction and Security Discourse* (London: Routledge, 2009); David C. Kang, *China Rising: Peace, Power, and Order in East Asia* (New York: Columbia University Press, 2009); Randall Schweller and Xiaoyu Pu, "After Unipolarity: China's Visions of International Order in an Era of U.S. Decline," *International Security* 36, no. 1 (Summer 2011): 41–72.

9. Andrew J. Nathan and Andrew Scobell, *China's Search for Security* (New York: Columbia University Press, 2012); David Shambaugh, *China Goes Global: The Partial Power* (New York: Oxford University Press, 2013).

10. Amitav Acharya, *The End of American World Order* (Cambridge, UK: Polity, 2014), 50.

11. Mark Leonard, "Why Convergence Breeds Conflict: Growing More Similar Will Push China and the United States Apart," *Foreign Affairs* 92, no. 5 (September/October 2013): 125–35. Other authors who believe China seeks to fundamentally alter the world order include Jacques, *When China Rules*; Charles Kupchan, *No One's World: The West, the Rising Rest, and the Coming Global Turn* (New York: Oxford University Press, 2012); and Michael Pillsbury, *The Hundred-Year Marathon: China's Secret Strategy to Replace America as the Global Superpower* (New York: Henry Holt, 2014).

12. G. John Ikenberry, "The Future of the Liberal World Order: Internationalism after America," *Foreign Affairs* 90, no. 3 (May/June 2011): 57. Other works offering similar arguments include Yong Deng, *China's Struggle for Status: The Realignment of International Relations* (New York: Cambridge University Press, 2008); and Marc Lanteigne, *China and International Institutions: Alternate Paths to Global Power* (London: Routledge, 2005).

13. Emilie M. Hafner-Burton, *Forced to Be Good: Why Trade Agreements Boost Human Rights* (Ithaca, NY: Cornell University Press, 2009), esp. chaps. 1, 6.

14. Tanisha Fazal, *State Death: The Politics and Geography of Conquest, Occupation, and Annexation* (Princeton, NJ: Princeton University Press, 2007).

15. Among others, see Thomas Risse, Stephen C. Ropp, and Kathryn Sikkink, eds., *The Power of Human Rights* (New York: Cambridge University Press, 1999); and Kathryn Sikkink, *The Justice Cascade: How Human Rights Prosecutions Are Changing World Politics* (New York: W. W. Norton, 2011). However, a realist explanation is also possible; see Andrew J. Nathan, "China and International Human Rights: Tiananmen's Paradoxical Impact," in Jean-Philippe Béja, ed., *The Impact of China's 1989 Tiananmen Massacre* (London: Routledge, 2010), 206–20.

16. For example, nuclear states can preserve their advantage by banning proliferation of nuclear weapons to nonnuclear states; states not possessing the capability to develop space weapons can diminish the advantage of states that possess space weapons or the capacity to develop them by banning the use of space weapons.

17. Injoo Sohn, "Between Confrontation and Assimilation: China and the Fragmentation of Global Financial Governance," *Journal of Contemporary China* 22, no. 82 (July 2013): 642.

18. Martin Dimitrov, *Piracy and the State: The Politics of Intellectual Property Rights in China* (New York: Cambridge University Press, 2009).

19. Shirley Kan, "China and Proliferation of Weapons of Mass Destruction and Missiles: Policy Issues," CRS Report for Congress, Order Code RL31555 (2007).

20. Waheguru Pal Singh Sidhu, Pratap Bhanu Mehta, and Bruce Jones, eds., *Shaping the Emerging World: India and the Multilateral Order* (Washington, DC: Brookings Institution, 2013).

21. China gained by seeing certain weapons banned that it did not want to use or to see used, such as chemical and biological; from nonproliferation by seeing its advantage over nonnuclear states sustained; from disarmament by seeing its nuclear disadvantage relative to the United States and Russia diminished; from promoting nuclear free zones by creating a disincentive for the use of nuclear threats by other nuclear powers; and so on. For more arguments along these lines see Nathan and Scobell, *China's Search for Security*, chap. 11. Other factors included American lobbying and China's "social learning" from other states. See Evan S. Medeiros, *Reluctant Restraint: The Evolution of China's Nonproliferation Policies and Practices, 1980–2004* (Stanford, CA: Stanford University Press, 2007); and Johnston, *Social States*.

22. Nathan and Scobell, *China's Search*, chap. 12.

23. For example, see Abram Chayes and Antonia Handler Chayes, "On Compliance," *International Organization* 47, no. 2 (Spring 1993): 175–205.

24. For example, Medeiros, *Reluctant Restraint*; Dimitrov, *Piracy and the State*; Elizabeth Economy, *The River Runs Black: The Environmental Challenge to China's Future* (Ithaca, NY: Cornell University Press, 2005).

25. Rosemary Foot, *Rights beyond Borders: The Global Community and the Struggle over Human Rights in China* (Oxford, UK: Oxford University Press, 2000); Ann Kent, *China, the United Nations, and Human Rights* (Philadelphia: University of Pennsylvania Press, 1999).

26. Jonathan E. Sanford, "Currency Manipulation: The IMF and WTO," CRS Report for Congress, January 28, 2011, at http://www.fas.org/sgp/crs/misc/RS22658.pdf, accessed April 2, 2013; also see Foot and Walter, *China, the United States, and Global Order*.

27. Michel Aglietta, "Prospects for the International Monetary System: Key Questions," in Jan Wouters, Tanguy de Wilde d'Estmael, Pierre Defraigne, and Jean-Christophe Defraigne, eds., *China, the European Union, and Global Governance* (Cheltenham, UK: Edward Elgar, 2012), 157.

28. Medeiros, *Reluctant Restraint;* John W. Garver, *China and Iran: Ancient Partners in a Post-Imperial World* (Seattle: University of Washington Press, 2006).

29. Ka Zeng, Conclusion, in Ka Zeng and Wei Liang, eds., *China and Global Trade Governance: China's First Decade in the World Trade Organization* (London: Routledge, 2013), 283.

30. Xiaowen Zhang and Xiaoling Li, "The Politics of Compliance with Adverse WTO Dispute Settlement Rulings in China," *Journal of Contemporary China* 23, no. 85 (2013): 144.

31. Marcia Don Harpaz, "Sense and Sensibilities of China and WTO Dispute Settlement," in Zeng and Liang, eds., *China and Global Trade Governance,* 233–60.

32. Gerald Chan, Pak K. Lee and Lai-Ha Chan, *China Engages Global Governance: A New World Order in the Making?* (London: Routledge, 2012), chap. 7.

33. Chan, Lee, and Chan, *China Engages*, chap. 6.

34. Chan, Lee, and Chan, *China Engages*, chap. 4.

35. Nathan, "China and International Human Rights," in Béja, ed., *The Impact.*

36. For example, the US Navy engages in "freedom of navigation operations" to promote its own interpretation of the norm of freedom of navigation, while some other states, including China, engage in operations to harass US vessels conducting such operations. The maritime forces of China, Japan, and various Southeast Asian states engage in actions to promote their states' interpretations of how customary international law and the UNCLOS apply to contested territorial claims in the East and South China Seas.

37. Aryeh Neier, *The International Human Rights Movement: A History* (Princeton, NJ: Princeton University Press, 2012).

38. Kennedy and Cheng, *From Rule Takers;* Kent, *Beyond Compliance*; Foot and Walter, *China, the United States, and Global Order.*

39. On Chinese passivity see Jan Wouters and Matthieu Burnay, "China and the European Union in the World Trade Organization: Living Apart Together?," in Wouters et al., *China, the European Union and Global Governance,* 88–90. On Chinese helpfulness see James Scott and Rorden Wilkinson, "China in the WTO," in Kennedy and Cheng, *From Rule Takers.*

40. Aaditya Mattoo, Francis Ng, and Arvind Subramanian, "The Elephant in the 'Green Room': China and the Doha Round," Peterson Institute for International Economics Policy Brief no. PB 11–3 (May 2011), at http://www.iie.com/publications/pb/pb11-03.pdf, accessed May 8, 2013.

41. The former position is expressed by Arvind Subramanian in *Eclipse: Living in the Shadow of China's Economic Dominance* (Washington, DC: Peterson Institute for International Economics, 2011); the latter by most contributors in Eric Helleiner and Jonathan Kirshner, eds., *The Great Wall of Money: Power and Politics*

*in China's International Monetary Relations* (Ithaca, NY: Cornell University Press, 2014).

42. Sohn, "Between Confrontation and Assimilation," 630–48, quotation from p. 640.

43. Tong Zhao, "China's Role in Reshaping the Global Nuclear Non-Proliferation Regime," *St Antony's International Review* 6, no. 2 (2011): 67–82.

44. Rana Siu Inboden and Titus C. Chen, "China's Response to International Normative Pressure: The Case of Human Rights," *The International Spectator: Italian Journal of International Affairs* 47, no. 2 (June 2012): 45–57.

45. Andrew J. Nathan, "The Authoritarian Resurgence: China's Challenge," *Journal of Democracy* 26, no. 1 (January 2015): 156–70.

46. Katrin Kinzelbach, *The EU's Human Rights Dialogue with China: Quiet Diplomacy and Its Limits* (London: Routledge, 2015).

47. *Counter-Terrorism and Human Rights: The Impact of the Shanghai Cooperation Organization* (New York: Human Rights in China, 2011), at http://www .hrichina.org/en/publications/hric-report/counter-terrorism-and-human-rights -impact-shanghai-cooperation-organization, accessed March 1, 2015.

48. Wuthnow, *Chinese Diplomacy*; Allen Carlson, "More Than Just Saying No: China's Evolving Approach to Sovereignty and Intervention since Tiananmen," in Alastair Iain Johnston and Robert S. Ross, eds., *New Directions in the Study of China's Foreign Policy* (Stanford, CA: Stanford University Press, 2006), 217–41.

49. Rosemary Foot, "The Responsibility to Protect (R2P) and Its Evolution: Beijing's Influence on Norm Creation in Humanitarian Areas," *St Antony's International Review* 6, no. 2 (2011): 47–66.

50. Marc Lanteigne and Miwa Hirono, eds., *China's Evolving Approach to Peacekeeping* (London: Routledge, 2012).

51. *China Media Bulletin: A Weekly Update of Press Freedom and Censorship News related to the People's Republic of China* 33 (September 22, 2011), distributed by email.

52. Violet Blue, "WCIT-12 Leak Shows Russia, China, Others Seek to Define 'Government-Controlled Internet,'" December 8, 2012, at http://www.zdnet.com /article/wcit-12-leak-shows-russia-china-others-seek-to-define-government -controlled-internet/, accessed March 3, 2015.

53. Bill Hayton, *The South China Sea: The Struggle for Power in Asia* (New Haven, CT: Yale University Press, 2014); see China's declaration upon acceding to the UNCLOS at http://www.un.org/Depts/los/convention_agreements/convention _declarations.htm#China%20Upon%20ratification, accessed May 18, 2012.

54. Foot and Walter, *China, the United States, and Global Order.*

55. Andrew Jacobs, "Plans to Harness Chinese River's Power Threaten a Region," at http://www.nytimes.com/glogin?URI=http%3A%2F%2Fwww.nytimes.com

%2F2013%2F05%2F05%2Fworld%2Fasia%2Fplans-to-harness-chinas
-nu-river-threaten-a-region.html%3Femc%3Dtnt%26tntemail1%3Dy%26
_r%3D1, accessed May 5, 2013; Brahma Chellaney, *Water, Peace, and War: Confronting the Global Water Crisis* (Lanham, MD: Rowman and Littlefield, 2013).

56. Sebastian Heilmann, Moritz Rudolf, Mikko Huotari, and Johannes Buckow, "China's Shadow Foreign Policy: Parallel Structures Challenge the Established International Order," *China Monitor*, Mercator Institute for China Studies, at http://www.merics.org/fileadmin/templates/download/china-monitor/China_Monitor_No_18_en.pdf, accessed March 3, 2015.

# 8

# CHINA'S RISE AND ECONOMIC INTERDEPENDENCE

## Helge Hveem and T. J. Pempel

Countries that are economically interdependent are disposed to behaving peacefully toward one another, more so than they would absent such interdependence. This is the view that Immanuel Kant articulated in what has subsequently become a widely applauded thesis. When applied to China, the Kantian peace thesis holds that China's increasing integration with the global economy is placing the country in a situation of ever-expanding economic interdependence. In more concrete terms, the Kantian argument would hold that its dependence on exports and foreign investments and imports of technology and natural resources, as well as its huge investments in bonds in the United States and Europe, push China toward taking a peaceful approach when it deals with other nations, including other great powers. Yet China's economic engagement is hardly characterized by simple dependence. Its dependence on, for example, the United States as an export market is partially or fully balanced by US dependence on Chinese investments to finance deficits and on Chinese labor to produce high value-added products at low (although increasing) costs. This increasing US-China interdependence should simultaneously reduce any US predisposition to use force in any effort to check China's rise. In other words, the world's two biggest economies are in a position of mutual dependence vis-à-vis one other, the end result of which is a reduced likelihood of overt conflict between them. Such a situation is also referred to as one of "complex interdependence."[1]

The implication of the Kantian thesis for Chinese policy making is that its leadership has little room for choosing options other than to seek compromise and agreement with its economic partner countries whenever the potential for major conflicts risks escalation. The same is true for the United States in its dealings with China.

The Kantian peace thesis—that high economic interdependence exerts strong pressures for both sides to achieve peaceful solutions—has a lot to say for it, but it has to be checked against powerful arguments from several other theoretical contentions and against changes in key aspects of the interdependence relationship. For one thing, economic interdependence may be asymmetric, with partner A being dependent on partner B to the point that A remains vulnerable to B's use of power. Before returning to the support for the peace thesis in the China case, a review of the options will be helpful. Some of them will complement and condition the liberal-institutionalist perspective, which is in fact the contemporary version of the Kantian peace view.

## ON THEORY

First, consider the role of security in relation to national sovereignty and prestige in shaping state behavior in the economic sphere. Many China watchers have strongly held beliefs in the realist tradition, that is, that Chinese leaders will prioritize national security and prestige above economic interests, or, when the two are considered simultaneously, they will be reluctant to rule out conflict even at the expense of costly economic losses. These beliefs largely build on a historical argument that falls into two parts. One piece of the classical realist argument contends that history has shown that rising powers will challenge the status quo and eventually get into direct military conflicts with declining hegemonic powers. As Graham Allison (among others) has pointed out, history teaches us that ever since Sparta took on Athens, changes in relative power more often than not have led to violent conflict between a waning hegemon and a rising contender(s). This is known as the "Thucydides' trap."[2] Other historical examples from the seventeenth to the twentieth century are cited to bolster this general point, though the argument is structural and rests simply on the distribution of national resources and the consequent global balance of power.

Even nondeterministic realists, who stress the potentially offsetting importance of compatibility of ideologies and domestic political systems, lean heavily toward the high probability of overt conflict as a result of such power shifts.[3] Yet it is not possible to induce from a historical perspective alone whether or not China *will* tend toward aggressive rather than peaceful external behaviors, since counterexamples exist. For one, the United States peacefully replaced Britain as the dominant power in the early twentieth century. More-over, Japan and Germany both rose quickly but peacefully in the aftermath of World War II and did little to upset the ongoing American-dominated status quo. The nineteenth- and twentieth-century experiences of Napoleonic France, imperial Japan, and both Wilhelmine and Nazi Germany, when the existing world order was challenged by force, all ended disastrously for the challengers—which suggests further that any current rising power would be wise to conclude that the historical odds are against victory for the newcomer in all-out military efforts to upend the status quo.

Equally challenging to the presumption that conflict is inevitable during a major power shift is the fact that nuclear weapons present a "new" phe-nomenon making direct great (nuclear) power conflicts highly unlikely. Cer-tainly, during the Cold War the United States and the Soviet Union worked assiduously to avoid direct conflicts with one another despite their mutual animosity (and with far less economic interdependence between them than now exists between the United States and China). Similarly, the United States and China have cooperated to exert some control over North Korea's nuclear ambitions and Iran's nuclear program, and to ensure demilitarization of East China Sea disputes as well as taking the leadership in addressing problems of global climate change.

A second major challenge to the Kantian peace theory relates to partic-ular regional aspects of the toxic possibilities emanating from a power shift that animates contemporary East Asia, despite the region's complex economic interdependence. The most prominent are China's desire to end a "century of humiliation" and the corrosive legacies of recent regional history. China seeks to deny the United States easy military access to waters around China as well as embarrass and punish Japan—the region's most powerful postwar state—for its actions in China from 1931 to 1945, as well as that country's alleged contemporary failure to address what Chinese officials consider to be a "correct interpretation of history" by which Chinese officials seem to mean "accepting China's interpretation of history." Toxic historical legacies damage the relationship between South Korea and Japan as well and animate China's escalating maritime claims in the East China and South China Seas.

Within China, as Odd Arne Westad argues, the sense of history is "inscribed in China's mental terrain" and "history therefore influences Chinese ways of seeing the world in a more direct sense than in any other culture."[4] Chi-na's historical memories of what it often refers to as "one hundred years of humiliation" dovetail with its strategic efforts to replace Japanese influence in the region, and tensions are further compounded by efforts within Japan to whitewash the negative history of the two countries' early-twentieth-century interactions. Certainly, numerous Chinese strategic planners frequently refer to the changing balance of regional and global power, to the economic sluggishness of Japan, and to the alleged decline of the United States (particularly following the global financial crisis of 2008–2009) and the consequent Chinese need to prepare for future clashes between itself as the rising power and the United States as the declining hegemon.[5]

Overt warfare and direct confrontation are not the only alternatives to "peace," however. In between harmonious cordiality and shooting wars lie a host of options whereby states can muster force in the exercise of "coercive diplomacy." Even if East Asia were able to avoid shooting wars, there is no guarantee that China and others in East Asia will not move ships around, threaten boycotts, test weapons systems in menacing ways, carry out xenophobic public demonstrations, engage in cyberwar, and other menacing behaviors.

A third factor that also does not lead to a clear hypothesis is the international structure. Within realism, this factor has been emphasized in the Waltzian tradition's preference for balance of power over hegemony; other realists prefer hegemony as a necessary structural condition for international peace. While it may be safely assumed that few Chinese leaders prefer a hegemonic world that would uphold America's preeminent power, many might well be happy to see China regain at least some of its own previous *regional* hegemony. It is unclear whether Chinese leaders would be content with, or even prefer, a balance of power structure. If they were to seek the latter, would they then work to achieve a bilateral hegemonic structure where the United States and China share global power predominance (i.e., a G2 world), or would they opt for the kind of balance of power that was created in 1815 among several great powers? As China has emphasized by strengthening its position both militarily and economically on the Asian continent and in East Asia in particular, could such regional efforts in themselves lead to conflict despite economic interdependence within that region?

It is unclear whether a regionally superior China would be content with a regional rather than a global hegemonic power position. China certainly is attempting to enhance its regional influence today—both economically and politically—though Chinese leaders are less likely to say they want military hegemony. Rather, they contend that their aim is to prevent US military hegemony from impeding China's, and the rest of Asia's, legitimate pursuit of development, autonomy, and sovereignty. But skepticism abounds concerning China's longer-term goals. Will enhanced regional influence over the next three to five years provide an impetus toward greater Chinese aspirations and enhanced global influence in twenty years?

The fourth factor to consider is the role and importance of international institutions. On the surface, institutional arrangements appear to reinforce economic interdependence and contribute to reduced chances of conflict. As Andrew Nathan points out in his chapter, especially after becoming a member of the World Trade Organization (WTO), China has adjusted to international regimes in trade, investment, and related issue areas after opening up to the global economy. It is also formally committed to behave in accord with an increasing number of other international institutions. China treats WTO trade claims against it as legitimate; China has joined a common treaty with Japan and the Republic of Korea that will constrain its behavior on intellectual property; it abides by UN resolutions despite frequently opposing the adoption of many it finds problematic; it has entered into various regional free trade agreements that constrain pure market forces; and it appears quite committed to the general financial reporting rules of the International Monetary Fund and the Basel II Accords. To international relations (IR) institutionalists, and in particular those in the liberal institutionalist tradition, the fact that China is part of this web of international institutions conditions its policy choices and makes more plausible the Kantian peace argument about the likelihood of nonconfrontational behavior. So far China has accepted most "basic" structural rules while seeking to make modifications within the existing institutional frameworks rather than challenging the fundamental legitimacy of those rules entirely. In other words, many of its actions suggest that it could well rise without offering major challenges to the institutions that the Western powers created from Westphalia onward and which the United States still leads.[6] Whether this pattern will continue in the medium- to long-term future remains quite obviously an open question.

Thus this argument should be accepted only conditionally. As China rises it will certainly want changes in some aspects of today's status quo, illustrated, for instance, by its efforts to reduce "dollar dominance" in favor of enhanced Asian reliance on more IMF drawing rights, by expanding reliance on the *yuan* (or *renminbi*, which means "people's money") in certain trade deals, by the Chiang Mai Initiative Multilateralization (CMIM) arrangements that limit strict IMF rules over East Asian financial deals, and the like. China is by no means a pure status quo power in regard to existing institutions; in the future, as its power grows, it is likely to chaff even more at rules it finds unduly constraining. As the yuan was included at the end of 2015 in the IMF's Special Drawing Rights, a basket of main currencies used as the IMFs unit of account, it is, however, possible that the new status will leave Chinese authorities with less flexibility to manage the exchange rate and more exposure to market forces.

Certainly China has shown that it opposes and will continue to oppose plurilateral agreements that it fears are set up against it, such as the Anti-Counterfeiting Trade Agreement (ACTA), which was negotiated in secret by the United States, the European Union (EU), and a selection of other countries in an effort to strengthen enforcement of measures against fraud, counterfeiting, and other breaches of international property rights not covered by the TRIPS Agreement of the WTO.[7] Furthermore, in response to the slowness in adjusting voting rights within the IMF and the World Bank to reflect China's increased economic muscle, as well as dissatisfaction with the powerful role played by Japan in the Asian Development Bank (ADB), China moved with the other BRICS in 2013 to create the New Development Bank (NDB) and has forged an Asian Infrastructure Investment Bank (AIIB) with some fifty plus members, both of which would offer central financial roles to China in institutions that at least supplement if not directly challenge the existing financial regime. China has also launched the Silk Road Fund, which was backed by another development bank. The Shanghai Cooperation Organization (SCO) was begun at China's initiative and includes four central Asian republics, China, and Russia, and serves as something of an "anti-NATO" in the analysis of some.[8]

These broad arguments strive to capture and predict behaviors at the global level. In attempting to assess issues related to China, however, it is vital to recognize that in the short term, at least, China's most pressing foreign policy concerns are concentrated within its immediate neighborhood. Therefore, the regional position and policies of China must be assessed in greater detail. The regional level is where security and economy aspects interact most clearly today and where they are most likely to have the most dramatic future effects. It is certainly where China is currently most active.

The role and importance of domestic politics and institutions need to be mentioned as a final set of considerations. The focus here will be primarily on how domestic politics and institutions may interact with and influence issues of economic interdependence. Here there are three broad arguments to consider. The first involves generational change: certainly the Deng and Jiang regimes put a premium on furthering China's domestic economic development and regional cooperation, stressing its peaceful rise while attempting to assuage regional worries. Domestic economic development continued to be the major focal point in the November 2013 Third Plenum. In the last two to three years, however, China has taken a more assertive posture on various diplomatic and military issues, particularly regarding East Asia. This leaves open whether or the extent to which the new Xi Jinping leadership will devote its efforts to continuing the Deng-Jiang focus on economic development while downplaying military prowess or on pushing forward with more assertive policies such as the massive island reclamation projects and confrontational challenges to Vietnam and the Philippines in the South China Seas. On the other hand, China's economic slowdown and dramatic stock market drop in late 2015 have forced the leadership to turn their attention to alleviating domestic economic troubles. Foreign assertiveness may well be a "luxury" enjoyed by leaders only so long as a successful national economy bolsters their legitimacy.

At the same time, there is a possibility for the "externalization of domestic conflict."[9] That is, if or when there is increased social conflict, enhanced populist nationalism, or challenges to the leadership's legitimacy at home, will governmental leaders be tempted to exacerbate external conflicts or engage in overseas adventurism as a tactic to defuse domestic discontent? (This may account for some of China's more recent assertiveness, as internal dissent and criticism of the CCP swells in strength.) Given the frequency of domestic popular protests in China as well as Communist Party concerns about continuing to legitimize its rule, the search for domestic tranquility may well become a predominant and conflict-inducing driver of China's foreign behavior.

China's relative growth in wealth and power has produced an increased self-confidence among the population as well as among the leadership. At the same time, recent events suggest that the leadership has become seriously concerned about the growing attention to the systemic corruption that has accompanied economic growth, especially among leaders of the CCP. The Bo Xilai revelations and the *New York Times* stories about the wealth of the family of Wen Jiabao are but the most spectacular public exposures of such corruption. It should be no surprise that Xi has been engaged in systematic Party cutbacks on conspicuous expenses and has made official corruption a major target of his presidency leading to numerous high-level officials being subjected to arrest.

As a final caveat, remember that the theoretical propositions outlined above are mostly structural in nature. Even as these proposition may differ on specific concrete predictions, all begin with premises about human agents responding rather "automatically" to their presumably overwhelming force. This discussion, while accepting some of the powers of structural constraints, will also emphasize the importance of human choice—the role of agency. Agency trumps structure if and when the type of leadership and leadership preferences are decisive for policy outcomes. In view of the fact that the leadership has recently changed in practically all of the political regimes across North and East Asia and the Asia-Pacific, it is particularly important to discuss the role of such agency. In other words, the almost simultaneous coming to power of Xi Jinping, Shinzo Abe, Park Geun-hye, and Kim Jong-un, combined with the reelection of Barack Obama and Vladimir Putin, invites particular attention to individual roles and policy preferences along with the roles and preferences of their inner circle of advisers—plus their interactions with one another. The major US foreign policy redirections that took place during the George W. Bush administration, the big swings in Japanese foreign policy following the replacement of Liberal Democratic Party (LDP) governments by the Democratic Party of Japan, and the vast policy changes between South Korea's two "liberal" presidencies and the conservative regimes of Lee Myung-bak and Park Geun-hye that followed are important reminders that structures can explain only so much. The election of a Republican president in the United States in 2017 could also represent a major change.

# STRUCTURE: BEYOND SECURITY

In assessing the current and medium-term probabilities for achieving either a Kantian-style peace or increased confrontation, three key structural changes are likely to shape events: 1) the end of cold war bipolarity; 2) enhanced capital mobility and consequent changes in national economic strength; and 3) the potential importance of institutions, including those at the regional level.

## The End of Cold War Bipolarity

China-United States relations changed from implacable hostility during the 1950s and 1960s into "frenemies" as a consequence of, among other things, Richard Nixon's visit to China in 1972; diplomatic recognition of the Chinese government by the United States, along with normalization of PRC-Japan and PRC-South Korea ties; China's accession to the UN Security Council; China's strategic cooperation as a balance against the Soviet Union; and Deng Xiaoping's radical overhaul of the underlying organization of the Chinese economy. The collapse of the Soviet empire between 1989 and 1991 reduced the strategic incentives for US-China cooperation but bilateral relations between the two continued to be generally positive for the subsequent two decades.

The military balance overwhelmingly favored the United States. Indeed, the first Iraq War, carried live on CNN, convinced numerous Chinese security analysts that the technological superiority of US weapons vastly outshone anything China had even imagined up to that point. That conclusion bolstered internal arguments for avoiding any direct military confrontations with the superpower or in the Asia-Pacific more generally. In its foreign relations China successfully negotiated a number of unresolved land boundaries with most of its fourteen neighboring states.

In fact, many security analysts in China viewed the US "hub and spoke" system in Asia in a positive light. A strong US presence in the region had long demonstrated America's s ability to provide "offshore balancing" among the region's often fissiparous neighbors; moreover, the United States showed few signs of coveting any Asian territories. Instead, the alliance system has assured Chinese security planners that the country's most worrisome potential threat, Japan, would be unlikely to engage in any significant military buildup, which in turn freed China from a costly regional arms race that could deflect the focus from domestic economic development. In addition, China needed US support for its entry into the World Trade Organization (which it gave in December 2001). For all these reasons there was little incentive for contentious security relations between the two countries.

That situation has changed in important respects. As China's economy has grown exponentially, the United States has been embroiled in two exceptionally costly and economically draining (and indecisively lost) wars in Afghanistan and Iraq. The global financial crisis of 2008–2009 left the United States bleeding gallons of financial blood, the consequences of which continue to be inflicted on its national economy and its diminished level of global prestige. Meanwhile, China (and most of East Asia) emerged from the crisis economically far less damaged.[10] The Chinese program of military modernization has steadily improved the sophistication of the Chinese air force and navy, including the recent acquisition by the PRC of its first aircraft carrier. Chinese strategic planners have become increasingly conscious of the fact that even though the United States continues to enjoy a vast overall superiority in weapons and military spending, China has increased its asymmetrical warfare capabilities, particularly maritime ones, in and around its immediate borders. This has led US planners to worry about China's enhanced "anti-access, area denial" capabilities, that is, the growing ability of China's military to deny the US navy or air force their previous levels of absolute freedom to operate in areas proximate to China's borders.

Meanwhile, security tensions in Northeast Asia have been exacerbated by the collapse of the Six Party Talks and North Korea's missile testing and nuclear program, as well as by its continued military and cybersecurity provocations, by the deterioration in ROK-DPRK relations (particularly during the presidency of Lee Myung-bak), by the nationalistic tensions between Japan and the ROK, and by China's quasi-military challenges to the status quo of disputed islands in the South China Sea and the East China Sea.

China initially drew closer to the DPRK through enhanced investments and trade as well as by Chinese efforts to protect the DPRK from UN resolutions condemning it for its many provocations. Such actions were linked to ideological compatibility while also serving to restrain US influence, protect the DPRK as a geopolitical buffer, and prevent a surge of DPRK refugees into China. As DPRK actions became more provocative, however, powerful voices within China began to suggest that it was time for planners to become more draconian in their dealings with North Korea as a way to ensure a more tranquil security and economic environment with the United States and with the major countries of East Asia.

Meanwhile, the US "pivot" toward Asia, its continued bilateral security ties, and the Pentagon's embrace of the air sea battle concept have increasingly been interpreted within China as a coordinated effort to contain China's growth and its efforts to emerge from its "hundred years of humiliation." A US presence that was once welcomed is increasingly interpreted as a catalyst for a deteriorating security climate.

In short, while the end of cold war bipolarity initially fostered a reduction in tensions over an unchallenged US hegemony, American hegemony has, in more recent years, come under a Chinese challenge. In addition, although China and the Soviet Union never saw eye to eye during the Cold War, their bilateral relations have moved closer through joint participation in the Shanghai Cooperation Organization, through their mutual support for regimes in Syria and Iran, through their separate anxieties about US power in the Asia-Pacific, and through their adamant insistence on limited UN interventions that challenge any country's sovereignty (although China has found it difficult to embrace Russia's takeover of Crimea). Two energy agreements made in 2014 are expected to link Siberian gas to Northern China and provide a large share of China's total gas consumption from 2018 on.[11]All of these suggest the possibility that the new Chinese leadership and reelected Russian president Putin will continue to strengthen their ties and that some of the long-dormant cold war bifurcations between their two countries will return.

Thus, recent events suggest both cooperation and contestation in Asia. But whereas the prevailing trends from the early 1980s into the mid-2000s moved toward enhanced economic interdependence, rising institutionalization, and security cooperation, recent events provide a strong body of evidence supporting realist and neorealist expectations that crisis and confrontation between the United States and China, as well as among and between regional actors, have become more rather than less likely.

## The Increased Role and Power of Global Finance

The classical Kantian argument, that economic interdependence promotes reduced security tensions, as well as much of the literature that followed in its wake put primary emphasis on cross-border trade in products. Yet trade in products has become only a minor portion of modern global economic activity. Dwarfing and also shaping trade today are the forces of global financial transactions of various kinds, public financial and monetary policies, foreign direct investments (FDI), subcontracting agreements, and cross-border production and transnational value chains fostered by both direct investments and non-equity modes of international production.[12] Although these elements are interrelated, they will be discussed separately.

Each day over $5 trillion in capital moves across national borders with the stroke of a few computer keys, a figure that has risen nearly 25 percent from five years ago.[13] Such movements have not been seriously stifled by the 2008–2009 financial crisis. Still heavily sourced from the industrialized United States, Japan, and Western Europe but increasingly channeled through Asian centers, these monies provide a powerful structural constraint over the actions of individual governments. After Bill Clinton's election, he allegedly was told by Secretary of the Treasury Robert Rubin that certain economic policies Clinton wished to pursue would be impossible due to the overriding power of the bond market.[14] The US government's huge debt—nearly $4 trillion at the time—meant that bond investors in the United States and abroad held substantial economic power constraining political options. The enhanced amounts of global debt and the problems that key countries face in handling sovereign debt catapult the power of global capital even higher. The world has become "financialized."[15]

Nothing drove home the power of global financial markets more clearly than the near-total global collapse in the wake of the Lehman Brothers shock. Only a massive $700 billion US bailout of the financial industry, followed by collective G20 stimulus packages, prevented complete collapse. The US actions, ironically, were taken by a US administration previously wedded to allowing "markets" to operate without governmental intervention. In an era of financial deregulation, so-called bond vigilantes—bond market investors who protest particular monetary or fiscal policies that they consider inflationary by selling their bonds, thus increasing yields—have acquired the collective power to enforce powerful limitations on the economic actions of governments, particularly when those governments have opted to "plug in" to global financial markets, as both China and the United States have certainly done.

The 2008 crisis hit the United States hard, and the crisis soon spread from the United States to Europe and elsewhere without exacting severe damage on most Asian economies (except for some short-run downturns in exports). The crisis thus contributed to an image that China and other BRIC countries had gained a relative advantage from what was widely considered an American-European financial crisis. Indeed, China was almost completely unconnected to the massive amount of derivative trading, credit default swaps, securitized home mortgages, and other high-risk products that laid the United States low. China's creditor status insulated it from external pressure for adjustment that other countries often experience.[16] And China's massive stimulus package in the wake of the crisis was vital to recatalyzing global demand and averting a more serious meltdown. However, neither China nor other BRIC countries emerged unscathed from the crisis. True, in 2014 three Chinese banks ranked at the top of the Forbes 2000 list of global companies and a fourth was among the top ten. But, for reasons having much to do with internal policies and its economic stimulus and little to do with global financial markets, China's banks, along with regional governments and other key institutions, now face a debt exposure level comparable to many Western countries. The property market poses a particular challenge with the real possibility of a Chinese property bubble that by fall 2015 appeared to be rapidly losing air.

Still, it is highly unlikely that a Lehman-style collapse will happen in China; the CPP and the state have been circumspect in limiting the penetration into China by global financial institutions and by circumscribing the convertibility of its currency. The Chinese state retains powerful weapons to assist the country's banks and stock markets in avoiding a traditional financial crisis, and any speculative efforts by non-Chinese investors will be inevitably met by strict capital controls and Beijing's financial firewall of $4 trillion USD in reserves. The stock market plays a much lesser role in China than in the Western economies. Moreover, China's economic resources provide the country's leaders with a powerful political instrument for exerting influence. Indeed, enhanced economic muscle may well reduce any temptation to rely on purely military force in the effort to achieve political ends. At the same time, the two-way flow of capital into and out of China will simultaneously provide increasingly powerful incentives for the country's political leaders to consider the economic consequences of any foreign policy and to minimize external conflicts. China's role and potential influence in international financial and monetary affairs is clear in two respects: as a provider of balance-of-payments financing for deficit countries around the world and as a major creditor country. *The Economist* refers to China as the new lender of last resort.[17] Beyond this, Chinese economic power has grown unevenly in other respects, and it has been only partially visible in monetary politics.[18] In addition, its domestic financial system and policy making are not exactly transparent.[19] While it is clearly investing heavily abroad in bonds, manufacturing, and services, in resource extraction, and in land for food production, its policies on financial liberalization—reform of the global financial system—and the issue of reserve currency appear as more fluid.

Financial liberalization is under way, as illustrated in its capital account reform of 2014, but full liberalization lies years ahead—if it ever happens. Chinese leaders remain deeply concerned with controlling capital flows.[20] Policies in this area may be said to follow Deng's famous mantra, "feeling the stones while crossing the river." It is obvious that the Party and state institutions are in command of the crossing and will stop or retreat if necessary. Banks are thus "political" in their lending practices, often covering up bad performances by favored clients.[21] But as policy makers begin to feel the need to make the domestic financial system more efficient *inter alia* in order to better serve private savings and the SMEs (which are often neglected under the present system's bias toward the big companies), a more market-based national finance system will develop. A large number of market economy measures are already applied. Authorities have even decided to make Shanghai a global finance center by 2020, a competitor to not only Hong Kong and Singapore but also London and New York. The implications for China's finance policies and the extent to which it will liberalize financial transactions involving foreign players are not clear. It may be appropriate to refer to the Mundell-Fleming model of macroeconomic policy making, based on the argument that a country cannot simultaneously have a stable currency rate, free capital flows, and free interest rates policy.[22]

China now operates in a global financial and monetary system in which the United States has traditionally dominated and where, because of the special place of the dollar, America still exercises considerable structural power. But this position appeared to be changing once China allowed the *renminbi* (RMB) to be subject to "managed flexibility." Since 2010 the *yuan* has thus eclipsed the dollar to become the dominant reference currency for East Asia. Also, a number of currencies, even some outside of Asia, move with the RMB to a larger extent than they move with the dollar.[23] At the regional or Asia level, it has been active in promoting its currency. It has signed bilateral local currency settlement agreements with the other BRIC countries, with South Africa, and with several Asian countries.[24] In the case of several Asian trading partners, payments are settled in RMB.

Despite these developments, Chinese monetary policies have been primarily oriented toward setting the exchange rate of the *yuan* vis-à-vis the US dollar, largely in order to support Chinese trade interests. After a long period of nonconvertibility, the *yuan* was made convertible for trade in most goods and services from 1990 on, although it is still not convertible for bond trading and the government retains control of broad bands within which the *yuan* can move. The continued significance of such government oversight was demonstrated in fall 2015 as the *yuan* suddenly fell after the government permitted enhanced flexibility in rates. But the weaker *yuan* was also seen as likely to boost Chinese exports at the expense of competitors at a time when the government was also pressing hard to sustain economic growth.

As noted above, China also has pressed for a reform of the IMF to give it greater influence in IMF decision making. This was most notably articulated in a 2009 statement by the governor of the Peoples Bank.[25] However, although China has, generally speaking, gained increased influence in international monetary affairs through its new banking initiatives such as the New Development Bank and the Asian Infrastructure Investment Bank noted above, Chinese policies regarding the IMF have not been very activist in practice; on concrete issues it has often seemed to favor the status quo.

In a relational power perspective, the significance of cross-border linkages that are forged by foreign direct investment (monies invested in hard assets, as opposed to the faster-moving liquid capital that crosses borders during the purchase of stocks, bonds, and currencies) is particularly important. Northeast Asia in particular has seen a massive cross-border FDI splurge in the last decade, much of it driven by investors from within the region. Average annual FDI into Asia during the period of 1990 to 1997 was $102 billion; for 2002 to 2006 it had risen to $221 billion; in 2007 it was $681 billion; and by 2013 the East Asia region was the destination for roughly one-third of the world's total FDI.[26] As the United States and Europe staggered to escape the wreckage wrought by the global financial crisis, Asia continued to grow, in both absolute and relative terms. Even as global FDI dropped dramatically as the result of the crisis, the flow of FDI to China in particular continued to increase, reaching a record level of $124 billion in 2013. Moreover, FDI in the services sector surpassed that of manufacturing for the first time. China was the second-largest host country in terms of incoming investments (after the United States), but the largest when totals for Hong Kong (third-largest destination for FDI at $74 billion) are added to those of the PRC (see fig. 8.1).

The role of Hong Kong both complicates an analysis of FDI in and out of China and underlines the importance of a regional perspective on FDI flows. Hong Kong is a world-class hub for FDI; the stock of ingoing FDI is almost the size of China's. It is also a transit place for channeling FDI into China; the stock of FDI in China held by Hong Kong–registered investors accounted for about 44 percent of the total, in both 2004 and 2012. A large share of these investments were held directly and indirectly by PRC citizens, but it's unclear how much. The same precautionary observation is even more appropriate when it is acknowledged that a large amount of investments into

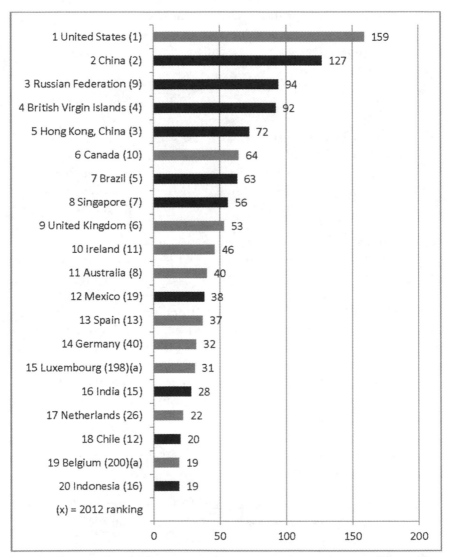

**Figure 8.1** Top Fifteen Countries in 2013 for FDI Inflows (figures in billions of US dollars)

Source: Adapted from United Nations Conference on Trade and Development (UNCTAD) World Investment Report 2014, 4. Note: British Virgin Islands is excluded because, by definition as an offshore financial center, most FDI inflows there are in transit to another country.

China originates in two tax havens in the Caribbean: 6.5 percent of all FDI into China in 2002, and 11.5 percent in 2012.[27]

While the total global FDI stock in China increased from roughly $501 billion USD to $1,343,559 billion USD from 2003 to 2012, Chinese stock investments abroad rose from roughly $33 billion to $532 billion over the same period.[28] In 2003, 68 percent of outgoing FDI stock had been invested in Hong Kong; the percentage was still 57 in 2012. Bearing in mind that a large part of these investments involves using Hong Kong as a transit for investing globally, not only for reinvesting in China, they add to a growing amount of outgoing investments from the mainland. In 2013 investment outflows from China increased by 15 percent year-on-year to $101 billion, close to balancing incoming FDI and almost double the flows in 2008 and the third highest in the world after the United States and Japan (see fig. 8.2). When a large, but unknown amount of Chinese-held FDI from Hong Kong is added, Chinese foreign investments are even larger. This development was spurred by several mega-deals, such as the $15 billion takeover of the Canadian oil and gas company Nexen by China's state-owned entity CNOOC Ltd., as well as the $5 billion Shuanghui-Smithfield acquisition in the food industry.[29] It is clear that China is becoming increasingly

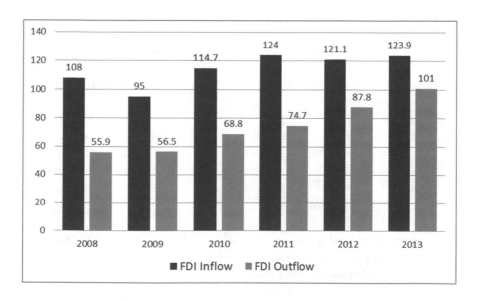

**Figure 8.2** Incoming and Outgoing FDI in China ($ billions)

Source: UNCTAD, *World Investment Report 2014*; and *China Daily*.

integrated with global investment markets, despite the precautions related to the role of FDI in Hong Kong in reinvesting outgoing Chinese capital back into China.

Particular interest has been devoted to the most important Chinese state arm in global FDI and the biggest Chinese and the world's fourth biggest sovereign wealth fund (SWF): the China Investment Corporation. Its capital was some $650 billion USD in late 2014, of which about $200 billion had been invested abroad. The company has taken stakes in several high-profile assets, including London's Heathrow Airport. It takes advice from several foreign experts who are currently members of its advisory council.[30] While the Chinese Investment Corporation is positioned in several foreign economies and may exert influence in some particular companies, it also is under pressure from Chinese authorities to cut losses after being criticized for mismanagement by the top Chinese auditor.[31]

An increasing and considerable portion of the FDI being invested in Northeast and Southeast Asia is coming from other East Asian countries. This is partly a consequence of the rising importance of transnational production networks or value chains across East Asia, and certainly their importance in China. These value chains are interregional and global value chains (GVCs) as well as regional production networks (RPNs), and sometimes a combination of the two. In these GVCs and RPNs, transnational corporations "move the product, not the factory." Through foreign investments or non-equity forms, including various types of contracts, GVCs locate the various stages of the production process across several countries. In so doing they pour ever-increasing amounts of money and effort into separating the production of final products into component parts that can be produced in multiple countries within Asia and elsewhere. This can be seen in the structure of foreign trade: intermediate products—imports that go into production for export—make up 28 percent of total global trade and Asian RPNs drive that percentage up.[32]

A good illustration is the iPhone, arguably one of the fastest-growing products in today's world and one that is controlled by the most valuable global company in 2014, Apple Inc. An illustration (see Figure 8.3) published in a joint OECD-WTO publication offers a concrete view of the value chain that produces the iPhone, the direction of production and the value of the intermediate products and technology components that go into the assembly plants in China, and the distribution of value among producing countries.[33] Figure 8.3 demonstrates the importance of regional production platforms, the relatively low value of China's contribution, and the high return to the owner of the trademark and technology. It also reflects the fact that FDI is not always the core means of controlling transnational

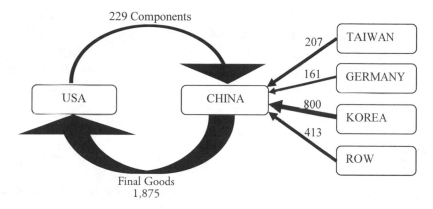

**Figure 8.3** The iPhone value chain (values in millions of US dollars)

Note: Assuming that 10 million iPhones are exported from China to the US, the iPhone trade represents a trade deficit of USD 1,646 million for the US economy (this is simply calculated as the difference between US exports of intermediate inputs to China–USD 229 million–and US imports of assembled iPhones–USD 1,875 million). In gross terms, there is only a deficit between China and the US.In (relatively crude) value-added terms, however, China adds only a small share of domestic value-added to the iPhone corresponding to the value of the assembly work. As highlighted in the list of costs presented in the figure, most of the components of the iPhone are sourced from economies outside China. In (relatively crude) value-added terms, the figure shows that the US trade deficit is not only with China but also with Chinese Taipei, Germany, Korea and the rest of the world (ROW). The overall trade deficit (vis-à-vis the world) stays unchanged at USD 1,646 million.

Source: OECD-WTO (2013) Trade in Value-Added. *Concepts, Methodologies, and Challenges,* 7.

relations. In the iPhone case, control is exercised mainly through long-term and extremely specified production contracts (i.e., subcontracting). This has implications for the relationship between the United States and China, which will be examined in the next section.

To sum up, high lending volumes, cross-national investments, contractual relations, and trade among countries may indeed push players toward a Kant-ian peace. The argument that increased trade per se reduces the probability of conflict is proved problematic by history, but it also does not take into account the increased complexity of today's international economic relations. Understanding the extent to which global financial flows and increased FDI will exert greater discipline over political leaders and affect trade is a far more complicated task.[34] Yet even if they do discipline political leaders, it is not clear that such discipline would automatically be mobilized in favor of peace and the avoidance of all forms of conflict. Certainly, extensive Japanese assets in China proved to be no deterrence to the escalation of tensions over the Senkaku-Diaoyu Islands; instead, Japanese assets in China provided a convenient target for massive government-supported demonstrations that caused millions in property damage. In this sense it is clear that economic interdependence alone does not automatically reduce security conflicts, even if they prove to be a barrier to full-scale war.

## Political Institutions

A third factor must be considered when assessing the changing security climate. China has been a vigorous joiner of virtually any and all global and regional institutions. The country is locked in as a permanent and presumably loyal member of a host of well-established global institutions, from the United Nations, the World Bank, the WTO, and the IMF to the G20, as well as being active in such ad hoc cooperative efforts like those against pirates off the coast of Somalia and terrorists in Mali. At the same time, within East Asia there has been a substantial rise in regional institutions, particularly since the Asian financial crisis.

Within East Asia, China is a member of the Association of South East Asian Nations (ASEAN) Plus 3 (APT) and the financial process it has spawned, the Chiang Mai Initiative Multilateralization (CMIM), which was designed to buffer the region against potential currency crises. It also concluded a tripartite investment treaty in 2012, with Japan and the Republic of Korea agreeing to regulate their cross investments. China also takes part in several current efforts to set up multilateral investment agreements in the region, some that include Oceania.[35] Contrary to what many have argued, China even appears to have accepted the investor-state dispute settlement institutions introduced by NAFTA and currently under negotiation as part of the bargaining taking place over the proposed Transatlantic Trade and Investment Partnership (TTIP). In fact, China has signed investment agreements with broad and binding consent to investment arbitration for more than fifteen years. And, in November 2014, it concluded the China-Australia Free Trade Agreement (ChAFTA), which includes investment arbitration.[36]

China has joined the ASEAN Regional Forum (ARF) and signed the Treaty of Amity and Cooperation (TAC), the latter of which is critical to formal engagements with ASEAN. It was the convener of the Six Party Talks until they collapsed; it continues to encourage resumption of the talks. It has been an active proponent of various regional bond market initiatives, as well as the Shanghai Cooperation Organization, the East Asia Summit, and numerous Track II diplomatic processes, to mention only a few of the most prominent regional bodies.[37] Various institutional arrangements also exist between China and the United States, perhaps the most important being the US-China Economic and Security Dialogue that began in 2009 by Presidents Obama and Hu. This dialogue consists of two tracks: economics and security. Multiple issues are systematically addressed along each track, with the security track being set up to deal with four major issues: bilateral relations (such as exchanges); international security (such as counterterrorism and nonproliferation); global (such as energy and global institutions); and regional (such as the DPRK).

By and large China has abided by institutional rules, though as noted earlier it has periodically sought to alter the prevailing rules currently in place. Various studies have suggested that membership in such bodies has begun to "socialize" China into accepting various global norms. Edward Steinfeld has gone so far as to claim that in such ways China is "playing our game."[38] Institutions in and of themselves do not ensure that agreements will be reached nor that cooperation toward a common and nonaggressive agenda will ensue. But surely they have demonstrated some positive influence in those directions. Whether or not such institutional constraints will continue to shape Chinese behavior, or, more important, whether they will shape the behavior of all participants in the direction of peace and cooperation in the future, again is an open question. There is still some way to go to have China fully integrated in the kind of institutions discussed here, and China itself will be seeking to decide where and how far it goes.

## ECONOMIC INTERDEPENDENCE: THE KEY BILATERAL RELATIONSHIP

All of this leads to a discussion of the increasing economic interdependence between China and the United States as well as between China and its other major trading partners. What elements are the mark of an interdependent relationship? Assuming that such a relationship develops in a nonlinear fashion, what challenges will it face, and what are the prospects for its success? What in particular characterizes the relationship between China and the United States, and where will it go? Finding answers to the latter question is clearly the key to understanding the contemporary global political economy, sometimes referred to as the G2.

In the first phase after Deng Xiaoping's 1979 opening (and up to the early 2000s), the relationship between the two countries was one of asymmetry and dependence: China needed the United States as a market for its goods and as a source of capital, technology, and organizational expertise. The relationship then became one of greater mutual dependence as the United States became ever more dependent on China for debt financing and cheap goods to meet the consumer needs of an increasingly poorer section of the population. Still, mutual economic dependence does not guarantee that conflicts are peacefully settled.

For that to be the case, the relationship should be one of complex interdependence. Complex interdependence among nations is characterized by a connection through multiple channels (e.g., governmental and nongovernmental, formal and informal) and multiple issue areas to be addressed in which no issue area is dramatically more important than any other (i.e., military security does not dominate). Complex interdependence also excludes the use of military force, but only among regional or alliance partners and not outside them, such as against a rival.[39] In the absence of hierarchy among issue areas, goals will vary by issue as will the distribution of power and the type of political processes that are at work. Special interests, well-organized actors, and determined bureaucracies may shape goals and strategies of governments. Such forces are at work in both countries' cases. True, the centralizing power of the CCP and the state in China should make for a congruence of goals across issue areas, while there is more disunity in the institutionally pluralistic United States. Although the foreign perception of China as a unitary state may be somewhat exaggerated,[40] as Linda Jakobson shows in her chapter, Chinese leaders have relatively better prospects for making use of a linkage strategy in dealing with economic partners, that is, linking one or more issue areas in order to strengthen a bargaining position.

The power potential of Country A increases the more Country B is vulnerable to changes in Country A's behavior, that is, it can create quick and significant costs for B that B cannot easily avoid. If ever this was the case—such as when China's dependence on the export of goods to the United States in the 1990s made it vulnerable to US policy changes—is it still the case? Or have the tables been turned? Three aspects of the bilateral economic relationship—finance and exchange rate policy; foreign direct investment and the nature of the industrial relationship; and trade—are particularly important in addressing this question.

Essentially the current relationship between the United States and China rests on the purchases by the Chinese government of US debt instruments, mostly Treasury bills. (This is in addition to the heavy purchase of Chinese exports by US consumers.) The US debt in 2011 was roughly $14.1 trillion. Some 32 percent of that total was held largely for things like the Social

Security trust fund and other government obligations. Of the remainder, 46 percent was held by foreign governments, of which China was by far the largest single holder with more than $1.2 trillion in bonds, notes, and bills.

Former Secretary of the Treasury Lawrence Summers categorized this interdependence as "mutually assured financial destruction." China loses if the United States fails to buy its exports; the United States loses if China becomes a more reluctant purchaser of its debt. As Robert Keohane and Joseph Nye explain, this is complex interdependence in a nutshell: partner B refrains from making use of its capacity to exploit A's vulnerability in one area as long as A refrains from using its capacity to hurt B in another area. The fact that Chinese agencies hold close to 10 percent of all US debt should make the United States feel, if not vulnerable, then at least sensitive to Chinese policy makers, especially if the latter were inclined to withdraw their holdings. On the other hand, the Chinese would stand to lose if the US economy and the dollar were weakened due to such an act.[41]

What matters most, however, is the bilateral relationship between the two countries. The exchange rate of the *renminbi* has received the most attention within the United States for several years. US policy makers and indeed several economists have vigorously criticized China for setting the rate artificially low in order to push its exports and create a competitive advantage for Chinese producers. Such voices were raised again when the Chinese currency fell sharply in fall 2015. Looking at the facts, this charge appears exaggerated. While the RMB depreciated by 2.5 percent against the dollar in 2014, the decrease happened after several years of appreciation. In real trade-weighted terms, the RMB appreciated by over 6.5 percent in 2014. Taking a longer perspective, "no country's real effective foreign exchange rate has appreciated more than China's since 2005, when the Peoples Bank abandoned the hard fix to the dollar. Since July of 2005, the RMB has appreciated by over 50 percent against the exchange rates of its trading partners."[42]

Though Western (including US) investors started to invest massively in China before the turn of the millennium, Chinese investments abroad were practically nonexistent before 2000. From 2003 on, however, statistics demonstrate an exponential increase. But, as shown in Figure 8.4, the United States has not been the main target of this investment; the European Union, or rather Hong Kong as a transit hub, has been the recipient, for reinvesting either in China or in countries outside the three major Western powers. Only 3 percent of Chinese FDI stock abroad was invested in the United States in 2012, as compared to 6 percent invested in the EU and practically nothing invested in Japan. Australia and Africa are equally more important homes for Chinese FDI, a reflection of China's resource-acquiring strategy.

Industrial and trade relationships are more or less one and the same thing, reflecting the fact that trade patterns are a result of relocation of industrial production. In fact, a large share of US imports of products from China comes from affiliates of US corporations that have invested in manufacturing on the Chinese mainland or from Chinese firms working under long-term contracts with US-based corporations. Close to 90 percent of US foreign trade is accounted for by corporations who are *both* exporters *and* importers.[43] As mentioned earlier, transnational non-equity as well as FDI activity has grown considerably over several decades. These have become central elements in organizing international production and trade lines. US direct investments and outsourcing and licensing contracts into China have grown considerably since the 1990s, with cumulative FDI (stock) reaching about $60 billion USD in 2010. But much of the relationship is covered by non-equity modes of operation.

As can be seen from Figure 8.4, Chinese FDI into the United States, on the other hand, has risen considerably but is still comparatively small, with the stock of Chinese FDI estimated at some $15 billion USD in 2013. From 2003 to 2010 the Chinese made over two hundred individual investments in the United States, whereas some few attempted investments failed due to US regulatory intervention. This did not apply to Lenovo's partial takeover of IBM nor the 2013 takeover of meat-producing Smithfield Company; it involved other cases in the energy sector and in infrastructure. In such cases the Congressional Committee on Foreign Investment in the United States (CFIUS) has decided that the proposed investment posed important challenges to vital American interests, particularly when they bordered on being or were found to be a threat to national security.[44] Chinese authorities, by comparison, have not formally blocked many large US investments in China. While China is still a very small foreign investor in the United States, the stock of Japanese FDI in the United States is estimated at $286 billion in 2012, against a $62 billion dollar stock of US investments in Japan.[45]

The best measure of industry-trade interdependence is probably the foreign value added in exports. This represents the extent to which the GDP contribution of trade is absorbed by other countries upstream in the value chain or the extent to which a country's exports are dependent on import content. The United Nations Conference on Trade and Development (UNCTAD) has introduced the GVC participation rate to help explain this process.[46] For East and Southeast Asia, the GVC rate is 56 percent (which is the same as the global average); China's alone is 59 percent, divided evenly between upstream and downstream. The US GVC rate is 45 percent, mostly downstream; and

Japan's is 51 percent. The EU, however, tops China with a 66 percent GVC rate divided roughly equally between upstream and downstream.[47]

The picture that emerges from these statistical data is mixed: China is more involved than the United States in GVCs and thus is arguably the more dependent on them, but at the same time China is less involved than are Germany and the United Kingdom. In terms of bilateral relationships and trade volumes, the largest extraregional GVC flows are those between the United States and Germany; second are between China and Germany. Sino-German interdependence appears to be greater than that between China and the United States.

While there are important reasons to assume that the relationship will remain interdependent, there are also dynamic factors that may challenge it. It is safe to assume that the Chinese will attempt to develop manufacturing capabilities beyond the type of value distribution represented by the OECD-WTO illustration referenced earlier and will actively seek to appropriate a growing share of value added, thus moving up the technological gradient. China's expressed ambition to become a fully developed economy with a strong position in high-tech manufacturing and services is likely to be an increasingly important concern to US decision makers, political as well as corporate. So far, Chinese industrial development has been quite dependent on imports of know-how and technology from abroad, not the least from the United States, Germany, and its other large regional trading partners including Japan, South Korea, and Taiwan. But China's real dependence is less the need for capital and more the necessity of gaining foreign technology, know-how, and access to export markets that come along with it. Although there have been many failures, still, a number of Chinese companies, through adaptation and transfer of technology contracts, have acquired know-how and have subsequently transformed that know-how into substantial manufacturing capability with automobiles, electronics, and software. Almost all the large foreign manufacturers and ICT (information and communication technology) corporations have also set up R&D laboratories in China and are likely to continue to do so as long as China's ambitious higher education programs bear fruit. But these programs face serious challenges and may still remain dependent on foreign innovation and know-how for years to come.[48] At present, China's innovation policy and its perceived threat to American competitiveness is causing conflict in US-Chinese economic relations. The role of standardization, intellectual property rights, and government procurement practice are at the center of this conflict.[49] If China really continues to succeed in "climbing the ladder" of industrial competence, the balance

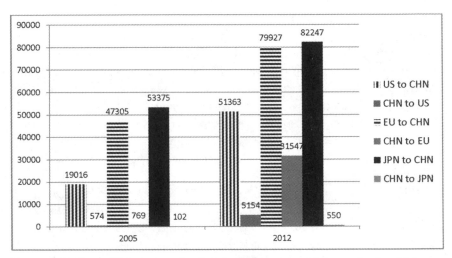

**Figure 8.4** Bilateral Investment Stock Relations between China and other Major Economies, 2005 and 2012 (values in millions of US dollars)

Source: UNCTAD, *Bilateral FDI Statistics*, 2014.

of today's interdependence will surely change and begin to be characterized more by competition than complementarity. It may even shatter completely.

Of equal importance is the high economic interdependence between China, South Korea, and Japan, which has been rising rapidly. In volume terms China is Japan's and South Korea's biggest export market. As in the US case, this is very much the result of Japanese and Korean investments in production entities located in China. Figure 8.4 shows the substantial jumps in bilateral trade among the three major Northeast Asia powers, particularly since the late 1990s.

Until the early 2000s the United States had remained the largest export market for both Japan and South Korea, its two major allies in Northeast Asia. This has changed as China has replaced the United States as the major recipient of goods coming from both countries. In 2002 China–Hong Kong became South Korea's largest export market.[50] As well, by 2001 China was the ROK's number one target of investment and a major recipient of Japanese investments at the same time. Clearly China is enmeshed in both a global and intraregional interdependence with the United States and Germany, and Japan and South Korea as key partners. Or, to place these developments into historical perspective, the United States now faces a broad regional network of increasing intraregional trade, capital, and money flows reminiscent of the order that existed in East Asia during the late nineteenth and early twentieth centuries. Today's pattern suggests no rupture with the past, nor even a return to it as some observers, such as Angus Maddison, argue when they point to the dominant position that China and India enjoyed in international markets centuries ago.[51] Peter Katzenstein astutely assesses the complex developments now manifesting themselves in China's economic rise as a "recombination of old and new patterns and components."[52]

It is, of course, not automatically clear that such FDI, production, trade, and other economic interdependence will mitigate any emerging security tensions. As pointed out earlier, it is not even certain that economic interdependence inoculates countries against the possibility that such tensions might turn harmful or violent. But surely such interdependence is likely to be a powerful force in shaping both China's and the United States' foreign policy decisions, as well as those of other countries in the region. Given the complex nature of this multinational interdependence, political leaders in all countries will almost certainly be reluctant to act in ways that ignore it.

## THE US PIVOT: THE EAST ASIAN REGION

The Obama administration has committed itself to a "repositioning" or "pivot" toward Asia. Obama first articulated this shift in a November 2011 speech in Canberra, Australia. His goals involved ending the Bush administration's heavy commitment of US funds, troops, and leadership attention to the Middle East and Afghanistan; on increasing the importance of revitalizing the US domestic economy; and on the centrality of Asia-Pacific relations to the achievement of those goals. Early reactions to "the pivot" gave undue attention to the US alliance structure and the plans to reposition additional naval forces in East Asia. This spawned many facile conclusions, not least within China, that the pivot was all about "containing China." In fact, while bilateral alliances remain a core component of US policies, and many American policy makers indeed fret about the rapid modernization of Chinese military power and its recent assertiveness on a host of previously quiescent issues, the pivot is seen by the White House as being far more nuanced and multidimensional than a simple bolstering of military force in the region.

The broad outlines of this more nuanced policy were further spelled out in Secretary of State Hillary Clinton's November 2011 *Foreign Policy* article, "America's Pacific Century." As she put it, "[o]ne of the most important tasks of American statecraft over the next decade will . . . be to lock in a substantially increased investment—diplomatic, economic, strategic, and otherwise—in the Asia-Pacific region . . . [b]ecause the Asia-Pacific region has become a key driver of global politics." Clinton emphasized the "six key lines of action: strengthening bilateral security alliances; deepening our working relationships with emerging powers, including with China; engaging with regional multilateral institutions; expanding trade and investment; forging a broad-based military presence; and advancing democracy and human rights."[53]

The multipronged nature of American involvement has been manifested by, among other things, the frequent visits to Asia by top US leaders; the US decision to sign the ASEAN Treaty of Amity and Cooperation; the appointment of a US ambassador to ASEAN; the behind-the-scenes efforts to encourage regime change in Myanmar; American entry into the East Asia Summit and its reinvigorated participation in the ASEAN Regional Forum and the Asia-Pacific Economic Cooperation (APEC) forum; multilateral cooperation in police, disaster relief, and counterterrorism efforts; and the vigorous pursuit of outgoing investments to the region and the more explicit embrace of geoeconomics as a strategy to pursue within the region. The latter would include the bilateral Strategic and Economic Dialogue with China, the Korea-US free trade pact (KORUS), and the vigorous pursuit of a Trans-Pacific Partnership trade agreement. At the same time, any domestic American political divisions might combine with looming economic problems to make an American emphasis on geoeconomics difficult to achieve. US policy makers are particularly likely to face major hurdles in trying to utilize what was once a key tool of American foreign policy, namely, national economic and financial muscle. Domestic economic disagreements run the risk of removing a key tool from America's foreign policy tool kit and they add to doubts about US power. As Adm. Mike Mullen, the departing chairman of the Joint Chiefs of Staff, declared; "The most significant threat to our national security is our debt." He is hardly alone in his concern. Many other US military and diplomatic experts now wonder if domestic economic turmoil will eviscerate America's global influence. In contrast to China, a US strategy of issue linkage will not be easily achieved, largely as the consequence of domestic political fissiparousness.

This means that prior American power to steer East Asia's regional developments will likely be replaced by greater autonomy for those regional powers and their entrepreneurs. As noted earlier, regional production networks and other intraregional activities have continued to increase their role in production processes across East Asia and beyond. While RPNs are more developed within North America (NAFTA) and Europe (EEU), they are growing faster in Northeast and Southeast Asia, with China increasingly as the hub. Moreover, the growing tendency of currencies in the region to align with the RMB and the fact that China is the principal trade partner for most of the ASEAN countries and for Australia are also clear indications of an economic power shift toward China.

However, intraregional integration in the financial sector remains limited.[54] Even after the experiences of the 1997–98 Asian financial crisis and the more recent 2008-2009 global financial crisis there is still not a well-developed regional bond market. Debt investments are still limited because a "national bias" in such capital flows prevails.[55] Dollar inflows continue to dominate. Investments from outside the region hit a new peak in 2013, particularly in China. This peak was probably caused by a search for a higher yield on capital than investors can get in the Western financial markets. Concerns with increased inflationary pressure on the Chinese economy will likely lead to stricter regulation of inflows.[56] Explanations of behavior in the economic sphere are usually posited in a rationalist framework: actors seek to optimize or maximize profits or other goals that derive from self-interest. However, identity and other cultural predispositions also influence behaviors, although concrete roles are hard to assess. While the message of his best-selling book (*When China Rules the World*) is a gross exaggeration, Martin Jacques makes a valid point when he emphasizes the influence of the global Chinese diaspora.[57] Their numbers are at least 40 million, they are geographically widespread, and they facilitate economic transactions between China and the countries where they reside. Diasporadic Chinese play an influential role in countries as far afield as Peru but their role is most prominent within East Asia, most notably as entrepreneurs in countries such as Indonesia, Malaysia, and Thailand.

An even more important part of the diaspora involves Chinese residing in Taiwan and China–Hong Kong. Over the last two decades these places have turned more of their attention toward China, which has led to deeper economic relations. As pointed out already, Hong Kong has developed into a hub for capital transactions to and from China, and as a site for "shadow banking" and reverse FDI. With regard to Taiwan, extensive economic relations that have developed between the island and the mainland are working the way the Kantian thesis might assume, though they are worrisome to many politically minded Taiwanese.

Finally, a Chinese diaspora exists even in Australia. But China's relationship with the large island partner to the south is primarily shaped by their respective interests in trade in natural resources. The relationship is definitely different from what it was when the two were on opposite sides and even engaged in direct combat during the Korean War. Australia established diplomatic ties with China only in 1972 with a change from a Conservative to Labor Party government. While there had been some trade between the two before then, trade took off after 1972 as China's opening and growth promotion strategy turned it from being self-sufficient to becoming dependent on importing minerals in the 1990s. China has turned into Australia's primary trade partner, taking almost 30 percent of Australia's total merchandise exports in 2011–2012 and accounting for almost 20 percent of Australian imports that same year.[58] Australia's share in Chinese foreign trade is much smaller, and China has certainly spread its import dependence across many countries. However, though alternative sources of resource imports do exist, China's demand for iron ore and other strategic minerals is high and growing so fast that guaranteed access to Australia's minerals is a must. Without it China's current infrastructure program would not be feasible. On the flip side of the argument, Australia's and in particular Western Australia's mining economy's dependence on the Chinese market is equally strong. The relationship between the two countries is perhaps not as stable politically as the relationship between the United States and Australia, but it is a possible illustration of complex economic interdependence.[59]

This complex relationship is subject to periodic tough bargaining, such as when Chinalco, the state-owned Chinese aluminum company, was barred from acquiring a larger share in the Anglo-Australian giant mining company Rio Tinto Zinc, even though Chinalco has held close to 10 percent of Rio Tinto's shares for some time. If the acquisition had succeeded it would have been the largest Chinese FDI in history and would have had a major strategic impact on the global mining industry. It failed, however, for two main reasons. First, the asset that China has used so well over the two or three preceding years—that is, China's financial strength during and after the financial crisis of 2007–2008—to allow them to offer financing and buy into firms with an acute need for capital has gradually eroded as financial markets and commodity prices recovered. Second, Rio Tinto's shareholders and Australian politicians joined forces in opposing the deal despite intensive lobbying by Chinese leaders, and the other large Anglo-Australian mining corporation, BHP Billiton, helped organize opposition to the deal partly, it appears, because its leadership hoped to merge with Rio Tinto.[60]

This brief analysis makes clear that economic interdependence has increased across East Asia in ways that transcend simple trade in products: the countries have indeed become one another's principal trade partners but they are also important locations for FDI and production networks that now flourish across the region. Actors are primarily motivated by self-interest, and this motivational mechanism has only been strengthened as East Asia has been turned into the world's growth engine. However, cultural factors such as identity may also play a role in promoting interdependence between China and countries with a sizeable Chinese diaspora.

Geopolitics seems to stimulate self-interest, not least within the major powers. An ongoing example is the US-led negotiations on the Trans-Pacific Partnership that are being challenged by the China-promoted Regional Comprehensive Economic Partnership (RCEP). Though both countries deny any overt power-enhancing motives in their competing trade pursuits, the TPP clearly excludes China while including a bevy of countries seeking to hedge against Chinese influence. The RCEP, in turn, hinges on ASEAN and those countries that have a free-trade agreement with it—which the United States does not. As the United States succeeded during autumn 2015 to have a negotiated agreement to establish the TPP, it looks like it has won the first round against China. How China will respond remains to be seen. Moreover, TPP has yet to be ratified in the US Congress.

## NEW LEADERSHIP, NEW POLICIES?

The key bilateral relationship has not yet reached the level of complex interdependence in which both parties accept that the other has leverage over itself and agrees to "swap" on a mixture of issues (and, by implication, put aside the use of military power). For complex interdependence to be stable, both parties must have a degree of knowledge about, and trust in, the other party's true long-range intentions and its decision-making habits in situations that might provoke conflict. China and the United States have not yet reached that level of interdependence.

The most difficult question the United States faces is obviously what influence the current Chinese leadership *may* have on China's foreign economic policy as well as the reactions and actions of other leaders in the region. It must be recognized that structural analysis provides only broad parameters within which individual choices (foolish or wise) can still be made. This discussion will conclude by describing four possible perspectives for China's future policy development posture: liberal, nationalist, populist, and recombination outcome.

The *liberal* outcome follows the logic of the liberal-institutionalist perspective. China continues to accept the rules and norms of current political-economic institutions because it is in its own best interests to do so—or in the best interests of its newly rich citizens, many of whom appear in top leadership positions. The individuals and networks that constitute the CCP's power base and the Party itself continue to maintain sufficient control over the domestic economy by making necessary concessions to the middle class and other important interest groups. The country has seen increasing demand among its educated middle class for greater individual freedoms, not necessarily for political reasons but certainly as a precondition for being innovative and productive. These holders of power are primarily found among those controlling privately owned businesses in China as well as state sector managers and workers who have strong vested interests in the foreign economy and within the Communist Party. The leadership responds to demand for continued and greater emphasis on well-working foreign relations in the economic sphere.

The *nationalist* outcome involves a China that turns inward. This introspective nationalism may be caused by an ideational turn in the leadership, wherein the fifth-generation leaders become so self-confident about China's international status and their ability to support it politically and militarily that they advance a more assertive foreign economic policy. They demand constitutive and substantive changes in international institutions and become less willing to compromise on what they define as Chinese national interests. This scenario may depend on China's ability to successfully "climb the ladder" of competencies in the knowledge economy and technological developments, thus gaining increased independence from foreigners without having to confer greater individual freedoms on the middle class. This scenario presupposes a contraction of the economy that creates greater social unrest at home and contributes to rising regional military tensions. In other words, this scenario stresses a leadership that has a particularly narrow and zero-sum view of national unrest.

The *populist* outcome would result from a serious decline in the leadership's ability to meet popular demand for continued wealth creation and diffusion if the economic growth rate drops radically or job creation stagnates. Leadership may opt to search for foreign scapegoats to divert popular attention from domestic problems; if a "suitable" regional conflict is not available, leadership may choose to create one. Joseph Schumpeter referred to this kind of militaristic populist aggressiveness as "atavism," and it would certainly constitute aggression.[62] Contraction of economic transactions with foreign countries along with the likelihood of military tensions with neighbors would result.

The *recombination* (or "mixed") outcome scenario largely follows the thinking that P. J. Katzenstein advances, where the process of China's rise and participation in the global economy overlaps with and benefits from global and international processes. These processes represent common standards for a global market "civilization" of which the Chinese have long been a part; after all, Chinese merchant capitalism was integrated early into the world economy. But China's current evolution also contains elements that are distinctive of its own civilizational polity.[63] China has been both a "recipient" of the norms, rules, and procedures established by Western-based institutions and structures and a "sender" through cultural channels (e.g., the spread of Confucius institutes), economic and financial presence abroad, and political messages that address its history of problematic relations with other countries (Japan in particular) and reaffirm its national interests in striking bargains with them (the United States). While to a large extent China has accepted the rules and procedures established in global institutions after the Second World War, it has also set its mark on revising the rules that now dominate within many international institutions regionally and even globally.

Which scenario is the most likely? From Tiananmen to well after China's entry into the WTO, the Chinese leadership was widely seen as pursuing the liberal path, responding to US expectations that China become a "responsible" great power. But increased economic strength has emboldened a more assertive China that increasingly manifests its national interests in foreign policy and projects its aspirations to exert more complex strategies in the service of changing goals.

Not surprisingly, the answer to the question thus depends on several factors, all of which are characterized by uncertainty: What happens to China's economic growth strategy? How does its relationship with the United States and other major economies develop—into more or less asymmetric interdependence? Will agency trump structure in shaping policy regarding governing economic interdependence relations? If so, how do leaders in the respective major economies view these relations and how should they react to changes in them? What are the possible short-term effects of changes in leadership in the region? In particular, how is the relationship between Xi's and Abe's administrations going to develop?

Slower economic growth, which in 2015 appears to be the trend, may create increased social pressure, which in turn may trigger tendencies towards nationalism. At the same time there are other trends visible: the economy is transformed from labor-intensive manufacturing for exports to more varied production that increasingly serves the home market, signaling a move from a predominantly industrial to a more service-based economy. Both trends will affect interdependence relations.

Following the argument presented at the beginning, we do not believe that the liberal scenario—the closest to Kantian peace theory—is in any way inevitable. Rather, the most likely scenario is the recombination outcome, where China's integration into the current global system continues but as a varied geometry; this will be accompanied by demands for constitutional and substantive changes in the institutions that govern the Chinese system and are modified by—or, as Katzenstein puts it, recombined with—the reappearance and reassertion of traditional elements from the era of the "Middle Kingdom."

## NOTES

1. For a presentation of the concept see Robert O. Keohane and Joseph N. Nye, *Power and Interdependence* 4th ed. (Boston: Longman, 2012), or the original from 1977.
2. Graham T. Allison, "Thucydides' Trap Has Been Sprung in the Pacific," *Financial Times,* August 22, 2012.
3. See Aaron L. Friedberg "The Future of U.S.-China Relations: Is Conflict Inevitable?," *International Security* 30, no. 2 (2005): 7–45; Aaron L. Friedberg, *A Contest for Supremacy: China, America, and the Struggle for Mastery in Asia* (New York: Norton, 2011); Jonathan Kirshner, "The Tragedy of Offensive Realism: Classical Realism and the Rise of China," *European Journal of International Relations* 18, no. 1 (2012): 53–75; John J. Mearsheimer, *The Tragedy of Great Power Politics* (New York; Norton, 2011); Cristopher Layne, "Kant or Cant: The Myth of the Democratic Peace," *International Security* 19, no. 2 (Autumn 1994): 5–49; and T. J. Pempel and Chung-Min Lee, eds., *Security Cooperation in Northeast Asia: Architecture and Beyond* (London: Routledge, 2012).
4. Odd Arne Westad, *Restless Empire: China and the World Since 1750* (London: Bodley Head, 2012), 2.
5. For a discussion of the debates within China on how to deal with its rise and the alleged decline of the United States see David Shambaugh, *China Goes Global: The Partial Power* (Oxford: Oxford University Press, 2013), 13–44.
6. For an account of this view see John Ikenberry, "The Rise of China and the Future of the West," *Foreign Affairs* 87, no. 1 (2008): 23–37; Robert Ross and Zhu Feng, eds., *China's Ascent: Power, Security, and the Future of International Politics* (Ithaca, NY: Cornell University Press, 2008); David Shambaugh, *Power Shift: China and Asia's New Dynamics* (Berkeley: University of California Press, 2005).
7. See Helge Hveem, "Policy Capture, Convergence, and Challenge: The European Union and the Doha Amendment to the TRIPS Agreement," in H. Hveem and C. H. Knutsen, eds., *Governance and Knowledge: The Politics of Foreign Direct Investment, Technology, and Ideas* (London: Routledge, 2012).
8. Richard Weitz, "China—Russia's 'Anti-NATO'?," *The Diplomat,* July 4, 2012, available at http://thediplomat.com/2012/07/is-the-shanghai-cooperation-org-stuck-in-neutral.
9. See, e.g., Christopher Gelpi, "Democratic Diversions: Governmental Structure and the Externalization of Domestic Conflict," *Journal of Conflict Resolution* 41 no. 2 (April 1997): 255–82; Michael D. Ward and Ulrich Widmaier, "The Domestic-International Conflict Nexus: New Evidence and Old Hypotheses," *International Interactions* 9, no. 1 (1982): 75–101; Susan L. Shirk, *China: Fragile*

*Superpower* (New York: Oxford University Press, 2008); Jack Levy, "Domestic Politics and War," *Journal of Interdisciplinary History* 18, no. 4 (Spring 1988).

10. T. J. Pempel and Keiichi Tsunekawa, eds., *Two Crises, Different Outcomes: East Asia and Global Finance* (Ithaca, NY: Cornell University Press, 2014).

11. *Bloomberg Business*, November 10, 2014.

12. UNCTAD, *World Investment Report 2012* and *World Investment Report 2013* (Geneva, Switzerland: United Nations). Non-equity modes are, e.g., licensing, outsourcing, contract manufacturing, and other forms of contractual relationship. See UNCTAD, *World Investment Report* for 2011.

13. See the table titled "Global FX Volume Reaches $5.3 Trillion a Day in 2013: BIS," Reuters, September 5, 2013, at http://www.reuters.com/article/2013/09/05/bis-survey-volumes-idUSL6N0GZ34R20130905.

14. Robert Rubin and Jacob Weisberg, *In an Uncertain Time: Tough Choices from Wall Street to Washington* (New York: Random House, 2003).

15. Thomas I. Palley, "Financialization: What It Is and Why It Matters," The Levy Economics Institute working paper no. 525 (2007).

16. Benjamin Cohen, "The China Question: Can Its Rise Be Accommodated?," in Eric Helleiner and Jonathan Kirshner, eds., *The Great Wall of Money: Power and Politics in China's International Monetary Relations* (Ithaca, NY: Cornell University Press, 2014), 23–44.

17. *Economist*, January 31, 2015.

18. Helleiner and Kirshner, *Great Wall of Money*.

19. *Economist*, February 4, 2010.

20. Arne Jon Isachsen, "Penge-og valutapolitikk i Kina" (Monetary and currency policy in China), Centre for Monetary Economics, BI Norwegian School of Management, working paper series no. 2 (May 2011).

21. Arthur Kroeber book review in *China Economic Quarterly*, December 2010.

22. Robert A. Mundell, "Capital Mobility and Stabilization Policy under Fixed and Floating Exchange Rates," *Canadian Journal of Economic and Political Science* 29 no. 4 (November 1963): 475–85.

23. Arvind Subramanian and Martin Kessler, "The Renminbi Bloc Is Here: Asia Down, Rest of the World to Go?," PIEE working paper series nos. 12–19 (Washington, DC, 2012).

24. Yang Jiang, "The Limits of China's Monetary Diplomacy," in Helleiner and Kirshner, *Great Wall of Money*, 178.

25. Zhou Xiaochuan, "Reform of the International Monetary System," March 23, 2009, available at http://www.bis.org/review/r090402c.pdf.

26. UNCTAD, *World Investment Report 2015*.

27. Calculations based on UNCTAD's *Bilateral FDI Statistics 2014* (Geneva, Switzerland: United Nations). While the FDI stock from the two into China in 2012

was $155 billion, Chinese FDI into the two tax havens amounted to $61 billion, that is, roughly 20 percent of the stock of ingoing FDI from them that year. Members of the Chinese elite apparently are among the investors. According to the International Consortium of Investigative Journalists, this group includes Xi Jinping's family. See *New York Times*, June 3, 2014.

28. UNCTAD, *Bilateral Trade Statistics 2014*.

29. "China the Largest in Asia and the World's Top Recipient of FDI Set to Be Net Investor," *Rightway*, June 25, 2014, at http://right-waystan.blogspot .ca/2014/06/china-largest-in-asia-and-worlds-top.html.

30. These include James D. Wolfensohn, the former director of the World Bank, and Knut Kjær, the former and first director of the Norwegian state's Pension Fund Global.

31. *Financial Times*, June 18, 2014.

32. UNCTAD, *World Investment Report 2013*.

33. "Trade in Value-Added: Concepts, Methodologies, and Challenges (Joint OECD-WTO Note)," Paris/Geneva, 2013, 7. At http://www.oecd.org/sti /ind/49894138.pdf.

34. Daniel W. Drezner, "Bad Debts: Assessing China's Financial Influence in Great Power Politics," *International Security* 34, no. 2 (2009): 7–45.

35. UNCTAD, *World Investment Report 2013*.

36. Axel Berger and Lauge N. Skovgaard Poulsen, "The Transatlantic Trade and Investment Partnership: Investor-State Dispute Settlement and China," *Columbia FDI Perspectives* 140 (February 2, 2015).

37. "Track II" diplomacy is a term used in contrast to traditional "Track I" diplomacy, in which government officials represent their governments explicitly and are empowered to enter into government-to-government agreements. Track II refers to diplomatic efforts at a less formal level, typically involving a mix of government officials and nongovernment individuals attending in their private capacity. The goal of Track II is to achieve greater informality and explore possible solutions to problems without having the actual power to reach formal agreements.

38. Edward Steinfeld, *Playing Our Game: Why China's Rise Doesn't Threaten the West* (Oxford: Oxford University Press, 2012).

39. Keohane and Nye, *Power and Interdependence*, 24–25.

40. See Helge Hveem, Carl Henrik Knutsen, and Asmund Rygh, "State Ownership, Political Risk, and Foreign Direct Investment," in Kjell A. Eliassen, ed., *Business and Politics in a New Global Order* (Oslo: Gyldendal, 2013).

41. Drezner, "Bad Debts."

42. According to Bank of International Settlements, quoted in *China Economic Watch*, January 23, 2015.

43. Andrew B. Bernard, J. Bradford Jensen, and Peter K. Schott, "Importers, Exporters, and Multinationals: A Portrait of Firms in the United States that Trade Goods," in Timothy Dunne, J. Bradford Jensen, and Mark J. Roberts, eds., *Producer Dynamics: New Evidence from Micro Data* (Chicago: University of Chicago Press, 2009).

44. Karl P. Sauvant, *Investing in the United States: Is the U.S. Ready for FDI from China?* (Cheltenham: Edward Elgar, 2009).

45. UNCTAD, *Bilateral Investment Statistics 2014*.

46. According to UNCTAD, the GVC participation rate of a country equals the share of its exports that is part of a multistage process; it is the foreign value added used in a country's exports (upstream perspective) plus the value added supplied to other countries' exports (downstream perspective) divided by total exports. The GVC is also an indication of the level of vertical specialization of economies, that is, the extent to which economic activities in a country focus on particular tasks and activities within those GVCs.

47. UNCTAD, *World Investment Report 2013*.

48. For a critical review of the several "rise of China and US decline" theses and a discussion of these challenges, see Michael Beckley, "Why America's Edge Will Endure," *International Security* 36, no. 3 (Winter 2011): 41–78.

49. Dieter Ernst, *Towards Greater Pragmatism? China's Approach to Innovation and Standardization*, East-West Center policy brief no. 18 (Honolulu, August 2011).

50. *China Daily*, February 2, 2002.

51. Angus Maddison, *The World Economy: A Millennial Perspective* (Paris: OECD Development Centre, 2006).

52. Peter J. Katzenstein, "China's Rise: Rupture, Return, or Recombination?" in P. J. Katzenstein, ed., *Sinicization and the Rise of China: Civilizational Processes beyond the East and West* (London: Routledge, 2012), 6.

53. Hillary Clinton, "America's Pacific Century," *Foreign Policy*, November 2011, at http://foreignpolicy.com/articles/2011/10/11/americas_pacific_century.

54. Cyn-Young Park, "Asian Financial Integration: How Much Has It Come True?," *Asian Development Bank Blog*, June 24, 2013, at http://blogs.adb.org/blog /asian-financial-integration-how-much-has-it-come-true.

55. Ivan Azis and Sabyasachi Mitra, *Why Do Intra-Regional Debt Investments Remain Low in Asia?*, Office of Regional Economic Integration, policy brief no. 1 (June 2012).

56. *Financial Times*, April 12, 2013.

57. Martin Jacques, *When China Rules the World: The Rise of the Middle Kingdom and the End of the Western World* (London: Allen Lane, 2009).

58. *Australia-China Free Trade Agreement Negotiations*, Australia Department of Foreign Affairs and Trade (2010), retrieved from http://www.dfat.gov.au//dfat.gov.au/geo/china/fta/.

59. See Keohane and Nye, *Power and Interdependence*, for the analysis of the US-Australia relationship at the time.

60. Xueli Huang and Ian Austin, *Chinese Investment in Australia: Unique Insights from the Mining Industry* (London: Palgrave Macmillan, 2012); J. D. Wilson, *Public and Private Sources of Governance in Global Production Networks: The Case of the Asia-Pacific Steel Industry*, Ph.D. diss., Australian National University, Canberra, 2011.

61. Shintaro Hamanaka, "Trans-Pacific Partnership versus Regional Comprehensive Economic Partnership: Control of Membership and Agenda Setting," Asian Development Bank working paper series on Regional Economic Integration, no. 146 (December 2014).

62. Joseph Schumpeter, *Imperialism and Social Classes* (New York: A. M. Kelley, 951).

63. Katzenstein, "China's Rise?," 27.

# 9

# XI JINPING AND THE CHALLENGES TO CHINESE SECURITY

## Robert S. Ross and Mingjiang Li

Since 2009 East Asia has become more volatile, with tensions and disputes arising in the Korean Peninsula, the East China Sea, and the South China Sea. All of these security flashpoints have involved China. China's heavy-handed security policy has deepened the apprehensions of many regional states toward China, so much so that by 2012 China's relations with the United States and much of the region were in a worse state than they had ever been in the previous two decades. Not even its economic importance as an exporter of inexpensive goods, as an investor, or as an official aid provider could establish a stable foundation for a more benign and amicable image of China.[1]

China attempted to repair its relations with the United States in 2013. Early in the year it adjusted its policy toward the Korean Peninsula, and in July Xi Jinping met with US president Barak Obama in California. These developments led to improved US-China relations and greater stability in East Asia. In particular, U.S.-China military diplomacy improved. In April 2013 the United States, China, and other Pacific nations reached an agreement on the Code for Unplanned Encounters at Sea, or CUES, at the Western Pacific Naval Symposium.[2] In July the navy of the People's Liberation Army (PLA) participated in the US-led Pacific-Rim multilateral exercises for the first time. During President Obama's visit to Beijing in November 2014 the two countries signed two memorandums of understanding (MOUs), one titled "On the Rules of Behavior for the Safety of Air and Maritime Encounters" and the other "On Notification of Major Military Activities."

Nonetheless, by late 2103 and in 2014 Chinese policy one again challenged the regional order and led to renewed US-China tension and regional apprehension over Chinese intentions. China's declaration of an air defense identification zone in the East China Sea, its oil drilling near Vietnam, and its reclamation activities in the South China Sea led to renewed apprehension over China's strategic intentions.

Chinese officials and analysts have repeatedly singled out collusion between its neighbors and Washington as the source of China's conflict-ridden relations from 2009 to 2015. They argue that China was mostly reacting to the "provocative" moves by neighboring countries. Although in some cases China may have been reacting to challenges from other countries, including the United States, some Chinese policies—such as the deployment of the Haiyang Shiyou 981 oil rig in waters near the Vietnamese-claimed Paracel Islands and the ongoing massive land reclamation projects at the Spratlys—cannot be described as simply reactive and are more aptly described as "overassertive." China's policy has not only alienated its neighbors; it has contributed to the US "pivot" to East Asia and a US challenge to Chinese security.

During the time when China pursued its "peaceful rise" strategy by maintaining a low profile (*taoguang yanghui*), foreign policy making was relatively easy. Beijing focused on minimizing conflict with the United States and on promoting regional stability.[3] As China's economic and naval capabilities have grown, however, the Chinese leadership has actively pursued its regional security and sovereignty interests and sought regional stability and good relations with its neighbors and the United States.[4] This is a far more difficult task than simply peaceful rise, and it is Xi Jinping's enduring foreign policy challenge. This challenge will be especially difficult in the context of China's increasingly complex regional environment and the persistence of nationalism and the politics of foreign policy making.

This paper discusses the changes in China's security policies and the impact of Chinese security policy on the regional security landscape and on China's own strategic situation. It also discusses the several factors that have led to the instability in China's East Asian security policy. The biggest challenge to China's regional security has been the mismanagement of its expanding regional capabilities, in part due to domestic politics, including the impact of nationalism and bureaucratic interests on policy making.

## RESPONDING TO THE PIVOT, 2009–2012

In March 2009 Chinese ships harassed the USS *Impeccable* that was operating within China's exclusive economic zone (EEZ). In December of that same year China engaged in contentious diplomacy during the United Nations Climate Change Conference. Following the January 2010 announcement of US arms sales to Taiwan, China for the first time suspended US-China diplomatic dialogues and announced sanctions on US corporations engaged in defense cooperation with Taiwan. In March it seemed to align with Pyongyang after North Korea sank the South Korean naval ship *Cheonan*. In July Beijing protested loudly against US–South Korean naval exercises in international waters in the Yellow Sea. In September it retaliated against Japanese detention of a Chinese fishing boat captain after the boat had rammed a Japanese coast guard ship sailing in disputed waters. In November and December Chinese diplomats railed against Norway and other Western democracies and then imposed economic sanctions on Norway after the Nobel Prize Committee awarded the Peace Prize to Chinese democracy activist Liu Xiaobo.[5]

The Obama administration responded with policies that challenged Chinese security. It increased defense cooperation with South Korea through an expanded US troop presence in South Korea, by boosting the size and frequency of US–South Korean joint military exercises, and by agreeing to four new US-Korea defense agreements. From July 2010 to the end of the year US Secretary of State Hillary Clinton twice visited Hanoi and called for a US-Vietnam "strategic partnership" and Secretary of Defense Robert Gates visited Vietnam.[6] In December the US Navy held its first engagement with the Vietnamese Navy and the two countries held annual exercises through 2015. In 2012 Secretary of Defense Leon Panetta visited Cam Ranh Bay and announced, "Access for United States naval ships into this facility is a key component of this relationship and we see a tremendous potential."[7]

The United States also changed its policy toward the maritime disputes in the South China Sea. Prior administrations had merely asserted a US interest in freedom of navigation and peaceful resolution of the disputes. During visits to Hanoi in July 2010 and to Manila in November 2011 Clinton called for "collaborative" and "multilateral" negotiations among the claimants, thus supporting the ASEAN call for multilateral negotiations to resolve maritime disputes, in contrast to China's preference for bilateral negotiations. In 2012, Clinton charged that China's territorial claims exceeded the limits allowed by the law of the sea.[8]

Chinese leaders may have understood that its own heavy-handed diplomacy had contributed to the US pivot, but they nonetheless viewed the pivot as a US effort to "encircle" or "contain" China.[9] Moreover, they viewed US support for the Philippines and Vietnam as having emboldened both of those countries to challenge Chinese sovereignty in the South China Sea. At the 2011 East Asia Summit in Bali, Premier Wen Jiabao warned external forces against getting involved in the South China Sea dispute, regardless of the reason. He said that the South China Sea dispute had existed for many years and should be resolved through direct negotiations among the claimant states.[10] In August 2012 China accused the United States of "stirring up trouble" just as the region was trying to resolve the disputes and calm the situation."[11]

In reaction to US policy, China reduced its cooperation with US interests. In February 2012 it cooperated with Russia and against US policy over Syria, leading Clinton to call the Chinese veto of the UN Security Council resolution condemning Syria "despicable."[12] China also resisted the US-sponsored UN sanctions against Iran, compelling the United States to impose sanctions outside the UN framework. In February 2012, just after the European Union and the United States announced new sanctions against Iran, several Chinese oil companies agreed to increase their imports from Iran. And from 2010 to 2012 China offered little assistance to US policy toward North Korea and showed little interest in convening the Six-Party Talks on nonproliferation.[13]

# XI JINPING'S FOREIGN POLICY

Thus, in late 2012 the Xi Jinping leadership encountered deteriorated US-China relations and US policy that challenged Chinese security along its periphery. Xi's challenge was to restore cooperation with the United States so as to reduce US pressure on Chinese security. Xi characterized his diplomatic initiative toward the United States as an effort to promote "a new type of great power relations," but China could not pursue regional stability and improved US-China relations at the expense of Chinese security and sovereignty in East Asia. Rather, Chinese foreign policy aimed to persuade Washington to ease its support for regional opposition to Chinese policy while China continued to defend its security interests. This proved to be a difficult challenge.

## The Korean Peninsula

Chinese interests in North Korea include stability and peace on the Korean Peninsula, the survival of the North Korean regime and its role as a strategic buffer zone for China's relations with the United States, and North Korean denuclearization. These goals do not necessarily converge. Beijing has preferred the goal of stability and survival of the North Korean regime over denuclearization, and its policy priorities have often led it to adopt policies that conflict with the expectations and interests of South Korea, Japan, and the United States.

China's divergent interests were especially evident in its response to the sinking of the *Cheonan* warship and the bombing of Yeonpyeong Island in 2010. Beijing's neutral or even pro-Pyongyang stance in the aftermath of these two events contributed significantly to South Korean anger toward China and to US and Japanese distrust of Chinese intentions. When the United States, Japan, and South Korea held naval exercises to deter further aggressive actions by North Korea, the Chinese leadership, especially PLA leaders, ratcheted up their rhetorical opposition to increased US military presence in Northeast Asia. North Korea's sinking of the *Cheonan* and its shelling of Yeonpyeong Island resulted in diminished Sino–South Korean cooperation and led to a stronger US military presence in South Korea, both of which challenged Chinese security in Northeast Asia.

Renewed instability on the Korean Peninsula in early 2013 and the simultaneous emergence of a new South Korean leadership and John Kerry's appointment as US secretary of state encouraged Xi Jinping to change China's policy toward North Korea. In the aftermath of Pyongyang's third nuclear test in February, Beijing leveled increasingly harsh criticism of North Korea and effectively isolated it in the midst of the tensions. In January China cooperated with the United States in drafting the UN Security Council resolution to impose additional sanctions on North Korea.[14] Then, in April, as further tensions mounted, Premier Li Keqiang met with Kerry in Beijing. Li opposed "troublemaking" on the Korean Peninsula and warned that "to do that is nothing different from lifting a rock only to drop it on one's own toes."[15] China then welcomed the US chairman of the Joint Chiefs of Staff, Martin Dempsey, to Beijing. In a meeting with Dempsey, the vice chairman of the Chinese Central Military Commission, Gen. Fang Fenghui, directly criticized North Korea's nuclear program.[16] As President Xi Jinping declared at the annual Bo'ao Forum in early April, "No one should be allowed to throw a region and even a whole world into chaos for selfish gains."[17] In June 2013, in a significant policy shift, Beijing agreed to strengthen UN surveillance of North Korea's adherence to sanctions and to impose new sanctions on North Korean entities.[18]

China also imposed economic sanctions on North Korea. In an unusual move, the Bank of China announced that it had cut off dealings with the Foreign Trade Bank of North Korea. There were also reports that China had frozen some North Korean bank accounts in the Chinese border cities of Dandong and Hunchun, that it had closed a North Korea foreign exchange bank, and that it had increased inspections of North Korean exports to China.[19]

Chinese isolation of North Korea continued through 2015. In March Beijing reportedly rejected North Korea's application to be a founding member of the Asian Infrastructure Investment Bank.[20] In September North Korean leader Kim Jong-un did not appear at the Chinese celebration of the seventieth anniversary of the end of World War II. Kim sent one of his deputies, Choe Ryong-hae, secretary for the Korean Workers' Party, to the events in Beijing. Choe did not meet Xi personally.

China has also expanded cooperation with South Korea. In March 2013 Xi wrote a personal letter to the recently elected South Korean president, Park Geun-hye.[21] Xi then telephoned Park and suggested an early Sino–South Korean summit. As tensions began to escalate in April, China agreed to establish a hotline with South Korea.[22] In April Wu Dawei, China's special representative for Korean peninsula affairs, traveled to Seoul and to Washington, where he met with both Kerry and Dempsey. Meanwhile, Chinese foreign minister Wang Yi welcomed the South Korean foreign minister, Yun Byung Se, to Beijing. In June 2013 Park Geun-hye visited Beijing for a summit meeting with Xi Jinping. In a joint statement, the two sides stated that "nuclear weapon development seriously threatens peace and stability in Northeast Asia, including the Korean Peninsula." They affirmed their commitment to carrying out the UN sanctions against North Korea and their support for reconvening the Six-Party Talks.[23] In contrast, throughout this period China had nothing positive to say about North Korea and conducted no public diplomacy with North Korea. The contrast with past Chinese behavior is striking. Whereas China had welcomed Kim Jong-il during a visit to Beijing in the aftermath of North Korea's sinking of the *Cheonan* in 2010, by 2013 China had sided with South Korea against North Korea.[24]

Since 2013 China has continued to develop cooperation with South Korea. In July 2014, Xi paid his fifth visit to Seoul since Park was elected president. During Xi's visit, China and South Korea jointly criticized North Korea's nuclear weapons program and agreed to form working groups to delimit the boundary of the exclusive economic zones in the Yellow Sea. They held their first delimitation working group meeting in January 2015.[25] President Park visited Beijing again in September 2015 to join China's commemoration of the end of World War II despite American opposition. In contrast, through early 2016 there had yet to be a China–North Korea summit meeting since Xi's rise to the presidency.

The Xi Jinping leadership also used the 2013 crisis to enhance cooperation with the United States. In July 2013, following his meeting with Foreign Minister Wang Yi at the ASEAN Ministerial Meeting in Brunei, John Kerry emphasized that the United States and China are "absolutely united" that North Korea "must" give up its nuclear weapons. He reported that China had assured him that it had made "very firm statements and steps" in support of denuclearization.[26]

Thus, Beijing has diplomatically isolated North Korea and threatened North Korea with economic isolation. But North Korea is less stable today than at any time since the end of the Korean War. The new North Korean Worker's Party leader, Kim Jong-un, is young and inexperienced and he lacks a reliable political base. Kim has also carried out a series of destabilizing leadership transfers among the North Korean military, which suggests that elite politics in North Korea are highly unstable and that he may be vulnerable to significant challenges. Meanwhile, the North Korean economy remains on the verge of collapse. Given its concern for border stability, China thus continues to support the North Korean economy with sufficient economic assistance to prevent regime collapse.[27]

But even while Beijing has supported political stability in North Korea, it has also developed an economic "engagement" policy in the hope of promoting gradual political and social change in North Korea. Chinese border trade with North Korea in such consumer goods as cell phones, televisions, video players, and refrigerators, and cross-border infrastructure development contribute to an erosion of Pyongyang's social and economic controls and to the determined development of societal pressures against the government's oppressive policies.[28]

Pyongyang's warmongering diplomacy and dangerous brinkmanship will continue to be a major source of instability in Northeast Asia. Moreover, Washington will continue to challenge China's growing cooperation with South Korea. For example, through 2016 Washington has continued to press South Korea to deploy the US THAAD missile defense system, which China insists would undermine its security.[29]

## Japan and the East China Sea

The East China Sea maritime territorial dispute between China and Japan has also challenged Chinese diplomacy. Before 2010 the dispute had been managed under the precondition that Beijing did not directly challenge Japan's administrative control over the Diaoyu/Senkaku Islands. In 2008 Beijing and Tokyo reached an in-principle agreement for joint development in the East China Sea, and the two countries held several rounds of talks on the implementation of the agreement.[30] The maritime law enforcement personnel of the two countries enjoyed quite good interactions; Chinese and Japanese coast guard officers traded cigarettes and played Mahjong together during their patrol activities.[31]

But in September 2010 the Japanese coast guard arrested the captain of a Chinese fishing boat operating in the territorial sea surrounding the Senkaku/Diaoyu Islands after the captain had rammed his boat into the coast guard ship. Japan charged the captain with violating Japanese domestic law. China responded with strident measures: it demanded the unconditional release of the fisherman and it severed high-level political exchanges. As tension mounted, China stopped rare earth exports to Japan, which Japan understood to be Chinese economic sanction. Beijing also restrained Chinese tourism to Japan. As the dispute dragged on, China arrested four Japanese businesspeople. Japan eventually released the Chinese fisherman before he was tried and only then did China release the four Japanese business people.

A new round of Sino-Japanese tension developed in September 2012 when the Japanese government purchased three of the Senkaku/Diaoyu Islands to preempt the Tokyo governor, Shintaro Ishihara, from purchasing the islands. The Japanese government maintained that if Ishihara had purchased the islands he would have encouraged Japanese nationalists to land and build structures on the islands, which in turn would have created bigger problems in Japan-China relations. The Chinese were never convinced by the Japanese explanation for its nationalization of the islands and argued that the Japanese government could have taken other administrative measures to stop Ishihara from the purchase.

Beijing reacted with harsh countermeasures. These included a suspension of high-level political meetings with Japan, toleration of violent anti-Japan demonstrations in over one hundred cities in China, imposition of economic penalties against Japan, the addition of the islands to the official weather forecasting program, the drawing of territorial baselines around the islands, and most important, the start of an unprecedented program of regular patrols by Chinese government civilian ships in the territorial waters near the islands. According to a report issued by the Japanese coast guard, from September 2012 to March 2013 China's maritime surveillance ships were present in the territorial sea of the islands for 35 days and in the contiguous zone of the islands for 136 days.[32]

The tense atmosphere over the Diaoyu/Senkaku Islands significantly increased the possibility of naval skirmishes between China and Japan. On February 5, 2013, the Japanese ministry of defense disclosed that a Chinese warship had used its fire-control radar against a Japanese helicopter on January 19 and again on January 30 against a Japanese destroyer.[33] The Chinese Ministry of Defense stated that in both cases the PLA naval ship had simply used normal monitoring and warning measures, not fire-control radar. It further argued that the root cause of the incident was the short-distance tagging and monitoring behaviors of Japanese jet fighters and warships during the PLA Navy's regular training exercises. China further charged that Japan had made irresponsible statements about normal Chinese naval exercises to play up the "China threat" and denigrate China's image.[34] Zhang Zhaozhong, a military analyst at China's National Defense University and a popular media commentator, noted that the Chinese warship's use of fire-control radar would be an internationally accepted operation if the Japanese jet fighter or warship had entered within ten nautical miles of the safety zone of the Chinese frigate in the high seas.[35]

The truth of the fire-control radar incident will be mired in mystery for some time because of the lack of technical evidence from the Japanese side. If the PLA naval ship had indeed used its fire-control radar, such "hostile intent" could have been (mis)interpreted as a prelude to an attack and led the Japanese ship to preempt an imminent "onslaught" and thus create unintentional hostilities.[36]

On April 23, 2013, eight Chinese maritime law enforcement vessels entered the waters of the Diaoyu/Senkaku islands and "successfully expelled" a group of Japanese nationalists trying to land on the islands. On April 26, 2013, the PRC Foreign Ministry spokesperson stated, "It is an issue about China's territory and sovereignty, and therefore, a matter of "core interest."[37] By 2015 Chinese patrols of the islands' territorial waters had become routine, with approximately two such patrols each month through 2015. Beijing had established a "new status quo" in the East China Sea.[38]

Chinese diplomatic hostility toward Japan increased after Shinzo Abe became Japan's premier in December 2012. Abe's resistance to any concessions toward China on the islands, the April 2013 visit by Abe's cabinet and more than one hundred conservative legislators to the Yasukuni Shrine, where Japanese World War II class-A war criminals are enshrined, and Abe's hesitation to accept Japan's 1995 apology for its atrocities during World War II have hardened Beijing's resistance to improved Sino-Japanese cooperation.

The United States has been reluctant to interfere in the Sino-Japanese conflict. Nevertheless, it made it clear that it would not allow the US-Japan alliance to erode in the face of Chinese pressure on Japan. In November 2013 China declared an air defense identification zone (ADIZ) over the East China Sea that encompassed the Diaoyu/Senkaku Islands. In itself the ADIZ did not challenge the regional order. Japan, Russia, South Korea, and even Taiwan all had established ADIZs. But after over a year of tension between China and the United States and its allies, China had challenged US resolve to resist Chinese pressure.

The US response was uncompromising. In February 2014, US White House and state department officials singled out China for causing regional instability and possessing extreme territorial claims, and they warned that should China declare an ADIZ that included the South China Sea, the US Navy could adjust its "presence and military posture" in East Asia.[39] In April, during a visit by President Obama to Japan, the United States reaffirmed three times that the US-Japan alliance covers defense of Japanese administered territories, including the Diaoyu/Senkaku Islands. Washington had challenged China's insistence that the United States should not interfere in the Sino-Japanese territorial dispute and it had encouraged Japan to resist Chinese pressure. Heavy-handed Chinese policy had undermined Chinese security by driving Japan and the United States closer.[40]

Thus, even as China continued to patrol within twelve miles of the Diaoyu/Senkaku Islands, it softened its Japan policy. A turning point in Sino-Japanese relations occurred during the Beijing APEC meeting in October 2014. After long negotiations the two countries reached a four-point statement, which ambiguously addressed the territorial dispute and the history issue.[41] The statement helped China save face and made it possible for many more positive developments in bilateral relations.

Soon after the APEC meeting China and Japan began discussion of crisis management mechanisms for the East China Sea. Then, in March 2015 they held their first security issues meeting in four years.[42] China also invited Japan to join as a founding member the proposed Asian Infrastructure Investment Bank (AIIB) and suggested that Japan could hold the top-ranking vice president position.[43] The Chinese, Japanese, and South Korean foreign ministers also met together for the first time since Abe's election as Japanese prime minister.[44] In October Chinese Prime Minister Li Keqiang traveled to Seoul for the first China-Japan-South Korea trilateral meeting in three years. Nonetheless, through 2015 Beijing had yet to agree to hold an official Sino-Japanese summit.

But Xi Jinping's long-term ability to manage the Sino-Japanese territorial dispute will be challenged by Chinese nationalism. In 2012 Chinese scholars questioned Japanese sovereignty over the Ryukyu Islands, including Okinawa, on the grounds of faulty World War II postwar arrangements and various international documents.[45] Maj. Gen. Jin Yinan, director of the Institute for Strategic Studies at the National Defense University, stated that no international treaty recognizes the forceful occupation of the Ryukyus, a former vassal state of China, and thus the ownership of Ryukyu is still an open question.[46] In May 2013 the *People's Daily* argued that during the negotiations of the Treaty of Shimonoseki following the 1894–1895 Sino-Japanese war, the sovereignty issue of the Ryukyus was not unambiguously settled.[47] Soon China's nationalist netizens insisted that Japan had illegally occupied the Ryukyu Islands, including Okinawa.[48]

Moreover, Chinese nationalism will likely face repeated provocations from Japanese nationalism. Prime Minister Abe's ambiguous statements regarding Japan's atrocities during World War II and his Yasukuni Shrine policy were simply the most recent reflections of increasing Japanese nationalism. With the passage of new security bills by the Japanese Diet in September 2015, Japan is poised to exercise collective security rights and expand its security role in the Asia-Pacific and beyond. Thus the combination of Chinese nationalism and Japanese nationalism exacerbates the difficulty Xi will encounter in asserting Chinese territorial claims while at the same time trying to improve Sino-Japanese and US-China cooperation.

## Maritime Disputes in the South China Sea

In May 2009 China submitted its controversial nine-dash line map of the South China Sea to the UN Commission on the Limits of the Continental Shelf (CLCS). This was the first time that the Chinese government had included such a map in an official document. Many Southeast Asia countries suspected that that China was determined to control the entire maritime zone within the nine-dash line, which encompasses about 80 percent of the entire South China Sea. Then, in an apparent response to US alignment with the ASEAN countries against China on the disputed maritime territories at the July 2010 ASEAN Regional Forum, Chinese foreign minister Yang Jiechi said, "China is a big country and other countries are small countries, and that's just a fact."[49]

There has also been increased tension over energy resource exploration in the South China Sea. Beijing has been accused of using forceful diplomacy to intervene in the oil and gas exploration activities of Vietnam and the Philippines in their claimed EEZs. In 2012 Vietnam passed a maritime law that declared sovereignty and jurisdiction over the Paracel and Spratly Islands. To counter this, China established on a South China sea island a prefectural-level city, Sansha, to administer the islets, sandbanks, and reefs near Xisha, Zhongsha, and Nansha Islands. Following the policies of Vietnam, the Philippines, and Malaysia, state-owned China National Offshore Oil Corporation invited exploration bids for nine offshore blocks in the South China Sea near Vietnam. In 2012 China also issued new passports imprinted with maps that implied Chinese sovereignty over the entire South China Sea, which incited strong protests from the Philippines and Vietnam.

## China, the Philippines, and the Spratly Islands

In January 2012 Manila submitted the Sino-Philippine South China Sea maritime dispute over their overlapping EEZ claims to the Permanent Court of Arbitration of the UN Convention on the Law of the Sea (UNCLOS), challenging Chinese insistence that the dispute should be negotiated bilaterally and not "internationalized." A key request in the Philippines' submission was for the arbitration panel to determine the legality of China's nine-dash line. China has refused to participate in the legal procedure but the United States and many other regional countries supported the submission.[50] In October 2015 the UNCLOS arbitration panel agreed with the Philippines that the court has jurisdiction over the conflict.

Then, in April 2012, Philippine Navy ships approached Scarborough Shoal to detain Chinese fishing boats moored in the lagoon. When they were alerted by the Chinese fishermen, China's marine surveillance ships intervened and blocked the lagoon before the Philippine ships could detain the boats. During the prolonged standoff, Chinese vice-foreign minister Fu Ying warned the Philippines that China had "made all preparations to respond to any escalation of the situation by the Philippine side." The *Global Times*, a populist Chinese newspaper affiliated to the official *People's Daily*, reinforced Fu's remarks by warning that China had not ruled out the possibility of using force to resolve the conflict. It added that China should "teach a lesson" to the Philippines and that "if the standoff escalates into a military clash, the international community should not be completely surprised."[51] China also imposed sanctions on banana exports to China and Chinese tourism to the Philippines.[52]

The standoff was resolved when both countries' ships left the area. Chinese ships, however, soon returned to the disputed waters and blocked all fishing access to the lagoon.[53] In a situation that is similar to its dispute with Japan, China's reaction to its dispute with the Philippines sought more than a restoration of the status quo. China continues to block all access to the lagoon, creating a *fait accompli*.

In 2014, as the Sino-Philippine conflict continued, China began construction of maritime facilities on the disputed Spratly Islands as well as storage and communication facilities that will enable expanded Chinese patrols of the disputed waters in the South China Sea. Up to August 2015, China had reclaimed 2,900 acres of land on the 7 reefs under Chinese occupation. China is also building three airstrips at three of the reefs.[54]

Chinese land reclamation projects have strengthened both the Chinese presence in disputed waters and its claims to disputed territories, but they also challenge the security and sovereignty claims of other claimant states and raised concern in the United States that China would significantly militarize the islands.[55] In 2014–2015, the US took high-profile actions to ensure the freedom of navigation in the area. On May 20, 2015, a US Navy P-8 Poseidon surveillance aircraft flew close to Fiery Cross Reef. US naval officers suggested that American warships should sail within 12 nautical miles of China's manmade islands. These developments led some observers to believe that Sino-US relations have reached a "tipping point."[56] Then, in October 2015 a US warship sailed within 12 miles of Subi Reef, where China was constructing an airfield.

As is the case in Sino–South Korean and Sino-Japanese relations, China has not managed its competing interests well in defending its sovereignty claims and security interests in East Asia, while minimizing US-China conflict and US efforts to bolster cooperation with its allies. In response to sustained Chinese pressure on the Philippines and following China's declaration of its East China Sea ADIZ, the United States bolstered US-Philippine alliance relations. During President Obama's visit to Manila in April 2014, the United States and the Philippines agreed to the Enhanced Defense Cooperation Agreement, which allows US forces to have access to Philippines camps on a rotational basis.[57] Then, as Chinese reclamation projects expanded and accelerated through early 2015, the United States frequently criticized Chinese "coercive" policies in disputed waters.[58] In April the United States more than doubled the number of troops participating in US-Philippine annual naval exercises.[59]

### Sino-Vietnamese Tension

China's territorial dispute with Vietnam escalated from 2009 to 2012. In 2008 Hanoi, along with the Philippines, refused to extend the 2005 agreement for China-Vietnam-Philippines joint oil exploration in disputed waters. Vietnam then officially challenged China's claim to both the Spratly Islands and the Paracel Islands with its 2009 United Nations submission and the June 2012 passage of its Law of the Sea legislation. Moreover, Vietnam developed military cooperation with the United States. Secretary of State Clinton's visits to Hanoi in 2010, the visits to Vietnam by Secretaries of Defense Robert Gates and Leon Panetta, and the annual US-Vietnam naval exchanges from 2010 to 2012 all suggested expanding not only US-Vietnam defense cooperation but also US support for Vietnam's challenges to Chinese sovereignty claims.

In 2011 and 2012 Chinese ships cut the cables of Vietnamese seismic survey ships and increased its naval presence around the Paracel Islands. In 2011 the situation was particularly tense, with Chinese nationalists, including PLA soldiers, demanding that China "punish" Vietnam.[60] On March 20, 2013, Chinese patrol boats confronted a Vietnamese fishing boat near the Paracel Islands.

Two Chinese patrol boats fired a flare at the boat, causing a fire that destroyed the boat's cabin.[61] Then in late April the local authorities in Hainan started organized cruise tourism to the Paracel Islands (*Xisha*). Of the three hundred or so tourists on board the *Coconut Fragrance Princess*, two hundred were government officials from Hainan province. The Vietnamese did not interpret the Chinese action as tourism, "but something more like imperialism."[62]

But as a Chinese foreign policy analyst explained, "Though Vietnam has asked for help from the United States to counterbalance China, it is fully aware that this is not easy to achieve."[63] Thus, by the end of 2012 Hanoi had begun to reduce its opposition to Chinese policy. It was cautious in its support for the Philippines and Japan and it jailed anti-Chinese nationalists. Vietnamese vice-minister of defense Nguyen Chi Vinh assured China that Vietnam rejected outside "intervention" in the territorial dispute and implicitly accepted China's opposition to the "internationalization" of the dispute by involving the United States.[64] In May 2013 China welcomed Vice-Foreign Minister Nguyen to Beijing. Nguyen assured China that Vietnam would "properly handle the South China Sea issue." In June Vietnamese president Truong Tan Sang traveled to Beijing to meet with Xi Jinping. He reported that a major objective of the summit was to reinforce "confidence" between China and Vietnam and that Vietnam aimed to raise relations to a "new height." Truong and Xi agreed they would "seek fundamental and long-term solutions" to their territorial disputes through "friendly negotiations." China and Vietnam also agreed to establish a naval hotline between their defense ministries in order to minimize tensions in disputed areas.[65]

Nonetheless, while seeking stable relations with China, Vietnam had refused to accommodate China's interest in bilateral management of the sovereignty dispute and Sino-Vietnamese tension reemerged. Sino-Vietnamese negotiations in early 2014 to reach a new agreement on joint exploration ended without success. Then, on May 27, China deployed the Haiyang Shiyou oil rig into disputed Sino-Vietnamese waters, leading to heightened maritime tension. In September Hanoi reached an agreement with New Delhi for joint oil exploration in waters also claimed by China, challenging Chinese sovereignty and internationalizing the maritime dispute. The next month Vietnam and India agreed on the sale of Indian naval ships to Vietnam. In December Hanoi then filed a statement with the international arbitration panel in support of the 2012 submission by the Philippines regarding its EEZ dispute with China and in January 2015 it opened discussion with Manila on establishing a strategic partnership.[66]

Vietnam also developed enhanced defense ties with the United States. In October the United States eased its long-time ban on arms sales to Vietnam.

Then, in April 2015 a US littoral combat ship docked in Danang to participate in the first formal US-Vietnam joint naval exercise.[67]

Thus far, however, Xi Jinping seems willing to tolerate Vietnam's independent security policy, so long as Hanoi does not "internationalize" the sovereignty dispute. In April 2015, after the US-Vietnam joint naval exercise, Xi
traveled to Hanoi to meet with Vietnam's Communist Party general secretary
Nguyen Phu Trong. The two leaders issued a joint communique that reaffirmed their commitment to cooperation. Most important for China, Hanoi
agreed to bilateral negotiations over the maritime dispute and met Beijing's
demand not to internationalize the dispute. The joint communiqué stressed

> effectively utilizing the Government-level negotiation mechanism on Viet-
> nam-China boundary and territorial issues, . . . actively studying transitional
> solutions that do not affect stances and policies of each side, including actively
> studying and discussing cooperation for common development . . . not taking
> actions that can further complicate and expand disputes.[68]

### China and ASEAN

China has forcefully asserted its sovereignty claims in the South China Sea
against Vietnamese and Philippine challenges and it has shown minimal
interest in moderating its polices. Moreover, the PLA Navy has signaled its
resolve to defend Chinese sovereignty claims throughout the South China
Sea. In March 2013 a PLA Navy flotilla moved into waters near the James
Shoal (*zengmu ansha*) located 80 kilometers (fifty miles) from Malaysia's
coast, which is claimed by both China and Malaysia, to conduct a combined
arms amphibious exercise. The crew held a shipboard ceremony to affirm
their vow to defend China's sovereignty in the South China Sea. Xi Jinping
then traveled to Sanya, where he boarded the amphibious ship and congrat-
ulated the returned sailors.[69]

But thus far China has persuaded ASEAN to avoid involvement in the
South China Sea territorial disputes. The forty-fifth ASEAN ministerial meeting held in Phnom Penh in July 2012 failed to issue a joint communiqué due
to disagreements on how to handle the disputes. It was the first time in the
ASEAN's forty-five-year history that the meeting did not issue a joint communiqué. Cambodia, in supporting China's position, blocked the Philippine
effort to have the ASEAN meeting support Manila's position vis-à-vis China
on the dispute. Then, in April 2013, the ASEAN Summit issued a consensus communiqué that did not mention the dispute. Since then ASEAN has
refused to take a position on the maritime disputes in the South China Sea.

At the ASEAN ministerial meeting in June 2013, the ASEAN states and China agreed to hold senior-level talks to implement fully the 2002 Declaration on the Conduct of Parties in the South China Sea (DOC) and to develop a more detailed Code of Conduct (COC). The agreement was reached despite Philippine objections, including foreign minister Albert del Rosario's criticism of China for its "massive" military presence in Philippine sovereign waters and for its violations of the DOC. Vietnam's foreign minister Pham Binh Minh, however, praised the results of the meeting and pledged to work with China on the implementation of the DOC and the development of the COC.[70] China had effectively isolated the Philippines in Southeast Asia regarding the maritime dispute.

But China's decision to deploy the Haiyang Shiyou oil rig changed the dynamics in the South China Sea disputes. Vietnam reacted strongly to China's initiative. The ASEAN countries issued a joint statement urging China to calm down the tensions. The United States and other external powers were also critical of China's provocation.

But by the end of the summer China took corrective measures. At the August 2014 meeting in Myanmar between ASEAN and China's foreign ministers, Chinese foreign minister Wang Yi proposed a dual-track approach to the management of the South China Sea disputes.[71] Wang Yi also proposed that China and ASEAN countries work together to seek common grounds in the ongoing talks on the COC.[72] In November Xi Jinping convened an unprecedented work conference on China's relations with its neighboring countries. The conference was attended by all Politburo standing committee members. It proposed the principles of "amity, sincerity, mutual benefits, and inclusiveness" in China's diplomacy with neighboring states.[73]

But when China began its South China Sea land reclamation projects in 2014, it came under renewed criticism from both ASEAN countries and the United States. The chairman's statement of the twenty-sixth ASEAN Summit, publicized on April 27, 2015, indicated that ASEAN countries were seriously concerned about China's land reclamation efforts and that such a move "has eroded trust and confidence and may undermine peace, security and stability in the South China Sea."[74]

China used economic diplomacy to minimize the effect of its strong defense of its sovereignty interests in the South China Sea. A month before its November 2014 work conference on regional diplomacy, just as it began to improve Sino-Japanese relations and its Southeast Asian diplomacy, China launched the establishment of the AIIB. Then in March 2015 China launched its "One Belt, One Road" infrastructure development strategy to integrate the Chinese economy with the economies of Southeast Asia (and Central Asia). The plan calls for China to spend US $40 billion for infrastructure projects in

China and throughout the region. These Chinese economic initiatives have been well received throughout Southeast Asia. Despite US opposition to the AIIB, in March 2015 all of the ASEAN countries became founding members of the AIIB.[75]

Most regional countries have expressed interest in China economic initiatives. Nonetheless, Beijing's economic diplomacy has not been able to mitigate regional suspicions of Chinese strategic intentions. Southeast Asia's maritime countries have all expanded naval cooperation with the United States, even as they have expanded economic cooperation with China. China's diplomacy continues to challenge Chinese interest in regional strategic stability.

## DOMESTIC POLITICS AND FOREIGN POLICY

Despite Beijing's overassertive diplomacy and the many setbacks for Chinese diplomacy, China has achieved important successes. Beijing has managed well North Korea's provocations, which in turn has contributed to improved relations with both Seoul and Washington. And, despite the multiple sovereignty conflicts in the South China Sea, since mid-2013 China has begun to stabilize relations with Vietnam and it has prevented ASEAN unity in support of the Philippines territorial claims. Nonetheless, the domestic sources of China's heavy-handed diplomacy remain powerful elements in Chinese policy making and it is uncertain that the Xi leadership will be able to develop pragmatic Chinese policy making.

### Popular Nationalism

As Joseph Fewsmith discusses in his chapter in this volume, popular nationalism has become a powerful voice in Chinese politics. Furthermore, as Barry Naughton discusses in his chapter, the Xi Jinping leadership faces significant and enduring domestic economic problems, which challenge the leadership's political legitimacy and limit its ability to constrain popular nationalism. Thus China's foreign policy has coincided with the growth of popular nationalism.[76] This is especially the case regarding popular attitudes toward Chinese maritime sovereignty. A 2009 survey jointly conducted by the *International Herald Leader* and three prominent Internet content providers in China revealed that as many as 90.4 percent of respondents were dissatisfied with China's efforts in protecting its maritime interests. When asked to identify the biggest threat to China's maritime security, 26.9 percent said it was China's insufficient attention to maritime security, 32.4 percent mentioned anti-China forces, and 20.7 percent referred to states with disputes with China.[77]

In a survey conducted by the *Global Times* in 2010, over one-third of the respondents noted that they would support the use of force to resolve the territorial disputes.[78] Twenty days after the Sino-Philippines standoff over the Scarborough Shoal in April 2012, a *Global Times* survey found that nearly 80 percent of respondents supported using military means in response to "provocations" and "aggressiveness" of other regional states in the South China Sea.[79] In a survey among urban residents in seven cities, the *Global Times* found that about 90 percent of the respondents support adopting all necessary means, including the use of force against Japan, to protect the Diaoyu (Senkaku) Islands.[80]

Chinese leaders are conscious of the dangers of the growth of ultranationalism and even xenophobia regarding domestic stability and foreign policy.[81] But they also are determined to use this nationalism to maintain the legitimacy of the Chinese Communist Party during a prolonged period of economic and social instability, including reduced GDP growth, financial instability, spreading popular protests, and the absence of a legitimating ideology. Xi Jinping seems particularly committed to joining his leadership with nationalism. He has personally promoted the phrase China Dream, the title of a 2010 popular nationalist book written by a senior colonel at the National Defense University, and to China's "rejuvenation" (i.e., reversal of the "century of humiliation"). Xi's "China dream" political campaign could encourage even greater nationalist sentiments and increase domestic pressure on the leadership to adopt nationalist foreign policies. Moreover, the Chinese military, including Chinese naval officers, have argued that a "strong army dream" and a strong navy should be part of the "China dream."[82] Xi's promotion of the "China dream" encourages Chinese citizens to become more vigilant against challenges to Chinese sovereignty from regional states. As a result, they will scrutinize acts by the Chinese government and look for any moves that indicate compromise or weakness.

Moreover, Chinese nationalism will likely be inflamed by regional developments. Growing anti-Chinese nationalism in Japan, the Philippines, and Vietnam suggests the likelihood that there will be future challenges to Chinese maritime interests in both the East China Sea and the South China Sea. Thus, Chinese nationalism could contribute to repeated episodes of deterioration of relations between China and its East Asian neighbors.

## Bureaucratic Interests and China's Maritime Policy

China's expanding naval capabilities and rising nationalism have provided new opportunities for bureaucratic interests to shape a more forceful Chinese foreign policy. As discussed in Linda Jakobson's chapter in this volume, in this "fragmented" policy-making context agencies can use policy debates and mass nationalism to justify their policy preferences.

The final report of the Eighteenth Party Congress in October 2012 stated that China will continue to "increase its capabilities in exploring marine resources, develop marine economy, protect the marine bio-environment, resolutely safeguard national maritime rights and interests, and build a strong maritime power."[83] This portion of the report was likely prepared by the State Oceanic Administration (SOA) under the jurisdiction of the Ministry of Land and Resources. More generally, the SOA has pushed for the expansion of China's interests in the maritime domain. For instance, it has persistently labeled the nine-dash line in the South China Sea as its outer limit of law enforcement (*zhifaxian*). It also has supported China's expanded civilian government maritime presence within twelve miles of the Diaoyu/Senkaku Island. The SOA also boasted that China has made significant achievements in protecting China's maritime interests, arguing that China has established effective control over the Scarborough Shoal.[84]

The PLA leadership, especially the navy's leadership, has also expressed an expansive view of China's maritime security interests. In the words of Adm. Jiang Weilie, commander of the PLA Navy's South Sea Fleet, the more than 3 million square kilometers of maritime territory is important for the realization of China's sustainable development, for the grand revival of the Chinese nation, and for the China dream. He further emphasizes that unlike the traditional view of the Chinese map (a rooster), China's territory now looks like a torch (with the territory in the South China Sea being the handle of the torch).[85]

# CONCLUSION

Heightened regional tensions and escalated conflicts over disputed territories in East Asia since 2009 have reflected many factors. Beijing was certainly not solely to be blamed. But the conflicts of interest between China and its neighbors have combined with China's growing military capabilities and economic power, with intensified Chinese nationalism, and with fragmented policy making to produce Beijing's heavy-handed approach to regional security. All of these factors have contributed to increased regional tensions and to deteriorated relations between China and its neighbors and the United States.

The Xi Jinping leadership has also made considerable progress in defending Chinese security and sovereignty interests in East Asia. China enjoys strong relations with South Korea. The regular presence of Chinese ships in the vicinity of the Diaoyu/Senkaku Islands has strengthened its sovereignty claim, even while it is stabilizing its relations with Japan. China's occupation of disputed territories and its land reclamation projects in the South China Sea have strengthened its legal and political positions vis-à-vis the Philippines and Vietnam. Its diplomacy has also cautioned Vietnam from challenging Chinese sovereignty. And China's diplomacy, including its foreign economic policies, has contributed to stable and cooperative relations with all of the ASEAN states except for the Philippines.

Nonetheless, China's heavy-handed policies and its frequent and assertive overreaction to other states' provocations have contributed to heightened regional concern over Chinese intentions and have contributed to heightened tension between China and the United States. Since Xi Jinping assumed leadership of the Chinese Communist Party in October 2012, the United States, in response to Chinese challenges to US allies, has significantly expanded diplomatic and defense cooperation with its security partners throughout East Asia, including with Japan and the Philippines, posing a greater challenge to China's security and its "peaceful rise."

China's growing civilian, maritime, and naval presence in the western Pacific Ocean and the South China Sea will continue to generate significant strategic pressure on the region's states and will arouse growing US concern for the effect of Chinese naval power on US allies and the regional balance of power.[86] Thus, for China to consolidate its recent gains and avoid recurring cycles of instability, Beijing will have to better manage its national power.

In September 2015 Xi Jinping conducted his first state visit to the United States. Xi attempted to reassure the Americans that China would not challenge the US predominant role in the world and emphasized cooperation in Sino-US relations. The two countries reached broad agreements on a wide range of global issues, including climate change, international development, reforms of financial institutions, and various other nontraditional security matters. They also made some progress in managing their differences over cyber security. Xi vowed that "the Chinese government will not, in whatever form, engage in commercial theft and hacking against government networks."[87] The two countries also agreed to set up a dialogue mechanism and carry out judicial cooperation on illegal cyber activities.

Xi's visit may have helped contain the negative spiral in bilateral relations, but the differences over regional security and the South China Sea maritime disputes remained unresolved and Washington seemed unconvinced by Xi's reassurances. Regional security issues continue to pose a considerable challenge to the Xi Jinping leadership. Not only must China manage the competing interests of peaceful rise and active defense of Chinese interests; it must also contend with the combination of rising domestic nationalism, reduced Party legitimacy and fragmented policy making. Should Xi Jinping fail to manage the growing complexities of Chinese foreign policy, East Asia will face continued instability and China will face the prospect of greater resistance to its rise.

## NOTES

1. See, for example, "Can't Buy Me Soft Power: China's Economic Might Is Not Doing Much for Its Popularity Elsewhere in Asia," *Economist*, April 27, 2013. For an alternative view see David Kang, "Paper Tiger: Why Isn't the Rest of Asia Afraid of China?" *Foreign Policy*, April 25, 2013, at http://foreignpolicy.com/2013/04/25/paper-tiger/.

2. Jeremy Page, "Pacific Navies Agree on Code of Conduct for Unplanned Encounters: Agreement Comes after Rise in Territorial Tensions," *Wall Street Journal*, April 22, 2014, at http://www.wsj.com/articles/SB100014240527023040499045795173427791 10078.

3. For a discussion of the origins of this policy and the more recent policy debates, see Chen Dingding and Wang Jianwei, "Lying Low No More? China's New Thinking on the Taoguang Yanghui Strategy," *China: An International Journal* 9, no. 2 (September 2011).

4. For a discussion of the impact of China's growing capabilities on Chinese foreign policy and regional security see Robert S. Ross, "The Revival of Geopolitics in East Asia: Why and How?," *Global Asia* 9, no. 3 (fall 2014).

5. On this period, see Jeffrey A. Bader, *Obama and China's Rise: An Insider's Account of America's Asia Strategy Paperback* (Washington, D.C.: Brookings Institution Press, 2013); Michael D. Swaine, "China's Assertive Behavior," part 1: On "Core Interests," *China Leadership Monitor*, no. 34 (2011), at http://carnegieendowment.org/2010/11/15/china-s-assertive-behavior-part-one-on-core-interests; Michael D. Swaine and M. Taylor Fravel, "China's Assertive Behavior, part 2: The Maritime Periphery," in *China Leadership Monitor*, no. 35 (2011), at http://media.hoover.org/sites/default/files/documents/CLM35MS.pdf.

6. See Clinton's call for a "strategic partnership" at http://www.state.gov/secretary/rm/2010/10/150189.htm.

7. See "U.S.-Vietnam Naval Exercises Begin Amid Sea Tensions," http://www.bloomberg.com/news/articles/2014-04-07/u-s-vietnam-naval-exercises-begin-amid-se-asian-tension; "Media Availability with Secretary Panetta in Cam Ranh Bay, Vietnam," June 3, 2102, at http://archive.defense.gov/transcripts/transcript.aspx?transcriptid=5051.

8. See Clinton's press availability on July 23, 2010, in Hanoi at http://www
   .state.gov/secretary/rm/2010/07/145095.htm; Marc Landler, "Offering to
   Aid Talks, U.S. Challenges China on Disputed Islands," *New York Times*, July
   23, 2010, at http://www.nytimes.com/glogin?URI=http%3A%2F%2Fwww
   .nytimes.com%2F2010%2F07%2F24%2Fworld%2Fasia%2F24diplo.html
   %3F_r%3D0; and interviews with Clinton administration official. On Clinton's comments in the Philippines, see Thomas Lum, "The Republic of the
   Philippines and U.S. Interests," Congressional research Service, RL33233,
   April 5, 2012; Shaun Tandon, "Clinton Uses Warship to Push Philippines
   Alliance," *Defense News*, November 16, 2011, at http://www.defensenews.com
   /article/20111116/DEFSECT04/111160306/Clinton-Uses-Warship-Push
   -Philippines-Alliance. Also see "China's Sea Claims Exceed What's Allowed by
   International Law, Says Clinton," *Philadelphia Daily Inquirer*, May 25, 2012, at
   http://globalnation.inquirer.net/37841/china%E2%80%99s-sea-claims-exceed
   -what%E2%80%99s-allowed-by-international-law-says-clinton.
9. See, for example, Liu Qing, "Mei Guo zai Yatai Zhanlue Bushu de Xin Bian-
   hua," (The new change in US strategic deployments in the Asia Pacific), *Xiandai
   Guoji Guanxi* (Contemporary international affairs) 5 (2011): 16; Wang Fan,
   "Meiguo de Dongya Zhanlue yu dui Hua Zhanlue" (US East Asia strategy and
   its China strategy)," *Waijiao Pinglun* (Foreign affairs review) 6 (2010): 21.
10. *Renmin Ribao* (People's daily), "Wen Jiabao's speech at the Fourteenth
    China-ASEAN Summit and the Commemorative Summit for the Twentieth
    Anniversary of the Establishment of China-ASEAN Dialogue Partnership,"
    November 19, 2011, at http://politics.people.com.cn/GB/1024/16307513
    .html.
11. Qin Gang, spokesperson of the Ministry of Foreign Affairs of China, made
    the response on August 4, 2012. See http://www.fmprc.gov.cn/mfa_eng/xwfw
    _665399/s2510_665401/2535_665405/t958226.shtml.
12. Steven Lee Myers, "Nations Press Halt in Attacks to Allow Aid to Syrian Cities,"
    *New York Times*, February 24, 2012, at http://www.nytimes.com/glogin?URI
    =http%3A%2F%2Fwww.nytimes.com%2F2012%2F02%2F25%2Fworld%
    2Fmiddleeast%2Ffriends-of-syria-gather-in-tunis-to-pressure-assad.html%
    3Fpagewanted%3Dall%26_r%3D1.
13. "Iran to Increase Oil Export to China to 500K BPD in 2012," *China Daily*,
    February 18, 2012, at http://bbs.chinadaily.com.cn/thread-732456-1-1
    .html; Mark Landler, "China Is Excluded from Waivers for Oil Trade with
    Iran," *New York Times*, June 11, 2012, at http://www.nytimes.com/glogin?
    URI=http%3A%2F%2Fwww.nytimes.com%2F2012%2F06%2F12%2
    Fworld%2Fmiddleeast%2Fchina-not-issued-waiver-for-oil-trade-with-iran

.html%3F_r%3D1. China's lack of support for the Six-Party Talks is based on an extensive survey of the Chinese media for 2011 and 2012.

14. Rick Gladstone, "U.N. Resolution to Aim at North Korean Banks and Diplomats," *New York Times*, March 5, 2013, at http://www.nytimes.com/glogin?URI=http%3A%2F%2Fwww.nytimes.com%2F2013%2F03%2F06%2Fworld%2Fasia%2Fchina-said-to-back-new-sanctions-against-north-korea.html%3F_r%3D0; Robert A. Wampler, "Will Chinese Troops Cross the Yalu?," *Foreign Policy*, April 11, 2013, at http://foreignpolicy.com/2013/04/11/will-chinese-troops-cross-the-yalu/. For a Chinese discussion of the opportunity presented by the transition from Clinton to Kerry, see editorial, "Huanying Keli, Xiwang Ta yu Xilai bu Tong" (Welcome Kerry, hoping he is not the same as Clinton), *Huanqiu Shibao* (Global times), April 4, 2013, at http://opinion.huanqiu.com/editorial/2013-04/3828126.html.

15. Xinhua News Agency, April 13, 2013, at http://news.xinhuanet.com/english/china/2013-04/13/c_132306244.htm.

16. Karen Parrish, "Dempsey Urges More Strategic Dialogue between China, U.S.," American Forces Press Service, April 22, 2013, at http://www.defense.gov/News-Article-View/Article/.

17. Jane Perlez and Choe Sang-Hun, "China Hints at Limits to North Korea Actions," *New York Times*, April 7, 2013, at http://www.nytimes.com/glogin?URI=http%3A%2F%2Fwww.nytimes.com%2F2013%2F04%2F08%2Fworld%2Fasia%2Ffrom-china-a-call-to-avoid-chaos-for-selfish-gain.html%3Fpagewanted%3Dall%26_r%3D0.

18. "China Agrees to Bigger U.N. Panel on N.K.," *Korea Herald*, June 24, 2013, at http://www.koreaherald.com/common_prog/newsprint.php?ud=20130624000445&dt=2.

19. Lingling Wei and Jay Solomon, "China Publicly Cuts Off North Korean Bank," *Wall Street Journal*, May 8, 2013, at http://www.wsj.com/articles/SB10001424127887323372504578468403543236068.

20. "China Rejects North Korea Request to Join Asian Infrastructure Investment Bank," at http://www.upi.com/Top_News/World-News/2015/03/31/China-rejects-North-Korea-request-to-join-Asian-Infrastructure-Investment-Bank/4481427814172/.

21. Wampler, "Will Chinese Troops Cross the Yalu?."

22. "Top Diplomats of S. Korea, China to Set Up Hotline Amid North Korea Tensions," *Yonhap*, April 24, 2013, at http://english.yonhapnews.co.kr/national/2013/04/24/11/0301000000AEN20130424014700320F.HTML.

23. Lim Soo-Ho, "Park Geun-Hye's Northeast Asia Policy: Challenges, Responses and Tasks," *SERI Quarterly*, April 2013, 15–21. The text of the joint statement

is at Xinhua News Agency, June 27, 2013, at http://news.xinhuanet.com /world/2013-06/27/c_116319763.htm.

24. "Tokyo's Actions Push Seoul and Beijing Closer," *Korea Joongang Daily*, April 26, 2013, at http://koreajoongangdaily.joins.com/news/article/article .aspx?aid=2970744.

25. "Park, Xi Boost Security, Business Ties," *Korea Herald*, July 3, 2104, at http:// www.koreaherald.com/view.php?ud=20140703001232; Zhao Shengnan, "Preparatory Talks on Maritime Border to Be Held with South Korea," *China Daily*, January 30, 2015, at http://usa.chinadaily.com.cn/epaper/2015-01/30/content _19450217.htm.

26. Karen DeYoung, "Kerry Praises China on North Korea Efforts, but Criticizes Its Action on Snowden," *Washington Post*, July 2, 2013, at http://www .washingtonpost.com/world/asia_pacific/kerry-praises-china-on-north-korea -efforts-but-criticizes-its-action-on-snowden/2013/07/01/be70f822-e271-11e2 -aef3-339619eab080_story.html; see Kerry's press availability at http://www .state.gov/secretary/remarks/2013/07/211397.htm; see Wang Yi's statement at http://news.xinhuanet.com/english/china/2013-07/01/c_132502499.htm.

27. Cheng Xiaohe, "China's Northeast Asia Policy in the Xi Jinping Era," *SERI Quarterly*, April 2013, 23–29. On economic developments see Jeremy Page, "China Builds Up Its Links to North Korea," *Wall Street Journal*, June 6, 2013, at http://www.wsj.com/articles/SB10001424127887324069104578527080945326710.

28. James Reilly, "China's Market Influence in North Korea," *Asian Survey* 54, no. 5 (September-October 2014).

29. Alastair Gale, "Seoul, U.S. Split on North Korea Nuclear Threat," *Wall Street Journal*, April 13, 2015, at http://www.wsj.com/articles/seoul-u-s-split-on -north-korea-nuclear-threat-1428913567. Also see Liu Chong, "Meiguo Yun-niang zai Han Bushu 'Sade' Xitong Banxi" (Analysis of US deployment of THAAD system in South Korea), *Xiandai Guoji Guanxi* 5 (2015).

30. The two countries did not officially sign any agreement. The agreement was largely informal and the two governments simultaneously announced the agreement in the form of a press release. According to various Chinese sources, Beijing reached the agreement with Japan in order to secure Japan's support for the 2008 Beijing Olympics.

31. Interview with a senior officer at the East Sea branch of the China Maritime Surveillance, February 2013.

32. "Riben Fabu Zhong Ri Haishang Duizhi Qingkuang" (Japan publicizes Sino-Japan standoffs in the sea), *Lianhe Zaobao*, May 13, 2013.

33. *Duowei Xinwen*, February 5, 2013, at http://global.dwnews.com/news/2013 -02-05/59114353.html.

34. See "Rìben jian ji jin juli genzong jianshi shi zaocheng zhong ri hai kong anquan wenti de genyuan (Japanese ships and planes close tracking and monitoring is the root cause of Sino-Japanese sea and air security issues) at http://news.xin huanet.com/politics/2013-02/09/c_124340696.htm.

35. "Zhuanjia: Yong Leida Suoding Duifang Yingdui Qi Tiaoxin Fuhe Guoji Guanli" (Using illumination radar on the other provoking Party conforms to international norm), *Huangqiu Shibao*, February 7, 2013.

36. Koh Swee Lean Collin, "Tensions in the East China Sea: Time to Contain Naval Stand-offs," *RSIS Commentary* 26 (February 8, 2013), at http://www.rsis.edu.sg /rsis-publication/idss/1916-tensions-in-the-east-china-sea/#.VTevJNLBwXA.

37. http://www.soa.gov.cn/xw/hyyw_90/201304/t20130423_25497.html; http:// www.soa.gov.cn/xw/hyyw_90/201304/t20130423_25499.html; "Japanese, Chinese Defense Officials Meet to Ease Tensions over Senkakus," Asahi Shimbun, April 27, 2013, at http://ajw.asahi.com/article/asia/china/AJ201304270049. Note that the official transcript of the spokesperson's remarks removed this sentence. The amended statement read that "China resolutely upholds the nation's core interests, including national sovereignty, national security, territorial integrity etc. The Diaoyu Islands issue touches on China's territorial sovereignty." Foreign Ministry spokesperson Hua Chunying press briefing, April 26, 2013, at http://www.fmprc.gov.cn/web/.

38. On the frequency of Chinese ships entering within twelve miles of the islands, see M. Taylor Fravel and Alastair Iain Johnston, "Chinese Signaling in the East China Sea?," *Washington Post*, April 12, 2014, at https://www.washingtonpost.com /blogs/monkey-cage/wp/2014/04/12/chinese-signaling-in-the-east-china-sea/.

39. Geoff Dyer, "US Blames China for Rising Tensions in South China Sea," *Financial Times*, February 9, 2014, at http://www.ft.com/cms/s/0/cdc09e14-91a7 -11e3-8fb3-00144feab7de.html; testimony by Assistant Secretary of State for East Asia Danny Russel before the U.S. House of Representatives, US Department of State, "Maritime Disputes in East Asia," February 5, 2104, at http:// www.state.gov/p/eap/rls/rm/2014/02/221293.htm.

40. Bonnie Glaser and Jacqueline Vitello, "US-China Relations: China's Maritime Disputes Top the Agenda," *Comparative Connections*, May 2014, at http://csis .org/files/publication/1401qus_china.pdf.

41. "China, Japan Reach Four-Point Agreement on Ties," http://news.xinhuanet .com/english/china/2014-11/07/c_133772952.htm.

42. "China, Japan Agree on Crisis Management," http://www.chinadaily.com .cn/china/2015-01/29/content_19442675.htm; Martin Fackler, "Japan and China Inch toward Mending Ties," *New York Times*, March 19, 2015, at http:// www.nytimes.com/glogin?URI=http%3A%2F%2Fwww.nytimes.com%2F 2015%2F03%2F20%2Fworld%2Fasia%2Fjapan-china-security-meeting.

html%3Fsmprod%3Dnytcore-ipad%26smid%3Dnytcore-ipad-share
%26_r%3D1.

43. "China Offered Japan No. 2 Post at New Bank," *Nikkei Asian Review*, April 15, 2015, at http://asia.nikkei.com/Japan-Update/China-offered-Japan-No.-2 -post-at-new-bank.

44. "Wang Yi Talks about Trilateral Foreign Ministers' Meeting among China, Japan, and the ROK," at http://www.fmprc.gov.cn/mfa_eng/zxxx_662805/t1247994 .shtml.

45. Chen Degong and Jin Dexiang, "Riben Dui Liuqiu Wu Hefa Zhuquan" (Japan has no legal sovereignty over Ryukyu)," *Huanqiu Shibao*, October 9, 2010.

46. "Shaojiang: Diaoyudao Wenti Taixiao Ying Xian Taolun Liuqiu Zhuquan Guishu" (Major general: the Diaoyu islands issue too small; need to discuss the ownership of sovereignty over Ryukyu), see http://mil.huanqiu.com/Observation /2012-07/2911162.html.

47. Zhang Haipeng and Li Guoqiang, "Lun Maguang Tiaoyue yu Diaoyudao Wenti" (The treaty of Shimonoseki and the Diaoyu Islands issue), *Renmin Ribao*, May 8, 2013. Li Guoqiang, one of the authors of the *People's Daily* article, explained later that he was not arguing that Ryukyu belonged to China historically, only that the main purpose was to put pressure on Japan on the Diaoyu Islands issue. See "Liuqiu Zai Yi Ling Ri Jinzhang, Zhongguo Dangbao Fabiao Jianrui Guandian" (Re-discussing the Ryukyu issue makes Japan nervous; China's Party newspaper publicizes sharp viewpoint), *Huanqiu Shibao*, May 9, 2013, at http:// world.huanqiu.com/exclusive/2013-05/3915193.html.

48. In the 1950s Beijing had strongly supported Japan's sovereignty claim over Okinawa. In an editorial published by the *People's Daily* in March 1958, Beijing accused the American occupants of Okinawa of fabricating news reports that China was set on claiming Okinawa. The editorial noted that China had always strongly and consistently supported the complete return of Okinawa to Japan. See the editorial "Wuchi de Niezao" (Shameless fabrication), *Renmin Ribao*, March 26, 1958.

49. John Pomfret, "U.S. Takes a Tougher Tone with China," *Washington Post*, July 30, 2010.

50. The Philippines submission is available at file:///C:/Users/Robert/Desktop/ Notification%20and%20Statement%20of%20Claim%20on%20West%20 Philippine%20Sea.pdf.

51. Damian Grammaticas, "China Bangs the War Drum over South China Sea," BBC News, May 10, 2012, at http://www.bbc.co.uk/news/world-asia -china-18016901.

52. See James Reilly, "China's Unilateral Sanctions," *Washington Quarterly* 35, no. 4 (Fall 2012): 129.

53. See Bonnie Glaser, "Trouble in the South China Sea," *Foreign Policy*, September 17, 2012, at http://foreignpolicy.com/articles/2012/09/17/trouble_in_the _south_china_sea.

54. Gordon Lubold, "Pentagon Says China Has Stepped Up Land Reclamation in South China Sea," *Wall Street Journal*, August 20, 2015, at http://www.wsj.com /articles/pentagon-says-china-has-stepped-up-land-reclamation-in-south-china -sea-1440120837.

55. David E. Sanger and Rick Gladstone, "Piling Sand in a Disputed Sea, China Literally Gains Ground," *New York Times*, April 8, 2015, at http:// www.nytimes.com/glogin?URI=http%3A%2F%2Fwww.nytimes.com %2F2015%2F04%2F09%2Fworld%2Fasia%2Fnew-images-show-china -literally-gaining-ground-in-south-china-sea.html%3F_r%3D0.

56. See David Lampton's view at "China and the United States: A Conversation with David M. Lampton," Asia Foundation, July 29, 2015, http://asiafoun dation.org/in-asia/2015/07/29/china-and-the-united-states-a-conversation -with-david-m-lampton/.

57. Jim Garamone, "U.S.-Philippine Pact Expands Defense Cooperation," American Forces Press Service, US Department of Defense, April 28, 2014, at http:// www.defense.gov/News-Article-View/Article/.

58. See, for example, Testimony by Assistant Secretary, Bureau of East Asian and Pacific Affairs, House Committee on Foreign Affairs, Subcommittee on Asia and the Pacific, February 5, 2014, at http://www.state.gov/p/eap/rls /rm/2014/02/221293.htm; and "Remarks by Secretary Carter and Nakatani at a Joint Press Conference," US Department of Defense, April 8, 2015, at http:// www.defense.gov/News/News-Transcripts/Transcript-View/Article/607035.

59. Seth Robson, "US More Than Doubles Troops for Philippine Balikatan Exercise," *Stars and Stripes*, April 8, 2015, at http://www.stripes.com/news/pacific/ us-more-than-doubles-troops-for-philippine-balikatan-exercise-1.338953.

60. Edward Wong, "China Navy Reaches Far, Unsettling the Region," *New York Times*, June 14, 2012, at http://www.nytimes.com/glogin?URI=http%3A%2F% 2Fwww.nytimes.com%2F2011%2F06%2F15%2Fworld%2Fasia%2F15china .html%3F_r%3D1; Jane Perlez, "Dispute Flares over Energy in South China Sea," *New York Times*, December 4, 2012, at http://www.nytimes.com/glog in?URI=http%3A%2F%2Fwww.nytimes.com%2F2012%2F12%2F05% 2Fworld%2Fasia%2Fchina-vietnam-and-india-fight-over-energy-explora tion-in-south-china-sea.html%3F_r%3D0; M. Taylor Fravel, "China's Strategy in the South China Sea," *Contemporary Southeast Asia* 33, no. 3 (December 2011); and personal author interviews with Chinese military officers, June 2011.

61. Chinese authorities acknowledged that the Chinese vessels had fired but called the discharges "warning shots." See Wu Dengfeng, "Sowei 'Zhongguo

Haijun Jianting Qiangji Yue Yuchuan' Yishi Chun Shu Niezao" (The so-called "Chinese naval vessels fired on Vietnamese fishing boats" is pure fabrication), Xinhua News Agency, March 26, 2013, at http://news.xinhuanet.com /mil/2013-03/26/c_124506582.htm; the Vietnamese foreign ministry statement is at http://www.mofa.gov.vn/en/tt_baochi/pbnfn/ns130326202046/view.

62. Didi Kirsten Tatlow, "Chinese Cruise to Disputed Paracel Islands Angers Vietnam," *International Herald Tribune*, April 30, 2013.

63. Li Xiaokun and Zhang Yubin, "Li Underlines Vietnam Ties," *China Daily*, May 13, 2013, at http://www.chinadaily.com.cn/china/2013-05/11/content _16491673.htm.

64. Nguyen Chi Vinh, "Promoting Peace to Defend Territorial Sovereignty and Build the Country," *Quon Doi Nhan Dan* (People's army newspaper), at http://en.qdnd .vn/editorial/promoting-peace-to-protect-national-sovereignty-and-build-the -country/222008.html.

65. China-Vietnam joint statement at Vietnam News Agency, June 21, 2013, at http://en.vietnamplus.vn/vietnam-china-issue-joint-statement/46121.vnp; Xinhua News Agency, June 18, 2013, at http://news.xinhuanet.com/english/china /2013-06/19/c_124874471.htm; Xinhua News Agency, June 19, 2013, at http://news.xinhuanet.com/english/china/2013-06/19/c_124874471.htm.

66. "China, Vietnam Launch Consultations on Sea-Related Joint Development," Xinhua News Agency, January 9, 2014, at http://news.xinhuanet.com/english /china/2014-01/09/c_133032429.htm; Vu Trong Khanh and Nguyen Anh Thu, "Vietnam, India to Expand Oil Exploration in Contested South China Sea," *Wall Street Journal*, September 15, 2014, at http://www.wsj.com/articles/viet nam-india-to-expand-oil-exploration-in-contested-south-china-sea-1410777168; Sanjeev Miglani, "India to Supply Vietnam with Naval Vessels Amid China Disputes," Reuters, October 28, 2014, at http://in.reuters.com/article/2014/10/28 /india-vietnam-idINKBN0IH0L020141028; "First Meeting of Philippines–Viet Nam Joint Commission on Concluding a Strategic Partnership Held in Manila," Philippine Department of Foreign Affairs, January 30, 2015, at http://www .gov.ph/2015/01/30/1st-meeting-of-philippines-viet-nam-joint-commission -on-concluding-a-strategic-partnership-held-in-manila/. On Vietnam's submission to the UN arbitration panel in support of the Philippines, see the Vietnamese foreign ministry statement at http://www.mofa.gov.vn/en/tt_baochi/pbnfn /ns141212143709. For a statement of the Chinese position that in the absence of an agreement with Vietnam on joint exploration it will unilaterally develop South China Sea resources, see "Expert Suggests China Drill Alone If Neighbor Continues Troublemaking," *China Daily*, May 30, 2014, at http://news .xinhuanet.com/english/china/2014-05/30/c_133373018.htm.

67. Michael R. Gordon, "U.S. Eases Embargo on Arms to Vietnam," *New York Times*, October 2, 2014, at http://www.nytimes.com/glogin?URI=http%3A%2F% 2Fwww.nytimes.com%2F2014%2F10%2F03%2Fworld%2Fasia%2Fus-eases -embargo-on-arms-to-vietnam.html%3F_r%3D0; Sam LaGrone, "U.S. and Vietnam Start Limited Naval Training on Twentieth Anniversary of Estab- lishing Diplomatic Relations," *USNI News*, April 6, 2015, at http://news.usni .org/2015/04/06/u-s-and-vietnam-start-limited-naval-training-with-vietnam -on-20th-anniversary-of-establishing-diplomatic-relations.

68. The text of the communique is at *Vietnam Plus*, April 8, 2015, at http://en.viet namplus.vn/vietnam-china-issue-joint-communique/74208.vnp.

69. Jeremy Page, "Chinese Ships Approach Malaysia," *Wall Street Journal*, March 27, 2013, at http://www.wsj.com/articles/SB100014241278873246851045 7 8386052690151508; An Bajie, "Xi Visits Fleet, Praises Sanya Sailors," *China Daily*, April 12, 2013, at http://www.chinadaily.com.cn/china/2013-04/12 /content_16394757.htm.

70. See Reuters, June 30, 2013, at http://www.reuters.com/article/2013/06/30 /us-asean-southchinasea-idUSBRE95T03V20130630. The statement by del Rosario is at http://www.dfa.gov.ph/index.php/newsroom/dfa-releases/197 -secretary-del-rosario-expresses-concern-over-militarization-of-the-south-china -sea. On Vietnam's statement see http://en.vietnamplus.vn/vietnamese-fm -hails-outcomes-of-amm46/46569.vnp. The joint communique is at http:// www.asean.org/images/2013/news/joint%20communique%20of%20the%20 46th%20asean%20foreign%20ministers%20meeting%2046th%20amm%20 -%20final%20-%2030%20june%202013.pdf.

71. "Wang Yi: Handle the South China Sea Issue through the 'Dual-Track' Approach," Chinese Foreign Ministry, at http://www.fmprc.gov.cn/mfa_eng /zxxx_662805/t1181523.shtml.

72. "China-ASEAN Strategic Partnership Enter New Stage," *China Daily*, August 10, 2014, at http://www.chinadaily.com.cn/china/2014-08/10/content_18280226 .htm.

73. "Xi Jinping Chuxi Zhongyang Waishi Gongzuo Huiyi Bing Fabiao Zhongyao Jianghua" (Xi Jinping attends the central foreign affairs conference and delivers an important speech), November 29, 2014, at http://news.xinhuanet.com/politics /2014-11/29/c_1113457723.htm.

74. See the ASEAN summit statement at http://www.asean.org/images/2015 /april/26th_asean_summit/Chairman%20Statement%2026th%20ASEAN% 20Summit_final.pdf.

75. The AIIB's opening document is at http://aiibank.org/detail-06.html. On the funding commitments, see Tom Mitchell, "China Cannot Believe Its Luck over

New Investment Bank," *Financial Times*, April 6, 2015, at http://www.ft.com/cms /s/2/1c73b174-d9df-11e4-9b1c-00144feab7de.html; and Jane Perlez, "Stampede to Join China's Development Bank Stuns Even Its Founder," *New York Times*, April 2, 2015, at http://www.nytimes.com/glogin?URI=http%3A%2F%2F www.nytimes.com%2F2015%2F04%2F03%2Fworld%2Fasia%2Fchina -asian-infrastructure-investment-bank.html%3F_r%3D0.

76. Jonathan Saul, "Chinese Firms Drop Iran As Latest U.S. Sanctions Bite," Reuters, July 1, 2013, at http://www.reuters.com/article/2013/07/01/iran -shipping-idUSL5N0F43CH20130701; John Irish and Michelle Nichols, "U.S., Russia Agree on Syria U.N. Chemical Arms Measure," Reuters, September 27, 2013, at http://www.reuters.com/article/2013/07/01/iran-shipping -idUSL5N0F43CH20130701.

77. Robert S. Ross, "The Domestic Sources of China's 'Assertive Diplomacy,' 2009– 10: Nationalism and Chinese Foreign Policy," in Rosemary Foot, ed., *China Across the Divide: The Domestic and Global in Politics and Society* (Oxford: Oxford University Press, 2013).

78. "Zhongguo Gongmin Haiquan Yishi Jueqi" (Chinese citizens' awareness of maritime rights increases), *Guoji Xianqu Daobao* (International herald leader), April 21, 2009.

79. "Baifenzhi Sanshiliu Dian Wu Guoren Renwei Biyao Shi Wuli Jiejue Zhoubian Lingtu Zhengduan" (36.5 percent of Chinese believe it's okay to use military force to resolve territorial disputes with neighboring countries if necessary), *Huanqiu Shibao*, November 11, 2010.

80. See "Nanhai Jushi Weimiao Bacheng Zhichi Junshi Huiying Nanhai Wenti" (Delicate Situation in the South China Sea: 80 percent of the people support use of force), at http://news.enorth.com.cn/system/2012/05/05/009169236.shtml.

81. "Huanqiu Yuqing yu Tai Mindiao Xianshi: Liang'an Duoshu Minzhong Zhichi Baodiao" (Global times and Taiwanese public survey: The majority of people across the Taiwan Strait support efforts to protect the Diaoyu islands), *Huanqiu Shibao*, July 19, 2012.

82. See the discussion in "Zhongguo Guanfang Jiaoting 'Dongjing Da Baozha' Yanhua" (China officially halts selling "bombing Tokyo" fireworks), *Lianhe Zaobao*, February 7, 2013, at http://www.zaobao.com.sg/photoweb/pages4/fire works130207.shtml.

83. See, for example, Luo Zheng, "Haiyang Qiangguo, Shixian Zhongguo Meng de Biran Xuanzhe" (Maritime power inevitable choice for achieving China dream), *Jiefangjun Bao* (Liberation army daily), March 9, 2013, at http://www.81.cn /jfjbmap/content/2013-03/09/content_29680.htm; Cao Zhi and Li Xuanliang, "Jiefangjun daibiao zai shenyi zhengfu gongzuo baogao shi biaoshi, jiakuai tuijin guofang he jundui xiandaihua, yuanman wancheng dang he renmin fuyu

de gexiang renwu" (PLA delegates talk about accelerating the modernization of national defense and the armed forces and fulfilling various tasks given by the Party and the people when reviewing the government work report), Xinhua News Agency, March 6, 2013, at http://news.xinhuanet.com/2013lh /2013-03/06/c_124425221.htm; Bai Ruixue, Gao Yi, and Gan Jun, "Nanhai Da Nianbing: Zhuanfang Yuanhai Xunlian Biandui Zhihuiyuan Jiang Wei-lie" (Large-scale training in the South China Sea: An exclusive interview with Jiang Weilie, commander of the South Sea Fleet distant sea training formation), Xinhua News Agency, April 1, 2013, at http://news.xinhuanet.com/mil/2013 -04/01/c_124530104.htm.

84. See the Eighteenth Party Congress report at http://news.china.com.cn/politics /2012-11/20/content_27165856_7.htm.

85. "2013 Nian Zhongguo Haiyang Fazhan Baogao: Queli Dayang Shiwu (China's maritime development report: Establishing power status in oceanic affairs), *Changjiang Ribao* (Changjiang daily), May 9, 2013, at http://intl.ce.cn/qqss /201305/09/t20130509_24363433.shtml.

86. "Nanhai Jiandui Silingyuan: Haiyang Guotu Shi Minzu Fuxing Zhongyao Bufen" (Commander of South Sea Fleet: Maritime territory an important part for national rejuvenation), *Jiefang Junbao*, April 9, 2013.

87. See, for example, Ristian Atriandi Supriyanto, "The US Rebalancing to Asia: Indonesia's Maritime Dilemma," *RSIS Commentary* no. 073/2013, April 24, 2013, at http://www.rsis.edu.sg/wp-content/uploads/2014/07/CO13073.pdf.

# Conclusion

## NEW LEADERS, STRONGER CHINA, HARDER CHOICES

Jo Inge Bekkevold and Robert S. Ross

In this volume we have explored the challenges facing China's new leadership and have analyzed its room for maneuver, both at home and abroad. We have analyzed how demography and the main characteristics of China's new leadership, its formal political structures, and its culture may constrain or empower its leaders, and we have discussed the challenges of economic growth and social stability. Furthermore, we have outlined several dimensions of China's foreign policy challenges, including the fragmentation of foreign policy decision making in China, the influence exerted on China's foreign policy by economic interdependence and international regimes, and the challenges to China's security.

Xi Jinping and his team not only differ in many ways from previous generations of Chinese leaders; they also face a different and more complex set of challenges. We hope the chapters in this volume generate a broad understanding of the many challenges facing China's new leaders.

## CHINA'S NEW LEADERSHIP

The majority of the new generation of leaders entered the Chinese political elite in 2002 as members at the Central Committee of the CCP. Two candidates, however, had central committee membership at the Fifteenth Party Congress in 1997: Xi Jinping and Li Keqiang. As many as twenty of the twenty-five members of the Eighteenth Politburo brought leadership experiences they had gained in the provinces. Hence, China's new leaders are already a highly experienced group of politicians who are well versed in the often complicated landscape of Chinese policy making.

The average age of the Eighteenth Politburo membership is only marginally different from that of its predecessors, with ages ranging from the elder members born in the late 1940s to the younger members born in the early 1960s. This relatively large span suggests that it is not helpful to use the term "fifth generation" as a label for the new leadership group. Due to the norm of expected retirement at age sixty-eight, at least eleven Politburo members, including five standing members, will retire at the next Party Congress in 2017. This suggests that during Xi Jinping's expected ten-year term policy implementation challenges will come from people belonging to different factions, and that the Nineteenth Party Congress will be an important milestone in Xi's effort to secure an even more prominent position for his allies and his policies.

Many in this new generation of leaders are "princelings," i.e., the sons and daughters of prior Chinese leaders either by birth or by marriage. Princelings enjoy great advantages in China but the downfall of Bo Xilai is a stark reminder that they are not also untouchable. Moreover, as Bo Zhiyue notes, youth league cadres in fact often reach the higher echelons of Chinese politics at younger ages than princelings.

The majority of China's new leaders had their education interrupted by the Cultural Revolution, and almost one-third of the members never attended college on a full-time basis. The current Politburo has the fewest number full-time college degrees. Politburo members who did receive an undergraduate or graduate degree were more likely to be humanities or social sciences majors rather than science or engineering majors. This trend distinguishes this generation from the two previous generations of leaders. China is no longer led by so-called technocrats and few of the top leaders have foreign experience. Nonetheless, even though thousands of Chinese students have returned to China with degrees earned at American Ivy League universities and many of these "returnees" fill important positions in Chinese politics and in the bureaucracy, China's new top leadership is less internationally orientated than previous generations of leaders.

A majority of the Eighteenth Politburo members went through their formative years during the Cultural Revolution. An important question is how this experience affects their political behavior. For instance, has the chaos of the Cultural Revolution imprinted a preference for a lighter or a tougher policy preference regarding dissent and social unrest? What about preferences for economic policies and market reforms? Bo Zhiyue believes that some members of the new leadership may be tempted to imitate Mao's disposition to being both a nationalist and a populist and they could promote "assertive" foreign policies, a development addressed also by Joseph Fewsmith as well as Mingjiang Li and Robert Ross in their respective chapters in this volume.

## GROWING EXPECTATIONS AND NATIONALISM

When Hu Jintao came to power in 2002, China was ranked as the world's sixth largest economy; its GDP was only slightly larger than Italy's GDP.[1] In 2012, Xi Jinping took charge of the world's second-largest economy. China's economic growth has been impressive and has contributed to widespread expectations of great domestic and foreign policy achievements.

China's leaders themselves assume that China's new economic muscle entitles it to a position of greater international respect, an assumption that influences Chinese foreign policy making. On the one hand China insists on its status as a developing country in the WTO and regarding climate change talks, and in an effort to downplay its great power status it has never embraced the G2 idea. On the other hand, China has also emphasized the importance of the BRICS and the G20. In 2008, in the midst of the financial crisis when the economies of the United States, Japan, and most EU countries were in free fall, Beijing hosted the most expensive Olympic Games ever. In 2010 it hosted the most spectacular international EXPO in modern times. Due to its Keynesian stimulus investment program, China maintained a high economic growth rate.

These developments had an impact on Chinese leaders' worldview. Barry Naughton observes that an "air of triumphalism" has crept into Chinese attitudes and that it was "a particular point of pride" when the size of the Chinese economy surpassed that of Japan and became the second-largest economy in the world. This air of triumphalism is one explanation for China's "assertive" foreign policy in 2010, when China's strategic thinking seemed to gradually shift in the context of the global financial crisis. Chinese triumphalism may also have bred economic complacency and resistance to a necessary change of its economic growth model.

There are growing expectations of China from the international community. As the Chinese economy has continued to grow, other countries have raised the bar for Chinese contributions to the global economic order. The international community expected more of China in resolving the global financial crisis and in reaching agreement at the 2009 Copenhagen conference on climate change. Regarding security affairs, other countries expect

China to play a larger role in resolving international conflicts, including the North Korean and Iranian nuclear issues. These heightened expectations make it more difficult for China's new leaders to shape foreign policy.

Furthermore, the Chinese people have also developed their own higher expectations of the government's ability to deliver on welfare and public goods. For instance, second-generation migrant workers demand higher salaries and better working environments, as well as housing and education for their children. Because the public knows the government has more resources for public welfare, government failure to deliver public benefits has led to increased skepticism and distrust and sometimes social unrest. The widespread availability of social media has contributed to people's willingness to voice their dissatisfaction on such issues as pollution, food security, corruption, and local government abuse, all of which challenge the central government in new ways. By proclaiming the "China dream," Xi Jinping has raised the level of expectations even higher.

Growing economic expectations and the changing state-society relationship challenge the government, and the leadership remains preoccupied with social stability. In his chapter, Fewsmith identified three types of responses from the Chinese government to maintain social stability and the legitimacy of the Party – patriotic education, strengthening the domestic security apparatus, and building a more service-oriented government. The fact that the government spends more on domestic security than on national defense illustrates the leadership's heightened attention to maintaining social stability.

Finally, the Chinese people expect their new leaders to take a stronger position on foreign policy issues, one that reflects China's new position as a great power. Narratives of nationalism and humiliation influenced by the patriotic education campaign reinforce these expectations. In her contribution Linda Jakobson writes that China's leaders appear to be constrained by public opinion and the views of the online netizen community, especially during times of international crisis. She also points to scholars, observers, and actors operating on the margins of China's foreign policy institutions, all of whom push for a stronger defense of Chinese sovereignty. Joseph Fewsmith suggests that Chinese leaders have allowed domestic problems to influence foreign policy more so than ever before and they use foreign tensions to distract attention from domestic problems. According to Fewsmith, rather than celebrating its economic miracle, many Chinese people still brood on the injustices of the past; this type of nationalist sentiment may constrict the space China has to adjust its foreign policy. Moreover, China's slowing economy, domestic instability, growing nationalism, and strong patriotism have combined with growing nationalism in Japan, the Philippines, and Vietnam, and territorial disputes in the region, so that it is likely that China will face a more difficult relationship with other countries in the region.

## SUSTAINING ECONOMIC GROWTH

China is ranked as the world's second-largest economy based on gross domestic product (GDP). But based on a GDP per capita, China ranks as number seventy-nine. China's GDP per capita of USD ($7,571) in 2014 was at the same level of countries such as Azerbaijan, Botswana and the Dominican Republic, and far below the United States GDP per capita of USD$54,369.[2] The OECD GDP per capita average was USD$38,914 in 2014.[3] For China to increase the welfare of its people and become a truly great power, it does not need to continue to grow by double-digit amounts, but it will need to sustain a relatively high growth rate for at least another two or three decades. China's economic growth of 7.3 percent in 2014 and slightly above 6.5 percent in 2015 is still impressive and does not suggest an economy in crisis. In fact, economists had expected that China's growth rate would decline to six to seven percent.

However, there is a consensus among observers of China's economy that it will be increasingly challenging for China to sustain its current high-growth figures, at least based on its current model of development. The International Monetary Fund has advised that Chinese "failure to change course and accelerate reforms" will "increase the risk of an accident or shock that could trigger an adverse feedback loop."[4]

Barry Naughton discusses four main reasons why the economic policy trajectory China has followed over the last 2–3 decades is not sustainable. First, China's failure to improve the quality of Chinese economic institutions will erode productivity. Second, although investment-led growth has served the Chinese economy well, the limits to investment-driven growth are beginning to appear. The rushed 2008 stimulus program during the global financial crisis exacerbated this trend. Third, a restructuring of China's financial system is already long overdue, and China will need to address the problem of its fast-increasing debt. Finally, China's surplus labor in the countryside is diminishing and wages are increasing. With past Asian growth "miracles," the arrival of the "Lewis turning point" in the labor market often presaged the end of very high growth periods. At the same time, China's working-age population is declining. These structural changes in China's labor force will inevitably lead to slower growth.

Managing the transition from investment and export-led growth to greater reliance on consumption-led growth is a huge challenge. When Asia's earlier "miracle economies"—Japan, Korea, and Taiwan—transitioned from very high growth phases, each faced major challenges to their growth models. China plans to upgrade its economy and move into high technology and other more sophisticated sectors, and it has already launched a massive government program of investment in education, research, and development. The difference is the role of the private sector: in other Asian miracle economies, the private sector played a more prominent role than what is the case in China today.

Chinese development of the high-technology sector requires access to foreign investments, technology, management expertise, and markets. But as Fewsmith points out, the challenges of social stability and legitimacy suggest an increasingly inward-looking trend in Chinese politics as the government favors a Chinese path that sees the outside world as threatening. Moreover, the global financial crisis strengthened the perception among many leaders in China's foreign policy elite that China no longer needs to acquiesce to outsiders' demands. A more inward-looking policy will hamper China's ability to climb the value-added ladder and maintain high growth.

China possesses an able and professional economic policy team that well understands how China can transition to a new growth model. But elsewhere in China's political system, recent Chinese economic successes have contributed to a new complacency and a resistance to change. The strength of "special interests groups" now makes serious reform extremely difficult and may hamper China's economic development. The ambitious economic reform program that Xi Jinping launched at the Third Plenum in November 2013 shows that China's new leadership understands well the challenges with China's economic model. However, the task of rolling out and implementing this reform agenda remains a huge challenge.

## IMPLEMENTING REFORMS

According to the World Bank's Governance Indicator Project (one of the most comprehensive data sets available, comparing governance in different countries from the mid-1990s to today), over the last decade China has steadily improved both its government effectiveness and the quality of its government regulatory system.[5] China has nearly caught up with the lower-ranked European countries on governance effectiveness. One important reason for this achievement is China's increasingly professional bureaucracy. For example, Zhou Xiaochuan, the head of China's central bank, Lou Jiwei, minister of finance, and Liu He, head of the Finance and Economics Leadership Small Group General Office, form a triumvirate that is quite capable of running an economic reform program, In addition, government careers are an attractive option for students in China's elite universities, so that China's bureaucracy is increasingly staffed with sophisticated personnel.

A further source of confidence is the rapid increase in government revenues. Naughton finds that Chinese budget revenues increased from 10.8 percent of GDP in 1995 to 22.6 percent of GDP in 2012. In (current) US dollars, the value of Chinese budgetary revenues increased from $75 billion in 1995 to $1,862 billion in 2012; this may enable an increase in government spending on, for example, infrastructure, education, and welfare policies that contribute to consumption.

Moreover, at the Eighteenth Party Congress, the number of standing members of the Politburo was reduced from nine to seven in an effort to strengthen its effectiveness and decision-making procedures, and three new government bodies have been established that will enable Xi to better coordinate and implement policy. The new Central Leading Group on Comprehensively Deepening Reforms that was introduced during the Central Committee Third Plenary meeting in November 2013—and headed by Xi Jinping himself—is an effort to strengthen the coordination of the overall reform program. The first meeting of the new body was held in January 2014. Xi is also head of the new National Security Commission as well as a new Small Leading Group on the Internet and Informatization.

Xi Jinping has positioned himself as a more powerful leader than most observers of Chinese politics had anticipated. He is moving beyond being just first among equals. Zheng Yongnian and Weng Cuifen raise the possibility that this new concentration of power in the hands of one strong leader could undermine the established practice of collective leadership and balance among competing political camps, and lead to an intensified power struggle.

A challenge identified by several of the authors in this volume is that even though Xi has gained strong political authority, the power to make decisions does not guarantee that the decisions will be implemented efficiently and according to plan. Barry Naughton refers to the important distinction between initiating reform and consolidating reform, and that reform consolidation requires a different set of leadership skills than does initiating reforms. China will need to strengthen the efficiency of the government bureaucracy in order to be able to implement and enforce any new policies. Zheng Yongnian and Weng Cuifen argue that despite recent administrative reforms, the still-complicated Party-state relationship has a negative impact on public administration efficiency. They also argue that China's weak judiciary system and widespread corruption undermine good governance. Without further institutional reforms, the new leadership will not be able to govern society effectively.

Another challenge affecting policy implementation is the crisis in local governance. Staff professionalism and efficiency have increased in central agencies, but this is not necessarily the case at the local levels. Fewsmith argues that the crisis in local governance has actually gotten worse as local governments are often more driven by profit and economic considerations than driven by providing public goods. Decentralization of the Chinese governing authority would normally be viewed as a positive development, but in the absence of institutions that are able to constrain and supervise local governments, excessive opportunities for corruption and abuse of power have appeared. For example, pervasive land acquisitions by local government bureaus have triggered severe mass incidents and protests among the local populations.

Regarding economic reform, policy institutions are designed to support China's high-investment imperative. Reforming economic institutions to serve a consumption-driven model will require changing the attitudes and incentives of officials who are in control of the central agencies in Beijing and a shift of power to officials residing in the districts and townships in the provinces. Undoubtedly this will be a protracted process. Despite the 2009 adjustments to the cadre management system and the development of incentives for the cadres to improve social management and public services, nothing yet exists to provide a strong motivation for local leaders to change course; they have continued on the traditional path of high economic growth as the main objective.

The country's leadership will also be challenged by the imperative of managing social instability. The shift to a more service-oriented government under Hu Jintao and Wen Jiabao achieved some results, but the new leadership will contend with ongoing implementation problems. China's current government structure cannot effectively manage social instability and in fact it seems to add to the risk of instability. The outdated cadre management system and the lack of accountability expected from officials create opportunities for corruption which in the end only contribute to instability. Thus the "strike hard" campaigns against crime and the rapid increase in the mandate of the social stability system only serve to heighten societal discontent and unrest.

Zheng and Weng argue that the political conflicts caused by parallel Party and state systems alienate both the Party and the state from society and blur the lines between state and market and between state and society. This has implications for both the transition to a new economic model and for effective social policies. But they point to the diminished role of the Central Political and Legal Commission (CPLC) as a positive development. When Zhou Yongkang was head of the CPLC (2002–2007), a task force for maintaining social stability was established and the Party strengthened its influence over the judicial system, which only led to serious power abuses. The current downgrading of the CPLC may contribute to improved legal procedures and social management. On the other hand, the March 2013 "Document No. 9" identified seven ideological trends that must be resisted, including constitutional government, civil society, and judicial independence, and the Party has recently issued a sequel to Document No. 9. At the same time as China's new leaders are trying to roll out the most ambitious market economy reform program in China ever, signaling a move to the right of the political spectrum, China's leaders are tightening the space for liberal ideas, so that the old struggle between change and stability, between an open society and a more closed, inward-looking, controlled society, continues to linger in Chinese politics.

# SHAPING FOREIGN POLICY

The second part of this volume highlighted the challenges the Chinese face in the area of foreign policy making. These challenges include developments in China's foreign policy bureaucracies, within Chinese politics and society, and in the international arena.

## The Fragmentation of Foreign Policy Making

Linda Jakobson's research analyzes how a wide range of institutions, corporations, and individuals influence Chinese foreign policy. She also observes that a diverse group of foreign policy perspectives exist among officials and institutions within the foreign policy apparatus as well as among quasi-independent opinion leaders. These trends contribute to fragmentation in China's foreign policy.

The existence of multiple foreign policy actors is normal in most countries, but the combination of a "stovepipe syndrome" in China's government system with a relatively weak ministry of foreign affairs that lacks political leverage contributes to turf battles and a lack of foreign policy coordination. This lack of coordination in turn contributes to conflicts in China's maritime disputes with Japan and in the South China Sea, as agencies adopt tough stances on foreign policy issues to strengthen their positions within the system. Although China has centralized its maritime law-enforcement agencies to enhance coordination, it also has established a more powerful maritime security agency that is better able to defend China's interests regarding maritime sovereignty and economic disputes.

Furthermore, as Stenslie and Chen write in their chapter, China's foreign policy is very often characterized by "fire-fighting" and reactive policies, which undermines China's ability to take a more proactive and leading role in international diplomacy. The politically weak foreign policy bureaucracy also impedes the effective coordination of policy making. It is significant that Yang Jiechi, the state counsellor in charge of foreign affairs, was not included in the Politburo of the Eighteenth Central Committee. Ultimately, when it comes to foreign policy issues, Chinese foreign ministry officials must defer to military officers and Politburo members who rank higher than they do in the Party organization.

Poor policy coordination that affects Chinese diplomacy is reflected in the frequently independent role of the PLA in carrying out weapons tests and military exercises. Moreover, the continued modernization of the People's Liberation Army could lead to greater demands from the armed forces for a more prominent role in foreign policy. Chinese military leaders have argued that a strong army and a strong navy should be part of Xi Jinping's "China dream." Zheng and Weng remind us that as the personal authority of Party leaders decreases, leaders must rely more on institutions to control the military. One important development in this regard was the passing of the National Defense Law in 1997; another was the National Defense Mobilization law in 2008, promulgated by the National People's Congress in the aftermath of the Sichuan earthquake. The more recent law gave the state council a legal basis and authority to mobilize the military for responding to natural disasters and to coordinate peacekeeping missions. Nevertheless, the power to prepare and mobilize for war and the final control of the PLA rests within Party-PLA relations, where politics remains decisive.

The new National Security Commission was established in 2013 in part to address the problem of fragmentation and to strengthen Xi Jinping's authority over policy making. But Linda Jakobson emphasizes that despite his significant authority, Xi is not able to manage every important foreign policy decision and that systemic problems and fractured authority still leave substantial room for various actors to push their own agendas and influence policies. Furthermore, it remains to be seen if the National Security Commission will mainly coordinate domestic security issues and manage social stability, or if it will also be authorized to coordinate foreign policy making.

## Status Quo or Revisionist Rising Power?

As China's economic and military rise is changing the global distribution of power, does the Chinese leadership see a place for China within the current international order, or does it want to significantly shape and change the international system as it grows stronger? There are, of course, no clear-cut answers to these questions. Such factors as the international balance of power, economic interdependence, international regimes, and the policies and actions of other countries will all contribute to China's foreign policy decisions and actions.

China is often accused of seeking to overturn the international order. Many observers point to China's establishment of the Asian Infrastructure Investment Bank (AIIB) as the latest example of China's challenge to the global economic order. However, Andrew Nathan as well as Helge Hveem and T. J. Pempel find that China's rise does not threaten the liberal international order. Nathan shows that China has over the past decades joined an impressively high number of international regimes and supervising bodies. This "joining" represents a dramatic shift from the Maoist era, when China did not participate in most international organizations. Nathan also notes that China's joining behavior is remarkable compared with that of another rising power, India. Nonetheless, China is still a newcomer to many international regimes, which helps to explain its sometimes low-profile and reactive policies.

China's national interests have been the main driver for it to join these organizations because it is easier to influence and change the global order or a particular organization or regime from within. For the most part, though, China has adhered to already established regimes. Although its compliance with its obligations varies across regimes, international regimes in turn have influenced China's foreign policy. China is an outlier in some regimes, such as in global finance, human rights, and the law of the sea, and it resists the concept of responsibility-to-protect (R2P) and humanitarian intervention. Hveem and Pempel as well as Nathan acknowledge that China will push for a revision of certain rules and norms of international regimes in line with China's national interests and seek changes in the international status quo, such as in the international monetary system, where the dollar dominates as the reserve currency. But they all argue that China is more likely to join and increase its influence within existing regimes than seek to overthrow the system.

## Assertive or Peaceful Rise?

China has not been engaged in war since 1979, and China's rise has thus far certainly been a peaceful rise. A power shift on the scale of China's rise today has often led to conflict and even war. History, of course, never repeats itself, but China's rapid economic and military rise continues to create uncertainty in the region, and in the United States, about its intentions.

Nathan clearly show that China attaches great importance to the contemporary international order, even though its increasingly active participation is driven by national interests. As China now is the world's largest trading nation, the second-largest host country of incoming foreign direct investment (FDI) and one of the largest home countries for outgoing FDI, international economic stability is critical to China's economic prospects.

Based on this, Hveem and Pempel argue that interdependence with the global economy may contribute to China's "peaceful rise" strategy. However, Hveem and Pempel remind us that economic relations between China and the United States have not yet reached a level of complex interdependence, and they write that in between harmony and war exist a wide range of policy options, including far more coercive Chinese diplomacy.

In fact, Mingjiang Li and Robert S. Ross find that when Xi Jinping assumed leadership of the Chinese Communist Party in November 2012, China's relations with much of East Asia and with the world were in a worse state than they had been anytime during the previous two decades, and the worst with the United States since 1989. Hu Jintao's diplomacy had alienated its neighboring countries and contributed to a pivot by the United States toward East Asia, all of which increased pressure on China's security.

Xi's first opportunity to manage China's security situation and US-China relations occurred in early 2013 following North Korea's nuclear and missile tests. Xi managed China's Korea policy differently than Hu Jintao had done, aligning China with South Korea and the United States against North Korea's nuclear program and thus contributing to improved Sino-US relations. Furthermore, as Mingjiang Li and Robert Ross argue, in 2013 Xi managed to improve China's relationship with the United States while establishing a "new status quo" in its relations with Japan in the East China Sea and with Vietnam and the Philippines in the South China Sea.

However, the sources of China's more assertive diplomacy have remained powerful elements in Chinese policy making. In 2013–2014 China's announcement of its air defense identification zone for the East China Sea and its land reclamation projects in the South China Sea contributed to another cycle of heightened US-China conflict. Xi faces an increasingly complex domestic policy-making environment and persistent widespread nationalism, so he is willing to play the nationalism card himself. Protecting China's sovereign rights has become a nationalist mantra that Xi can use to justify his country's assertive behaviors. But he walks a tight line as he tries to consolidate his recent gains and avoid recurring cycles of Chinese foreign policy assertiveness and regional instability.

# LEADERSHIP IN CHINESE POLITICS
# AND FOREIGN POLICY

In 2012 Xi inherited a domestic and foreign policy agenda that had continued the development of the Chinese economy and Chinese national security but also fundamentally challenged the interests of the Chinese Communist Party. Domestic instability and the erosion of effective governance, imbalances in the Chinese economy, and heightened instability in East Asia posed serious challenges to the Chinese leadership's ability to develop and implement effective policies. These domestic and international challenges have necessarily shaped Chinese policy making since the Eighteenth Party Congress. But every contributor to this volume has argued that leadership does make a difference. The succession of power from Hu Jintao to Xi Jinping has led to many important changes in China's domestic and foreign policies and affected the prospects for China's prosperity and security.

In domestic politics Xi has relied more than Hu Jintao did on the suppression of public criticism of the leadership, ostensibly to maintain social and political stability while using overt nationalist propaganda to enhance the legitimacy of the Chinese Communist Party. In this political context he also has set the most ambitious agenda for Chinese economic reform since the 1990s and has called for a far-reaching macroeconomic rebalancing. Together these initiatives, if effectively implemented, could set China on the path of stable long-term economic growth. Overall, in domestic affairs Xi has been a more decisive leader than Hu Jintao was, with important consequences for Chinese politics and economics.

Xi has been an equally decisive leader in foreign policy making. Whereas Hu developed a counterproductive assertive foreign policy program that was reactive to both domestic nationalism and international developments, Xi's foreign policy has been characterized by initiatives that have proactively shaped China's strategic environment. He significantly adjusted China's North Korea policy while resisting challenges to Chinese interests in the East China Sea and in Southeast Asia. The creation of the National Security Commission and the Leading Small Group for Deepening Reform, both headed by Xi himself, will likely improve the coordination and implementation of policies in two important sectors and strengthen Xi Jinping's personal authority.

The emergence of strong leadership in Beijing has not eliminated the contradictions in Chinese domestic and foreign policies, however. Most fundamental is the contradiction between the interests of the Chinese Communist Party and the Chinese state. The Party's interest in survival has led to its increased reliance on nationalism and repression to sustain domestic stability and Party legitimacy. But it is far from clear that Party interests are compatible with economic development. Effective reform and rebalancing can exacerbate unemployment and undermine domestic stability and repression, while nationalism can stifle economic innovation and international economic cooperation. Similarly, a reliance on nationalism for Party legitimacy interferes with the development of pragmatic and moderate foreign policies that promote a stable East Asian international environment—a prerequisite to China's future security and economic development.

As China grows stronger, China's leaders have gained a richer policy tool kit, but each policy decision also carries greater repercussions, both at home and abroad. Xi Jinping and his leadership team face a more complex set of challenges and harder choices than previous leaders. Thus, Xi Jinping's greatest challenge is the management of the interconnected but frequently contradictory demands of Party survival and national interests. For single-party authoritarian governments, this challenge has frequently been overwhelming. Whether China's authoritarian political system can effectively manage the contradiction between Party interests and state interests depends on both the severity of the challenge and the strength of its leaders. If Xi Jinping manages to push through the necessary reforms needed to consolidate a new economic model and maintain regional stability, he will most likely go down in history as a great Chinese leader.

If Xi Jinping gives priority to the revival of ideological mobilization, Party control over the economy and society, nationalism and China's great power status, and seeks to maximize his own personal power rather than focus on pragmatic policy making, China will face increasingly uncertain prospects.

## NOTES

1. International Monetary Fund, *World Economic Outlook Database, April 2013*, at http://www.imf.org/external/pubs/ft/weo/2013/01/.
2. International Monetary Fund, *World Economic Outlook Database, October 2015*, at http://www.imf.org/external/pubs/ft/weo/2015/02/.
3. *OECD States Extracts* at http://stats.oecd.org/.
4. People's Republic of China, "2013 Article IV Consultation," Country Report No. 13/211, July 17, 2013, at http://www.imf.org/external/pubs/ft/scr/2013/cr13211.pdf.
5. See World Bank statistics at http://info.worldbank.org/governance/wgi/index.aspx#home.

# CONTRIBUTORS

Jo Inge Bekkevold is the head of the Centre for Asian Security Studies at the Norwegian Institute for Defence Studies. He has lived in China for more than ten years as a diplomat and trade analyst. His research focuses on Chinese foreign policy and security policy, on Sino-Russian relations, and on naval developments in Asia. His publications include *Arctic: Commerce, Governance and Policy*, with Uttam Kumar Sinha, and *Security, Strategy and Military Change in the Twenty-First Century: Cross-Regional Perspectives*, with Ian Bowers and Michael Raska.

Bo Zhiyue, a leading authority on Chinese elite politics in the world, is director of the New Zealand Contemporary China Research Centre and professor of political science at Victoria University of Wellington, New Zealand. He has published more than 150 book chapters and articles and is the author of a trilogy on China's elite politics, including *Chinese Provincial Leaders: Economic Performance and Political Mobility since 1949* (2002); *China's Elite Politics: Political Transition and Power Balancing* (2007); and *China's Elite Politics: Governance and Democratization* (2010).

Chen Gang is a research fellow at the East Asian Institute of the National University of Singapore. Since joining the institute in 2007, Chen's research and publications have focused on China's politics and foreign policy. He is a consultant to the Singapore Government on political and economic issues in East Asia.

Joseph Fewsmith is a professor of international relations and political science at Boston University. He is the author or editor of seven books, including, most recently, *The Logic and Limits of Political Reform in China* (Cambridge University Press, 2012). He is one of the seven regular contributors to the *China Leadership Monitor*, a quarterly web publication that analyzes current developments in China.

Helge Hveem is professor emeritus of the Department of Political Science, University of Oslo. He is the former director of the International Peace Research Institute in Oslo, the Centre on Development and the Environment, and the Centre for Technology, Innovation, and Culture at the University of Oslo. He has also served as a senior research consultant for the UNCTAD Secretariat.

Linda Jakobson recently took up the position of visiting professor at the US Studies Centre at the University of Sydney and founded China Matters, a not-for-profit public policy initiative that aims to advance nuanced policy debates in Australia about China. Prior to that she served as East Asia Program Director of the Lowy Institute for International Policy. She has lived and worked in China for twenty years. Jakobson has published extensively on China's foreign and security policy, including six books on Chinese and East Asian society.

Mingjiang Li is an associate professor at S. Rajaratnam School of International Studies at Nanyang Technological University in Singapore. He is the author or editor of twelve books and numerous journal papers and book chapters.

Andrew J. Nathan is Class of 1919 Professor of Political Science at Columbia University. He is the author, with Andrew Scobell, of *China's Search for Security* (Columbia University Press, 2012), and the co-editor (with Larry Diamond and Marc Plattner) of *Will China Democratize?* (Johns Hopkins University Press, 2013).

Barry Naughton is the So Kwanlok Professor of Chinese Affairs and Economics at the Graduate School of Global Policy and Strategy at the University of California, San Diego. He is the author of *Growing Out of the Plan* (1995) and *The Chinese Economy: Transitions and Growth* (2007). His most recent book, coedited with Kellee Tsai, is *State Capitalism, Institutional Adaptation, and the Chinese Miracle* (Cambridge University Press, 2015).

T. J. Pempel is the Jack M. Forcey Professor of Political Science at the University of California, Berkeley. His research focuses on comparative politics, Japanese political economy, and Asian regional issues. His most recent book, coedited with Keiichi Tsunekawa, is *Two Crises: Different Outcomes* (Cornell University Press, 2015).

Robert S. Ross is a professor of political science at Boston College and Associate, John King Fairbank Center for Chinese Studies, Harvard University. His recent publications include *Chinese Security Policy: Cooperation and Conflict at Sea* and *Twenty-First Century Seapower: Cooperation and Conflict at Sea.*

Stig Stenslie is the assistant deputy general and head of the Asia division of the Norwegian defense staff. He received his Ph.D. in political science from the University of Oslo. He has held visiting fellowships at, among others, the Norwegian Institute for Defense Studies in Oslo, the National University in Singapore, and Columbia University in New York. His most recent publication is *Forty-Nine Myths about China*, coauthored with Marte Kjær Galtung.

Weng Cuifen has conducted research at the East Asian Institute of the National University of Singapore. She is currently in the doctoral program in management and organization at the business school of the University of New South Wales, Australia. Her main research interests are public policy and the internationalization of business firms in contemporary China.

Zheng Yongnian is a professor and the director of the East Asian Institute at the National University of Singapore. He is also the editor of *China: An International Journal* and *East Asian Policy*. His research focuses on China's elite politics, nationalism, political economy, and international relations.

# INDEX

*Figures, notes, and tables are indicated by f, n, and t respectively.*